CW01658940

INSIGHT GUIDES

IRELAND

INSIGHT GUIDES
IRELAND

CONTENTS

Introduction

History & features

Places

Travel tips

TRANSPORT

A – Z

FURTHER READING

Maps

LEGEND

Insight on
Photo story

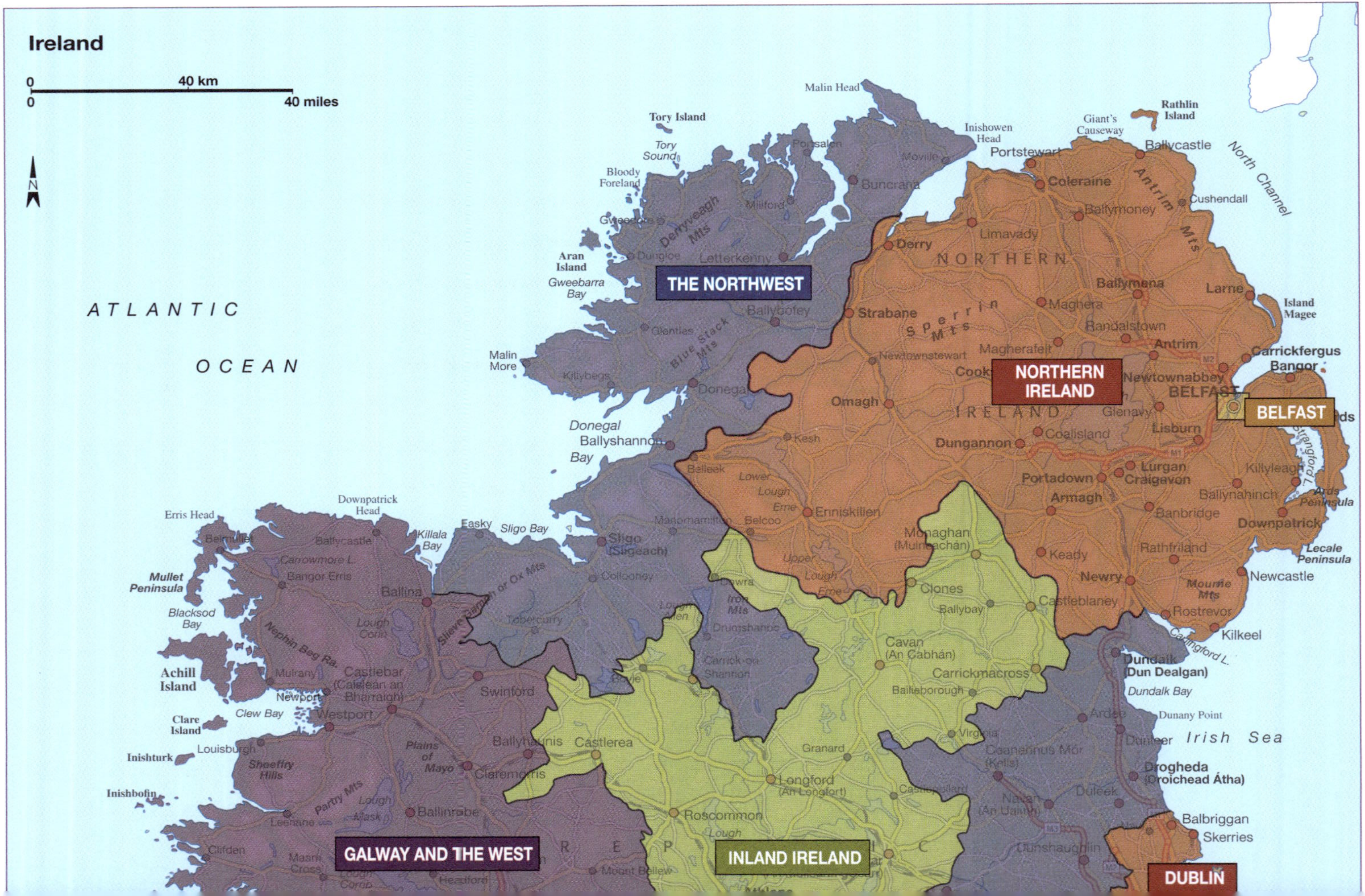
Ireland
0 40 km
0 40 miles
N
ATLANTIC OCEAN
North Channel
Irish Sea
NORTHERN IRELAND
BELFAST
DUBLIN
THE NORTHWEST
INLAND IRELAND
GALWAY AND THE WEST
Rathlin Island
Ballycastle
Cushendall
Antrim Mts
Giant's Causeway
Portstewart
Coleraine
Ballymoney
Larne
Island Magee
Carrickfergus
Bangor
Ards Peninsula
Strangford L.
Lecale Peninsula
Newcastle
Kilkeel
Mourne Mts
Rostrevor
Carlingford L.
Ballymena
Antrim
Newtownabbey
Lisburn
Randalstown
Maghera
Magherafelt
Cookstown
Dungannon
Coalisland
Portadown
Lurgan
Craigavon
Armagh
Banbridge
Ballynahinch
Downpatrick
Killyleagh
Rathfriland
Newry
Keady
Inishowen Head
Limavady
Derry
Strabane
Sperrin Mts
Newtownstewart
Omagh
Enniskillen
Lower Lough Erne
Upper Lough Erne
Belleek
Kesh
Belcoo
Monaghan (Muineachán)
Castleblaney
Carrickmacross
Clones
Ballybay
Cavan (An Cabhán)
Bailieborough
Dundalk (Dún Dealgan)
Dundalk Bay
Dunany Point
Ardee
Drogheda (Droichead Átha)
Balbriggan
Skerries
Navan (An Uaimh)
Kells
Dunshaughlin
Longford (An Longfort)
Granard
Roscommon
Castlerea
Carrick-on-Shannon
Drumshanbo
Malin Head
Moville
Buncrana
Milford
Letterkenny
Derryveagh Mts
Dungloe
Tory Island
Tory Sound
Bloody Foreland
Aran Island
Gweebarra Bay
Glenties
Blue Stack Mts
Ballybofey
Donegal
Donegal Bay
Ballyshannon
Killybegs
Malin More
Sligo (Sligeach)
Collooney
Tobercurry
Ox Mts
Sligo Bay
Easky
Killala Bay
Ballina
Lough Conn
Swinford
Claremorris
Ballinrobe
Plains of Mayo
Castlebar (Caisleán an Bharraigh)
Westport
Newport
Mulrany
Clew Bay
Nephin Beg Ra.
Bangor Erris
Carrowmore L.
Downpatrick Head
Erris Head
Belmullet
Mullet Peninsula
Blacksod Bay
Achill Island
Clare Island
Louisburgh
Inishturk
Inishbofin
Sheeffry Hills
Leenane
Partry Mts
Lough Mask
Clifden
Maam Cross
Headford

EXCURSIONS FROM DUBLIN
THE SOUTHEAST
CORK AND SURROUNDINGS
THE SOUTHWEST
LIMERICK AND THE SHANNON REGION
IRELAND
Dun Laoghaire
Bray (Bré)
Greystones
Wicklow (Cill Mhantáin)
Wicklow Mts
Arklow (An tInbhear Mór)
Gorey
Cahore Point
Enniscorthy (Inis Córthaidh)
Wexford (Loch Garman)
Rosslare
Rosslare Harbour
Carnsore Point
Saltee Islands
Kilmore Quay
Hook Head
New Ross (Ros Mhic Thriúin)
Waterford (Port Láirge)
Tramore
Kilkenny (Cill Chainnigh)
Bagenalstown
Carlow
Tullow
Athy
Naas
Kildare
Portarlington
Portlaoise
Mountmellick
Durrow
Roscrea (Ros Cré)
Birr
Cloghan
Borrisokane
Lough Derg
Nenagh (An tAonach)
Templemore
Thurles (Durlas)
Slieveardagh Hills
Cashel (Caiseal)
Clonmel (Cluain Meala)
Carrick-on-Suir (Carraig na Siúire)
Dungarvan (Dún Garbhán)
Mine Head
Youghal (Eochaill)
Knockadoon Head
Tallowbridge
Knockmealdown Mts
Cahir (An Chathair)
Tipperary
Galtee Mts
Fermoy
Mitchelstown
Cobh (An Cobh)
Crosshaven
Cork (Corcaigh)
Ballincollig
Kinsale
Old Head of Kinsale
Mallow (Mala)
Kanturk
Macroom
Bandon
Clonakilty
Galley Head
Skibbereen
C. Clear Island
Dunmanway
Bantry
Ballydehob
Bantry Bay
Glengarriff
Kenmare
Kenmare River
Beara
Bere Island
Sheep's Head
Mizen Head
Dursey Head
Skellig Islands
Iveragh
Waterville
Cahersiveen
Valentia Island
Bray Head
Blasket Islands
Dingle
Dingle Bay
Brandon Head
Camp
Killorglin
Carrantuohill 1041
Killarney (Cill Airne)
Castleisland
Tralee (Trá Lí)
Tralee Bay
Kerry Head
Ballyheige
Listowel
Ballybunion
Loop Head
Mouth of the Shannon
Carrigaholt
Kilrush
Donegal Point
Tarbert
Abbeyfeale
Newcastle West
Rathluirc
Kilmallock
Croom
Patrickswell
Limerick (Luimneach)
Tulla
Ennis
Ennistymon
Cliffs of Moher
The Burren
Ballyvaughan
Black Head
Galway Bay
Inisheer
Inishmaan
Inishmore
Aran Islands
Gorumna Island
Kinvara
Loughrea
Slieve Aughty Mts
Slievefelim Mts
Celtic Sea
St George's Channel
M7
M8
M9
M11

THE BEST OF IRELAND: TOP ATTRACTIONS

△ **Georgian Dublin**. The city retains some of its Georgian heritage – for example, the characteristic doors – but the real appeal is the Dubliners' vibrancy and sense of fun. See page 117.

▽ **The Giant's Causeway**. This astonishing assembly of more than 40,000 hexagonal basalt columns on the north coast is a natural wonder. See page 300.

△ **Glendalough**. Round towers are a striking reminder of Ireland's Golden Age when, after the fall of the Roman Empire and Europe plunged into the Dark Ages, monks in Ireland ('the Land of Saints and Scholars') kept alight a lone beacon of learning and civilization. See page 143.

▽ **The Glens of Antrim**. The nine steep valleys with their seemingly magical waterfalls in Glenariff Forest Park reminded the novelist William Makepeace Thackeray of 'Switzerland in miniature'. See page 298.

△ **The Wild Atlantic Way**. This scenic drive takes in the famous Ring of Kerry – expect a panorama of coast and mountain, lush vegetation and sandy beaches. See page 193.

△ **Traditional Irish Music**. This has influenced so many styles of music around the world, and can be heard at its authentic best everywhere from street buskers to sessions in city and country pubs. See page 67.

▷ **Connemara**. The far west of Ireland is iconic – a landscape of wild, rocky bog land, its deeply indented coastline covered in autumnal shades of seaweed, its stunted pine trees struggling for a foothold and mirrored in the surprisingly blue water of its many loughs. See page 227.

△ **The Burren**. The moon-like plateau in Co. Clare contains ancient tombs and a remarkable variety of rich flora. See page 214.

▷ **The Aran Islands**. An unspoiled Irish-speaking community, beaten by the Atlantic, the islands are a haven for animals and wildlife. See page 229.

▽ **The Rock of Cashel**. Towering above Tipperary's green plain is a dramatic cluster of romantically ruined stone buildings, dating to the 12th and 13th centuries and the former stronghold of the Kings of Munster. See page 167.

THE BEST OF IRELAND: EDITOR'S CHOICE

Kiss the Blarney Stone to gain the gift of the gab.

BEST FAIRS AND FESTIVALS

Bloomsday. Fans of James Joyce's Ulysses celebrate 16 June (the day on which it is set, in 1904) by proceeding around Dublin in period costume. Alcohol is consumed. See page 140.

Fleadh Nua. Fleadh means festival, and during May in Ennis, *Fleadh Nua* (*Nua* means new or modern) attracts thousands of traditional musicians, amateur and professional, with the music continuing at night in bars. See page 209.

The Auld Lammas Fair. The oldest fair in Ireland, dating from 1606, held in Ballycastle, County Antrim, still sees traditional horse trading alongside a busy trade in dulse (edible seaweed) and yellowman (hard toffee). See page 299.

ONLY IN IRELAND

Newgrange, County Meath. This ancient passage tomb predates the Egyptian pyramids by centuries. See page 147.

Kissing the Blarney Stone. Even if it doesn't bestow the 'gift of the gab', it's a dizzying experience. See page 177.

Trinity College, Dublin. With its cobbled court-yards, elegant Georgian buildings and bustling student population, it has a unique ambience. See page 119.

The Ring of Kerry. A day-long drive around the coastal scenery of Kerry's southwesterly peninsula, renowned for its combination of lush subtropical vegetation, and rugged seascapes. Visit a series of pretty seaside villages while offshore the rugged Skellig Rocks hover mysteriously on the horizon. See page 193.

Cruinniú na mBád. Traditional wooden boats with brown sails, laden with turf, race across Galway Bay in August. See page 216.

Croagh Patrick. Thousands of pilgrims, many of them barefoot, walk up Mayo's 'holy mountain' on the last Sunday in July, as did their grandparents before them. See page 231.

Derry's walls. The last walled city to be built in Europe is the centre of a vibrant cultural life. See page 274.

Dubai Duty Free Irish Derby. Held in June at the Curragh Racecourse in Co. Kildare, this is the most popular event on the busy horseracing calendar. See page 330.

Bloomsday Ulysees re-enactment Glasnevin Cemetery.

BEST TRADITIONAL PUBS

The Crown Liquor Saloon. 46 Great Victoria Street, Belfast. Its ornate Victorian interior is cared for by the National Trust. See page 310.
The Auld Shebeen. Abbey Street, Ballina, County Mayo. Town-centre bar with music nightly. Good food.
Hargadon's. 4–5 O'Connell Street, Sligo. A great 'brown' pub (furniture, floors, walls, ceilings: brown). Good food, music. See page 255.
MacCarthy's. Main Square, Castletownbere, Beara, County Cork. The front is a grocery shop, used by local trawlermen; behind it is MacCarthy's Bar. See page 190.
O'Neill's Pub and Kitchen. Suffolk Street, Dublin 2. An old-style pub, with a warren of 'snugs'.
Morrissey's. Main Street, Abbeyleix, County Laois (on the N8 Dublin–Cork road). Opened as a grocer's in 1775.
Tigh Neachtain. Cross Street, Galway, has stubbornly retained its old-fashioned painted wooden interior. Music.

LUXURY HISTORIC HOTELS

Cashel Palace Hotel. With views of the Rock of Cashel, this fully refurbished 1732 manor oozes tradition. Rooms are as fine as the dining in Michelin-starred The Bishop's Buttery. The spa is a veritable treat, too. See page 167.
Adare Manor. The former home of the Dunraven Earls, this opulent manor is the ultimate luxury with Michelin restuarant The Oak Room and olde world bar. See page 206.
The Merchant Hotel. The grand cupola and chandelier give a nod of what to expect. Rooms are Victorian or Art Deco style while cocktails, jazz and gastro pub fare delight. See page 318.

Cashel Palace Hotel, Tipperary.

Traditional pubs showcase traditional music.

TOP MUSEUMS AND GALLERIES

National Museum. A wealth of priceless Irish treasures, including Celtic antiquities, Bronze Age gold jewellery and early Christian crosses. See page 123.
National Gallery. Paintings by Vermeer, Rembrandt, Poussin and Goya, plus a major collection of Irish art. See page 124.
Chester Beatty Library. Exquisite collection of Islamic and Far Eastern art housed in a wing of Dublin Castle. See page 128.
Irish Famine Museum. Strokestown, County Roscommon. Visit for a compelling account of the Great Hunger (1845–49), which devastated Ireland. See page 245.
Hunt Museum. Limerick. Celtic and medieval treasures in historic Customs House on the River Shannon. See page 203.
The Model. Sligo. Converted 'model school' houses superb collection of paintings by Jack Yeats. See page 256.
Ulster Folk and Transport Museum. Reconstructed houses and cottages bring Ulster c.1910 to life. Transport ranges from huge locomotives to the DeLorean sports car (one of which featured in the film *Back to the Future*). See page 296.
Dublin City Gallery The Hugh Lane. Imposing 18th-century town house in the Palladian style; collection of Impressionists plus 19th- and 20th-century Irish art. See page 133.

RECOMMENDED FOR FAMILIES

Viking Splash Tours. Use amphibious vehicles for a hilarious orientation tour of Dublin by land and water. (Departs St Patrick's Cathedral and St Stephen's Green) www.vikingsplash.com.

The Ark. Eustace Street, Temple Bar, Dublin. This cultural centre for children has a gallery and workshop space. See page 126.

Carrick-a-Rede Rope Bridge. Ballycastle, County Antrim. Spans a 60ft (18-metre) gap between mainland and Carrick-a-Rede Island. Strictly for thrill-seekers. See page 300.

Dublinia. St Michael's Hill, Dublin. A reconstruction of life in medieval Dublin with high-tech displays. See page 129.

Malahide Castle. Escape from the city to 22 acres (9 hectares) of pleasure gardens with playground and pitch and putt course, and sweet treats at the Avoca Café. See page 139.

Cobh Heritage Centre. Cobh, County Cork. Compelling recreation of the emigrant experience. See page 178.

Muckross Traditional Farms. Muckross Park, Killarney. Walking tour of three farms inhabited by farming families and their animals, including a friendly pair of giant Irish wolfhounds. See page 192.

Bunratty Castle and Folk Park. Bunratty, County Clare. The huge 15th-century castle is authentically furnished, while the village is inhabited by real people and animals. See page 207.

Sheep and Wool Centre. Leenane, County Galway. Twenty breeds of sheep graze around the house, where craftspeople show how sheep's fleece is turned into wool. See page 231.

Fota Wildlife Park. Giraffe and wallabies roam free, while the cheetahs have a huge run in their cage. See page 177.

Titanic Belfast. Visitor centre built to the same scale as the fated ocean liner, and located beside the dry dock in which it was built: hours of fascinating multimedia exhibits on the ship and the men who built her. See page 313.

Cliffs of Moher. Trails lead to viewing points above the towering cliffs. See page 211.

Ulster Folk and Transport Museum.

BEST BEACHES

Irish beaches are generally undeveloped, with free car parking. Beaches are popular with walkers outside July and August.

Banna Strand. County Kerry. West-facing beach backed by dunes big enough to get lost on. Fine views over Tralee Bay. See page 198.

Brittas Bay. County Wicklow. White sand backed by dunes interspersed with small coves. Popular holiday spot for Dubliners. See page 144.

Curracloe Strand. County Wexford. Stood in for Normandy for the D-Day landing scenes in the 1998 film *Saving Private Ryan*. Stretches for 5.5 miles (9km). Nature trails and birdwatching hides to observe winter migrants. See page 154.

Lahinch. Surfers flock to Lahinch on the west coast of County Clare in search of huge waves offshore, but the waves on the beach, which is in the village centre, are ideal for beginners. See page 210.

Inch Strand. Dingle, County Kerry. Stretch of golden sand running for 5 miles (8km) on a spit of land protruding into Dingle Bay. See page 196.

Mullaghmore beach, County Sligo.

BEST CRAFT SHOPS

Avoca Handweavers. Killmacanogue, County Wicklow (also Dublin, Kenmare and Letterfrack). Flagship store of a family-run chain known for their jewel-coloured, handwoven rugs and throws. Also famed for fresh, wholesome food. www.avoca.com

Blarney Woollen Mills. Blarney, County Cork (also Killarney and Tipperary). Amid the leprechaun key rings and Guinness T-shirts is good, Irish-made clothing. www.blarney.com

Waterford Crystal Experience, The Mall Waterford. A 50-minute tour takes visitors through the various stages of production. Wide range of crystal on sale in the shop. www.waterfordvisitorcentre.com

The Kilkenny Design Centre. Kilkenny Castle. Well-designed Irish-made ceramics, jewellery, clothing and textiles. www.kilkennydesign.com

Judy Greene Pottery. Kirwan's Lane, Galway. The best of hand-crafted design: ceramics by Judy Greene, wood, textiles, glass and basket ware. www.judygreenepottery.com

Belleek Pottery. Co. Fermanagh. Fine bone china. See page 283.

Thomas Ferguson. 54 Scarva Rd, Banbridge, County Down. Wide range of goods in Irish linen for sale in Ireland's last remaining linen weaving factory. www.fergusonirishlinen.com

Belleek Pottery.

Walking in Connemara.

BEST WALKS

Ireland's scenery can be enjoyed on waymarked paths suitable for all levels of fitness.

The Grand Canal Way. Flat canal-bank walk from the Dublin outskirts to the little-visited Midlands (highest point, Lowtown, 280ft/85 metres). See page 101.

The Kerry Way. Passes through some of Ireland's most beautiful scenery between Glenbeigh and Killarney. See page 99.

The Slieve Bloom Way. Inland route close to the exact centre of Ireland. Quietly spectacular. See page 101.

The Ballyhoura Way. Easy walking on an inland pastoral route though low hills with views of the Golden Vale. See page 168.

Beara Way. A variety of coastal and mountain scenery on one of the southwest's less frequented peninsulas. See page 189.

The Sperrin Mountains. Sparsely populated area in the northeast of County Tyrone; bog, heather and moorland. See page 279.

MONEY-SAVING TIPS

Heritage Cards An OPW Heritage Card gives you unlimited admission to all 780 sites in the Office of Public Works scheme for one year. At €40 adult (€30 seniors, €90 family) it will pay for itself.

Hostels To save money, consider the options listed by Independent Holiday Hostels of Ireland (nine in Northern Ireland), with no curfew or membership needed. Some are in historic buildings; all are friendly and well run.Outside Dublin expect to pay €20 per night in a double room (in Dublin around €30). www.hostels-ireland.com

Bed and Breakfast If you are staying for more than one night, ask for a reduction on advertised price.

Early Bird or Special Value/market menus Many restaurants offer cheaper two or three-course menus before 6.30 or 7.30pm. If you are keen to sample some of Ireland's top-grade restaurants and hotels but fear it may wreck your budget, go for lunch rather than dinner. A good-value way to enjoy the ambience of Ireland's famous castle hotels is to drop by mid-morning for a coffee.

Bar Food is often a cheaper, and excellent, alternative to eating out in restaurants.

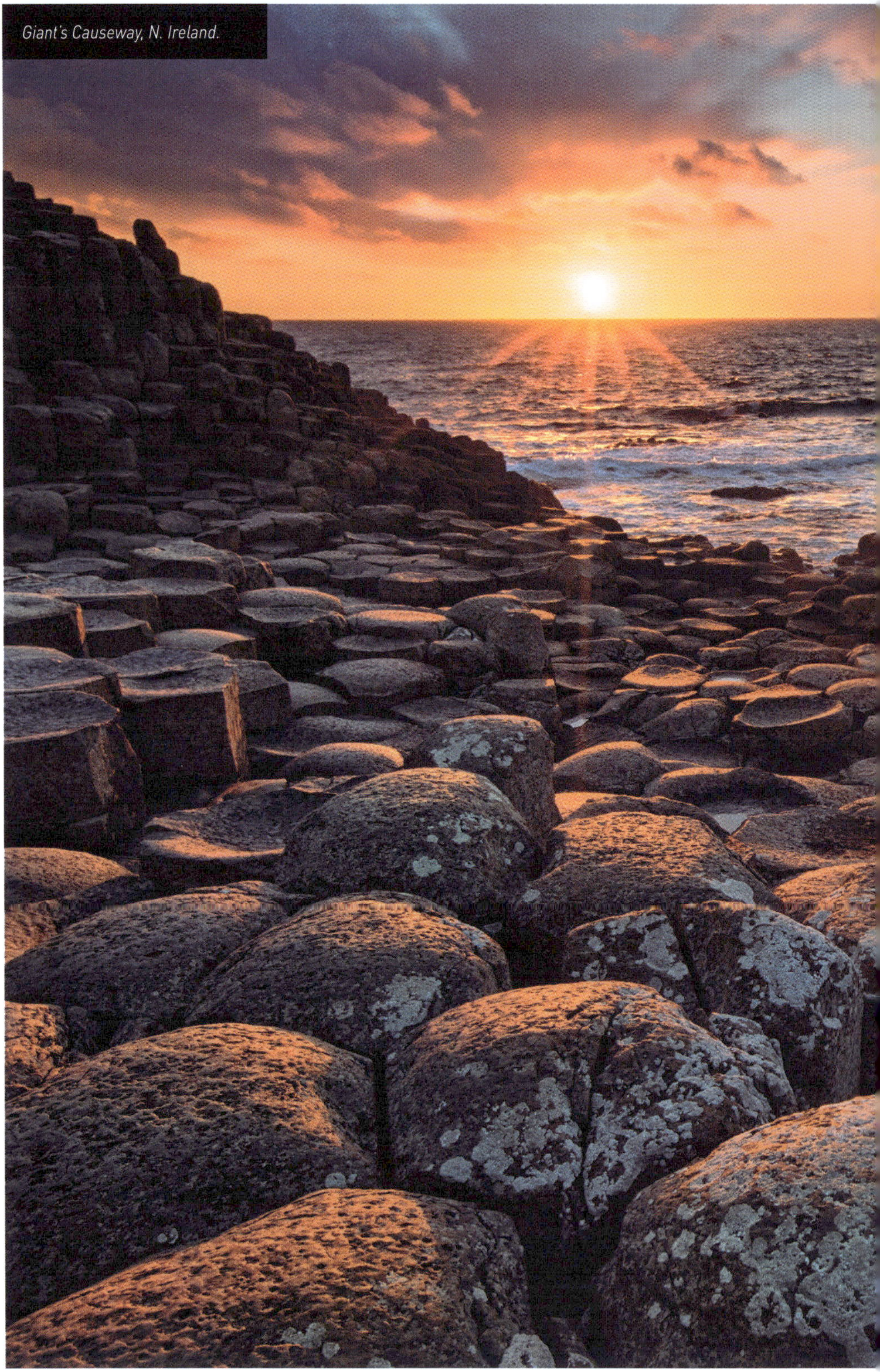

Giant's Causeway, N. Ireland.

Fanad Head lighthouse, Co Donegal.

The Samuel Beckett Bridge, Dublin city at sunset.

The Dark Hedges, County Antrim.

THE NEW IRELAND

Ireland has changed dramatically in recent years. The Republic has become a secular, multiracial, European state, while Northern Ireland has progressed from sectarian violence to power-sharing.

An alluring brand image has been created for Ireland over the years, portraying an unspoilt green land full of hospitable people, living life at a leisurely pace and possessed of an uncanny ability to have fun. Much of it is genuine – this is an ancient land full of human narrative and natural wonder – but there's a little bit of traditional 'Blarney' in the mix too.

A CHANGED SOCIETY

Today's visitors who enjoy having their preconceptions smashed will indeed have a grand time in Ireland, on both sides of the border.

A dramatic transformation has taken place in the Republic. Viewed 40 years ago by some as an economically-deprived, priest-ridden country whose most prolific product was emigrants, Ireland has gone full circle socially and economically since joining the European Union in 1972 (albeit with the odd wobble along the way). Adopting the euro in 2003 distanced the country decisively from its old imperial master, Britain, which clung to sterling. Irish culture, it found, travelled well, whether in the form of the comically clichéd 'Irish pub', which took root in 42 countries, or as cunningly modernised traditional music and dance extolled by Riverdance and the Pogues. The global success of artists ranging from stadium rockers U2 to indie singer-songwriter Hozier helped give Dublin a new hip identity, consolidated by its buzzing Temple Bar district. Most dizzying of all has been the revolution in social attitudes, with the conservative Catholic Church finally losing its stranglehold on an increasingly young, diverse and progressive population, stimulating several seismic changes in the law.

Generous tax breaks and a job market flooded with well-educated graduates encouraged multinationals – from Pfizer and other pharmaceutical companies, to Google and Facebook – to set up Irish operations, often basing their European headquarters in this hospitable English-speaking Eurozone country. Many of those who had emigrated returned to a new Ireland with a booming economy, and were joined by emigrants from eastern European countries and elsewhere, diluting the former homogeneous population of white, Irish-born Catholics. Embracing globalisation, the Republic took as its model not its fellow European countries, with their emphasis on the welfare state, but the US, with its stress on individual achievement. It was, the saying went, 'more Boston than Berlin'. Tipping its hat to US values, the low-fare airline Ryanair shamelessly modelled itself on America's Southwest Airlines, and became the biggest carrier in Europe.

BOOM, BUST, BREXIT

In 2009, the Republic suffered a crash and severe recession, when the global economic downturn revealed short-sighted and occasionally criminal behaviour by some Irish banks and developers. Projects paused and emigration again soared. Ireland introduced austerity measures and an 85-billion euro rescue package was agreed with the EU and IMF. By 2017, the economy had stabilised, unemployment was falling and the cobwebs were being blown off stalled developments. Ireland was back in business, and as a warning against future greed and irresponsibility, several disgraced bankers received prison sentences in 2018.

Meanwhile, Brexit too caused chaos given billions of euros of Irish trade goes to or through the UK each year. As a positive, some international companies relocated to Ireland to stay within the EU but the longterm economic impact on agriculture, food, trade and tourism is likely to be less so.

SOCIAL UPHEAVAL

Social change has accompanied Ireland's economic metamorphosis, recently at lightning pace. Divorce was not decriminalised in the Republic until 1995 and homosexuality until 1993. However, in recent years, revelations about paedophilia in the church, the cover up of child abuse by Catholic Bishops, and the exploitation of women in church-run 'Magdalen Laundries' have led to widespread anger, a sharp decline in attendance at Sunday Mass, and massive weakening of the church's influence in Irish society.

In 2015, Ireland voted by a landslide to legalise same-sex marriage – despite the Catholic Church's opposition – and in 2018, Irish people voted by 66.4 percent to remove the Eighth Amendment and allow abortion to be legalised, after a highly emotive referendum. Abortion remains illegal in Northern Ireland (even in cases of rape and fatal foetal abnormalities), but buoyed by their success in the south, civil rights campaigners are focussing on changing that, now with the support of Sinn Féin.

THE NORTHERN TRANSFORMATION

Once known for terrorism, Northern Ireland is increasingly seen as a great place to visit for outdoor adventurers, golfers, history, wildlife and art lovers. This is largely thanks to the 1998 Good Friday Agreement, which ended three decades of violence. The Republic amended its constitution, which had included a claim of sovereignty over Northern Ireland, the IRA laid down its arms and a devolved Northern Ireland Assembly was created, in which Unionist and Republicans leaders could share power. In 2007, the British army officially ended its operations in Northern Ireland, removing soldiers from the streets and making the border almost invisible. It's not all been easy, though. In 2017, the power-sharing deal in the Assembly collapsed, not to be restored until 2024, and uncertainty about border procedures post Brexit is continuing to cause concern.

IRELAND'S CONTINUING ALLURE

Ireland manages to combine modernity with traditional hospitality and unspoilt scenery. The weather may be wet and windy at times and the prices may be steep, but the people still have an outstanding capacity for friendliness and sense of fun that they are more than willing to share with their visitors.

Exploring Ireland's woodland on horseback.

THE IRISH CHARACTER

Justifiably famed for their hospitality, loquacity and wit, the Irish are generally gregarious people, with a love of laughter, conversation, culture, stories, poetry, politics and sport.

With trademark dark humour, Irish people take delight in seizing the stereotypes and jokes made against them, and turning them inside out. This trait is brilliantly exemplified in the much-loved TV sitcom, *Father Ted*, where all the characters are grotesque exaggerations of one kind or another, to great comic effect.

Local stallholder in Dalkey.

EMBRACING CULTURAL IDENTITY

Millions of visitors respond to this captivating charm by falling in love with Ireland at first sight. An increasing number, be warned, choose to consummate this love affair by giving up their life elsewhere, and moving to Ireland full time. Yet many in Ireland consider that the colossal social and economic changes that have taken place (see page 21) have eroded the traditional Irish values of courtesy, hospitality, spontaneity, sportsmanship and sense of fun.

English as spoken in Ireland is influenced by the grammar and vocabulary of the Irish language.

These critics argue that Ireland is selling its soul in return for a rootless cosmopolitanism, ruining the attraction of its unspoilt countryside by ill-thought-out and badly designed developments (planning permission has gotten much stricter), while ignoring the widening gap between the rich and the poor.

Certainly, the Republic, with its car-dependent, increasingly suburban commuter lifestyle, and its preference for British and American TV and film, has become more like everywhere else. But enough people have realised the danger of diluting Ireland's unique cultural identity, and are working hard to promote a pride in, and affection for, all things Irish, including the language, the music, even the football team, and the (sometimes elusive) idea of a less stressful way of life. Visitors, therefore, once they have recovered from the shock of discovering how expensive everything is – don't take Oscar Wilde's dictum, that those who live within their means suffer from a lack of imagination, seriously (he died penniless) – are likely to find that the time-honoured sense of hospitality has survived, sustained by an innate gregariousness.

THE TWO IRELANDS

After achieving the status of a dominion within the British Empire, an event followed by a bloody civil war, the new Irish Free State (declared 6 December 1922, Ireland didn't officially become a republic until 1949) signalled its priorities in its currency, with coins displaying emblems evoking a rural idyll and Celtic mythology: pigs, hens, hares and salmon.

But since those seismic events in the early 20th century, there has been two Irelands. One consists of the 26 counties of the Republic, generally seen as a friendly and easy-going destination. Then there are the Six Counties of Northern Ireland, still part of the United Kingdom, a more complex place to characterise, where society is more fragmented and scarred by the decades of modern conflict known as The Troubles, which raged between 1968 to 1998 and still bubble close to the surface at certain times. The border between North and South, which became much less visible post the 1998 Good Friday Agreement, has come back into sharper focus since Brexit.

Celebrating Bloomsday at the James Joyce Centre.

In terms of personality, the Northern Protestant is often regarded as being more earnest, more unimaginative than the Northern Catholic, who is in turn seen as less outgoing, less impulsive than the Southern Catholic. In reality, like all such stereotypes, these are absurd over-simplifications with grains of truth running through them. Perhaps because of their recent history, Irish people do tend to be relatively politically aware, and quite philosophical about life.

The German writer Heinrich Böll identified two turns of speech most characteristic of the Irish: 'It could be worse' and 'I shouldn't worry'. In a world where worries proliferate daily, Ireland retains its optimism. A popular poster when Ireland was experiencing the economic devastation that followed the boom, featured the optimistic slogan 'Keep going, sure it's grand' – an Irish version of the British wartime advice 'Keep calm and carry on'. It would be a mistake to read this as having blind faith in the status quo, though, as the reaction to the scandals in the Catholic Church revealed. Long held back by conservative values imposed on them by the church, the Irish enthusiastically threw off the shackles when multiple members of the once all-powerful institution were revealed as hypocrites, bullies and, in too many cases, abusers.

Shannon locals make the most of river life.

A STRONG THEATRICALITY

Occasionally contradictory and quick to change, the Irish character is an elusive concept to pin down. Unarguably, there is a nationwide love for good stories and a bit of drama, and Irish raconteurs have an almost reckless tendency towards exaggeration. This characteristic is a key feature in the darkly funny series *Black Books* penned by Dylan Moran, and also in the pantomime-esque (and polarising) *Mrs Brown's Boys*, the reflective *Moon Boy* and irreverent *Derry Girls*. But there's an introversion, too, the proneness to melancholy captured by George Bernard Shaw in *John Bull's Other Island*, a play set in the land of his birth: 'Your wits can't thicken in that soft moist air, on those white springy roads, in those misty rushes and brown bogs, on those hillsides of granite rocks and magenta heather. You've no such colours in the sky, no such lure in the distance, no such sadness in the evenings. Oh the dreaming! the dreaming! the torturing, heartscalding, never satisfying dreaming, dreaming, dreaming.'

You can sometimes sense this aspect of the Irish character in a pub when, after the talk – once called 'a game with no rules' – has achieved an erratic brilliance, the convivial mood abruptly changes to one of wistful melancholy.

The Irish are as much at home with sorrow as with laughter. This characteristic, sometimes manifesting itself as a natural pessimism, is the same one that makes Irish sporting fans such good losers. This was much remarked on during Ireland's disastrous performance at Gdansk in Euro 2012, as the Irish side headed for a 4-0 defeat by Spain. In about the 86th minute of the game the fans en masse broke into a beautiful and melodic rendition of *The Fields of Athenry*, one of the saddest songs in the repertoire, recalling the deportation to Australia of a man who stole to feed his family during the Great Famine. The intention was to encourage the team, who were outclassed by the eventual champions, but it was also seen as demonstrating the fans' very Irish resignation in the face

Street performers in Galway.

WHY DUBLIN IS DIFFERENT

Just as London is not representative of England, nor New York of the US, so the gap has widened between Dublin and the rest of the country. Dublin has long been Ireland's most populated and most cosmopolitan city, home to the largest jobs pool, best restaurants, stores and entertainment. While 30 years ago, almost everyone you met in the capital's streets or pubs would be Irish – drawn from all counties of the island – immigration has diluted that homogeneity as Ireland has evolved into a multiracial society, but again, this is much more evident in the city. To fully experience Ireland and the Irish character, you have to travel beyond the bright lights of Dublin.

of an unavoidable defeat. It is significant that the same sad song is also often sung by fans at rugby matches. While the demographic of the crowd is very different than at a football (soccer) match, the intrinsic character of the nation remains the same.

VIOLENCE AND VENDETTAS

The poet Louis MacNeice, described Ireland as a nation 'built upon violence and morose vendettas'. This less flattering aspect of the Irish personality was nicely summed up by another poet, Seamus Heaney, writing in 1975 at the height of the sectarian violence euphemistically referred to as 'the Troubles' in a poem entitled 'Whatever You Say, Say Nothing'. The title in fact came from a poster common in Belfast at the time, beginning 'Loose-talk costs lives' warning people that their conversations might be monitored by security forces. As another great Irish poet, W.B. Yeats in the poem 'Remorse for Intemperate Speech' (1931) reflected on the notorious Irish ability to bear a grudge: Out of Ireland have we come. / Great hatred, little room, / Maimed us at the start. / I carry from my mother's womb / A fanatic heart.

The history of this 'wretched little clod, broken off a bigger clod, broken off the west end of Europe,' as Shaw called it, encouraged it to view itself as a victim of colonialism, which lies behind the moral authority that singers such as Bono and Bob Geldof assumed when they lectured world leaders face-to-face on the need to get to grips with the causes of world poverty. Enya's easy listening take on traditional Celtic rhythms, *Only Time*, was judged poignant enough to be used as the soundtrack to TV replays of the collapse of the World Trade Center. More modern incarnations can be felt in folk band Amble's hit song *Lonely Island*, a haunting song evoking an old man's return home to Ireland and his disillusionment with what it is today.

TradFest is a lively gathering of musicians, singers and dancers.

AN ATTITUDE TO LIFE

In an age that esteems brand awareness, Ireland's international image is a potent one. It contains an echo of an 18th-century pace of life that is not lost, a psychological climate in which a racehorse attracts more glances than a Rolls-Royce. It's this attitude to life that makes Ireland such a rewarding place to visit. As the US-born novelist J.P. Donleavy, expressed it winsomely in *The Ginger Man*: 'When I die I want to decompose in a barrel of porter (dark beer) and have it served in all the pubs of Dublin. I wonder would they know it was me?'

IRELAND IN THE MOVIES

While Irish films once played on stereotypical images aimed at the lucrative Irish-American market, these days they are more likely to be about rock bands than red-headed colleens.

Ireland's first dedicated cinema, the Volta in Dublin's Mary Street, was opened in 1909 by James Joyce. But the country had no film studio until 1958, when Ardmore Studios opened in Bray, County Wicklow. It was thus left to Hollywood to portray Ireland to the world, and it did so by peddling whimsicality to the huge audience of Irish Americans who had a sentimental attachment to the pastoral ideal most potently portrayed in John Ford's *The Quiet Man*. The Irish, who were in reality facing hardship and chronic emigration, didn't object to such a portrayal: indeed, they built a tourist industry on it.

More recently, Ireland's social and political reality has assumed centre stage. Several films have tackled the Troubles, including Neil Jordan's *The Crying Game*, Jim Sheridan's *In the Name of the Father* (1993) and *Some Mother's Son* (1996), starring Helen Mirren. Perhaps the best film about the Irish War of Independence (and the internal conflict that followed it) is Ken Loach's *The Wind That Shakes the Barley* (2006), shot on location in rural Cork and starring Cillian Murphy.

The movie that did most to cement the image of the Irish as fighting boyos with a pre-feminist outlook was John Ford's 1952 production The Quiet Man, in which John Wayne slugged it out with Victor McLaglen and Maureen O'Hara in a virulently green landscape. Americans loved it – and unexpectedly, so did the Irish.

Neil Jordan's 1996 biopic Michael Collins, was dubbed Ireland's first national epic film, though it was US funded. Jordan sacrificed historical detail for dramatic impact, but Liam Neeson conveyed the romanticism and ruthlessness that characterised Ireland's struggle.

Alan Parker's faithful 1999 version of Angela's Ashes, Frank McCourt's boyhood memoir of growing up in Limerick, was felt locally to have overstated the level of poverty. Others complained that pain was driven out by glossy photography and sentimentality.

Veteran Hollywood director John Huston, who came of Irish stock and had a home in Ireland, captured the country's streak of Chekhovian melancholy in his last film, The Dead (1987), adapted from a classic short story by James Joyce.

Once (2006) – with Marketa Irglova and Glen Hansard - was funded by the Irish Film Board and cost €130,000. The touching tale of a Dublin busker and his Czech girlfriend has taken over €20m worldwide, and won an Oscar for Best Song. The Broadway musical (2012) won eight Tonys.

The Quiet Girl.

Fresh Voices

Lenny Abrahamson is one of Ireland's success stories. His debut film was the darkly comic tale of two hapless Dublin junkies *Adam and Paul* (2004); *Garage* (2007) tells the story of a lonely garage attendant in a country town and won a prize at the Cannes Film Festival; *What Richard Did* (2012), starring Jack Reynor, focuses on a group of privileged South Dublin teenagers; and *Room* (2015), based on Emma Donoghue's book of the same name, tells the disturbing story of a boy and his mother held captive.

John Carney played bass in Irish rock band The Frames before moving into filmmaking. His romantic musical drama *Once* (2006) enjoyed enormous success, with an Academy Award for Best Song. *Sing Street* (2016) is a musical comedy set in 1980s Dublin in which a teenage boy meets the girl of his dreams and starts a band in the hopes of impressing her.

The Guard (2011), an Irish cop comedy written and directed by John Michael McDonagh, and starring Brendan Gleeson and Don Cheadle, is great fun, and *Song of the Sea* (2014), an animated film about a selkie (shapeshifting seal folk) and various characters from Irish mythology, is excellent for younger viewers. Brendan Gleeson and Colin Farrell, stars of McDonagh's debut film *In Bruges* (2008), have been cast together again in tragicomedy *The Banshees of Inisherin* (2022), as lifelong friends whose friendship ends abruptly.

Grittier themes are dealt with in *Michael Inside* (2017), about a young man from a Dublin housing estate who ends up in prison, written and directed by Frank Berry, and *Black 47* (2018), a film about the Great Famine. *Aisha* (2022), starring Letitia Wright and Josh O'Connor, tackles asylum in Ireland through the eyes of a Nigerian refugee.

Colm Bairéad's coming-of-age film *The Quiet Girl* (*An Cailín Ciúin*, 2022) is about a neglected nine-year-old sent away from her dysfunctional family to distant relatives, and stars Catherine Clinch in the title role. It has made history as the first Irish-language film to make the Oscar shortlist for International Feature Film.

Another, film on the horrors of the Magdalene Laundries, *Small Things Like These* (2024) starring Cillian Murphy tells the story from the perspective of a coal merchant in the 1980s.

Bloody Sunday memorial march, Derry, 1994.

BLOODY
SUNDAY
JUSTICE

DECISIVE DATES

c.8000 BC
Ireland's first people arrive. Archaeological evidence of Mesolithic hunter-fisher-gatherer people discovered at Mount Sandel dates from this period.

4000 BC
The Neolithic period sees the arrival of the first farmers. The 6,000-year-old Céide Fields in north Mayo are the oldest in the world.

3000 BC
Megalithic tombs appear.

2500 BC
The Bronze Age arrives in Ireland with metallurgists from the Pontic Steppe.

From 500 BC
The La Tène style of art appears in Ireland.

c.AD 300
Stone-carved inscriptions appear in the 'Ogham alphabet', a rune-like script.

Statue of King BrianBorú at Dublin Castle.

An Ogham stone.

431
The Pope sends Palladius as the first bishop to Ireland.

c.432
St Patrick (later one of Ireland's three patron saints) comes back to Ireland as a missionary. At 16, he had been abducted from Britain and taken to Ireland, but later fled to France.

795–841
Viking attacks begin. After more than 40 years of pillaging the Norsemen establish their first longphort.

976–1014
BrianBorú, crowned king of Munster in 976, and high king of Ireland in 1002, defeats the Vikings near Clontarf in 1014 but is later slain in his tent.

From 1169
Anglo-Normans – sent to Ireland by the English King Henry II after a request from Dermot MacMurrough, the deposed king of Leinster – conquer large areas of the island and settle there. A system of feudalism is introduced and castles built.

1366
The Statutes of Kilkenny represent an attempt by the English crown to stop its Norman barons from assimilating, marrying Irishwomen or speaking the Irish language.

From 1541
England's Henry VIII declares himself king of Ireland and begins asserting British supremacy over the Irish chieftains.

1607
The most powerful of the Irish chieftains flee to Spain (called the Flight of the Earls), marking the end of Gaelic supremacy.

1608
James I starts the systematic settlement of Protestant Scots and English (known as the Plantation of Ulster).

1641–53
A rebellion by Irish Catholics against the English settlement policy is initially successful. In 1649, after his victory in the English Civil War, Oliver Cromwell conquers Ireland in a merciless campaign.

1690
England's Catholic King James II loses his throne to William of Orange at the Battle of the Boyne, and the period known as the Protestant Ascendancy begins.

1691
The Irish Parliament in Dublin passes the Penal Laws, which

James I was responsible for the Plantation of Ulster.

exclude Catholics from public office, deprive them of their property and their right to vote.

1791
Influenced by the revolutions in France and America, the United Irishmen movement is formed in Belfast. Its leading light, Wolfe Tone, is a Protestant coachbuilder's son.

1800
The Act of Union makes Ireland part of the United Kingdom. The Irish Parliament in Dublin is dissolved and Ireland is represented by a 100 MPs in the House of Commons in London.

1829
A Catholic politician, Daniel O'Connell (known as 'the Liberator'), forces the British parliament in London to pass a law emancipating Catholics.

From 1840
Nationalist movements gain strength (Irish Republican Brotherhood founded in 1858, Irish National Land League founded in 1879). There is a renewed interest in Gaelic culture (the Gaelic League is formed in 1893).

1845–49
The Great Famine deprives more than one-third of the Irish population of their main source of nutrition. An estimated 1 million people die and another 1 million emigrate.

From 1880
The Land League and the Irish Home Rule Party led by Charles Stuart Parnell employ parliamentary means in their struggle for Irish autonomy and land reform. In 1886, the first of several draft resolutions for Irish independence is rejected.

1905–08
The group known as Sinn Féin (We Ourselves) is formed 'to make England take one hand from Ireland's throat and the other out of Ireland's pocket'.

1912
Almost three-quarters of all Ulster Protestants sign a solemn pledge to stop all attempts at autonomy 'by all necessary means'. The Ulster Volunteer Force is formed in 1913 to enforce the pledge.

1916
On 24 April around 1,800 volunteers, led by Pádraig Pearse and James Connolly, occupy public buildings in Dublin and declare the formation of an Irish Republic. The Easter Rising is put down six days later. Britain's harsh response strengthens the nationalist cause.

Daniel O'Connell.

1918–23
Sinn Féin wins an overall majority in UK elections and announces the formation of an Irish Parliament in Dublin, with Éamon de Valera as president; the British government sends in troops, leading to the Irish War of Independence (also known as the Anglo-Irish War; 1919–21). In 1922, the Dáil narrowly accepts the

Engraving of a family evicted from their farm in the 1880s.

Anglo-Irish Treaty for the foundation of an Irish Free State excluding the Six Counties of Ulster with Protestant majorities. Civil war ensues and the pro-Treaty Free State government prevails.

1937
The Free State (now called Éire) adopts its own political constitution.

1939
Éire declares its neutrality during World War II. Germany tries to damage Britain's interests by supporting the IRA.

1949
Éire leaves Commonwealth to become the Republic of Ireland.

1969–70
A demonstration by the Northern Irish Civil Rights Movement is attacked by the British army. The IRA splits into two factions in 1970. The Provisional IRA intensifies its armed struggle in Northern Ireland.

1972
Thirteen demonstrators are shot dead by British soldiers on Bloody Sunday. The parliament in Belfast is dissolved and Northern Ireland is ruled directly from London.

1973
The Republic joins the European Economic Community (EEC) along with Great Britain.

1990
Mary Robinson becomes the first woman president of Ireland.

1997
In the Republic, divorce becomes legal. Mary McAleese, a Northerner by birth, becomes president.

1998
A Northern Ireland peace treaty is signed by all parties, including Sinn Féin. David Trimble and John Hume receive the Nobel Peace Prize. A car bomb in Omagh kills 29.

1999
An all-party Assembly with limited powers sets up in Northern Ireland. The Republic drops its claim to sovereignty over the North.

Éamon de Valera, opposing the 1922 treaty that divided Ireland.

Mary Robinson.

2002
The Republic adopts the euro. In the North, rule from London is reimposed.

2005
The IRA declares that its war is over and its weapons destroyed. The legendary Northern Irish footballer, George Best, dies.

2007
In Northern Ireland Ian Paisley's Democratic Unionist Party (DUP) and Gerry Adams's Sinn Fein Party agree to work together.

2008
Taoiseach Bertie Ahern, resigns and hands over to Brian Cowen. The effects of the international financial crisis hit home, and the recession begins.

2010
The government decides that Irish tax payers will bail out the banks. Many homeowners are left in negative equity or on reduced pensions. Several bishops resign following revelations of the Catholic

Church's failure to protect children from sexually abusive priests.

2011
Fine Gael wins a landslide victory and forms a coalition with the Labour Party with Enda Kenny as Taoiseach. Michael D. Higgins, a former Labour Party TD, an Irish speaker from Galway and a published poet, is elected president. At Ireland's first-ever Citizenship Ceremony, 73 new citizens from 24 countries are sworn in.

2012
Mass demonstrations follow the death of Savita Halappanavar in a Galway hospital from a septic miscarriage, despite her repeated requests for a termination. Emigration of unemployed young people to Canada and Australia grows apace.

2013
Taoiseach Enda Kenny issues a formal apology on behalf of the state for its part in the Magdalene Laundries. Austerity increases, a property tax is introduced, and banks start to negotiate with mortgage defaulters.

2014
The Protection of Life During Pregnancy Act comes into effect in the Republic of Ireland. Tens of thousands march as anti-water charges protests begin.

2015
The Republic of Ireland votes 'yes' in same-sex marriage referendum. Anti-water charges protests continue.

Posters for the 2018 abortion referendum.

2016
Centenary commemorations for 1916. General elections show a rise in support for independent candidates, as well as a resurgence of support for Fianna Fáil. After two months of negotiations, a minority government is formed with Enda Kenny as taoiseach. The European Commission orders Ireland to recover up to 13 billion euros from Apple in back taxes. Northern Ireland and Scotland vote to remain in the EU, but leave vote wins the majority of votes in England and Wales.

2017
Discovery of a mass grave containing the remains of nearly 800 babies at the former Tuam Mother and Baby Home. Enda Kenny resigns and Leo Varadkar (Fine Gael) becomes Taoiseach.

2018
Over 66 percent of Irish voters say 'yes' to repealing the Eighth Amendment and legalising abortion. Michael D Higgins is re-elected as president. Ireland wins the Six Nations rugby tournament with a Grand Slam.

2020
The Covid-19 pandemic hits the world.

2021
Same-sex marriage is legalised in Northern Ireland. The Northern Ireland Protocol comes into force.

2025
A new government is formed under Taoiseach Micheál Martin and Simon Harris as Tánaiste.

Unionist mural in the Newtownards Road area of east Belfast.

St Matthew from the Book of Kells.

IRELAND'S INVADERS

The Anglo-Normans decided to stake a claim, and that's when the trouble really began.

Most of Ireland's dramatic past is integrally bound up with the extraordinary relationship it has endured with the powerful island to its immediate east. Much of the country's history, in a nutshell, has been shaped by its resistance to England's attempts to dominate, subjugate or exploit the island of Ireland in one form or another, for various political or economic reasons. The irony of the latest twist in the tale, with the Irish Border (created by the UK government in 1922) frustrating Britain's hard Brexit plans, is not lost on locals.

THE FIRST CONQUESTS

Ireland's first people were Mesolithic hunter-fisher-gatherers. In the 1970s, a campsite dated to 7900–7600 BC was discovered at Mount Sandel, in County Derry. While there are no visible remains, to-date it's the earliest known human settlement in Ireland.

The island's first conquerors arrived from Anatolia (present-day Turkey) around 4000 BC. These early farmers displaced the island's earliest people, and have left a rich legacy of megalithic burial chambers. The Newgrange passage-grave overlooking the Boyne River in Country Meath, is thought to be 5,000 years old.

Giants, gods, magicians and monsters abound in Ireland's origin myth the 'Book of Invasions' ('Leabhar Gabhála'); a collection of poetry and prose compiled in the 11th century.

In turn, metallurgists from the Pontic Steppe supplanted the Neolithic builders around 2500 BC and may have introduced Goidelic (a Q-Celtic language) to Ireland. A 2015 DNA study revealed a significant genetic affinity between these Bronze Age people and modern Irish, Scottish and Welsh people. Beautifully crafted leaf-shaped swords and gold ornaments, such as the Lunula, have been preserved. The La Tène style of art appears in Ireland from 500 BC but the evidence for further mass migration is sparse.

Prehistoric monument Newgrange, built in the Neolithic period.

VIKINGS RAIDS IN 'THE LAND OF SAINTS AND SCHOLARS'

When the fall of the Roman Empire plunged Europe into the Dark Ages. Ireland, in contrast, entered its golden age, becoming a lone beacon of learning and civilisation – 'The Land of Saints and Scholars'.

Christianity is believed to have been brought to the island by a Romano-British missionary, St Patrick, who had been kidnapped as a youth and taken to Ireland to tend sheep. Later, he travelled widely in France and Italy, returning to Ireland in AD 432 to spread the word of Christ. Today, he is fondly thought of as being responsible for having banished snakes from the island.

Viking raids plagued Ireland from the late 8th century until the early 11th century (see boxes pages 118 and 157), but the Norse tyranny was destroyed at the Battle of Clontarf in 1014 by High King Brian Ború, who saw himself as Ireland's Charlemagne. The Normans, led by the ambitious adventurer Strongbow, followed in their Viking ancestors' footsteps, and landed an invasion force in 1170. Having gained a toehold, they built a power base with fortified stone castles. Strongbow declared himself king of Leinster, which spurred England's Henry II (previously, little interested in Ireland) into action, and inaugurated an involvement between the two countries that was to last, with immeasurable bloodshed, for 800 years.

St Patrick in military dress on horseback.

SAVED BY THE MONASTERIES

Monasteries quickly became centres of learning across the country, with people coming to Ireland from Europe to study in them. Some were in isolated locations while others were close to strongholds of Irish kings who kept treasures there, in turn making the monasteries a target for plundering Vikings from the late 8th century onwards. Tall round towers, many still standing, were built to serve as lookouts, refuges and belfries. Intricately-carved sandstone High Crosses were built around churches to teach Bible stories. Also surviving are some of the monks' exquisite illuminated manuscripts such as the 'Book of Durrow' and the 'Book of Kells'.

NORMAN INFLUENCE

Over the next three centuries, the Normans, intermarried with the Irish, and expanded their influence. Many of the country's elaborate castles, such as Blarney in County Cork and Bunratty in County Clare, date from this time.

But, as the barons thrived, the English Crown's authority gradually shrank to an area around Dublin known as 'the Pale'. It was Henry VIII, determined finally to break the local nobles' power, who proclaimed himself 'King of this land of Ireland as united, annexed and knit for ever to the Imperial Crown of the Realm of England'.

When the nobles resisted, Henry seized their lands, resettling them with loyal 'planters' from England and Scotland.

His daughter, Elizabeth I, fought a series of wars in Ireland. As well as trying to impose the Reformation on the country, she wanted to protect England's right flank against an invasion from her principal opponent, Spain. Near the end of her reign, powerful Ulster chieftains, Hugh O'Neill, earl of Tyrone, and Red Hugh O'Donnell, earl of Tyrconnell, were defeated at the Battle of Kinsale.

William of Orange, who defeated James II at the Battle of the Boyne in 1690.

From 1609 onwards, Elizabeth I's successor, James I, planted English and Scottish settlers in six counties of Ulster. These new settlers were Protestants, firm believers in the Calvinist work ethic, and the religious mix they created led to strife in Ulster in the 19th and 20th centuries.

An early sign of the troubles ahead came in 1641, when Ulster Roman Catholics, hoping to recover their confiscated lands, rebelled at Portadown. The facts of the rebellion were rapidly overwhelmed by lurid tales of a drunken Catholic pogrom against the God-fearing settlers, with 12,000 Protestants knifed, shot and drowned, pregnant women raped, and infants grotesquely roasted on spits.

The Gaelic Irish had further cause to worry when, after Charles I was beheaded, the new Puritan Parliament in England began suppressing the Roman Catholic religion. Fanned by the flames of this resentment, a new Catholic revolt began to spread. This 'Great Rebellion' was ruthlessly suppressed by Oliver Cromwell, whose 20,000 Ironside troops descended and devastated the countryside. By 1652, about a third of the Catholic Irish had been killed and much of their land had been taken from them and handed over to Protestants.

When the monarchy was restored, Charles II disappointed Catholics by throwing his support behind the Protestants, on whom he depended for power. His successor, James II, himself a Roman Catholic, raised hopes by introducing an Act of Parliament that would have ousted the Protestant settlers, but, before it could be put into practice, James was defeated at the Battle of the Boyne (1690), near Dublin, by William of Orange. William had been called in by the English establishment to end James's 'Popish ways' and his success in doing so is still commemorated annually on 12 July with mammoth parades by Protestant Orangemen throughout Northern Ireland. From that day in 1690, Roman Catholics became a persecuted majority in Ireland. New anti-Catholic legislation, the Penal

Laws, barred them from all public life and much social activity.

THE LAND PROBLEM

Protestant Ascendency politicians, led by Henry Grattan, pushed for an independent legislature in Ireland. The threat of force was added in the shape of the Irish Volunteers, 80,000 strong by 1782. London caved in and agreed to a separate parliament in Dublin. However, the Catholic majority (three-quarters of the population) were still denied a political role and the extensive

Henry Grattan.

patronage at the disposal of the English parliament allowed it to manipulate policy in Dublin.

The government in London passed two Catholic Relief Acts giving Catholics limited voting rights and allowing them once more to own or lease land. As so often in Ireland, however, a well-meaning policy gave birth to anarchy. Catholics began buying land in Ulster, forcing up prices and alarming the Protestants, who formed a vigilante outfit, the Peep o' Day Boys, to burn out Catholics in dawn raids. The Catholics set up their own vigilante force, the Defenders. The lines of a long conflict were drawn.

Yet Ulster was the cradle in 1791 for a brave attempt by Protestants and Catholics to fight together for reform. Wolfe Tone, the son of a

> *By the middle of the 18th century, only 7 percent of Irish land was in Catholic hands, and peasants had the status of slaves.*

Protestant coachbuilder, set up the first Society of United Irishmen club in Belfast and a second soon opened in Dublin. It began well, largely as a debating society, but was suppressed within three years when British prime minister William Pitt feared an alliance between Ireland and France, with whom Britain was at war. Tone, condemning England as 'the never-failing source of all our political evils', fled to America.

Government anxiety increased when the United Irishmen, largely a middle-class Protestant group, began forging links with the Defenders, mostly working-class Catholics. And soon an even more threatening alliance was being forged: the United Irishmen persuaded Tone, who had been thinking of becoming a farmer near Philadelphia, to sail to France and rally support against Britain. Tone assured the French that their arrival in Ireland would trigger a national uprising, supported by the Irish militia, and on 16 December 1796 a French battle fleet of 43 ships set sail.

It was the weather that came to England's rescue. Severe storms dispersed the fleet, and the few troops who landed at Bantry Bay, on the southwest coast, were greeted rather unenthusiastically by the Irish peasants, who believed that the French really had been sent by the northern Protestants to suppress them further.

In the end, it was the United Irishmen who were suppressed. Pitt, fearing a second French expedition, imposed harsh martial law in Ulster. The army, four-fifths of whom were themselves Catholic Irish peasants, began arresting the organisation's outlawed leaders, identifying them as a result of information partly provided by informers, partly extracted through brutal beatings. Soon Ulster was in the grip of terror and the stage was set for a new group to enter the Irish drama. These were the Orangemen, whose role in Ulster remains central today.

The movement began in 1795 after a clash between Protestant Peep o' Day Boys and Catholic Defenders at the Battle of the Diamond, near Armagh, in which 30 men died. The Protestants, fearing worse was to come, reorganised as the

Orange Society, named after their hero, William of Orange, and preyed as lawless bandits on Catholics. In defeating the United Irishmen, the government was glad of their vicious support.

THE UNITED KINGDOM OF GREAT BRITAIN AND IRELAND

After the Irish Rebellion of 1798 (see page 41), and mindful of the likelihood of further ones, William Pitt proposed a full union between Britain and Ireland. The 300-seat Irish parliament in Dublin would be abolished and 100 seats for Irish representatives would be created within the Imperial Parliament in London.

Unsurprisingly, this proposal was met with resistance. The British government resorted to outright vote buying and on 28 January 1800 a majority of Irish Members of Parliament voted in favour of the proposed union. Ireland's parliament had, in effect, abolished itself.

On 1 January 1801, Britain and Ireland entered, in Pitt's phrase, their 'voluntary association' within the Empire with 'equal laws, reciprocal affection, and inseparable interests'.

'Horrors of the Irish Union – Botheration of Poor Pat or A Whisper Across the Channel', a 1798 cartoon.

THE GREAT REBELLION

Disaffection with English rule climaxed in May 1798 in a major rebellion. But by then so many of the United Irishmen's leaders had been arrested that most of the risings throughout the country were too poorly organised to succeed. The yeomanry reacted by torturing and shooting indiscriminately, often butchering the rebels after they had surrendered.

Within six weeks, it was all over. Perhaps 30,000 had died, giving birth in the process to countless ballads commemorating a small nation's struggle for freedom. Irish patriotism was taking root with a vengeance.

Napoleon Bonaparte, pressed by Wolfe Tone not to abandon French support for Ireland, belatedly agreed to another expedition, which set sail that August. But once again the French had been misinformed. When one party landed at Killala, County Mayo, having been led to expect enthusiastic, disciplined battalions, they found instead supporters whom they disdainfully regarded as rapacious simpletons.

In October, Tone himself tried to land in County Donegal with a party of 3,000 French, but they were beaten back by a Royal Navy force. Tone was captured and died in prison after an attempted suicide. His martyrdom was assured: several Gaelic football clubs are named in his honour and a trad band called the Wolfe Tones are well known for their rebel songs.

IRELAND'S FINEST RUINS

Visiting ruins not only unveils the drama of Irish history, it often takes you off the beaten path to unusually beautiful corners of the countryside.

To understand why Ireland has so many churches in ruins, consider its history. Located at the western edge of the known world, Ireland escaped conquest by the Romans, and continued to follow a pagan religion until the mid-fifth century, and the arrival of Palladius, St Patrick and other missionaries. It was a peaceful conversion, and pagan customs were absorbed into Christian ritual. The earliest monasteries became important centres of learning. Stone carving was used on High Crosses to tell the Gospel story to an illiterate population, and in architectural decoration.

In contrast, Christianity's subsequent history in Ireland has been turbulent. The monastery at Clonmacnoise, established on its vulnerable Shannon-side location in AD 545, had a typical fate, surviving numerous attacks from warring Irish clans, then Viking raiders, and then Normans, only to be destroyed by the English in 1552.

Gallarus Oratory was built between the 7th and 8th centuries and is the best-preserved early Christian church in Ireland.

THE PENAL LAWS

In the twelfth century the Anglo-Normans arrived. The Normans endowed continental monastic orders, including the Cistercians, and built abbeys on an ambitious scale. But these institutions were short-lived. From 1536 onwards, the Reformation led to the suppression of the monasteries, and by 1653 Oliver Cromwell had finished off the job. The infamous Penal Laws that followed prohibited Catholic participation in public life, and most of the ruined churches and abbeys were never rebuilt.

But because of the beauty of the stone carving, their scale – which ranges from ambitious to modest – and their typically tranquil locations, the ruins of these buildings are most rewarding to visit.

The beautiful and remote valley of Glencolumbkille, County Donegal, associated with St Columba (Latin) or Colmcille (Irish), runs down to the sea at Glen Bay and contains 15 Early Christian pillars and cross-slabs decorated with cross-motifs and geometric designs. At midnight on 9 June a barefoot pilgrimage around the sites begins.

When the monastery at Clonmacnoise, County Offaly, was founded by St Ciarán around AD 540, its Shannon-side location marked the boundary between the provinces of Leinster and Connacht.

Influences from both Burgundy and the west of England have been detected in the richly carved Cistercian abbey that is Boyle Abbey, County Roscommon. Rounded arches of the Romanesque style were in favour in the late 12th century, but in a later phase of building, pointed Gothic arches were introduced.

The beehive huts at Skellig Michael.

Skellig Michael

The monastery of Skellig Michael, 8 miles (13km) off the southwest coast, is dramatically situated on a barren rocky island. A UNESCO World Heritage Site since 1996, it is the most remarkable Early Christian site in Ireland, and can be visited by boat between May and September. Dating from around AD 800, the monastic remains are on a saddle of rock reached by climbing some six hundred stone steps. Six beehive huts, in which the monks lived, and two rectangular oratories, where they prayed, were built of dry stone on a cliff edge around a small garden area. They are surprisingly well preserved, given their exposed Atlantic location. Below the huts are the remains of a 12th-century church, and there are also early Christian cross slabs and hermitages. Shortly after AD 1200, the monks transferred to the mainland at Ballinskelligs. The monks, seeking to emulate the desert fathers in their isolation, survived on a diet of fish, seabirds and their eggs (which they traded with passing seafarers), and vegetables from their garden. The island was a place of pilgrimage for penitents until the 20th century.

A clifftop site on a narrow promontory makes a stunning location for the ruined 12th-century Ardmore Cathedral, County Waterford. Its sturdy Hiberno-Romanesque arches contrast with the slender, conical-roofed round tower. St Declan's Oratory and Well nearby date from the 9th century, and are still visited by pilgrims annually on 24 July.

THE MAKING OF A NATION

The union with Britain brought little happiness to either partner. And the divorce would involve more than a century of bitter bloodshed.

Like many of his contemporaries, Daniel O'Connell, a Catholic lawyer from a well-off Kerry family, had been educated in France, and the ideals of the French Revolution had influenced his thinking. Although he recognised that none of Ireland's basic problems had been solved by the union with Britain, he wanted no revolution in Ireland, not even a separation from the British Crown. What he campaigned for, with powerful oratory, was the right of Catholics to become Members of Parliament. Sir Robert Peel, Britain's prime minister, was forced to introduce a Catholic Emancipation Bill, which was passed.

Once in the House of Commons, O'Connell, by now 'the Liberator', began to rally support for his next cause: a repeal of the union. When his appeals struck few chords in Parliament, he took his arguments to his countrymen, holding 'Monster Meetings' throughout Ireland. One rally was attended by 300,000. The meetings resulted in his arrest for conspiracy. When he was released from prison months later, he was in failing health.

The formidable Daniel O'Connell, 'the Liberator'.

IRELAND'S GREATEST DISASTER

At that point, fate intervened in the form of the Great Famine that began in 1845. In reality, it wasn't a true famine at all, rather a failure of the potato crop. At its height, wheat and barley were being freely shipped to England, together with tens of thousands of cattle, sheep and pigs. But such produce was beyond the pockets of the peasants, whose every penny went towards paying rent to the series of middlemen – often as many as seven – who stood between them and their land's ultimate owner. All they could afford was the humble potato. When it was blighted, they starved.

Out of a population of 8 million, 1 million people died in the Great Hunger and well over a million set off in squalid emigrant ships for a new life in America, where they would pass down to future generations a deep anti-British resentment. Around a third of the land in Ireland changed hands as estates went bankrupt, but the new landlords, who were mostly Irish (of both religions, now that Catholics were allowed to buy land), were even harsher than their predecessors in increasing rents. O'Connell travelled to London and made an impassioned appeal to Members of Parliament for aid but his words fell on deaf ears. He retired to Italy, and died in 1847.

In 1848, a year which saw nationalist uprisings in several countries of Europe, the Young Irelander Rebellion took place in County Tipperary. It was a total failure, with little support from a weakened populace, but the leaders (subsequently arrested and transported) were later influential in setting up Irish nationalist movements in America, and the Irish Republican Brotherhood in Ireland, which later organised the Easter Rising.

THE BIRTH OF THE FENIANS

On St Patrick's Day, 17 March 1858, James Stephens, a Kilkenny railway engineer who had been a leading Young Irelander, founded a society that came to be known as the Irish Republican Brotherhood, dedicated to the idea of an independent democratic republic. An American branch was set up, called the Fenians after the ancient Gaelic warriors. The American Civil War, Stephens noted, had given his supporters their valuable experience of battle. After a skirmish in Canada, Fenian participants were referred to as 'The Irish Republican Army'. It was the IRA's first appearance on the world stage.

Stephens was deposed as leader after his failure to organise an army of liberation from the US, but by 1867, armed and well-drilled bands had been set up throughout Ireland to revolt. Some trains were derailed, marking the arrival in the country of a strategy that would shape Ireland's struggles: guerrilla warfare.

THE FIGHT FOR HOME RULE

But it was not violence that was to further Ireland's cause most at this time. The two principal engines of change were driven by William Ewart Gladstone, who came to power as Britain's prime minister in 1868, and Charles Stewart Parnell, an English-educated Protestant landowner from County Wicklow.

'My mission,' said Gladstone, 'is to pacify Ireland.' He began in 1869 by removing one chronic grievance. Since the Reformation, the Protestant church had been the established church in

A destitute family about to be evicted from their dwelling during the Great Famine of 1845.

ENGLAND AND THE FAMINE

The British government was not unaware of the Great Famine's effects. One MP described a large-scale eviction as 'the chasing away of 700 human beings like crows out of a cornfield'. England's refusal to provide relief is regarded by many today as a horrifying failure of imagination. Even compassionate and otherwise enlightened men lacked the vision to question the prevailing economic orthodoxy, the rigid belief that it would make matters worse to interfere with natural economic forces. The same principle was applied to the industrial working classes in England's factories, but their lot was less desperate.

Ireland, although it represented only a sixth of the population. Gladstone abolished this privileged position. Next, he introduced a land Bill designed to make it less easy for landlords to evict tenants. Sensing new hope, nationalists began to demand once more that Ireland should have its own parliament for Irish affairs, leaving international matters to the Parliament in London. This aspiration was known as Home Rule.

On reaching the House of Commons in 1875, Parnell, son of an Irish father and an American mother, scorned its cosy, club-like conventions and perfected filibustering techniques for blocking parliamentary business: proposing endless amendments, and making long speeches.

The one part of Ireland to benefit from the Industrial Revolution was Ulster, where linen and shipbuilding took off. Ulster Protestants saw their prosperity being threatened by anyone who wanted to weaken the link with England.

Parnell Monument, O'Connell Street, Dublin.

THE PROS AND CONS OF HOME RULE

Gladstone's 1881 Land Act was regarded as revolutionary. It granted fixity of tenure to tenants who paid their rent; laid down that a tenant should be paid when he vacated a holding for improvements he had made; and decreed that fair rents should be defined not by the landlord but by a Land Court. Progress seemed possible. But then Lord Frederick Cavendish, the new chief secretary for Ireland and Gladstone's nephew by marriage, was knifed to death in Dublin. Reform slid down the agenda.

Parnell's next move was to found the Irish National League to campaign uncompromisingly for Home Rule. A general election in 1885 gave him control of 85 of the 103 Irish seats in the House of Commons – and the balance of power between the Liberals and Conservatives. Home Rule became the main issue in English politics.

The Conservatives argued that Home Rule would still leave Parliament controlling international affairs, war and peace, even customs and excise. Yet many educated Irishmen, including nationalists, were resigned to remaining within the British Empire – as long as they could control their domestic affairs. Had Home Rule been granted in 1886, therefore, Ireland might well still be part of the United Kingdom, having 'a distinct but not separate identity' rather like Wales and Scotland. It is one of the big 'ifs' of Irish history.

With Michael Davitt, Parnell set up the National Land League of Ireland. Funds from America flowed in to help the victims of oppression and threats of violence, frequently carried out, gave teeth to the Land League and left it in control of some areas of the country.

ULSTER GOES ON THE ALERT

A million Protestants still lived in Ireland, almost half of them in the northeast area of Ulster, and Home Rule would have severely limited the power of this influential minority. These Ulstermen saw themselves as different, as indeed they were. Their Presbyterian tradition had always been more radical than the loose Protestantism of their southern coreligionists and had given them a formidable self-reliance – some would say stubbornness. Although security of tenure had always been greater in the northeast, the Protestant descendants of the 17th-century Scots settlers felt far from settled; they had retained an ineradicable tribal fear of being dispossessed of their lands by the Catholics, and it was largely their opposition to change that led to the first Home Rule Bill being voted down in 1886.

In southern Ireland, a literary revival was growing, creating a new appreciation of Celtic culture and myths and a new respect for the Irish language, hitherto regarded as a fast-dying vulgar tongue. W.B. Yeats, the son of a Protestant Irish artist, published collections of folk tales such as *The Celtic Twilight*, conferring a new dignity on the often-ridiculed Irish peasantry. A Gaelic League was set up, declaring itself the archer that would slay the plundering crow of the English mind, its arrow being the Irish language.

In the political arena, however, there were setbacks. Parnell lost political support when the scandal of his longtime affair with Kitty O'Shea, who had borne him three children, erupted in 1889. Parnell died from pneumonia two years later, after being soaked with rain at a political rally in Galway. Gladstone himself retired from the scene in 1893, aged 84, having failed to get his second Home Rule Bill, which had been approved narrowly by the House of Commons, through the Upper Chamber, the House of Lords. It was time for the baton of the Irish cause to pass to a new generation.

Ulster Unionists bring out the guns in 1912 to demonstrate their resistance to Home Rule.

THE 20TH CENTURY

As a new century dawned, a Conservative government in England held out no hope of Home Rule. Queen Victoria's visit to Dublin in 1900 and Edward VII's in 1903 were well received, but new forces of nationalism were being assembled by Arthur

Griffith, a Dublin printer and journalist, and John McBride, a Mayo-born republican who had fought the British in the Boer War. Griffith and McBride demanded 'an Irish Republic One and Indivisible'.

Two general elections in Britain in 1910 left the Liberals and Conservatives almost equally split in parliament. Once again, the Irish Party, now led by the moderate John Redmond, used its balance of power to press for a new Home Rule Bill. Such a Bill was introduced in 1912 by Prime Minister Herbert Asquith and looked likely to become law in the foreseeable future.

Sir Edward Carson, although born in Dublin, rallies Protestant Ulster against Home Rule.

The Protestants in Ulster began arming themselves. They found as leader a Dublin MP and lawyer, Sir Edward Carson, who had been solicitor general for England, Wales and Ireland and who had acted as prosecuting counsel against Oscar Wilde in 1895. What, asked Carson, was the point of Home Rule now that most Irishmen owned their farms, all major grievances had been removed, and even a Catholic university had been set up?

In 1913 recruiting started for a 100,000-strong Ulster Volunteer Force and large consignments of rifles were imported. The southerners responded by setting up a counter force, the Irish National Volunteers, whose badge carried the letters 'FF', for Fianna Fáil, a legendary band of warriors. The problem could be simply stated: the Protestants in the northeast wished to remain full British subjects and were prepared to fight to retain that status. The Catholic minority in the area, like the Catholic majority in the rest of the island, sought a more Irish identity. The two attitudes seemed irreconcilable.

Sir Winston Churchill, then a Liberal minister, was first to voice publicly one possible solution. Of the ancient province of Ulster's nine counties, six – those most heavily settled by Protestants in the early 1600s – might be excluded from Home Rule. Redmond, under pressure to get results, conceded that these Six Counties could 'temporarily' be excluded for six years, after which time he hoped the Unionists would see the wisdom of rejoining their fellow Irishmen. From the nationalists' point of view, it was a fatal concession.

THE EASTER RISING

In 1914 Britain became embroiled in World War 1 (see page 49), supported by many Irish volunteers acting on a promise of Home Rule once the war was won. However, the Irish Republican Brotherhood were distrustful, and unprepared to shelve their demands for independence for the duration of hostilities. They planned an uprising, supported by the Irish Citizens' Army (founded to defend striking workers against brutal police suppression, by James Connolly, a Scottish labour organiser born into a poor Irish family), 200 women of Cumann na mBan, and the remaining Irish Volunteers who had refused to join the British war effort, led by Pádraig Pearse, a schoolmaster. A consignment of weapons sent by Germany to help the rebels was intercepted by the British, and Volunteer leader Eoin MacNeill issued a command cancelling the uprising as a result, which led to severely depleted numbers when the Uprising began regardless, on the morning of Monday, 24 April 1916.

Pearse and Connolly, along with 400 others, armed with a variety of rifles and agricultural implements, took over the city's General Post Office (GPO) and solemnly read out the Proclamation of the Republic. Another 800 or so civilian soldiers took over a brewery, a biscuit factory, the Four Courts and other key places. Éamon de Valera, a young maths teacher born in America of an Irish mother and a Spanish father, led the occupation of a mill (see page 53).

The authorities were caught napping, but soon Dublin ground to a halt. Alarm and rumours spread. The poor looted stores and children ransacked sweet shops. A British gunboat on the River Liffey began to shell the rebel strongholds. The inevitable end, when it came, was swift. The British set fire to the area around the GPO. By the time Pearse surrendered on the Saturday, 77 rebels, 139 police and soldiers, and 374 civilians had died. The centre of Dublin lay in ruins. Martial law was imposed and 4,000 people jailed. Dubliners, by and large, were disgusted by the uprising, but this opinion swiftly changed when it was announced that 16 leaders were to be executed.

EXECUTIONS AND AMNESTY

On 3 May, the first three leaders (Pádraig Pearse, Thomas MacDonagh and Thomas J. Clarke) were shot at dawn. The next day, four more were shot (Joseph Mary Plunkett, William Pearse, Edward Daly and Michael O'Hanrahan). On 5 May, one more (John MacBride). On 8 May, four more (Éamonn Ceannt, Michael Mallin, Seán Heuston and Con Colbert). On 9 May, one more (Thomas

Dublin's O'Connell Street in ruins after being shelled by a British gunboat during the Easter Rising.

THE IMPACT OF THE GREAT WAR

Larger problems than Ireland loomed for Britain in 1914 with the outbreak of World War I. A deal was rapidly done under which politicians in London passed a Home Rule Act, together with an order suspending its implementation for the duration of the war or until such time as some kind of amendment could be added to take account of the concerns of Ulster Unionists.

Ireland was thus bought off, to the extent that a greater proportion of Irishmen – from both the north and the south – volunteered for the British army than any other part of the United Kingdom's population. Irishmen won 17 Victoria Crosses in the first 13 months of the war. Surely, the Irish nationalists reasoned, such courage would eradicate even Ulster Unionist worries about the reliability of their Catholic countrymen.

The reality was different. Sir Edward Carson, now a member of Britain's War Cabinet, saw the Ulster regiments' heavy losses in the war, particularly during the Battle of the Somme in 1916, as a subscription towards permanent membership of a grateful UK.

In Dublin, not everyone was prepared to wait until the war with Germany ended. Many still remembered the old adage that England's misfortune is Ireland's opportunity, and nationalists led by Arthur Griffith began grouping under the broad banner of Sinn Féin (meaning 'We Ourselves').

Kent was executed at Cork Detention Barracks). On 12 May, two more (Seán Mac Diarmada and James Connolly; the latter was tied to a chair before the firing squad as a bullet had fractured his ankle during the fighting). On 3 August 1916, one more (Roger Casement was hung at Pentonville Gaol in London). One of the men, 28-year-old Joseph Mary Plunkett, married his sweetheart Grace Gifford in Kilmainham Gaol seven hours before his execution. Horrified, public opinion swung behind the rebels. As Yeats memorably wrote in his poem about Easter 1916, 'All has changed, changed utterly, a terrible beauty is born'. That terrible beauty was Sinn Féin.

That Christmas, as a goodwill gesture, David Lloyd George, the 'Welsh Wizard' who was now Britain's charismatic prime minister, released 560 Irish internees from prison in England. Among them were Arthur Griffith, Sinn Féin's founder, and a 27-year-old west Cork man, Michael Collins, formerly a clerk working in London with the British civil service. Another batch of prisoners given amnesty at Easter 1917 included Éamon de Valera, who had survived his role in the Easter Rising thanks to his American citizenship. The cast was now in place for the climactic act of Ireland's drama.

THE RISE OF SINN FÉIN

In April 1918, panicked by a setback in the war in France, Britain finally extended conscription to Ireland, throwing in as a sop new Home Rule legislation based on partitioning the island. It was a foolish move. The Catholic Church's hierarchy condemned conscription – which turned out to be unnecessary anyway, as the war was soon to end – and the Irish Party walked out of the Commons. Sinn Féin, having found a rallying cry, won sweeping victories in the postwar general election of December 1918. The new MPs boycotted the Commons, forming their own parliament, Dáil Eireann, in Dublin's Mansion House. As president of their new 'republic', they elected de Valera, although he was still languishing in jail at the time.

On 6 December 1921, in London, Michael Collins signs the controversial treaty setting up the Irish Free State. Arthur Griffith is seated on the left.

Standing behind Sinn Féin were the Volunteers, known as the Irish Republican Army, who used violence as an effective weapon. They began killing anyone in uniform who stood in their way, then progressed to selective assassinations. Like so many Irish conflicts, this one rapidly took on some of the characteristics of a civil war. The corpses found labelled 'Spy – Killed by IRA' were usually those of Irishmen.

After an attempt was made in broad daylight on the life of the new viceroy, England suppressed Sinn Féin. Undeterred, the party did well in the municipal elections in January 1920.

When some of the boycotted police force resigned, they were replaced by auxiliary recruits from England, many of them demobilised soldiers, mentally damaged or hardened to killing by the battlefields of France. Known as the 'Black and Tans', they formed motorised squads and hit back quickly after any republican attacks. They became infamous for ill-discipline and savagery in their reprisals, which terrified the population, but grew support for the rebels.

On 21 November 1920, the first 'Bloody Sunday', Michael Collins ordered the assassination of 12 undercover British operatives (known as the Cairo Gang), most of whom were surprised by an attach early in the morning and shot in their beds. That afternoon, at a Gaelic football match in Dublin's Croke Park, police and an Auxiliary Division opened fire indiscriminately, shooting dead 14 civilians and injuring 60 more. In the countryside, families took to sleeping in hedgerows to escape the revenge killings. Guerrilla warfare spread, out of control.

Children in Dublin wave American flags to celebrate the ending of the Anglo-Irish War in 1921.

HUNGER STRIKES

Sinn Féin candidates stood for parliament at by-elections, and began winning. When jailed supporters had their demands to be recognised as political prisoners rejected, hunger strikes began. When one striker died after being force-fed, General Michael Collins organised a show funeral, massively attended. Arms were stockpiled. Lawlessness spread in rural areas. By the time the Irish Party's leader John Redmond died in March 1918, his hopes of bringing about Ireland's independence peaceably had evaporated. In a strange repetition, the hunger strike was again adopted by IRA prisoners in the 1970s and 1980s.

A DEAL IS DONE

In May 1921 Britain tried out a new idea, holding elections for two Irish parliaments, one in the North, one in the South. Sinn Féin swept the board in the South and the Unionists dominated the North. In October, a conference was called in London at which British and Irish leaders, faced with the prospect of an ongoing war of awful attrition, sat down to thrash out a settlement.

Notably, de Valera had sent Michael Collins to do the negotiating, knowing full well the compromises were going to be agonising. On 5 December 1921, at 2.20am, a deal was done. The island was to be divided. The consequences would be huge. 'Early this morning I signed my own death warrant' Collins wrote later that day.

DUBLIN AT WAR

Bullets and shellfire ripped the heart out of the city centre between the Easter Rising of 1916 and the end of the Free State's bitter and bloody civil war in August 1923.

Few ordinary Dubliners supported the small band of mostly middle-class intellectuals and their 1,200 supporters who, armed with a variety of rifles and agricultural implements, took over the city's GPO and other sites on 24 April 1916 and solemnly read out, to the apathy of bystanders, the 'Proclamation of the Irish Republic'. Many, indeed, saw the action as treacherous: World War I was at a critical point and many Irishmen were serving – and dying – in British regiments in France.

It was only when Britain, having crushed the revolt, began executing the rebels that derision for the upstarts turned to sympathy. Support for independence soared, but the compromise that led to Britain retaining six north-eastern counties divided the nation and led to a civil war in the new Free State in 1922. O'Connell Street was in flames again, with sixty dying in the first eight days of fighting. Between 1916 and 1922, three-quarters of the street was demolished, never to regain its former elegance.

Even today, two of Ireland's main political parties reflect the opposing sides in the Civil War, Fianna Fáil (Anti-Treaty) and Fine Gael (Pro-Treaty). At the time of writing, the two parties were working side by side as part of a coalition government, alongside the Green party showing that the desire to remain in office can even overcome political differences.

Armoured train at Inchicore Works in 1922.

The tram passing by was numbered 244. The ads on the tram are for Donnelly's Bacon, Hudson's Super Soap and the Metropolitan Laundry. An ad for Bovil can just be made out on another tram.

Irish revolutionary leader Michael Collins (1890-1922) working the crowd in Dublin in 1922.

Red Cross ambulance passing the G.P.O. on Sackville Street (later renamed O'Connell Street).

Artillery shelling of the Four Courts in an attempt to remove anti-treaty IRA - the start of the Irish Civil War.

A Delightful New Romance "THE HEART OF GLORIA" On Page 20 of Today's Post

The Boston Post

EXTRA

WEDNESDAY, AUGUST 23, 1922

REBELS KILL MICHAEL COLLINS
IRISH LEADER SLAIN IN AMBUSH

Murdered on Tuesday Afternoon During a Tour to Bandon, Near Cork, to Inspect Work of National Troops—Fearlessness in Moving About Country When Warned His Life Was in Danger, Led to Tragedy—Terrible Blow to Ireland Coming So Soon After Griffith's Death—Was One of World's Great Figures—Gave Life for His Country

HUSBAND'S TIP WINS HER FORD

Mr. Whitcomb Did Not Think Story Worth Much, But Wife Did and Now Has New Car

Sport Flashes

FATE'S WORST BLOW TO ERIN

Tragedy's Last Act Closes in Murder of Michael Collins---Knightliest Soul of Land

BY JOHN BANTRY

Assassination Followed an Unsuccessful Attempt on Collins' Life Sunday

Had Also Been Shot At on April 17, But Escaped Then Without Injury

DRAMATIC ARMY ORDERS

WON'T LET FELON UNLOCK OLD SAFE

BIG SEAPLANE SAMPAIO LOST

Partial front page of The Boston Post, 23 August 1922.

Éamon de Valera

In 1916, Éamon de Valera, a 33-year-old maths teacher, liberated a mill against the wishes of its workers, who felt that even in a republic people had to eat. Because he had been born in New York, of an Irish mother and a Spanish father, he was the only Easter Rising commandant not to be executed by the British.

Although president of Dáil Eireann in 1921, de Valera made the decision not to travel to London for negotiations on the Anglo-Irish Treaty and instead sent Michael Collins and Arthur Griffith. A deal was struck and signed on 6 December 1921 without his consent which led to the creation of the Irish Free State but left partition in place. The terms of it also meant that Ireland retained dominion status, swearing allegiance to the British Empire and its king instead of becoming a sovereign state. Public opinion was split and his absence from negotiations left him free to oppose the compromise, setting him against the pro-Treaty side in the civil war that followed.

The war ended in 1923, with the effective surrender of anti-Treaty forces, and he did not achieve power until he headed the Fianna Fáil government in 1932.

He built Fianna Fáil into a formidable populist party, keeping Ireland neutral during World War II and served three terms as Taoiseach. He went on to serve two terms as Irish president (1959–73) and died in 1975, aged 92.

Eamon de Valera c 1922-30.

LIVING WITH PARTITION

Instead of coming together, the Catholic South and the Protestant-dominated North ignored each other for 50 years. Then civil strife and terrorism erupted in the North.

To David Lloyd George's dexterous political mind, the fact that the Anglo-Irish Treaty gave everyone 'something' they wanted but nobody 'everything' they wanted meant it must stand some chance of success. This was a mistake and the first fruit of limited independence was a brutal civil war.

In some respects, the treaty gave the nationalists more than many had expected: a dominion status within the British Empire similar to Canada's. This was far greater freedom than Home Rule had ever promised. However, the British king remained head of the Irish state, which rankled; the British Navy retained a presence at key ports, and the country was split along an antiquated line that divided farms and families.

THE BORDER QUESTION

One particularly dark cloud cast a shadow over the deal. Six counties of Ulster – Antrim, Down, Tyrone, Fermanagh, Armagh and Derry – were retained within the UK, the British having recognised that even a world war had not softened the resolution of the Protestants. Sir Winston Churchill expressed the dilemma graphically: 'As the deluge subsides and the waters fall short, we see the dreary steeples of Fermanagh and Tyrone emerging once again. The integrity of their quarrel is one of the few institutions that's been unaltered in the cataclysm which has swept the world.'

To sell the division of Ireland to nationalists, the government added a proviso: a Boundary Commission would decide which Roman Catholic-dominated areas of Northern Ireland would later be incorporated into the Free State. This promise permitted pragmatic patriots such as Michael Collins to swallow the bitter pill of partition: after the Catholic areas of Tyrone, Fermanagh and south Armagh had been removed, they reckoned, what remained would be too small to be viable.

A farewell to the British Empire as Queen Victoria's statue is removed from outside Ireland's parliament building.

But Collins's hopes were not universally held. Ferocious arguments broke out, laying bare long suppressed personal animosities. On the one side stood the pro-Treaty supporters led by Arthur Griffith: on the other, the anti-Treaty forces massing behind Éamon de Valera. After a bitter 12-day parliamentary debate, the treaty was carried by 64 votes to 57. De Valera resigned as president of Dáil Éireann and was succeeded by Griffith.

It was too narrow a margin to ensure peace, especially since the Irish Republican Army, mirroring the split in the country, was marching in opposite directions; about half with Collins, transforming itself into the regular army of the Free State, and the other half refusing to recognise the new government, relying instead on force to win them a free and united Ireland.

By 1922, Dublin's O'Connell Street was in flames again, with 60 deaths in eight days. Northern Protestants, looking on, vowed to have nothing to do with any redrawing of borders, declaring: 'What we have, we hold.' Fighting broke out in Northern Ireland, too, with the death toll rising to 264 within six months.

The new president of Dáil Éireann did not live to see the end of the struggle: in August 1922, heavily overworked, Griffith collapsed and died. Collins had a more violent end, being shot dead in an ambush on the Macroom to Bandon road in his native County Cork. He had been expecting just such an outcome: after putting his name to the Anglo-Irish Treaty, he had written to a friend: 'Will anyone be satisfied with the bargain? Will anyone? I tell you this – early this morning I signed my death warrant.'

The Boundary Commission's recommended adjustments were never implemented. De Valera's view of the border as 'an old fortress of crumbled masonry, held together with the plaster of fiction' had proved false. Permanent partition had arrived.

FINE GAEL AND FIANNA FÁIL

The Civil War ended in 1923 with the anti-Treaty side's effective surrender. But it was to dominate every aspect of political life in the Free State for the next half-century. The country's two main political parties today, Fine Gael (founded 1933) and Fianna Fáil (founded 1926) are direct descendants of the pro- and anti-Treaty forces.

In 1927, de Valera returned to the Dáil at the head of Fianna Fáil. He came to power in the 1932 election, vowing to reinstate the ancient Gaelic language and culture, ushering in a new era of pious respectability, based firmly on Catholic values. The poet W.B. Yeats, a member of the Irish Senate, warned Éamon de Valera of the dangers of alienating northern Protestants by allowing the Catholic Church too much influence in the South. 'If you show that this country, Southern Ireland, is going to be governed by Catholic ideas and by Catholic ideas alone, you will never get the North,' said Yeats. 'You will put a wedge into the midst of this nation.'

In the following three decades, de Valera built Fianna Fáil into a formidable populist political movement, drawing support from small farmers, the urban working class and the newly moneyed. Fine Gael's heartland was among larger farmers and the professional classes. The Labour Party, which pre-dated partition, found it hard to build support: the trade unions, while nominally pro-Labour, often did deals with Fianna Fáil, and the Church's anti-communist propaganda encouraged a fear of the Left.

Éamon de Valera's vision for a new Ireland had a strong emphasis on rural values.

ENDLESS EMIGRATION

'Dev' as he became affectionately known, pursued a policy of economic nationalism, raising tariff barriers against England, which retaliated. A tax was even imposed on English newspapers. Yet not everyone was thrilled when, for example, Dev announced that Ireland was self-sufficient in shoelaces. Emigration, mainly to England and America, claimed yet another generation of younger sons unable to inherit the family farm and younger daughters unable to find husbands. In the early 1920s, an astonishing 43 percent of Irish-born men and women were living abroad. At the opposite end of the social scale from the farmhands, the once affluent Anglo-Irish – sometimes called the Protestant Ascendancy – fell into decline and their 'Big Houses' at the end of long, tree-lined avenues began to look dilapidated.

Many southerners began to question the wisdom of following their leader's 'Small is Beautiful' signposts. 'It was indeed hard,' said one

Éamon de Valera addresses a rally.

DE VALERA'S VISION

As the leader of Fianna Fáil, Éamon de Valera declared: 'No longer shall our children, like our cattle, be brought up for export.' He spelt out his vision for the Free State's future in a famous St Patrick's Day address, in which he described his ideal Ireland as 'a land whose countryside would be bright with cosy homesteads, whose fields and villages would be joyous with the sounds of industry, with the rompings of sturdy children, the contests of athletic youths and the laughter of comely maidens, whose firesides would be forums for the wisdom of serene old age'. A noble aim, but it didn't belong to the 20th century.

observer, 'to muster up enthusiasm for the carrageen moss industry, in the possible utilisation of the various parts of the herring's anatomy, down to the tail and the fin, in portable, prefabricated factories themselves made of herringbone cement along the west coast.'

But what was the alternative? Certainly not to imitate the UK, Dev insisted, and, to emphasise the point, he produced a constitution in 1937 which abolished the oath of allegiance to England's king, claimed sovereignty over all 32 counties of Ireland and underlined the pervasive influence of the Roman Catholic Church.

The new constitution created a curious equilibrium. The bishops in the South and the Orangemen in the North each exercised a sectarian and politically conservative pressure on their respective parliaments.

Although the unionists would have been happy to remain an integral part of Britain, Lloyd George, emphasising Ulster's 'otherness', had given them their own parliament, Stormont – built on the outskirts of Belfast in the style of Buckingham Palace, only grander. And they had lost no time in making their makeshift state impregnable. London, relieved to have solved the perennial 'Irish question', did nothing to stop them. Nor, fatally, did the Roman Catholics' elected representatives, who boycotted Stormont. The assembly, the unionists boasted, was 'a Protestant parliament for a Protestant people'. The historic hatreds between the two communities were left unhealed.

If anything, these sentiments intensified and deepened and the division widened. Taking advantage of the nationalists' boycott, the unionists made sure that the plum jobs and the best housing went to their own supporters. Two distinct communities developed: Protestant dentists pulled Protestant teeth, Catholic plumbers mended Catholic pipes.

An all-Protestant part-time special constabulary (the 'B' Specials) maintained close links with the Orange Order and helped the police keep dissension under control. The IRA, making little headway in Ulster, began a year-long bombing campaign in English cities in 1939.

WORLD WAR II

While Irish history was repeating itself, European history concocted another world war. The unionists felt their self-interest had been justified when, as soon as Britain declared war on Germany in 1939, de Valera announced that Southern Ireland would remain neutral. Behind the scenes, Winston Churchill, Britain's new wartime leader, offered de Valera a united Ireland at some point in the future if Ireland were to enter the war and allow the British navy to use its ports, but de Valera refused. To enter the war would leave Ireland – with no navy or air force – wholly dependent on the protection of its old enemy, England, and its long-term prospects if Germany won the war, which seemed entirely possible, would hardly be enhanced. That said, approximately 70,000 Irishmen joined the British armed forces.

Churchill's fears had not been unfounded. The Germans had been planning an invasion of Ireland, 'Operation Green', and intended as a springboard to an assault on Britain. In a handbook designed to brief their battalions, they noted that 'the Irishman supports a community founded upon equality for all, but associates with this an extraordinary personal need for

A Traveller family in 1970s Ireland.

THE TRAVELLING PEOPLE

There are probably more than 3,000 families of Travellers in Ireland, adding up to an estimated 25,000 people. Although they bear some resemblances to the Romany of France, Spain and Romania, they are entirely Irish in their ethnic origins – the true Romany, like the Romans, never reached Ireland.

Many lived in illegal campsites by roadsides, on waste ground, or on land cleared for development, and were frequently forced to move on. Until the 1960s, almost all Travellers lived in brightly painted horse-drawn caravans or in tents. They fulfilled a useful economic role in a society that was still mainly rural: mending utensils, making baskets and sieves, peddling knick-knacks, dealing in horses and selling scrap. By the 1990s, traditional caravans had been replaced by motor vans or more spacious modern caravans.

Today, most councils provide halting sites, and some Travellers have moved into rented housing, in search of a better education for their children, and a higher standard of living (Travellers have a far lower life expectancy than settled people). But many take to the road again come summer, making the traditional round of horse fairs, which is where you are most likely to encounter these often much-maligned people but you may also spot them in groups with a horse and trap or riding bareback on a main road.

independence which easily leads to indiscipline and pugnacity'.

Northern Ireland became a target. A ferocious night raid on Belfast in April 1941 killed more than 700 people. The unionists claimed that the neutral South's lack of a blackout helped German bombers pinpoint their targets in the darkened North. Another grudge was chalked up on the blackboard of Irish history.

Over the years even the name of the Free State had been fiercely argued about. Both the English and the Irish seemed to find 'Éire' ('Ireland' in Irish) acceptable. But in 1948 a coalition government fixed the name of the country as the Republic of Ireland. Britain declared that, as a result, Ireland was no longer part of the Commonwealth. At last, Ireland – or at least 26 counties of it – had officially regained its freedom.

The Rev. Ian Paisley protesting outside St Paul's Cathedral, London, in 1969.

THE GREEN CONSUMERS

In 1958, under the premiership of Seán Lemass (de Valera's successor), Ireland decided to rejoin the 20th century. He set out vigorously to create new jobs by opening up the economy to foreign investment, attracting light engineering, pharmaceutical and electronics companies.

The dream of de Valera (now president of Ireland) faded fast. Interest in Gaelic language and culture waned and the voice of management consultants was heard in the land. The Irish embraced consumerism with relish. Even the IRA failed to command much support in its fight for a united Ireland. A campaign of border raids between 1956 and 1962 netted a few arms hauls but then petered out. By 1965, it seemed the most natural thing in the world for Lemass to have a neighbourly meeting with Northern Ireland's prime minister, Captain Terence O'Neill. But it seemed shockingly unnatural to hardline unionists. Several Cabinet colleagues and a popular fundamentalist preacher, the Reverend Ian Paisley, reminded him that Ireland's constitution claimed jurisdiction over the Six Counties.

The upper-class O'Neill was ill equipped to cope with the Pandora's box that was opened just three years later. Inspired by other international protest movements in the late 1960s, including the Black civil rights campaign in the US, Catholics formed the Northern Ireland Civil Rights Association (NICRA) in 1967. They demanded fairer allocation of public housing, equal voting rights in local elections, the end of gerrymandering and the disbandment of the infamous 'B-Specials' (an all-Protestant auxiliary police force).

> *As Britain rebuilt its economic strength in the 1950s, Northern Ireland began to feel the benefit of its welfare state and industrial incentives, while the Republic remained essentially a humdrum agricultural economy.*

After marching on 24 August 1968 in County Tyrone, the NICRA planned a march in Derry on 5 October. The Apprentice Boys announced they too would march on the same day, along the same route, and well substantiated fears of violence led to O'Neill's government banning both. Several thousand civil rights protesters peacefully walked regardless, but they were met by rows of police officers from the Royal Ulster Constabulary (RUC), who arrived armed with batons and water cannon to violently break them up.

Television viewers around the world watched on in horror as the RUC took their truncheons to the demonstrators with what looked suspiciously like enthusiasm. Further marches unsurprisingly also ended in violence and O'Neill, having seen his dreams for a civilised relationship between the two Irelands consumed by the fires of sectarian hatred, was forced out of office by militant unionists.

Almost inevitably, the Protestants' annual march in August 1969, which passed the Catholic area of Bogside in Derry, again sparked off violence. Petrol bombs were hurled, along with broken-up paving stones. The police responded with CS gas. Fighting spread to the Catholic Falls Road and the Protestant Shankill Road in Belfast. The RUC, hopelessly out of its depth, appealed for reinforcements and, on 16 August, a reluctant British government sent troops on to the streets of Derry and Belfast 'in support of the civil power'. Intended as a brief intervention, 'Operation Banner' became the British Army's longest continuous campaign, finally coming to an end in July 2007.

Two armed soldiers inside a road block in Belfast in 1970.

WHY THE NORTH DISTRUSTED THE SOUTH

The 26 counties of Ireland remained economically and culturally stunted. Emigration reached epidemic proportions, triggered by the unattractive nature of life in rural Ireland, and also by the restrictions placed on entertainment. In 1954 a record 1,034 books were banned, and cinemagoers, if they wished to follow the plots of many films, had to cross the border to see the uncensored versions. London's more lurid Sunday newspapers published tamer Irish editions. In *Mother Ireland*, the novelist Edna O'Brien described the constricting parochialism and the awful predictability that led her to flee to London: 'Hour after hour I can think of Ireland, I can imagine without going too far wrong what is happening in any one of the little towns by day or by night ... I can almost tell what any one of my friends might be doing at any hour, so steadfast is the rhythm of life there.' Northern Protestants noted not only the southern state's poorer standard of living and also its intrusion into personal freedoms – its outlawing of divorce, for example, and its ban on the importation of contraceptives. Northern Ireland, Britain had pledged when the Republic left the Commonwealth, could remain part of the United Kingdom as long as a majority of its people wished. Since Protestants outnumbered Catholics by two to one in the Six Counties, that might mean forever.

IRELAND TRANSFORMED

As violence dragged on, the South left the North to its own devices and looked instead to Europe. The North eventually agreed to power-sharing and the Republic's economic boom turned to bust.

At first the British soldiers arriving in what was technically British territory were welcomed as a neutral force. Catholic housewives, many of whom had been preparing to take refuge in the Republic, plied them with endless cups of tea. Girls smiled sweetly at them. Perhaps, it seemed for a moment, all would be well. But it was already too late for such hopes, for this latest chapter of Ireland's Troubles had caused a fearful resurrection: that of the IRA.

As a fighting force, the Irish Republican Army (IRA) had virtually ceased to exist in 1962. By the late 1960s the declared aim of the small group of Marxists who constituted the rump of the IRA was to overthrow the conservative establishments in both parts of Ireland, then set up an ill-defined workers' republic. Lacking modern weaponry, they were acutely conscious of their failure to protect Catholic communities against Protestant mobs, a failure brought painfully home by graffiti which interpreted IRA as 'I Ran Away'. The movement split into two groups in 1969: the traditionalists (the 'Officials') and a new Provisional wing (the 'Provos'). Recruitment to the Provos soared when the British army embarked on late-night arms searches in Catholic areas of Belfast and soon the army, having arrived as mediator, was seen as the enemy.

VIOLENCE SPREADS

Initially the IRA focused on defending Catholic areas, but an offensive campaign began in 1971, with the objective of driving the British out of Northern Ireland. Ruthless guerrilla tactics included the use of snipers, booby-trapped vehicles and bombs across the UK. Protestant vigilante and terrorist groups such as the Ulster Defence Association and the Ulster Volunteer

A mural proclaims loyalties in Derry.

THE TWO TRIBES

Trust between nationalists and unionists in Northern Ireland had always been elusive because the two cultural traditions had so few points of contact. Protestant children attended state-supported Protestant schools, while Catholic children went to Catholic schools. Catholic children were taught Gaelic games, Protestants played cricket. Catholics learned Irish, Protestants didn't. Integrating the schools would have meant transporting children from one area to another and was difficult to implement because the Catholic Church in particular argued strongly that Catholic children must have a Catholic education.

Force matched violence with violence. The situation worsened dramatically when, on 30 January 1972, shooting broke out at an anti-internment rally in Londonderry (Derry) and 14 unarmed civilians were killed by paratroopers. The date became known as Bloody Sunday. The following month, an IRA bomb exploded at Aldershot Barracks in England, killing seven.

IRELAND JOINS EUROPE

As bombs and bullets ripped Northern Ireland's economy to shreds, the Republic was enjoying unprecedented prosperity. After the country's entry into the European Economic Community at the beginning of 1973, financial subsidies descended, as seemingly inexhaustible as Ireland's rain. Former farm labourers, much to their delight, found themselves earning good money assembling electronics components, and one euphoric trade minister dared to describe Ireland as 'the sunbelt of Europe'.

Culturally, too, the climate was brightening. Writers and artists, once forced to emigrate in search of intellectual freedom, were exempted from paying income tax on their royalties. Some well-known names, such as thriller writer Frederick Forsyth, moved to Ireland to take advantage of the concession. One or two more provocative authors found it peculiar that, while one arm of the government was allowing them to live free of income tax, another was banning their books.

LONDON TAKES CONTROL

In the North, the sky was darkening further. Britain abolished the 50-year-old Parliament of Northern Ireland, imposing direct rule from London, and tried unsuccessfully to persuade Protestant and Catholic leaders to set up a power-sharing executive. As atrocities multiplied, the death toll passed 2,500 and an entire generation reached adulthood without ever having known peace. Even well-tried nationalist tactics were failing to work anymore: a hunger strike in an Ulster prison was ignored by Britain's Prime Minister, Margaret Thatcher, and 10 men starved to death in 1981.

Economic recession, and the reluctance of industrialists to site factories in Northern Ireland, made unemployment seem as great an evil as terrorism. And in this respect the South was faring little better. As the effects of the 1970s oil crisis became felt, industrial unemployment rose and inflation neared 25 percent. Both governments were chasing the same investors. The North had the bad luck to win the tussle over who should build John DeLorean's gull-wing sports car: the Belfast factory closed after the UK had invested £17 million.

THE HAUGHEY ERA

At one stage during 1981–82, there were three elections in the Republic within 18 months. A complex system of proportional representation meant that Fianna Fáil minority administrations,

Charles Haughey and other leaders at the European Summit in Dublin, 1990.

now led by the charismatic Charles Haughey (see box page 62), alternated with Fine Gael–Labour coalitions. The last of these coalitions, from late 1982 to 1987, had one major achievement: it succeeded in negotiating, with British Prime Minister Margaret Thatcher, the Anglo-Irish Agreement. This gave the Irish Government a consultative role in the administration of Northern Ireland, while committing British and Irish law and security forces to work together against terrorism and reaffirming that the Six Counties would remain part of the UK as long as a majority of their people favoured that option.

It was a Haughey administration that eventually introduced fiscal measures brutal enough

Economic growth and foreign investment policy brought real, not fool's, gold to the end of the Irish rainbow. Mercedes and Toyotas sped foreign execs through rural lanes, adding more hazards to Ireland's unpredictable traffic.

to halt the Republic's economic deterioration. Public services were cut and unemployment soared, but the ground was laid for better times

An anti-abortion protestor holds up a placard outside the Marie Stopes clinic, the first private clinic to offer abortions to women in Belfast, in 2012.

in the 1990s. That decade was ushered in by the election as Ireland's president of the left-wing Mary Robinson, a leading lawyer and feminist who stood for liberal and pluralist values. In her seven-year term, she was to transform the presidency from being a dumping ground for retired politicians to a force for social change.

EU FUNDING

The European Union was largely responsible for the economy's upturn. Jobs were created and roads built as billions of pounds poured into the country from the European social fund. A sharp fall in interest rates gave rise to a boom in property development and construction. Cheques from Brussels made up almost half the income of Irish farmers. New wealth reduced the country's economic dependence on trade with its larger neighbour.

Ireland began promoting itself as the 'Silicon Valley of Europe'. Its combination of a youthful, well-educated workforce and generous grants and tax incentives lured more than 300 electronics companies to the Republic. Computer giants such as Dell and Intel began assembling computers and microchips there, while Microsoft established its European operations centre in Dublin.

The buoyant job market eroded the emigration figures, which had reached 30,000 a year in the 1980s – mainly to Britain and the US. Suddenly many of those who had gone in the 1980s came home, flaunting the experience they'd gained abroad and grabbing many of the new jobs. Refugees from destinations as diverse as Romania and Zaire, learning of Ireland's comparatively liberal immigration laws, arrived in Dublin. Applications for asylum, which had been only 30 to 40 a year at the beginning of the decade, soared to several thousand a year. As unemployment figures among the Irish dropped, people overcame their resentment of economic migrants from the EU, prepared to do the menial jobs spurned by the newly affluent Irish.

Happily, Europe loved Ireland just as much as Ireland loved Europe – if nothing else because its support acted as a useful counterweight to Britain's at times antagonistic attitude. Being small and remote lent enchantment, too: Ireland

THE HAUGHEY PHENOMENON

Once compared to a Renaissance potentate, Charles Haughey dominated politics in the Republic for two decades. In 1970, when minister for finance, he had been acquitted of conspiring illegally to import arms for use in Northern Ireland. As taoiseach, he lived flamboyantly beyond his means.

Suspicions grew about his financial probity and in 1992 he was forced from office. Five years later he was charged for having received while in office millions of pounds of undeclared funds from Ben Dunne, a supermarket tycoon. Condemned by *The Irish Times* as a 'symbol of the degeneracy of political culture,' he died in 2006 aged 80. He was given a state funeral.

could never have got away with offering corporate tax incentives that made a mockery of EU harmonisation if it had been a serious economic competitor to France or Germany.

The *Alice in Wonderland* nature of Irish politics was highlighted in 1997 by the election of Mary McAleese, a Belfast academic with strong nationalist sympathies, to the presidency. Being a citizen of Northern Ireland, Mrs McAleese could not cast a vote in the Republic's presidential contest, yet she could legally stand as a candidate – and win.

Tourism benefited as Ireland suddenly became a hip tourist destination. For the first time, a £30 million ad campaign, an initiative of a new joint marketing body, Tourism Ireland, promoted both the Republic and Northern Ireland as a joint destination.

CRIMINAL RACKETEERING AND TERRORISM

But the Emerald Isle hadn't become a Garden of Eden. Dublin in particular was bedevilled by racketeering, much of it centred on the drugs trade. The scale of the problem became apparent in 1996 when gangs gunned down Veronica Guerin, a leading investigative journalist.

In Northern Ireland, a peace agreement had been signed on Good Friday 1998 by all the main political parties, including Sinn Féin, and the Republic changed its constitution to renounce its territorial claim to the North.

But another shocking incident occurred on a Saturday afternoon in August 1998, when a car bomb exploded in Omagh's busy town centre killing 29 innocent people and injuring more than 200. A splinter group called the Real IRA, opposed to the Good Friday Agreement, claimed responsibility. Public reaction to this atrocity helped to spur on the peace process. Not until 2013 were two men found liable, following a civil action.

The Irish had few qualms about embracing the euro in 2002 (although Northern Ireland, as part of the UK, retained pound sterling). Suddenly the Irish discovered the joys of cheap credit, made possible by Europe's low interest rates, and embarked on a spending spree. Property prices spiralled, especially in and around Dublin, and in a bid to create affordable homes, the commuter belt expanded to estates built on the outskirts of towns an hour's drive and more from the city.

In 2005, the IRA formally declared that the armed conflict was over and that they had scrapped their weaponry. British troops left the streets of Northern Ireland in 2007.

PEACE BREAKS OUT

Although a low level of violence continued in both of Northern Ireland's communities, everyday life in Belfast seemed relatively normal. Clubbers from Britain and further afield discovered the city's vibrant nightlife, and the growth

Facebook's head office in Dublin.

> *During the boom years, Dublin-owned companies acquired expensive commercial properties in the UK and USA: it was remarked that skyscrapers built with Irish labour were now owned by the labourers' descendants.*

of low-cost airlines such as Ryanair enabled them to sample it.

Meanwhile, in the North, progress was being made on the political front. Having been stubborn enough to resist all compromises, the unionists' leader, the Rev. Ian Paisley told his supporters that his essential demands had been met and that he was now ready to join a power-sharing assembly with his former sworn enemies. Because no parliamentary 'opposition' was built into the system, co-operation was essential. So, as first minister, Protestant firebrand Paisley had to get on with his deputy, former IRA man Martin McGuinness, or the assembly would collapse. Amazingly, it worked.

PROPERTY BUBBLE BURSTS

The first rumblings of trouble in the financial sector surfaced soon after the resignation of Bertie Ahern in May 2008. By September, it appeared that the international financial crisis was affecting the Irish economy. However, it eventually emerged that the Irish economy was suffering a home-grown crisis, and was massively under-capitalised.

Former Taoiseach, Bertie Ahern.

Irish banking had been operating in an effectively unregulated environment, encouraging speculation by property developers, leading builders into dire trouble, precipitating mass unemployment as workers were laid off. Taxes were raised and salaries dropped, leaving few if any buyers for thousands of houses and offices built during the boom. Stringent mortgage rules and a lack of new units led to spiralling rents in Dublin, and an increase in homelessness.

The Fianna Fáil government decided to bail out the banks, leading to severe austerity. In the 2011 election Fianna Fáil suffered a massive defeat, and the centre-right Fine Gael Party formed a coalition government with the Labour Party under Taoiseach Enda Kenny. In 2016, with signs of a recovery blossoming, the electorate returned a hung parliament with Fine Gael eventually forming a coalition government with the Independents and Enda Kenny remaining as taoiseach for another term. Kenny resigned a year later, however, handing over to 38-year-old Leo Varadkar, Ireland's youngest ever taoiseach, who was also openly gay and of Indian descent. Varadkar's elevation coincided with the UK's withdrawal from the EU, which threatened uncertainty for the Irish economy and the fragile peace in Northern Ireland, as the border once again became a thorny issue.

THE GREAT DEBATE OVER ABORTION

In 1992, the Republic was asked to vote by referendum about abortion. The government's chief legal advisor had sought an injunction to prevent a 14-year-old rape victim going to England to have an abortion. To many, the proposal seemed hypocritical since an estimated 4,000 Irish women travelled to Britain each year for abortions. But after a vitriolic public debate, the Irish Constitution was amended to defend the right to life of the unborn.

The situation for medical practitioners remained ambiguous, and the issue resurfaced in 2012 when Indian dentist Savita Halappanavar died during a miscarriage in Galway, in spite of her requests for a termination. In 2014, a pregnant refugee, Ms Y, was denied the right to travel to the UK to seek a termination and was forced to deliver her baby by caesarean section. In 2014, a clinically dead pregnant woman was kept alive against the wishes of her family for several weeks, while the courts attempted to find a legal solution. The EU insisted that Ireland legislate to clarify the position, and the heated debate continued.

Against a backdrop of rapid social change and widespread disgust at the Church for covering up years of abuse, a referendum was held in 2018 and a landslide majority of over 66 percent voted to repeal the Eighth Amendment and legalise abortion. The issue remains a fraught one in the North, now the only part of the UK and Ireland where it remains illegal, including after rape.

A POPULAR PRESIDENT

In November 2011 Michael D. Higgins, a former Labour Party TD, took office as President, following a bitterly fought election campaign with seven candidates. Higgins brought dignity, erudition and warmth to the office, and is almost universally popular, leading to a second term after another election in 2018.

The Catholic Church suffered a strong decline in public esteem following revelations of its failure to protect children from sexually abusive priests, and to punish the abusers. Its anti-abortion stance, firmly restated following the death of Savita Halappanavar (see page 64), further increased the Church's unpopularity, as did revelations of the injustices perpetrated to unmarried mothers and other marginalised women in the Church-run Magdalen Laundries.

Lack of jobs in the construction industry and lack of opportunities for graduates led to a surge in emigration by young people, many headed for Australia and Canada, unsure for how long. In 2012, some 39,500 people between 25 and 44 years old left the country, while 52,700 immigrants arrived.

Following pressure from the EU, a property tax was introduced in 2013 and water charges in 2014. Banks agreed to negotiate with owner-occupiers in serious mortgage arrears, and to tackle the problem of negative equity. With pubs and retail outlets closing, 'ghost estates' crumbling, and most people feeling the pinch, morale was only slightly raised by a successful Irish presidency of the EU in 2013, and words of praise from the Troika for Irish efforts to regain financial stability.

By 2016, Ireland had started to show real signs of economic recovery. Prior to Brexit, the thorniest problem the government had faced was the hugely unpopular water charges and outraged citizenry. Monster rallies were organised around the country by the 'Right to Water' campaign (universal water charges were scrapped in 2017, with refunds promised to those who'd paid).

Post 2016, Brexit has become the biggest concern, both north and south of the border, which is itself once again a red-hot issue.

Ryanair boss Michael O'Leary.

THE ENVIRONMENT: IS IRELAND REALLY GREEN?

Ireland's green credentials are somewhat mixed. On the one hand, its per capita emissions of greenhouse gases are surpassed in the EU only by Luxembourg and Denmark, and emissions from transport have been growing as more cars take to the roads.

On the other hand, peat is gradually been phased out – the last power plant to exclusively use it went offline in 2020 – and renewable energy sources are increasing, with electricity generated from wind, hydro, biomass, landfill gas and biogas. Wind power is the fastest growing sector, with more than 300 wind farms across Ireland, and offshore farms in the Irish Sea. In 2022, wind turbines generated 34 percent of the Republic's electricity.

Although fertiliser use is decreasing, less than 2 percent of farmland is organically cultivated. The EU has an ambitious target of 25 percent by 2030. Irish consumers have opened their wallets to embrace organic farming.

A tax on polythene carrier bags was introduced in 2002 and shops such as supermarkets no longer provide single-use bags. The 22-cent tariff, collected by retail outlets, goes into an environmental fund. In 2005, the government introduced refuse charges for domestic waste, transforming the Irish into a nation of recyclers, along with in 2024 a Deposit Return Scheme for cans and plastic bottles. Ireland was also one of the first countries to ban smoking in public places, including bars.

Traditional music is played in many pubs.

MUSIC

Many kinds of music, from trance to traditional Irish music, are popular in Ireland. Whatever your taste, there are performances to enjoy all over the country.

Irish traditional music is organic, constantly evolving. It has always drawn on many influences and sources, absorbing, retaining and changing them. Over the centuries, hornpipes, polkas, barn dances, waltzes and other styles were imported from all over Europe and acquired a distinctly Irish flavour.

There are two basic types of Irish tune – the jig and the reel. The reel is the older and faster form, played in 4/4 time, while jigs have a 6/8 rhythm. Many thousands of different tunes make up the repertoire, which each musician performs in his or her unique style. Some airs and songs or how they are performed are associated with a particular area of the country.

Wherever you travel in Ireland you will encounter traditional music – from buskers performing on the streets to the hundreds of regular sessions (*seisiún* in Irish), running year-round all over the island – many with free admission.

Traditional Irish dancers.

TRADITIONAL VARIATIONS

Traditional music falls into two categories – instrumental and song. Instrumental music was originally dance music but gradually evolved and nowadays is also performed for a listening audience, as well as to accompany dancing. Musicians usually perform sets of, for example, two different jigs followed by a reel, which builds up excitement as the music speeds up.

There is also a very strong song tradition – including unaccompanied solo singing known as *séan nós,* usually performed in Irish, as well as accompanied songs in English. *Séan nós* is rooted in the Irish-speaking areas (Munster, Donegal and Connemara) with a distinct style unique to each area. *Séan nós has* influenced other genres due to its high emotional impact. Sinead O'Connor and The Hothouse Flowers both cite séan nós as an influence.

The harp, a national emblem, is the instrument most associated with Ireland but, while still widely played, you should not be surprised if you attend a music session where it does not feature. Other instruments include *uilleann* pipes, fiddle, flute, tin whistle, banjo, button accordion, *bodhrán*, harmonica and the spoons.

Uilleann pipes (pronounced *'ill-un'* or *'ill-yun'* and meaning elbow) are bellows-blown bagpipes, which evolved between the 18th and 19th century to their present form. The player performs seated, with the bag under one arm and the bellows under the other. The *bodhrán* (pronounced '*bow-raun*') is a hand-held drum made from goatskin, which has been popular since the 1960s. Ordinary spoons, in the hands of a master, produce a great sound, often setting the pace of a piece of music.

Comhaltas Ceoltóiri Éireann, founded in 1951, is the largest body involved in the promotion of Irish traditional music; its activities include concerts, festivals, competitions and summer schools, with workshops and classes in a range of instruments. It is well worth looking at its website: www.comhaltas.ie.

The remaining members of some groups formed in the 1960s continue to tour today – among them The Chieftains, one of the most influential in building the international appeal of Irish music. The group has collaborated with some of the biggest names in rock and pop, including musical legends Sting and Van Morrison, as well as with symphony orchestras and traditional groups. The Irish folk band The Dubliners retired in 2012, the band's 50th anniversary, following the death of the last original member, Barney McKenna. However, surviving non-original members have formed The Dublin Legends and now tour.

Uilleann is the Irish word for 'elbow', and refers to how the pipes are played.

REVIVAL OF INTEREST

While traditional music was always popular, it was a predominantly rural phenomenon until the 1960s, when there was a massive revival in interest, at least partly influenced by Irish music composer Sean Ó Riada (1931–1971), and the founding of companies including Claddagh Records by Garech Browne. Today, bands such as Beoga, Danu, ***Gráda*** and Téada, and artists like Caoimhín Ó Raghallaigh are introducing the music to a whole new generation.

Music composed in earlier times has been revived and given new arrangements. Works by, for example, Carolan, the 17th/18th-century itinerant blind harper and composer, are enjoyed today.

CELTIC FUSION

Irish music has fused with rock and roll, punk and other genres since the 1970s, when Horslips merged traditional music and rock. Some fusion artists have been very successful both at home and internationally – among them the anarchic Pogues, uncompromising Van Morrison and the wistful Enya.

Van Morrison's songs are often described as Celtic Soul. He was exposed to many musical influences, growing up in Belfast, as his father collected US jazz recordings and his mother was a singer. His work is thoughtful and combines elements of jazz and R&B with Irish traditions.

Enya was a member of successful Donegal group Clannad with her siblings, but today is a best-selling solo artist, although she rarely performs in public and has not toured since the late 1980's. The huge popularity of the Irish band, Kila, fusing music played on traditional Irish instruments with the strong and varied percussive beats of world music, is seen by many as evidence of the growing multicultural nature of Irish society.

POP AND ROCK

Showbands were an Irish phenomenon in the 1960s and 70s. Modelled on American big bands, they toured dance halls performing covers of American and UK chart hits. They died out with the arrival of television and the closure of most halls, particularly those in rural areas, but the tradition was later replicated by 1990s boy bands like Westlife and Boyzone, both manufactured and managed by Louis Walsh.

Irish bands and musicians such as Rory Gallagher, The Undertones (from Derry), Thin Lizzy (fronted by the brilliant Phil Lynott) and Bob Geldolf's Boomtown Rats made their mark in the 1970s and 80s, while My Bloody Valentine, Snow Patrol, Ash, the Divine Comedy, the Frank and Walters, Sinead O'Connor and the Cranberries were all big in the 1990s and into the naughties.

Of course, the most famous and successful of all Irish musicians on the contemporary scene is rock band U2, a four-piece that formed at school in Dublin and have retained the same line-up for over four decades. More recent Irish bands and artists to get your ears around include Damien Rice, Two Door Cinema Club, Hozier, Róisín Murphy and SOAK.

SINGING

The Irish love singing – and do so at any opportunity – just listen to them at a sporting event or on social occasions. Traditional songs fall into four categories: historic lays, fictional ballads, documentary come-all-ye's (so named as they start with 'Come all ye...') and lyric song in Irish or *sean-nós*. The majority of songs in the Irish language collected in the 19th and 20th centuries

Enjoying the craic in Ireland.

IRISH DANCING: ALIVE AND KICKING

Irish dancing enjoyed a renaissance when the Riverdance and subsequent Lord of the Dance shows became a worldwide phenomenon in the mid 1990s (after an beginning as interval entertainment during the 1994 Eurovision Song Contest). Now smaller in scale, these shows continue to tour worldwide.

Until Riverdance, Irish dance was seen by many as stiff ritual associated only with hard-fought competitions or *féis* (pronounced 'fesh'). The Riverdance effect has led to a worldwide boom. The World Irish Dancing Championship attracts some 4,500 competitors and supporters from 32 countries, and has even been held in Boston to facilitate the many American participants. Small fortunes are spent on costumes, wigs and tuition.

Its popularity has a simple explanation: Irish dancing is great fun. Similar to the square dance, the *ceílí* is the best introduction. There are four basic dance forms – the reel, light jig, slip jig and hornpipe – with variations. There are more than 100 different set dances.

The Irish word *ceílí* means a gathering of neighbours in a house to enjoy music, dance and storytelling and, while today they are held in halls or pubs, that welcoming atmosphere survives. Avoid those organised purely for tourists. Cairde Rince Céilí na hÉireann (Friends of Irish Céilí Dancing; www.ceilidancing.com) hold regular set-dancing classes and workshops throughout Ireland.

are love songs, most composed between 1600 and 1850. After that period, and the disastrous famine, there was a growing dependence on English and that is reflected in the songs – some are bilingual, but most are in English.

Traditional songs glorify the feats of warrior heroes like Finn Mac Cual and Brian Ború, or commemorate a disaster, such as a ship sinking, or are about the heartbreak of emigration, the Famine and deportation (for example 'The Fields of Athenry'). Rebel songs, as they came to be known, with titles including *'Kevin Barry'*, *'Boolavogue'*, 'Banna Strand' and the 'Foggy Dew', hark back to times of British oppression and Irish resistance. The band The Wolfe Tones, formed in the early 1960s and still playing, continues the tradition of singing rebel songs, which can also still be heard, sung by punters in pubs, across Ireland.

SINGERS

Christy Moore is a perennially popular solo artist, whose songs reflect contemporary concerns. In the past he was also a member of

Van Morrison.

Ronan O'Snodaigh of Kila.

WHERE TO FIND THE BEST MUSIC FESTIVALS

The **West Cork Chamber Music Festival** (June–early July), epitomises the specialist music festival: a beautiful location – Bantry House, overlooking Bantry Bay – and an intensive programme of international stars performing highlights from the chamber repertoire, public master classes, instrument making classes and a Young Musicians platform. The day starts at 10am with a Morning Talk and ends with a Late Great Show at 10.30pm, with four concerts in between, and events featuring young musicians. www.westcorkmusic.ie

Opera lovers in evening dress enjoy full-scale performances in late October–early November at the **Wexford Festival Opera** in Ireland's National Opera House. Three operas from the lesser-known repertoire feature every year, alongside a programme of recitals and orchestral concerts. www.wexfordopera.com

The **Killaloe Chamber Music Festival** running over the June Bank Holiday weekend features four days of concerts in County Clare. www.killaloemusicfestival.com

East Cork Early Music Festival (Autumn) uses historic local landmarks as venues for small ensembles, including Cloyne Cathedral, Ballymaloe House and Fota House. www.eastcorkearlymusic.ie

The **Sligo Baroque Music Festival** (Autumn) takes place in the Model over four days of concerts, workshops and talks. www.sligobaroquefestival.com

bands, including Planxty and Moving Hearts, whose recordings are still available. His younger brother, Luka Bloom, has also been successful.

Singer songwriter Glen Hansard (member of The Frames and The Swell Season), who had a supporting role in the hit 1991 musical comedy The Commitments, recently won an Academy Award for Best Song in the musical drama film *Once*. Irish-speaker Iarla Ó Lionáird, a producer and performer with the Afro-Celt Sound System, a musical group that fuses hip hop and techno with Celtic and West African music, is also the first *sean-nós* singer to break into the mass market.

Damien Dempsey is a Dublin singer-songwriter who is influenced by traditional music but uses his lyrics to critique the social problems in modern Ireland.

CLASSICAL MUSIC

The main classical performing groups are the National Symphony Orchestra of Ireland and the Ulster Orchestra, based respectively in Dublin and Belfast. Visitors to Ireland are often surprised at the low ticket prices for concerts featuring world-class orchestras. Also look out for performances by students and graduates of colleges of music, particularly when visiting Belfast, Dublin, Cork or Limerick.

This being Ireland, politics naturally gets a look-in. In the hope that music might be the fruit of love, the Cross Border Orchestra of Ireland brings together 130 Protestants and Catholics aged from 12 to 24, www.cboi.ie.

The most famous Irish classical composer is John Field (1782–1837) who invented the nocturne. His music was brought to audiences in the 20th century by Irish pianist John O'Conor.

Opera has always been popular. Ireland's national opera touring company, the Opera Theatre Company (www.opera.ie) tours all 32 counties.

Ulster Orchestra.

The Great Music in Irish Houses festival brings chamber music concerts to historic buildings, including the Casino in Marino, County Dublin; Kilruddery House, County Wicklow; and Emo Court, County Laois, www.greatmusicinirishhouses.com.

Josef Locke (1917–99), whose life was celebrated in the film *Hear My Song*, was the country's most famous tenor. Classically trained singers still lack career opportunities at home, however. Some have formed trios such as The Celtic Tenors, The Priests and The Irish Tenors.

THE IRISH WAY WITH WORDS

Whether in the theatre, the street, in parliament or even the pub, the Irish are renowned for having the true gift of the gab.

The Irish love telling stories, and many of them are very good at it – that's one of the reasons Irish writers are so popular all over the world and why an evening in a Dublin pub can be vastly entertaining.

Before the population of the country could express itself on paper, travelling storytellers – *seannachie* (pronounced 'shan-ah-key') – entertained and informed; their stock-in-trade included discursiveness, allusiveness, hyperbole and lots of high spirits. That tradition lives on today in the popularity of Irish stand-up comedians and broadcasters in the UK and abroad.

Mary Donnegan, a traditional Irish storyteller from Donegal, photographed in 1947.

WRITING IN IRISH

For centuries the Irish language survived despite invasions by the Vikings and Normans, and the arrival of English and Scottish planters. It was not until the mid-19th century that its use began to decline, to be replaced by English. This was due to the introduction of the National School system in 1831 and the effects of the Great Famine of 1845–49 and the mass emigration that followed. The erosion was dramatic: in 1835 there were an estimated 4 million Irish speakers, but by 1891 the number had tumbled to 680,200.

As Ireland established its independence in the 20th century, interest in the native language increased. Although its everyday use was confined mainly to the Gaeltacht areas, some writers, such as the acclaimed poet Michael Davitt (1950–2005), wrote almost exclusively in Irish, while others, like the satirist Brian O'Nolan (AKA Flann O'Brien or Myles na gCopaleen, 1911–66), produced work in both languages.

Yet how English is spoken and written in Ireland differs greatly from how it is used elsewhere. Here it is less precise and hard-edged, much more lyrical, often using phrases directly translated from Irish. The delight in words seems to spring from a sharpened sensitivity to a language that has never been entirely adopted.

THE IRISH LOVE OF LANGUAGE

If you travel on public transport in Ireland, you will see how much people enjoy reading. If you get to know Irish people, you will be surprised to learn just how many of them write poetry or try their hand at prose.

Public readings of poetry and prose are relaxed, enjoyable occasions where all are welcome. Writing competitions and festivals are hugely popular, many of them offering workshops with experienced writers, which are often over-subscribed. The Arts Councils on both sides of the border encourage writing by giving financial assistance.

LEARNING ABOUT WRITERS

To learn more about writers, go to the Irish Writers' Centre on Parnell Square and the Museum of Literature (MoLI) on Stephen's Green in Dublin (see page 122). In the Munster Literature Centre in Cork, visitors can discover short story writers Frank O'Connor and Seán Ó Faoláin, among others. The Seanchaí - Kerry Literary & Cultural Centre in Listowel, focuses on writers from that area, including the late John B. Keane, whose plays are hugely popular. The Verbal Arts Centre in Derry and the Creative Writers' Network, based in Belfast, both organise readings and workshops. Literary events featuring also take place in libraries, bookshops and arts centres all over– look out for posters or call in and ask.

It is often difficult to categorise Irish writers, as many work across various genres – poetry, novels, short stories, stage plays and screenplays.

NOTABLE WRITERS OF THE PAST

Jonathan Swift, satirist and author of Gulliver's Travels, playwright Richard Brinsley Sheridan and poet and dramatist Oscar Wilde are among Ireland's most successful writers.

John Millington Synge (1871–1909) used his knowledge of Irish to transform theatrical language in works including *The Playboy of the Western World* (1907), which caused a riot when first performed at the Abbey Theatre for its raw depiction of peasant life and the plot's moral complexities.

James Joyce rewrote the rules of prose with *Ulysses* (1922), a portrait of a day in the lives of three Dubliners. Bloomsday (16 June) is an annual celebration of this towering literary achievement. (see page 140).

Before the days of mass literacy, professional storytellers called seanachies (pronounced 'shan-ah-keys') travelled from house to house to entertain around the fire. The tradition is sometimes revived in today's pubs.

CONTEMPORARY WRITERS

With too many to name, a ruthlessly selective list would include:

John McGahern (1934–2006) wrote about a society moving from insular repression in his early work towards self-confidence and freedom in his final novels, *Amongst Women* (1990) and *That They May Face the Rising Sun* (2001). His second novel, *The Dark* (1965), was banned.

Christy Brown (1932–81) suffered from cerebral palsy and could only control the toes of one foot, but that didn't stop him from becoming

Dublin Writer's Museum

an artist and author. *Down All the Days* (1970) is heralded as a masterpiece, and his autobiography, *My Left Foot* (1954) was made into an award-winning film starring Daniel Day Lewis.

Brian Friel (1929–2015) is one of Ireland's most important playwrights. Born in Omagh, County Tyrone, some of his writing is influenced by politics in Northern Ireland. His most successful play is *Dancing at Lughnasa* (1990), which won three Tony Awards on Broadway. Among his other works are *Philadelphia, Here I Come!* (1964), Lovers (1967), and *Translations* (1980).

Paul Durcan (b. 1944) is a satirical and idiosyncratic poet. He is often compared to the poet and novelist Patrick Kavanagh (1904–67), who also attacked Irish society.

Roddy Doyle (b. 1958) is best known for his Barrytown trilogy, a humorously poignant portrayal of working-class life in modern Dublin, beginning with his debut novel *The Commitments* (1987), later made into a film. He won the Man Booker Prize in 1993 for *Paddy Clarke Ha Ha Ha*. In *The Dead Republic* (2010) he completes a picaresque trilogy through 20th-century Irish history that began with the brilliant *A Star Called Henry*.

Joseph O'Connor (b. 1963, brother of singer Sinéad) has written seven novels, first gaining international recognition with *Star of the Sea* (2002), which focused on the Great Famine and emigration. *Redemption Falls* (2007) draws on some of the same characters, and *Ghost Light* (2010) completes the trilogy.

Marian Keyes (b. 1963) a three-time Irish Book Award winner (*This Charming Man*, 2009, *Making It Up As I Go Along*, 2016, *Again Rachel*, 2022) has written numerous novels and a selection of non-fiction books, many dealing with alcoholism and mental health with surprising humour. She also won Author of the Year in the British Book Awards in 2022.

Listowel Writers' Week is an internationally acclaimed literary festival.

IRELAND'S BEST LITERARY FESTIVALS

The International Literature Festival Dublin welcomes the world's finest writers to the word-drenched capital city for a week of readings and debate. www.ilfdublin.com

Galway's Cúirt International Festival of Literature is a big event in a small, festival-friendly town, held over six days in late April. Past visitors include Nobel Prize winners J.M. Coetzee, Nadine Gordimer, Derek Walcott and Seamus Heaney. It's a convivial event, with masterclasses, launches, theatre performances, readings and debates. www.cuirt.ie

Listowel Writers' Week is a unique festival held in June in a north Kerry town that prides itself on its literary connections, including the late John B. Keane (*The Field*). Events include readings, launches and writing competitions. www.writersweek.ie

West Cork Literary Festival in Bantry has free lunchtime readings from writers, many who also offer afternoon masterclasses. It attracts some big names and an enthusiastic audience who enjoy the informal contact. Many people stay for all six days. www.westcorkmusic.ie/literaryfestival

Immrama Festival of Travel Writing, a mid-June weekend of literary events organised around a travel writing theme, is held in Lismore in west Waterford, the home of travel writer Dervla Murphy. www.lismoreimmrama.com

Author John Banville (b. 1945) from Wexford, writes intricately beautiful novels, including *The Sea*, for which he won the Booker Prize in 2005. Other books, including some written under the nom de plume Benjamin Black, have won numerous awards, and he is considered a contender for the Nobel Prize in Literature. Emma Donoghue's (b. 1969) *The Room*, a finalist for the Man Booker Prize, is now a film.

The tradition of short story writing lives on with Edna O'Brien, William Trevor and Colm Toibin. A younger generation led by Claire Keegan (b. 1968), Nuala Ní Chonchúir (b. 1972) and Kevin Barry (b. 1969) is making its voice heard.

POPULAR FICTION

Maeve Binchy (1940-2012), a former journalist with *The Irish Times*, was one of Ireland's best-loved writers. Among the bestsellers are *Circle of Friends* (1990) and *Light a Penny Candle* (1982).

Other fine writers include Cathy Kelly, Sheila O'Flanagan and romance writer Cecilia Ahern. Claire Keegan's novel *Foster* was adapted into the film *The Quiet Girl*, shortlisted for an Oscar.

Roddy Doyle.

Claire Keegan.

IRISH WINNERS OF THE NOBEL PRIZE FOR LITERATURE

George Bernard Shaw (1856–1950) spent most of his life in England. He wrote over 50 plays and revolutionised the theatre with dramas about ideas and issues. Works include *Man and Superman (1903)*, *Saint Joan* (1924) and *Pygmalion (1913)*, which inspired the film *My Fair Lady*.

W.B. Yeats (1865–1939), a hugely influential poet and dramatist, was a founder of the Abbey Theatre in Dublin. His plays are rarely performed today, but he is considered one of the most influential poets of the 20th century. Although patriotic, his relationship with the nationalist movement was complicated, as is reflected in some of his best-known poems.

Samuel Beckett (1906–89) spent most of his life in Paris where, during World War II, he worked with the French Resistance. He wrote mostly in French and then translated into English. His best-known play, *Waiting for Godot*, was first produced in 1953.

Seamus Heaney (1939–2013) was born in County Derry; his early works combine personal memories with images of Irish heritage and landscape. His collections *North* (1975) and *Field Work* (1979) explore the political situation, while later works, including *Station Island* (1984) and *Seeing Things* (1991) convey an individualistic and meditative mood. As a translator, his work includes *Sweeney Astray* (1983) from a medieval poem in Irish, and the Anglo-Saxon poem *Beowulf* (1999).

ARTS FESTIVALS

The economic boom gave Ireland traffic jams and housing estates, but it also led to a flourishing of the arts.

The Irish have an international reputation as entertainers. But the visual artists, musicians, dancers and actors who once had to emigrate to find work now have jobs at home, in these rollercoaster economic times. Most Irish towns have a busy multi-purpose arts centre with exhibition spaces and auditorium.

Participating in cultural activities is one of the most popular pastimes for visitors to Ireland, and this has led to an explosion in the number of arts festivals taking place around the country, livening things up for residents as well. The concept of 'the arts' involved is the broadest possible one, with comedy, cabaret, street performers and rock gigs sharing the programme with more conventional theatre, dance, classical music and readings.

Overseas visitors (especially Americans) throng the streets of Dublin on 17 March, many of them taking part in the city's massive St Patrick's Day parade. The St Patrick's Festival provides a full week of carnival, music and street theatre, but its highlight is still the traditional parade through the city centre.

FILM AND THEATRE

Autumn and winter are the time for film festivals – in Cork, Dublin and Belfast – and theatre festivals. In a country that loves to party, arts festivals are easy-going, unstuffy affairs, with many events held in pubs. The big summertime arts festivals – the Cork Midsummer Festival (June), the Galway International Arts Week (July) and the Kilkenny Arts Festival (August) – co-exist with lively festivals in smaller towns that present ambitious multi-disciplinary programmes of theatre, music, cabaret, comedy, street entertainment, children's workshops and visual art. The talent might be mainly local, or you might be surprised by a big international name. While the main events will usually have modest ticket prices, all arts festivals generate free entertainment, and an unforgettable party atmosphere – which also makes them great places to meet people.

Féile na Bealtaine celebrates the arrival of Summer with a music and arts festival in Dingle.

Street performers at Dublin's New Year Festival.

Earagail Arts Festival is a bilingual music and arts festival that takes place throughout Co. Donegal every July.

Fireworks at Galway International Arts Festival every July.

Galway: festival city

Galway is the closest Ireland gets to a city that never sleeps: its compact centre and lively pub scene make it an ideal festival venue. Its festival calendar is a challenging test of stamina: April heralds the Cúirt Literature Festival, five days of readings from Irish and international authors. If you think literary festivals are quiet, polite occasions, Galway will change your mind. July is the year's highlight, with the six-day-long Galway Film Fleadh (over 70 Irish and international features, with master classes, seminars and more) leading up to a 10-day extravaganza, Galway International Arts Week, the biggest such event in Ireland with hundreds of events taking place day and night. Does Galway then take a quiet break and catch its collective breath? Not on your life: it's straight off to the Galway Races Festival, which brings the city and its ring road to a standstill, so that the preferred way to travel to the race course is by helicopter. Some 48,000 revellers attend Ladies' Day. The merry-makers assemble again in late September for the Galway International Oyster Festival. Then, in order to get the younger generation into training, mid-October sees the week-long Báboro, Ireland's first arts festival purely for children.

Spraoi International Street Arts Festival in Co. Waterford sees the city transformed by dance and music performances that are free to visit over the August bank holiday weekend.

CONTEMPORARY ART

A new generation of Irish painters and sculptors has been making an impact.

Ireland's artistic reputation rests largely on the genius of its writers, but from the late 20th century, the visual arts flourished with Irish artists fetching unusually high prices at auction. Irish Art auctions were held regularly in London, New York and Dublin. Sotheby's Irish Art Sale began in 1995; its 2015 auction made sales of £1,831,375. Early 20th-century artists John Lavery, Roderic O'Conor, Jack B. Yeats, William Orpen and Paul Henry all command high prices. Orpen's *Portrait of Gardenia St George with Riding Crop*, sold for £1,983,500 at Sotheby's in 2001 and, is the most expensive Irish painting ever to sell at auction (bar the works of Francis Bacon, whose 1969 Triptych of Lucien Freud fetched $142.2m at Sotheby's New York in 2013). With the economic downturn, prices fell, but have since started to recover. Irish painting, especially landscapes, continues to be sought after by collectors worldwide.

These artists are being joined by the next generation, including Belfast's Gerard Dillon, Dublin's Patrick Collins, Louis Le Brocquy and Cork-born Patrick Scott. Galleries showing contemporary art are thriving in Dublin and Belfast, and younger artists are encouraged by both the Arts Council in Dublin, and the Arts Council of Northern Ireland. Irish art colleges are oversubscribed, with the University of Ulster at Coleraine having a particularly high reputation for post-graduate work in contemporary art. Irish artist, Sean Scully has gained an international reputation as an abstract artist.

Louis Le Brocquy's James Joyce, Study 64 (1977), from the Irish Museum of Modern Art.

ANCIENT INSPIRATION

There has of course always been visual art in Ireland, from the spirals, loops and geometric forms of the Stone Age passage and burial graves at Newgrange and Knowth, to the La Tène period of Celtic art, which arrived from mainland Europe around 500 BC. After the arrival of Christianity, artists and craft workers continued to enjoy a privileged position in society, producing elaborately bejewelled chalices and shrines, as well as exquisite illuminated manuscripts.

The latter led to some of the greatest achievements in the history of Irish art; works such as the 'Book of Durrow' and the 'Book of Kells', whose intricate ornamentation and seemingly endless inventiveness can still take your breath away.

Stone crosses and ornamental metalwork are the only artefacts to survive successive waves of invasions, civil wars and general upheaval which began with the arrival of the Vikings at the close of the 8th century and lasted well into the 17th century. While the prosperity of the 18th century produced some of Ireland's greatest architecture, it was influenced more by English and continental traditions than indigenous ones. The Royal Hibernian Academy (RHA) was established in Dublin in 1823, in the tradition of its London counterpart. Many Irish artists emigrated to London, and had a significant impact on English art – for example, James Barry (1741–1806), Daniel Maclise (1806–70), Francis Danby (1793–1861) and sculptors such as John Henry Foley (1818–74) and John Lawlor (1820–1901), who worked on London's Albert Memorial.

THE CELTIC REVIVAL

The Celtic Revival (*c.*1880–1930), with its use of the Celtic motifs from illuminated manuscripts, metalwork and monastic architecture, was an Irish version of the Arts and Crafts Movement, closely allied to the movement for Irish independence. The Honan Chapel at University College Cork is a prime example of this style.

Impressionism began to influence Irish art

Barrie Cooke's Megaceros Hibernicus (1983), from the Irish Museum of Modern Art.

CONTEMPORARY ARTISTS TO WATCH OUT FOR

Basil Blackshaw: Northern Irish artist known for his depiction of horses and dogs, and latterly barns, in sketch-like paintings that capture the essence.

Barrie Cooke: American-born and educated in England, Cooke lived in rural Ireland from the 1950s until his death in 2014. Later works, such as *Sewage Outlet, River Nore* (1992), depict water pollution.

Dorothy Cross: works mainly in three dimensions, sometimes in video and performance, and famously created a real 'ghost ship' in Dublin Bay.

Martin Gale: paints eerie super-realist landscapes that mirror the changes taking place in rural Ireland.

Brian O'Doherty: Irish-born polymath, who found fame in New York's as a conceptual artist, writer and critic.

Clare Langan: artist and cinematographer whose spectacular video work offers visions of a future in which civilization has been overwhelmed by nature.

Cleary Connolly: a Paris-based couple trained in architecture, producing interactive video art.

Anne Madden: paints on a massive scale, usually abstracts inspired by landscape or mythology.

Vivienne Roche: sculptor working on a large scale, often in welded steel, whose austerely beautiful work uses motifs from Viking and early Christian Ireland.

Sean Scully: painter, photographer, printmaker and sculptor whose abstracts are inspired by stone walls.

around the turn of the century, with the work of Nathaniel Hone, John Butler Yeats, John Lavery, Sarah Purser, Walter Osborne, William Orpen and, most importantly, Roderic O'Conor. Jack B. Yeats (1871–1957), brother of the poet William B. Yeats, stood head and shoulders above his contemporaries, and led the way in his adoption of Irish subject matter, favouring outdoor scenes of his native Sligo, circuses and horse races.

The best-known artist of the time was Paul Henry (1876–1958) who had studied at Whistler's studio in Paris before settling on Achill Island to paint archetypal images of the west of Ireland landscape, cottages set against monumental hillsides and tumbling grey skies, that were used as posters to advertise travel to Ireland. Events of the Civil War and the establishment of the Irish Free State were captured in a series of historical paintings by Sean Keating (1889–1997), and social realism became the dominant style.

Alice Maher's Berry Dress (1994), made from rosehips, cotton, paint and sewing pins, part of the collection of the Irish Museum of Modern Art.

ART IGNORED

Economic conditions, Ireland's cultural isolation during World War II and the dominant ethos of Catholic conservatism did not add up to a favourable climate for artistic activity in the mid-20th century. Stained-glass artists were among the few to flourish, including the Harry Clarke Studios, whose work can be seen in Dublin City Gallery – The Hugh Lane, six of Clarke's windows are also located in Bewley's Café on Grafton Street. It was hard to make a living in a country where art was not taught in most schools, and art colleges did not award degrees. This is the era that has given rise to the belief that Ireland has no visual art tradition.

> *Many Irish artists live in scenic areas and have revitalised hitherto underpopulated areas, counties Leitrim, Roscommon, Mayo, Sligo, Clare, Kerry and West Cork in particular.*

However, the first public gallery in the British Isles devoted to contemporary art was Dublin City Gallery – The Hugh Lane (formerly, The Municipal Gallery of Modern Art), established in 1908. Its collection of Irish and European late 19th- and early 20th-century art was an inspiration to many Dublin artists. Inspired by what they had seen, Louis Le Brocquy, Norah McGuinness, Evie Hone, Mainie Jellett and others travelled abroad and experimented with Cubism, Futurism and Dadaism, returning home to lead the modern movement in Irish painting. In 1943, they founded the Irish Exhibition of Living Art as a *salon de refusés* for those whose work was consistently rejected by the annual exhibition of the RHA. This evolved into an annual show called the Irish Exhibition of Living Art, which became a forum for artists whose influences were derived from the international language of visual art: Patrick Scott, Patrick Collins, Gerard Dillon, Nano Reid, Barrie Cooke, Cecil King and Tony O'Malley. Living Art also embraced video and performance art, and persisted into the 1980s.

The Irish Museum of Modern Art (IMMA) opened in 1991, but meanwhile the creation of an improved infrastructure for the arts, the establishment of tax exemption for artists in 1969 and the introduction in 1981 of the island-wide Aosdána scheme did much to improve working conditions for artists. There was an unprecedented growth in venues, subsidised exhibition spaces and commercial galleries during the boom years, both in Dublin, Belfast and the provinces, and a corresponding upsurge in artistic activity. Many artists, such as the Manchester-born Hughie O'Donoghue, returned from long or short stays abroad and set up studios in Ireland, some combining their artistic practice with teaching and lecturing.

INTERNATIONAL TASTE

Many of the younger generation of artists – Clare Langan, Linda Quinlan and Amanda Coogan, for example, working respectively in video, installation art and performance – produce work that is indistinguishable from their contemporaries in London, Paris or New York. Others continue to be inspired by landscape, even though their work may use forms belonging to the international contemporary art scene. Examples include Sarah Walker's coolly modernist wild flower grids, Charles Tyrrell's rigorous abstracts and Gary Coyle's dramatic photographs of Dublin Bay from a swimmer's perspective.

Other contemporary artists produce attractive landscapes and with genre scenes of Irish life. Their work can be found in local galleries.

Void, contemporary art space, Derry.

HOW IRELAND REWARDS CREATIVITY

Aosdána, an association of writers and artists, was set up in 1981 by Taoiseach Charles Haughey (1925–2006), who as finance minister in 1969, had introduced a tax exemption for writers and artists. Both initiatives were intended to lure home Irish artists living abroad. Haughey's cultural advisor, the poet Anthony Cronin, inspired by the Celtic respect for the *aes dána* – the men of talent – drew up the plan.

Membership, limited to 250 people, includes many of Ireland's artistic elite: Sean Scully opted in, but John Banville opted out. It was intended as recognition of artistic achievement. But to ensure that a new generation did not suffer the poverty of their predecessors, membership also awards an optional annuity of €17,180 to those earning under €25,000 annually. Thus, enabling members to work full time on creative projects.

The assembly meets once a year to elect new members, and debate resolutions, many concerning its own workings. It was originally limited to writers, composers or visual artists; architects and choreographers are now eligible, but not performing artists. Aosdána receives government funding of €2.7 million annually – a fraction of the arts budget. But in a nation famous for 'begrudgery', many consider this amount excessive, and Aosdána remains controversial.

FOOD

A new generation of homegrown chefs are forging an Irish culinary identity.

Ireland has long been promoted as 'Ireland, The Food Island', an ingenious marketing slogan invented by Bord Bia (The Irish Food Board). Ireland remains an agricultural country that produces far more food than it can eat. Its grass-fed beef and lamb produce superb meat and dairy produce and speciality foods including a completely unique range of farmhouse cheese that are exported throughout the world. Stand in any fishing port and see how foreign fish merchants covet the fresh seafood caught in the country's clean Atlantic waters.

Ireland is clean, green and fertile – a moist, temperate climate and the benign influence of the Gulf Stream deflect the cold temperatures of Northern Europe. Tourism is equally important, so there is a sophisticated hospitality industry.

Chef at work at Balloo House.

> *Many country house restaurants use produce from their own farms and gardens, rivers and game shoots. It's part of the fun to inspect the estate or the kitchen garden before dinner and guess what will be on the menu.*

EATING OUT

Ireland is not a low-cost destination. However, if good food is what you seek there is value for money to be had at all levels – if you know where to find it. The best value (as opposed to the cheapest) is offered on 'Early Bird' or 'Today's Market' dinner menus, fixed price two- or three-course menus, and (the Irish way to experience a meal in leading fine-dining restaurants without blowing your budget) at lunchtime.

The pursuit of individualism is strong in Ireland. This can make it difficult for visitors to tell whether an establishment offers formal/fine dining with set four or five course menus (with a price tag to match), or casual/informal food where you can order as much or as little as you like. You'll come across restaurants, bistros, brasseries, café/bars, wine/café bars, or just plain cafés, pub/restaurants, pubs with bar food, pub carveries and seafood bars. The only sure way to distinguish between the first three is to inspect the prices on the menu, which must, by law, be displayed outside.

Café/bars and wine bars usually offer informal meals where you can order as much or little as you wish; you rarely need to make a reservation. Some cafés are quite expensive, restaurants in all but name; most offer an all-day menu and (sometimes) a lunch menu.

DINING IN PUBS

Pubs vary even more widely – some have restaurants with full lunch and dinner menus. Others offer 'bar food' – a proper lunch and dinner menu with table service in some cases, and self-service in others. Many pubs advertise a 'carvery' lunch, a self-service meal featuring at least one joint of meat, carved to order, and other pre-cooked options, filling and inexpensive but unlikely to be a culinary highlight. The best option is seafood (oysters, prawns, crab or mussels) at one of the coastal pubs offering freshly landed catch.

HOTELS AND RESTAURANTS

If eating in a hotel restaurant seems a last resort, think again. As a result of intense competition, most four- and five-star Irish hotels place a great emphasis on dining and employ top chefs. Many have two restaurants, one fine-dining and another informal. Most are open daily – useful to know as many Irish restaurants close after Sunday lunch and do not open for dinner on Sunday or Monday nights. In tourist areas some restaurants concentrate on weekends and close for a couple of months in mid-winter.

Fresh seafood is one of Ireland's specialities.

CONTEMPORARY IRISH COOKING

A distinctive style of Irish cooking has emerged over the past 20 years. A new generation of serious chefs take pride in using indigenous foods and, supported by a growing number of artisan food producers making authentic foods using traditional methods, re-explore traditional Irish recipes and dishes. What has emerged is a lighter, modern style, innovative spin on traditional dishes but firmly based on Irish foods and themes. Leading chefs take enormous care to source Irish ingredients, wild or farmed using

WHAT IS EURO-TOQUES?

A sign to look out for is Euro-Toques (www.euro-toques.ie), a pan-European organisation with 3,500 members. Euro-Toques has more than 200 members in Ireland and has been influential in the creation of unique contemporary Irish cooking. All Euro-Toques support sourcing top-quality, non-GM, local and seasonal food and deliver dishes of flavour and authenticity. They aim to protect the quality, diversity and flavour of regional food and promote indigenous production methods. Their support in buying artisan food products has reawakened consumer appreciation and helped young artisan food producers to create a sustainable business.

traditional methods, and support the ever-growing number of artisan food producers.

Irish chefs continue to be trained in the classic tradition. Most go abroad for a few years for experience and bring back culinary influences from their travels and give them an Irish twist; the most ambitious compete to work under influential Irish chefs so the modern approach is not just confined to fine-dining establishments but can be found in many places. Talented young chefs have the confidence to open their own restaurants not just in Dublin and other cities but in provincial towns, villages and sometimes deep in rural Ireland.

In many fine-dining restaurants modern Irish cooking allows a natural mingling of traditional Irish produce with an innovative approach to the cooking and presentation of long-established Irish dishes. The result is a contemporary Irish cuisine that is 'entirely itself', an idiomatic expression. The good thing is that this approach to cooking is not confined to formal fine-dining restaurants but can be on offer in establishments all over the country (see page 83).

Temple Bar Food Market, Dublin.

THE BEST PLACE TO SAMPLE MODERN IRISH CUISINE

Cliff Townhouse, Dublin (www.clifftownhouse.ie), and **The House Restaurant**, Cliff House Hotel, Ardmore, County Waterford (www.cliffhousehotel.ie). Martijn Kajuiter's twin ventures are up there with the most exciting places to eat in Ireland, the latter has held a Michelin Star since 2010.

The Tannery, Dungarvan, County Waterford. Paul Flynn applies foodie trends to well-sourced Irish produce in an attractive warehouse space. www.tannery.ie

Ballymaloe House, Shanagarry, County Cork. Ireland's most famous country house hotel has advocated the use of fresh local produce since the 1970s. Book for Sunday buffet lunch. www.ballymaloe.ie

Gregans Castle, Ballyvaughan, County Clare. Discreet, understated Georgian country house overlooking Galway Bay with an outstanding chef. www.gregans.ie

La Fougère, Knockranny House Hotel, Westport, County Mayo. Seamus Commons presides over this relaxed hotel restaurant. www.knockrannyhousehotel.ie

MacNean House and Restaurant, Blacklion, County Cavan. Successful TV series, cookbooks, and a cookery school have not distracted Neven Maguire from his main job as chef in his family's business. Worth the detour. www.nevenmaguire.com

Deanes Restaurant, Belfast. Visit Deane and Decano, Deanes at Queens, and Deanes in Howard Street for Michael Deane's modern fare: www.michaeldeane.co.uk

ETHNIC RESTAURANTS

The Irish, wide travellers, have multicultural tastes. Thriving ethnic restaurants are plentiful. Immigration during the boom years has increased their numbers and diversity. Once you might have been lucky to find French, Italian, Chinese or Indian restaurants; now you can choose from a far wider range of cuisines: Nepalese, Japanese, Vietnamese, Indonesian, Belgian, Breton, Polish and Thai, as well as Indian and Chinese offering authentic regional cuisine. A particular trend has been the huge growth in informal restaurant/café/wine bars offering Spanish tapas, or using the tapas principle to showcase Irish artisan foods including farmhouse cheeses, black pudding, smoked chicken and locally produced charcuterie, which has flourished following immigration from Eastern Europe.

Tempting baked goods testify to the increased demand for artisan foods.

IRISH COUNTRY HOUSE COOKING

Some of the best dining can be experienced in Irish country houses, almost all located in rural areas. At the top end the facilities are on a par with four- or even five-star hotels, with restaurants and dining experiences to match. Most (although not all) at this level offer modern Irish cooking and menus, tend to be open to non-residents and often attract a loyal local following as well as tourists staying in self-catering accommodation. Other smaller country houses do not employ a large team of chefs. In these the cooking style and presentation is simpler, menus shorter, and feature traditional (even regional) dishes that place an emphasis on allowing natural flavours of carefully sourced local and seasonal foods to shine through.

FARM TO FORK

The Irish place high value on knowing where food comes from – the entire route from farm to fork – and, by and large, they want it to be from an Irish farm. To satisfy consumer demand, the name of a product, its producer or the locality in which it was produced, is often incorporated into a dish's menu description. There are a growing number of artisan producers offering traditional and speciality foods. The demand for organic food has grown too and is used as a selling point in many restaurants.

FÉILE BIA

'Bia' is the Irish word for food and the word 'Féile' means a festival or celebration. The thrust of this voluntary programme run by Bord Bia (The Irish Food Board) is for restaurants to source fresh, authentic Irish food. Members must inform customers about how their food is produced and its source; they must use meat, poultry and eggs from approved quality-assurance schemes. There are 1,450 Féile Bia members in Ireland. Some top restaurants are not members as they source their foods from unique, organic producers.

FARMERS' MARKETS

A visit to a farmers' market is a must. Look out for farmhouse cheese (each unique to the farm and the cheesemaker), cured, smoked, spiced and air-dried meats, dry-cured bacon, black and white puddings, speciality sausages and pâtés, fish and shellfish, mountain lamb, wild game, home-grown fruit and berries, traditional breads and baked goods, jams, chutneys and sauces. For information on local markets, go to www.bordbia.ie/aboutfood/farmersmarkets.

Country markets – smaller affairs held weekly in nearly 60 locations by a long-established cooperative – specialise in home baking and local produce.

PUBS

The counterfeit Irish pub has conquered the world. But the authentic pubs in Ireland, whose most intoxicating product used to be talk, are struggling to come to terms with a changed society.

Dublin's hostelries – there are about 800 of them – are a mix of the very old and the very new. Some are vast drinking emporiums offering live sport on huge screens and palatable food to more than 1,000 people; others are spit-and-sawdust drinking dens. It's the characterful old-school watering-holes that are really worth visiting: McDaids, O'Donoghue's, the Palace Bar, Mulligan's, the Stag's Head, the International and M.J. O'Neill's – to name but a few.

These classic Dublin bars are peopled with wisecracking philosophers sharing their observations with anyone who'll listen – or buy them a drink. Old wooden bars, with creamy pints of stout, remain untouched by the hand of the modernisers. They have a well-lived-in and well-drunk-in look and feel, often decked out in brass and mahogany, with antique mirrors proclaiming the merits of whiskeys long since defunct. Some such pubs look much as they did in 1850.

One hundred miles (160km) to the north, Belfast is also richly endowed with pubs. A rash of bars such as the 21 Social, The Cloth Ear, Revoluciòn de Cuba and Hellcat Maggies, are the contemporary, cool venues. But the most-visited remains the iconic Crown Liquor Saloon, now owned by the National Trust, with its wood-panelled snugs, gaslights, ornate tiles, woodcarvings and brasswork. Other venerable venues include White's Tavern, the Duke of York, Kelly's Cellars, the Garrick, the Morning Star, Bittles Bar, Madden's or the John Hewitt, named after a local poet.

A perfect pint of "the black stuff".

THE DRINKING CULTURE

A recent European Union survey showed that Ireland has one of the highest proportion of binge drinkers in any European country. Just over a third of people living in Ireland were reported to consume on average five or more units of alcohol in a single sitting – more than three times the EU average. And four out of five drinks are consumed in bars rather than at home, compared to only one in three in Germany, reinforcing the image of the Irish as social drinkers.

Despite this, the downfall of the Irish pub has often been predicted, and many smaller rural pubs in particular have been forced out of business (1,829 pubs in total disappeared between 2005 and 2021, with almost 350 closed due to the Covid-19 pandemic). But the country still supports over 8,000 pubs (6,600 in the Republic; around 1,500 in Northern Ireland), and the rural pubs that *have* survived remain the epicentre of small towns where the community still comes together for its social and neighbourhood business. The paint may be peeling in some, but traditionally, they have been places where people meet, not just to drink and hold parties or wakes, but to gossip, talk football, solve the world's political problems, try to pick a winner in the 2:30pm Leopardstown race meeting, tell tall tales or simply *céilí* the night away.

These traditions survive. From the regular sessions of the *seanchaí* (storyteller) in the Red House in Lismore, west Waterford, to Osbourne's pub in Clongeall, south Carlow; from O'Loclainn's in Ballyvaughan, County Clare, to Kate Lavin's in Boyle, County Roscommon; and from Blakes of the Hollow in Enniskillen, County Fermanagh, to the pub from Father Ted, Vaughan's in Kilfenora, the customs and atmosphere – like the best whiskey – remain undiluted.

Many bars – especially the part-grocery/part-pub ones – are family-owned and can trace their longevity back several generations, although only about 200 pubs have been in one family for at least 100 years. Some commentators have pointed out that if such a lack of stability of

Out drinking in Ireland.

HOW THE SMOKING BAN MADE AN IMPACT

The sight of smokers huddled up outside the doorways of pubs has become common all over the Republic of Ireland since 2004 as smokers were bnished outdoors (Northern Ireland's bars went smoke-free in 2007). Ireland was the world's first nation to introduce a smoking ban in pubs and many predicted ruin for one of the most convivial of meeting places.

There were a few acts of defiance against the ban, but the law, like a decent pint of Guinness, eventually settled down. Pubs in rural Ireland continued to close at an alarming rate, but the smoking ban did not play a significant part in their demise – the trigger was the same social upheaval that was forcing the closure of village shops and post offices in remote areas.

The drink-driving laws have also hit hard. The traditional tolerance for the jovial drunk eroded as the number of young people killed or injured in early-morning road accidents at the weekends spiralled to tragic numbers. The police took a strong stand by introducing random breath testing of motorists, and some publicans, conscious of the lack of public transport in outlying areas, turned themselves into taxi drivers, transporting customers home in a courtesy minibus. If any one thing symbolises Ireland's embrace of modern European values, this behavioural change may be it.

ownership were to be found in farming, it would be declared a national scandal. Fortunately the days of the characterful country pubs with a thatched roof and turf fire have still not disappeared, although many don't open until early evening as there are fewer daytime customers.

TRADITIONAL MUSIC

Informal traditional music sessions or set dancing have great appeal, though performance times can be erratic and the entertainment may not start before 10pm. Most sessions are held indoors but during a *fleadh cheoil* (music festival) when thousands flock into towns, the performers spill out on to the pavement and music flows down the streets.

Generally, music sessions fall into two categories. Some bars hold set-piece evenings that are turned on like a tap for the tourists; these occur regularly and are premeditated with a practised set list. Others are spontaneous where the players drop in for an unplanned evening and the result is a happy meeting of musical minds. The quality of the playing in both is equally good,

A music session in Co. Offaly.

EXPORTING THE IRISH BAR

If America can persuade the world to eat hamburgers, can Ireland persuade it to drink Guinness? More than 1,000 'traditional' Irish pubs, from Durty Nellie's in Amsterdam to Finnegan's in Abu Dhabi, from Shifty O'Shea's in Leicester, England, to O'Kims in Seoul, Korea, are trying to do just that.

Brewers such as Guinness set up companies to export the Irish pub concept. They'll help entrepreneurs anywhere in the world to design their hostelry – you can pick a standard model such as Country Cottage, the Victorian Dublin or the Brewery – and also aid them in locating authentic fittings and recruiting staff.

but the impromptu session often has the edge because the unexpected may happen.

The informal nature of it means that it's open to all-comers to strut their musical stuff whether playing, singing or dancing. Often these sessions are the ones that will be imprinted in visitors' minds. The memory of the haunting *Nancy Spain*, the well-worn words of *The Wild Rover* or *Whiskey in the Jar* and the intoxicating talk will all remain long after the recollection of a visit to a spanking new interpretative centre has faded to oblivion.

In some parts of the country, old customs live on; search hard and you will find in Cork city a few 'early houses' – pubs that open their doors at 7am to cater for night-shift workers including dockers and bakers, or those in search of 'the cure' (a remedy for the morning-after hangover). On a Monday morning around 9am as office workers throughout the city scurry to work, you may be startled to stumble across several bars in the docks area almost as busy as on a Saturday night.

THE MYSTIQUE OF GUINNESS

The respect paid to this national beverage, a stout, dark beer with a creamy white head, is genuine and not something conjured up by a marketing department. Brewed in Dublin since 1759, it is a temperamental drink, needing great care. Constant temperature in the cellars, the distance from cask to tap and the frequency of the flow are all important in the art of 'pulling a good pint'.

If the pint isn't good, it is sent straight back. Experts (namely anyone who drinks the stuff) love long discussions on the pint's quality. The visitor's best criterion is this: if the place is crowded with locals, then the pint is probably good. And you'll know a good pint when you get one that's as smooth as velvet. It won't taste like what passes for Guinness in Britain. In 2018 Guinness opened its first brewery in the US since 1954, in Baltimore.

Guinness is good for you – purportedly anyway.

SIX BARS WORTH TOASTING

Tigh Neachtain, Cross Street, Galway. A popular city centre bar with old-fashioned painted wooden interior and features. The building dates back to medieval times and the tiny snugs are more than 100 years old. There's an open fire in the back room and music.

Morrissey's, Main Street, Abbeyleix, County Laois. Opened as a grocery in 1775 and now solely a pub, it has the air of a venerable institution. It has dark walls, a pot-belly stove and rules forbidding cards, TV and singing.

Shoot the Crows, Market Cross, Grattan Street, Sligo. Opened in 1876, this long, narrow pub has retained its original wooden interior. Good music on Wednesday nights.

P.J. O'Hare's Anchor Bar, Carlingford, County Louth. P.J.'s has been in the family for 150 years and is decorated with pub mirrors and curios. On sunny Sunday afternoons the yard becomes a dance area.

Anderson's Thatch Pub, Elphin Road, Carrick-on-Shannon, County Leitrim. This inviting roadside pub dates back to 1760. The owner, who plays 11 instruments, holds music sessions on Wednesdays and Saturdays.

Nancy's, Front Street, Ardara, County Donegal. This tiny hospitable bar is now in the seventh generation of family ownership. Seafood, especially the chowder, is a speciality. Traditional music is played.

A SPORTING NATION

Wild, energetic and thrilling, native sports such as hurling and Gaelic football will get the adrenalin pumping on and off the field. Then there's the widespread love of horses and passionate rugby and soccer fans...

Sport enthusiasts will have a field day in Ireland, as all the major international sports are played to some extent and only a few, like soccer, athletics and hockey, are affected by the political division of the island. Overall, the most popular sports are still the native ones of hurling and Gaelic football. These are fast-paced, thrilling, high-voltage games, amateur in nature and organised around the parish and controlled by a body called the Gaelic Athletic Association (GAA).

The GAA was founded in 1884, in Thurles, County Tipperary by Michael Cusack, a fiery nationalist from the Burren in County Clare, who was immortalised by James Joyce as 'The Citizen' in *Ulysses*. Organised for a purpose that was political as much as sporting, the association's *raison d'être* was to revive the native games, under native control, as a means of strengthening national self-respect at a time when national morale was at low ebb.

At the end of the 19th century, most of those involved with the GAA were farmers, labourers and shopkeepers but by the 20th century the new Roman Catholic middle class fired up by a Celtic Revival joined the movement. In 1918, the GAA was included on a list of organisations banned by the British Government but despite this Gaelic games were still played. Today in an Independent Ireland they still hold a hallowed position in Irish culture and are intrinsically linked to the national identity.

HURLING

Hurling has been played in Ireland since prehistoric times and some of the country's oldest sagas tell of hurling matches that went on for days. It's the fastest of all field team games and its rules are relatively simple, although watching it for the first time can be a dizzying, bewildering experience as the ball hurtles around at breakneck speed and players swing their hurleys about, narrowly missing teeth and foreheads.

Hurling is a skilled game.

The hurley itself is made from ash and is around 3.5ft (1 metre) long with a paddle at the bottom that measures about 3ins (7.6cm) across at its broadest. The hard ball consists of yarn, tightly wound round a ball of cork and covered with leather, stitched along the outside in a ridge to facilitate handling. The object of the game is to get the ball either between the posts to score one point, or under the bar and past the keeper to score a goal (for three points). As a result, scores tot up fast on this game, making for exhilarating viewing.

What makes the game so crazy to watch is that the ball can be propelled along the ground *or* hit in the air, but it can only be taken into the hand if it has been caught in full flight – something that requires considerable skill. The rest of the time players scoop the ball up onto the hurley, from the ground, while running at full speed and carry it, balanced or bouncing, on the broad end before passing or scoring. Tricky? Yes. Exciting to watch? Absolutely. The main traditional hurling areas remain south of a line from Dublin to Galway, with a small pocket in the Glens of Antrim. Cork and Kilkenny are the top

The first mention of football in Ireland can be traced to 1308, when John McCrocan, a spectator at a football game at Newcastle, County Dublin, was charged with accidentally stabbing a player named William Bernard.

Gaelic football is spectacular: fast-paced and rough and ready.

GREAT SPORTING MOMENTS

Croke Park in Dublin has been home to the GAA for over 100 years and is the largest stadium in the country with capacity for over 82,300. Steeped in history, the venue lies at the heart of Ireland's troubled history and in 1920 British forces fired into the crowd at a Dublin vs Tipperary match and shot dead 14 spectators (including the Tipperary captain), an atrocity that became known as the original 'Bloody Sunday'.

Since those early days, the stadium has remained central to Irish sporting and cultural life. During the boom, Croke Park (www.crokepark.ie, pronounced 'croak') was transformed into one of Europe's finest venues, with a museum and stadium tour. Having been exclusively used for Gaelic Games, 2005 saw a defining moment as the GAA agreed to allow 'Croker' to host 'foreign games' of soccer and international rugby, while their usual stadium, then Lansdowne Road, prepared for redevelopment.

The most controversial match of all was the 2007 Ireland vs England rugby international: because of Bloody Sunday, many Irish fans objected to the British national anthem being sung in the stadium. On 24 February, with phenomenal media hype, the historic match kicked off with emotions running high. As the Irish anthem was sung, there was barely a dry eye in the house with Irish fans and players feeling the weight of history thick in the air. Ireland won by 43–13.

hurling counties, with Limerick claiming the cup for the last three years.

FOOTBALL, GAELIC-STYLE

Like hurling, Gaelic football is played by teams of 15-a-side. The layout of the pitch and methods of scoring are also the same as for hurling. Played with a ball similar to that used in soccer, the rules of Gaelic football are somewhat open to interpretation, subject to constant revision and applied with varying degrees of robustness by different referees (similar to rugby). Players

Breeding greyhounds is a minor industry.

can handle the ball, lift it off the ground with the foot, run with it (for five steps, when a bounce or pass must be performed), pass it between hand and foot (by kicking it, or fisting it), or play it with the feet on the ground, as in soccer. To tackle a player in possession, it's permissible to slap it from their hands. It is a spectacular game and attracts huge crowds.

Australian Rules, although played with an oval ball on an oval pitch, has features similar to those of Gaelic football. It's thought that Irish emigrants had a hand in influencing long kicking and the great leaps in the air to catch the ball. In an attempt to gain an international dimension for a game played only in Ireland (with the exception of Irish emigrants in the USA and Britain) the GAA has run tours to and from Australia, with games played under compromise rules. The fact that the Australian players are all professionals have so far given the contests more bite than was anticipated. Pros don't relish being beaten by amateurs.

The high point of the GAA year is in September with the All-Ireland hurling and football Finals in Dublin's Croke Park, which now incorporates a museum devoted to Irish sports. Tickets for the Finals do not go on sale to the general public and are distributed for purchase only through clubs and county boards.

HARES AND HORSES

Greyhound racing (on tracks) and coursing in enclosed fields with live hares are popular sports in Ireland. The fact that races are over in a matter of seconds is no deterrent to the small army of punters who attend. Coursing is a winter sport, which has come under fire from animal-rights campaigners because of cruelty to hares. Two dogs are released to chase a hare. Points are scored by deflecting the hare from its course, or by killing it before it gets to the escape exit. Protests have resulted in greyhounds being muzzled by law since 1993.

SPORTS IN ALL ITS GLORY

Casual perusal of the sports pages of any Irish daily newspaper will show that an extraordinary range of sports is covered, and a surprising number of people excel in a variety of sports at the highest level. The biggest achievement

THE SPLIT IN SOCCER

Soccer in Ireland is split by the internal political border. Since 1922 the island has fielded two international sides: Northern Ireland and the Republic of Ireland. Despite limited resources, Northern Ireland qualified for the World Cup both in 1982 and in 1986, while the Republic stood out in the 1988 European Championships finals and in the 1990 and 1994 World Cups. Both teams qualified for the UEFA Euro 2016 tournament hosted in France, but neither reached the 2018 World Cup finals. Because Ireland's domestic football leagues are small, many top Irish footballers make names for themselves in UK leagues.

in recent years was Ireland's Grand Slam and Triple Crown triumph in the 2018 Six Nations rugby tournament. To mention just a few other highlights: Sean Kelly dominated the world of cycling throughout the 1980s, and in 1987 Stephen Roche won the sport's ultimate prize, the gruelling Tour de France. In professional boxing, world titles were held by Barry McGuigan, Steve Collins, Michael Carruth and Dave McAuley. Dublin's Conor McGregor became the first UFC fighter in history to hold titles in two weight divisions simultaneously when he beat Eddie Alvarez for the UFC Lightweight Championship in 2016, and subsequently took up a booking career, losing his first fight against Floyd Mayweather Jr in 2017. Alex Higgins, Ken O'Doherty and Dennis Taylor all claimed the world championship at snooker. In 1998 Sonia O'Sullivan crowned an already illustrious career in athletics by winning both the 5,000-metre and 10,000-metre European championship titles, and Catherina McKiernan won four silver medals in the World Cross Country Championships. Top golfers on the international circuit include Darren Clarke, Dubliner Padraig Harrington, who won the Open in 2007 and 2008, also winning the PGA in 2008, and Northern Ireland's Rory McIlroy, who turned pro in 2007 on reaching the age of 16. In 2010 McIlroy had his first PGA tour triumph, winning the Quail Hollow Championship days before his 21st birthday, and since then he has thrice been European Tour Golfer of the Year in 2012, 2014 and 2015. Footballers George Best and Roy Keane were both considered world class players in their prime, as was rugby player Brian O'Driscoll.

In international rugby Ireland fields a team drawn from both Northern Ireland and the Republic of Ireland. Rugby is the one international sport (except for professional boxing) that unites all political elements on the island, at least temporarily. In July 2010 the newly built Aviva Stadium in Dublin's Lansdowne Road, home of both rugby and soccer internationals, with a seated capacity of 50,000, hosted its first rugby match.

The unusual sport of road bowling.

ROAD BOWLING

Road bowling is a strange game, played only in South Armagh, Cork and pockets of Waterford, Wexford and Limerick. It originates from the 16th century and, depending on who you listen to, was either introduced by William of Orange or came from Irish rebels who would roll English cannonballs they had stolen back to their camp.

Either way, the game is very simple: two players throw or bowl a heavy iron ball along an ordinary public road, and the winner is the one who covers a set distance with fewer throws. The bowl, or 'bullet', can be 28, 21 or 16oz (between 800 and 450 grams, and is believed to be of military origin: the original 'bowl' was probably a cannon ball. One of the skills of the game is the negotiation of a bend in the road, either by lofting the bowl over the corner or by curving the throw. If the bowl leaves the road, the player is penalised.

While it might not be the most organised of sports, road bowling attracts major betting activity and large sums of money change hands when noted players meet. Not only are bets laid on the result of the contest, but side-bets are also laid on individual shots.

Technically, it is illegal as sections of public roads have to be closed off to traffic during play but volunteers are happy to keep an eye out to wave vehicles through safely.

GOLF

Ireland may lack the sun-soaked allure of Bermuda or the cachet of the Caribbean, but it's one of the world's most exciting golfing destinations, with beautiful, technically challenging courses.

Always a popular golfing spot for players in the know, Ireland hit the world stage in a big way in 2006 with the hosting of the Ryder Cup at the sleek and luxurious K Club golf resort in County Kildare. Major international Irish names, such as Padraig Harrington, Darren Clarke, Graeme McDowell and Rory McIlroy have highlighted the skill of Irish golfers at international competitions. The Irish Open is part of the European tour and attracts record crowds. In 2016, Dun Laoghaire Golf Club hosted the Curtis Cup for women amateur golfers.

A VARIETY OF COURSES

Golfers are spoilt for choice. There's the drama of Doonbeg in County Clare, the elegance of Druid's Glen in County Wicklow, and the untamed magnificence of links courses, such as the Old Head of Kinsale in County Cork or the magnificent lake and mountain scenery of the Killarney Golf and Fishing Club, host of the 2010 Irish Open. Dotted throughout the land and outside all the major cities are internationally recognised courses, as well as smaller lesser-known spots that can be equally delightful to play on, depending on what you're looking for.

TOP CLUBS AND HIDDEN GEMS

Among the big hitters are Lahinch in County Clare; Ballybunion and Waterville in County Kerry; and the Royal County Down. If you're looking for a quieter course, then try a hidden gem like Enniscrone in County Sligo; Ballyliffin in County Donegal; Kenmare in County Kerry and Killerig in County Carlow.

There are also an impressive number of luxurious golf resorts where you can complement a round of golf with some fine dining, spa and leisure facilities, along with deluxe accommodation. Mount Juliet in County Kilkenny boasts a Jack Nicklaus–designed course and is famed for its 1,500 acres of lush, rolling landscape and exquisite Georgian house. Carton House, County Kildare, is an opulent castle hotel in a beautiful location, or if you fancy living it up like one of the landed gentry, Dromoland Castle has sumptuous rooms and fine food and wine. All three have hosted the Irish Open.

Rory McIlroy.

THE OLDER THE BETTER

Unsurprisingly for a country with over 440 courses, the Irish take golf seriously. The country's golf pedigree dates back to the late 19th century and clubs, courses and even clubhouses battle it out for the title of "oldest". The Curragh Golf Club in County Kildare is reputed to have the oldest course in Ireland dating back to 1852; the oldest club, The Royal Belfast Golf Club was founded in 1881 and the Ardglass Golf Club in County Down has the oldest clubhouse – parts of which date back to the 14th century.

TRADITIONAL ROOTS

While golf has attracted a new generation of hip, young swingers in the UK and the US, in Ireland the game is still rooted in tradition. There may not be as many Pringle sweaters on the courses as there used to be, but clubs like Portmarnock Golf Club in Dublin are stalwarts of the old-school and bastions of male privilege. This beautifully situated links, nestled into the curve of coastline formed by Howth Peninsula, refuses to relax its age-old rule that excludes women from becoming full members, although visitors of both sexes are warmly welcomed on the course as long as they have a certified handicap.

Ireland's small size means that it's easy to take in a few clubs in a short space of time. But give yourself plenty of time to meet your tee-off booking, too, as you can be seriously delayed behind wayward cattle along some rural backroads.

In terms of cost, green fees vary – the Arnold Palmer-designed Ryder Cup course at the K Club, charges €250 for a non-resident from May to September – but if you're looking for a cheaper round of golf, there are lots of smaller clubs around the country that will only set you back around €30 or so.

Remember to check with the specific club regarding rules as some can be somewhat picky about dress codes, and nearly all clubs require advance booking for play, particularly during the busy summer months.

The Royal Portrush Golf Club, Country Antrim.

IRELAND'S BEST COURSES

The K Club, County Kildare. Two parkland courses. The choice of plutocrats.

Portmarnock, Dublin. On a peninsula north of Dublin; holding out against women members.

Ballybunion, County Kerry. Tiger Woods warms up on the Old Course for a European tour.

Killarney Golf and Fishing Club. Three courses amid stunning lake and mountain scenery.

Lahinch, County Clare. Challenging links course on the Atlantic coast, famed for massive bunkers.

Royal County Down. Near Mourne Mountains. Tough.

Royal Portrush. County Antrim. The only Irish club to have hosted a British Open. Coastal location.

ANGLING

For a country surrounded by sea, with an abundance of lakes and a 8,500 miles of fish-rich rivers, Ireland is one of Europe's most popular angling destinations.

Ireland's mix of year-round rain, reasonably mild winters and gentle summers results in a profusion of cold and warm water species, so there's a really broad range of experiences on offer including salmon fishing, coarse fishing, pike fishing, sea fishing and trout fly-fishing right across the island.

While it's undeniably possible that you might be lucky enough to reel in a Mediterranean bass for your supper, you're probably more likely to have success with one of Ireland's native fish. Coarse fishing in Ireland isn't enormously popular with locals so the country's lightly fished freshwaters are teaming with species like pike, bream, tench, roach, eel and rudd. Admittedly, you're unlikely to be rustling up a gourmet dinner with a freshly taken rudd, but it's all about the experience, and coarse fishing in Ireland is contemplative and tranquil thanks to the haunting beauty of the magnificent landscapes.

From the big rivers like the vast River Shannon, which dominates the midlands, to the small crystal-clear waters of Ireland's loughs such as County Roscommon's Lough Gara, Ireland offers a diversity that few other countries can compete with, and coarse fishing is a sport that thrills regardless of your level or experience. Or you could always opt for a showdown with a pink-fleshed salmon, trout or sea trout, which hold an honoured place in Irish culture and folklore.

THE REEL REGULATIONS

You'll need a licence, though, which you can pick up from fishing tackle shops and fishery offices. And, as the majority of waters are either privately owned or owned by the state, you'll also need a fishing permit. There are strict bylaws and conservation measures governing coarse and salmon fishing, including bag limits, mandatory catch and release and gill tags. It's best to contact the relevant Regional Fisheries Board (for contact details for each region, check with the Central Fisheries Board; tel: 1890 347424; www.fishinginireland.info) close to the time of travel as these regulations change.

Angling in the south of Co. Dublin.

ON THE SEASHORE

Sea fishing in Ireland is a real thrill, with more than 4,000 miles (6,400km) of coastline covering landscapes that range from towering sea cliffs that plummet into the crashing Atlantic Ocean along the west and northwest coast, to the gentler waters of the sunny southeast. There are over 80 species in the waters and the warming influence of the North Atlantic Drift means that you can take fish from spring to autumn, which would usually be found only in the summer months elsewhere.

> *Pike fishing is a huge draw for competitive anglers – the largest line-caught pike in a lough is 39lbs 3oz (17.7kg) and a whopping 42lbs (19kg) in a river, but don't expect to hook one that size; most average 20lbs (9kg).*

Fishing in Co. Galway.

Whether you want to boat fish languidly on a warm August afternoon, wreck fish for conger, ling, pollack or coalfish, or take the sociable approach with a big-fun bout of deep-sea fishing on a chartered boat, you're guaranteed an exciting experience. Best of all, after a day bobbing around in sea spray, a night in the pub dissecting the day's catch over a pint of Guinness is a particular treat.

For many anglers, Ireland is a dream location for shore fishing and nothing beats the pure adrenalin-rush of battling with big surf on the west coast during one of the area's legendary storms. This isn't for the faint-hearted, though.

There are few parts of Ireland that can beat the wild untamed beauty of the Beara, Iveragh and Dingle peninsulas in the southwest. It's a beguiling part of the country, with a raw magnificence and a physical vitality that never fails to impress, and these rocky coastal shores provide the angler with one of the most picturesque fishing locations in the world. In terms of fish, you'll find species of wrasse and pollack ready for the taking. But arguably the most Irish of angling experiences has to be a battle with the enormous native pike. The quality of the clear, clean waters is attributed to the large numbers of pike in Ireland, and the fisheries of the Shannon, Lough Allen, Lough Derg, River Suck and River Inny are prolific with these legendary creatures, which average around 20lbs (9kg). The chance of reeling in a vast fish fires up anglers from across the world who are drawn to Ireland because of the unspoiled habitat that enables the fish to breed and swell to such an impressive size.

CONSERVATION EFFORTS

Conservation issues are evident in the ever-changing bylaws. In sea fishing, most cartilaginous fish are tagged and returned alive, and freshwater anglers are encouraged to limit the number of wild fish taken. The Central Fisheries Board can supply current details. The CFB also offers a free download of *Irish Sport Fishes – A guide to their identification*, and more besides.

WALKING IN IRELAND

'The men of Ireland are mortal and temporal, but her hills are eternal,' wrote George Bernard Shaw. As well as nurturing a rich store of mythology and folklore, the Irish hills offer spectacular opportunities for walkers.

From the top of Slieve-na-Calliagh (hill of the witch) in County Meath, it's possible, on a clear day, to look down across 18 Irish counties. No great effort is needed to reach the summit as it's only 911ft (275 metres), and you can drive to a small car park 10 minutes' walk from the top. If the spirit moves you, and you have the key, you can enter a cross-shaped chamber covered with a mound of stones. Inside, the stones are riotously decorated with ancient rock art carvings and radial line patterns including zigzags and spirals that, it is believed, mark the expected variations of the sunbeam with the drifting of the equinoctial rising sun.

Although not huge in European or world terms, the mountains of Ireland have a seductive and, in the case of Slieve-na-Calliagh, enigmatic quality. For walkers, the countryside offers a spectacular range of opportunities. From the high peaks of Cork and Kerry to the Glens of Antrim, and from the Donegal highlands to the small hills or drumlins (low rounded hills) of the midlands, the range of walking possibilities is enormous.

There are few mountains that need more than half a day to scale, but walking an entire range will take two days or more to complete. Most peaks have their own qualities of visual drama. Many, including the Twelve Bens in Connemara, the Mourne Mountains in County Down, or Ireland's most climbed holy mountain, Croagh Patrick, have a distinctive triangular symmetry. Brandon in Kilkenny and the quartzite cone of Errigal in Donegal have an implacable presence, yet are intimate and inviting, their significance to the people living around their foothills out of all proportion to their height. Others are more subtle and don't always emphasise their glories.

Sheep's Head Peninsula, County Cork.

USEFUL WEBSITES

For details of routes on waymarked walking trails, loop walks, trails in forest parks, national parks and city or town walks (known as *Sli na Slainte*) as well as information on walking festivals go to www.irishtrails.ie.

Seven pilgrim paths in Ireland follow medieval pilgrimage routes. Details: www.heritagecouncil.ie.

The Mountaineering Council of Ireland has a helpful website: www.mountaineering.ie.

To find out more information about looped walks, forest and nature walks, festivals and , as well as accommodation for walkers have a look at www.discoverireland.ie.

ORGANISED WALKS

Walking in Ireland has grown rapidly as an activity; it is big business and well organised. There are more than 30 national waymarked walking trails and over 100 walking clubs.

The clubs are all affiliated to Mountaineering Ireland (www.mountaineering.ie), the representative body for hill walkers and climbers in Ireland north and south. The waymarked ways offer 1,860 miles (3,000km) of marked walking routes and one of their most appealing aspects is that they are suitable for walkers of all ages and abilities. The network ranges from towpath strolls and walks along scenic coastal stretches, to circuits of the high mountainous peninsulas. You can take your pick from one of the shortest, the Cavan Way at 16 miles (26km), to the Kerry Way stretching to 133 miles (214km). These trails rarely rise above 3,000ft (900 metres). While there are a few rugged stretches over open mountain passes, the routes mainly follow disused roads, grassy trails or forest tracks. They are signposted with yellow arrows and a walking man to guide you through the countryside and over stiles and bridges.

Killarney National Park is a hiker's paradise

WHEN A WALK BECOMES A FESTIVAL

Wherever there's high ground you will find someone organising a walking lasting a weekend (or longer). Many walks are led by local guides knowledgeable about heritage sites and the archaeology, geology, wild flowers and birdlife of the area. There is also a social side with evening entertainment in the pubs.

There are more than 30 walking festivals in Ireland. These include the Ballyhoura International Walking Festival on the borders of Cork, Tipperary and Limerick, the Castlebar International 4 Days' Walks, the Sperrins and Killeter Walking Festival and the North Leitrim Glens Walking Festival. The Wee Binnians, which labels itself 'the social group that walks', holds a popular annual festival in the Mourne Mountains.

The Slieve Blooms, in the centre of Ireland, offer Eco Walks as part of their biannual weekends. This lesser-known range covers an astonishing 60,000 acres (24,000 hectares) spread across Laois and Offaly. The writer Hubert Butler once described the Slieve Blooms as 'a low, demure-looking range of hills, very suitable for middle-aged, unadventurous mountaineers with children and picnic-baskets.'

Launched in 2018, the Killarney Mountain Festival (www.killarneymountainfestival.com) features guided hikes along with lots of other outdoor adventures, speakers and live music. See also www.discoverireland.ie.

TOUGHER HIKES

For those wanting a greater challenge, there are much tougher day-long annual hikes across some of the bigger ranges organised by mountaineering clubs. The Maumturks Walk in Connemara each spring covers 15 miles (24km), while the Glover Highlander in Donegal is held in early September. Most clubs have programmes of walks throughout the year and welcome visitors.

The weather can change quickly in mountainous regions and it's easy for a walker to go astray, so check the forecast before setting out. The old red sandstone Mountains of Kerry are the most dangerous in Ireland and can be treacherous, as the mist can descend with no warning, severely limiting visibility. At 3,414ft (1,039 metres), Carrauntoohil is the country's highest mountain and attracts thousands of walkers annually.

It's essential to have proper gear: walking boots with ankle support, rainwear, warm clothes, gloves and hat, maps, compass and guidebook and sufficient snacks such as chocolate or fruit, as well as a warm or hydrating drink.

Planning an advance itinerary and working out a route using the Ordnance Survey (OS; www.osi.ie) maps is the safest way. You should also leave word with someone where you are going and your approximate return time. The OS maps in the Discovery Series, drawn up to 1:50,000 scale, will help you find ancient monuments, holy wells and castles as well as landmarks in towns and villages. You will also find on them scores of names tucked away into the crevices and foothills such as Crotty's Rock, the Colleen Bawn Cottage, and, at the summit of Slieve Gullion in south Armagh, Calliagh Berra's Lake. According to legend, any man who swims in the lake comes out visibly aged.

Magnificent scenery opens up in many mountainous areas such as Mayo's Doolough Pass, the Spelga Pass in south Down and the bleak but beautiful Gap of Dunloe in Kerry. But be careful as you drive on these remote roads – a PhD in these parts refers to 'Pot-hole Dodging'.

Waymarker on the Ring of Kerry.

> *An average of two people a year die on the MacGillycuddy's Reeks near Killarney. A mobile phone is useful in an emergency but network coverage is often poor. Check the forecast, dress appropriately, avoid walking alone and let someone know your plans.*

IRELAND'S TOP 10 WALKS

From The Brandy Pad and The Dingle Way to coastal walks and a climb up Diamond Hill, there are hikes to suit everyone in the Emerald Isle.

A favourite walk is **Errigal Mountain** (County Donegal). The most direct route starts from Dunlewy at the car park on the main R521. After crossing heathery slopes, you will reach firmer footing and it's relatively easy to pick your way to the top for a view of a large area of northwest Ireland.

The Brandy Pad (County Down). This route follows an old smugglers' path across the northern section of the Mourne Mountains. The whole walk, which is waymarked throughout and marked on maps, is 7 miles (11km). It's not overly strenuous and the reward is spectacular views across the highest range in Ulster.

The Dingle Way (County Kerry). For a taste of dramatic scenery you could walk all, or part, of the 110-mile (180km) Dingle Way on the Dingle peninsula. The walk begins in Tralee, leads west to Camp on the northern side, then loops round the peninsula, taking in the imposing Brandon Mountain, and dropping down to Clogher Head before turning back along the southern stretch of the peninsula.

Croagh Patrick (County Mayo). On the last Sunday in July you'll have trouble creating elbowroom for yourself amongst 30,000 pilgrims on their annual hike to the summit. A well-trodden path takes you to the chapel at the summit of this conical, aloof peak, from which you can view the islands in Clew Bay.

Burren Coastal Walk (County Clare). Along the stunning coastline from Black Head down to Doolin, you will cross a variety of terrain that includes limestone pavement, beaches, grass and sand dunes all offering pleasant walking among grey walls, stones and rocks. You will come across seabirds and rare arctic-alpine plants that flower in the spring and early summer. The five-hour walk also takes you across Fanore beach, a European Special Area of Conservation.

Diamond Hill (County Galway). The path to the top of Diamond Hill starts from the Connemara National Park visitor centre. The 5-mile (8km) route follows the Sruffaunboy Nature Trail before branching off towards the cone of Diamond Hill. From the cairn on the summit ridge at 1,460ft (442 metres) the view embraces islands, bays, beaches, loughs and mountains.

Sawel (County Derry). The large expanse of the Sperrin Mountains are in a sparsely populated region of north Tyrone. The walking covers bog, heather and moorland and will take you through quiet valleys and encounters with sheep and birds.

The Grand Canal Way (County Dublin and Midlands). This flat canalside walk leads westwards from the outskirts of Dublin through the central plains to the village of Shannon Harbour, covering a distance of 80 miles (130km). The walk offers a variety of wildlife, canal features and pretty villages to stop in for refuelling. You can pause to explore Ireland's finest monastic settlement at Clonmacnoise.

The Mourne Mountains in County Down were the inspiration for C.S. Lewis's Chronicles of Narnia.

The Slieve Bloom Way (counties Laois and Offaly). This 43-mile (70km) route covers a wide circuit of an isolated range of mountains in central Ireland and takes two days. It provides panoramic views from the paths and tracks through the bog land; the ascents of the hills are not too strenuous.

Carrauntoohil (County Kerry). The most popular route to the top of Ireland's highest mountain is via the Devil's Ladder, although it can be dangerous in wet weather. Walkers have to scramble through a wide gully with loose boulders that can easily dislodge. The return time is a minimum of five hours, so this one is for more experienced walkers.

IRELAND'S ARCHITECTURE

Ireland has a long and turbulent history, and its buildings reflect a catalogue of conquest, and also its roots as an agrarian economy with extremes of wealth and poverty.

'Never accept a commission in Ireland' a 19th-century English architect warned his colleagues. His fear was that only the most rugged buildings could withstand the Atlantic winds and rain. In the 20th century, two greater threats emerged: bitter warfare which would see great Anglo-Irish manors burnt to the ground, and the rapacity of 1960s property developers which would devastate Dublin's Georgian heritage.

Ireland's buildings reflect a history of conquest. From the 12th century, Anglo-Norman fortresses were built to intimidate. But Ireland proved hard to subjugate and fortified tower houses continued to be built until the end of the 17th century. In the 18th century, the British imported Palladian and Georgian styles, and neoclassical influences spread to humble farmhouses. But the crude thatched cottage didn't die: it evolved into the crude bungalows that disfigure the countryside today.

Dublin became a showpiece city in the 18th century, with areas such as Fitzwilliam Square (pictured) conveying an elegant simplicity that implied social status. It was clearly a European capital. By contrast, Belfast was an industrial city, whose rapid growth in the 19th century produced a few grand civic edifices but mainly utilitarian Victorian buildings.

Bantry House in County Cork is about as far as you can get from the cliché image of an Irish cottage, and hints at the lifestyle enjoyed by the Anglo-Irish aristocracy. When Richard White, 2nd earl of Bantry, inherited this Georgian house in 1845, he began turning it into a repository for the art and antiques he collected on his world travels. An amateur architect, he had a theatrical sense of design. Parallels with the Capitol Building in Washington DC reinforce the claims of Charles Frederick Anderson, who emigrated to the US and said he had a hand in both. Its collection of carpets, tapestries and furniture is open to the public, and it offers one of the best views over Bantry Bay.

Leamaneh Castle is a striking ruin of an extended tower house, dating from 1480 and attached to a 17th-century four-storey mansion. It can be found in the Burren area of County Clare, on route R476 from Kilfenora through Killinaboy.

Killruddery House in Bray, County Wicklow, is an example of a grand country house within easy reach of Dublin. Built in the 17th century, it was later remodelled along neo-Elizabethan lines. A conservatory was added in 1852, its walls being masonry instead of glass because it was meant to house not only plants but also the statues collected by its owner, William Brabazon, 10th earl of Meath.

The classic image of Dublin is of its elegant Georgian doorways. But comparatively few have survived: unchecked developers bulldozed many to create modern office blocks, and public support for preserving Ireland's architectural heritage was sometimes interpreted as nostalgia for the former colonial ruler.

Avondale House, a Georgian building in County Wicklow, was the birthplace of the politician Charles Stewart Parnell (1846–91). Now a museum, it is surrounded by a forest park.

The Fight for Old Dublin

Dublin in the 18th century was one of the ornaments of Europe, its Georgian buildings expressing a distinctive graciousness, the wide streetscapes framing distant mountain views, some of which can still be seen today.

Swaths of that heritage was damaged during the Easter Rising, the War of Independence and the Irish Civil War, and more was destroyed in the unregulated property speculation of the 1960s. Whole streets were razed and replaced by often-unsympathetic office blocks. Classic Georgian terraces vanished. Protests peaked in the late 1970s after an important Viking site at Wood Quay was obliterated to build offices for city officials.

The recent record has been better. Plans for a huge bus depot south of the River Liffey were shelved in the late 1980s, when the city authorities realised that the small shops, galleries and restaurants on the cobbled streets of Temple Bar had turned the area into a prime tourist attraction. So instead of bulldozing the area, it was partly redeveloped, and is now home to the Irish Film Institute (IFI), The Ark (a children's cultural centre), Meeting House Square (an outdoor venue), galleries and artists' studios.

Georgian door knocker in Dublin.

Cushendun, Northern Ireland.

Trinity College, Dublin.

RALEIGH

Titanic Belfast.

Thatched cottage and garden, Adare, County Clare.

INTRODUCTION

A detailed guide to the entire island and all its delights, with principal sites clearly cross-referenced by number to the accompanying maps.

What other city but Dublin, capital of the Republic of Ireland, could boast a General Post Office as a national treasure? Where else but Belfast, capital of Northern Ireland, could have transformed itself in so short a time from a city besieged by political unrest to a popular short-break destination? The stimulating thing about Ireland is that despite the many preconceptions, it's always full of pleasant surprises.

Open-minded visitors, best equipped with raincoats and sturdy walking shoes, will discover a beguiling land of hidden loughs and charming towns, ancient burial chambers and decorative stone crosses, round towers and ruined castles, surprisingly beautiful beaches and rolling green hills. This is a country in which racehorses are revered and where everyone says hello, regardless of whether they've ever laid eyes on you before.

Kerry beckons with opulent valleys, nurturing wild fuchsia and scented orchids; Killarney, with jaunting cars and oh so touristy leprechaun lore; Dublin, increasingly Americanised, may be the least lonely of capital cities; sprawling Cork quite the foodie heaven. Rivers teem with salmon like Galway's Corrib and the Blackwater that runs through Armagh and Tyrone while Cavan and Fermanagh's resplendent boating lakes are gloriously free of crowds. It may be a small country but, like a good pint of stout, it deserves to be savoured slowly. Sometimes it simply has to be. A signpost may present you with three ways of getting to a destination or it may show none. Ask for directions and you'll probably be assured 'it's just around the corner' – in Ireland everything happens in its own good time.

The tensions of the modern world have not bypassed Ireland but many big-city dwellers will find an overall slower pace of life here. And while the economic highs and lows of the last few decades have left residents with plenty to bend the ear about given half the chance, a remarkable capacity for enjoyment prevails, one that visitors are certain to find wildly infectious.

Ireland
0 40 km
0 40 miles
N
ATLANTIC
OCEAN
Mull of Kintyre
North Channel
Rathlin Island
Ballycastle
Cushendall
Giant's Causeway
Antrim Mts
Portstewart
Coleraine
Ballymoney
R. Bann
Ballymena
Larne
Island Magee
Carrickfergus
Bangor
Donaghadee
Newtownards
Strangford L.
Ards Peninsula
Newtownabbey
BELFAST
Antrim
Randalstown
Lough Neagh
Lisburn
Lurgan
Craigavon
Killyleagh
Ballynahinch
Downpatrick
Lecale Peninsula
Newcastle
Mourne Mts
Kilkeel
Rostrevor
Carlingford L.
Banbridge
Rathfriland
Portadown
Armagh
Keady
Newry
Castleblaney
Dundalk (Dun Dealgan)
Dundalk Bay
Dunany Point
Dunleer
Drogheda (Droichead Átha)
Irish Sea
Balbriggan
Skerries
Duleek
Naul
Ardee
Carrickmacross
Ceanannus Mór (Kells)
Navan (An Uaimh)
Dunshaughlin
Virginia
Castlepollard
Bailieborough
Cavan (An Cabhán)
Ballybay
Monaghan (Muineachán)
Clones
Coalisland
Dungannon
Cookstown
Magherafelt
Maghera
Glenavy
Limavady
Inishowen Head
L. Foyle
Moville
Derry
NORTHERN IRELAND
Sperrin Mts
Strabane
Omagh
Newtownstewart
Buncrana
Malin Head
Portsalon
Milford
Letterkenny (Leitir Ceanainn)
Ballybofey
R. Foyle
Derryveagh Mts
Tory Island
Tory Sound
Bloody Foreland
Gweedore
Dungloe
Aran Island
Gweebarra Bay
Glenties
Blue Stack Mts
Donegal
Killybegs
Malin More
Donegal Bay
Ballyshannon
Belleek
Kesh
Lower Lough Erne
Upper Lough Erne
Enniskillen
Belcoo
Iron Mts
Dowra
Drumshanbo
Lough Allen
Manorhamilton
Sligo (Sligeach)
Collooney
Boyle
Carrick-on-Shannon
Longford (An Longfort)
Granard
Mullingar (An Muileann gCearr)
Lough Ree
Roscommon
REPUBLIC
Castlerea
Ballyhaunis
Claremorris
Tuam
Sligo Bay
Easky
Enniscrone
Tobercurry
Slieve Gamph or Ox Mts
Killala Bay
Ballina
Swinford
Plains of Mayo
Ballinrobe
Lough Mask
Lough Conn
Castlebar (Caisleán an Bharraigh)
Westport
Downpatrick Head
Ballycastle
Carrowmore L.
Bangor Erris
Nephin Beg Ra.
Mulrany
Newport
Partry Mts
Clew Bay
Sheeffry Hills
Louisburgh
Leenane
Maam Cross
Clifden
Headford
Erris Head
Belmullet
Mullet Peninsula
Blacksod Bay
Achill Island
Clare Island
Inishturk
Inishbofin
M1
M2
M3

Dun Laoghaire
Bray (Bré)
Greystones
Wicklow (Cill Mhantáin)
Rathdrum
Arklow (An tInbhear Mór)
Wicklow Mts
Wicklow Mountains National Park
Mullaghcleevaun 848
Lugnaquilla 700
Rathcoole
Naas (An Nás)
Newbridge
Kildare
Monasterevin
Athy (Baile Átha Í)
Carlow (Ceatharlach)
Tullow
Carnew
Gorey
Cahore Point
Enniscorthy (Inis Córthaidh)
R. Slaney
Wexford (Loch Garman)
Rosslare
Rosslare Harbour
Carnsore Point
Saltee Islands
Kilmore Quay
Hook Head
New Ross (Ros Mhic Thriúin)
Bagenalstown
R. Barrow
Kilkenny (Cill Chainnigh)
Thomastown
R. Nore
Waterford (Port Láirge)
Tramore
Castlecomer
Portarlington
Portlaoise
Mountmellick
Durrow
Callan
Carrick-on-Suir (Carraig na Siúire)
Slievenamon
Dungarvan (Dún Garbhán)
Mine Head
Clonmel (Cluain Meala)
Thurles (Durlas)
Templemore
Roscrea (Ros Cré)
Birr
Cloghan
Cashel (Caiseal)
R. Suir
Cahir (An Cathair)
Knockmealdown Mts
R. Blackwater
Tallowbridge
Youghal (Eochaill)
Knockadoon Head
Tipperary
Galtee Mts
Fermoy
Midleton
Cobh (An Cobh)
Crosshaven
Nenagh (An tAonach)
Borrisokane
Portumna
Lough Derg
R. Shannon
Slievefelim Mts
Mitchelstown
Cork (Corcaigh)
Ballincollig
Kinsale
Old Head of Kinsale
R. Lee
Loughrea
Slieve Aughty Mts
Limerick (Luimneach)
Patrickswell
Croom
Kilmallock
Mallow (Mala)
Rath Luirc
Kanturk
Macroom
Bandon
R. Bandon
Clonakilty
Galley Head
Tulla
Gort
Kinvara
Kilcolgan
Ennis (Inis)
Newcastle West
Rathmore
Dunmanway
Skibbereen
C. Clear Island
(Gaillimh)
Galway Bay
Black Head
Ballyvaughan
The Burren
Ennistymon
Creegh
Tarbert
Abbeyfeale
R. Feale
Castleisland
Killarney (Cill Airne)
Glengarriff
Bantry
Ballydehob
Gorumna Island
Inishmore
Inishmaan
Inisheer
Aran Islands
Cliffs of Moher
Kilrush
Ballybunion
Listowel
Tralee (Trá Lí)
Kenmare
Donegal Point
Carrigaholt
Mouth of the Shannon
Loop Head
Ballyheige
Kerry Head
Tralee Bay
Camp
Killorglin
Carrantuohill 1041
Iveragh
Beara
Bantry Bay
Bere Island
Sheep's Head
Mizen Head
Kenmare River
Dingle
Dingle Bay
Brandon Head
Cahersiveen
Waterville
Skellig Islands
Dursey Head
Blasket Islands
Valentia Island
Bray Head
I R E L A N D
St George's Channel
Celtic Sea
M6
M7
M8
M9
M11
M18

Dublin City
0 250 m
0 250 yds
Tram Line and Station
Drumalee Road
Auburn Walk
Prussia Street
Aughrim Street
North Circular Road
Ross Street
Oxmantown Road
Ben Edar Rd
Manor St
Halliday Rd
Harold Rd
Ivar Street
Manor Place
Mount Temple Rd
Ard-Righ Rd
Sitric Road
Stoneybatter
Kirwan Street
O'Devaney Gardens
Aberdeen St
Infirmary Road
Montpelier Gardens
Montpelier Hill
Arbour Hill
Dept of Defence
Dublin Criminal Courts Complex
National Museum of Decorative Arts & History (Collins Barracks)
39
Incorporated Law Society
St Brendan's Hospital
Grangegorman Upper
Grangegorman Lower
LUAS Tram (Cross City Line)
Broadstone - DIT
Constitution Hill
King's Inns
Prebend Street
Western Way
Dominick
Brunswick Street North
King Street North
Church St Upper
Coleraine St
Beresford Street
Halston St
Blackhall Place
Queen Street
Smithfield
The Chimney
Bow Street
May Lane
Mary's
Greek St
Hendrick Street
Old Jameson Distillery
34
St Michan's
Four Courts
Phoenix Park
Parkgate Street
Anna Liva
Benburb Street
Museum
Wolfe Tone Quay
Ellis Quay
Smithfield
Arran Quay
St Paul
Hammond Lane
Church Street
Chancery Street
Chancery Pl.
Four Courts
35
Inns Quay
River Liffey
St John's Road West
Heuston Station
Heuston
Victoria Quay
Usher's Island
Usher's Quay
Merchants Quay
Island Street
Bonham Street
Usher Street
Bridgefoot Street
Guinness Brewery (St James's Gate Brewery)
LUAS Tram (Red Line)
Steevens Lane
St Patrick's Hospital
Irish Museum of Modern Art
Military Road
Bow Lane West
Watling Street
St Patrick's Tower
Oliver Bond Street
St Augustine Street
Bridge St
Brazen Head
Franciscan Church
Cook Street
John St West
St Augustine and St John
23
St. Audoen's Church
Dublinia
22
Winetavern St
High St
An Taisce (Tailors' Hall)
Back Lane
Cornmarket
Thomas Street West
St Catherine
National College of Art and Design
James's Street
Echlin St
St James's
Crane St
Thomas Court
Hanbury Lane
Basin St Lwr
James's
Rainsford Street
Meath Street
Francis Street
Iveagh Market
John Dillon St
Nicholas St
24
Guinness Storehouse
Robert Street
Bellevue
Earl St South
Swift's Alley
St Nicholas of Myra
Basin Street Upper
Kilmainham Gaol
Bond St
Newport St
Pim St
Marrowbone Lane
Summer St South
Pimlico
Meath Place
Carman's Hall
The Coombe
Dean St
Patrick St
20
Convent
St James's Hospital
Fatima
John Street South
Ardee St
Rialto
St James's Walk
Our Lady's Rd
Cork Street
Newmarket
Ward's Hill
New Row South
Chamber St
Mill Street
Fumbally Lane
New Street South
Rialto Street
St Anthony's Rd
Lourdes Rd
Rosary Rd
Cameron St
Brown Street South
Malpas St
Long
Reuben Street
Reuben Ave
South Circular Road
Donore Avenue
Donore Rd
Susan Terrace
O'Curry Road
St Thomas Rd
Clarence Mangan Road
Blackpitts
Clanbrassil Street Lower
Vernon
Daniel St
Lombard St
Dolphin's Barn St
Coombe Hospital
O'Donovan Road
DOLPHIN'S BARN

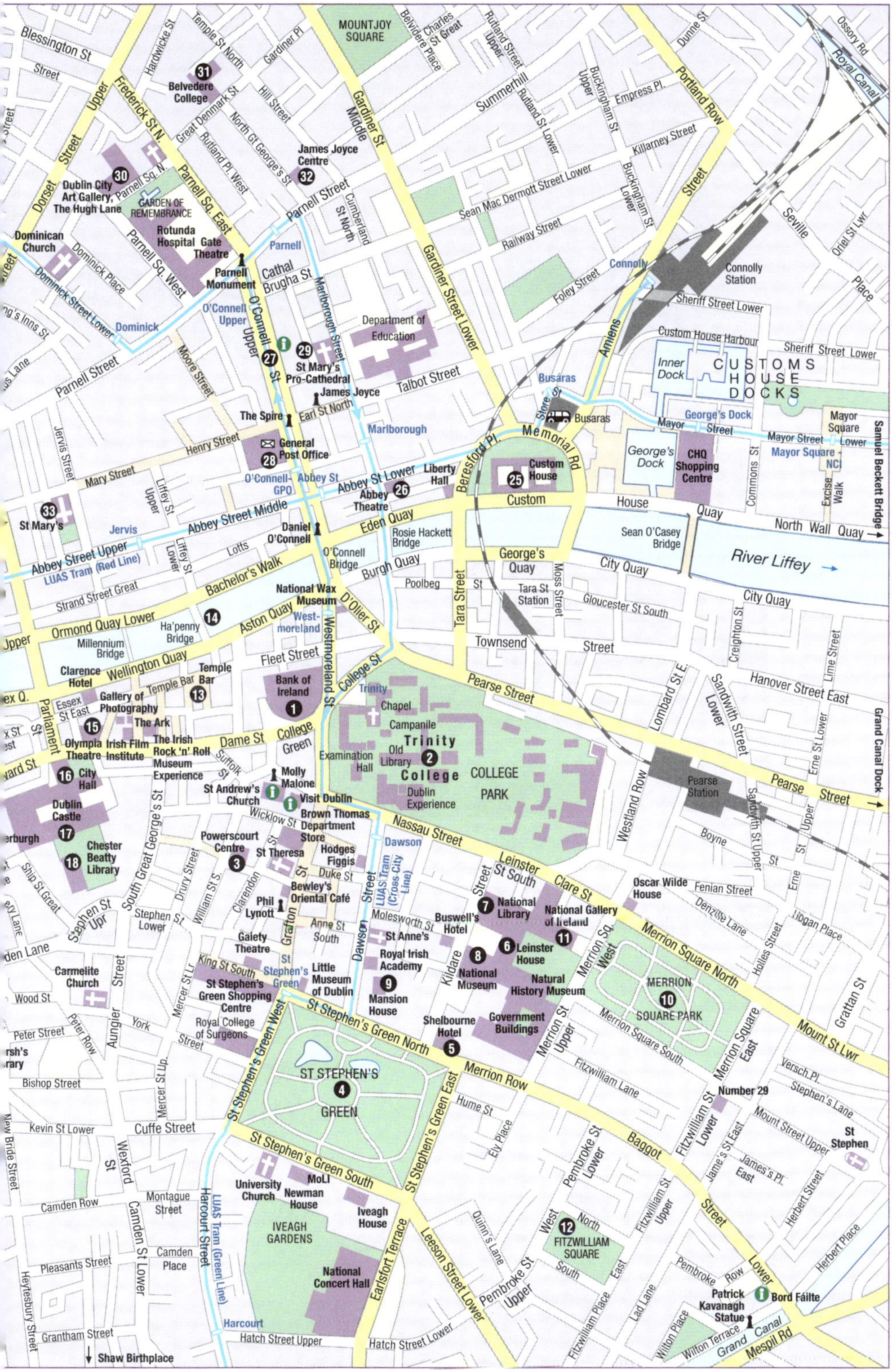

Blessington St
Street
Upper
Frederick St N.
Hardwicke St
Temple St North
31
Belvedere College
Great Denmark St
Gardiner Pl
Hill Street
North Gt George's St
Rutland Pl. West
MOUNTJOY SQUARE
Belvidere Place
Charles St Great
Rutland Street Upper
Gardiner St Middle
Summerhill
Rutland St Lower
Buckingham St Upper
Empress Pl.
Dunne St
Portland Row
Ossory Rd
Royal Canal
Dorset Street
Parnell Sq. East
Parnell Sq. N.
30
Dublin City Art Gallery, The Hugh Lane
GARDEN OF REMEMBRANCE
Rotunda Hospital
Gate Theatre
James Joyce Centre
32
Parnell Street
Cumberland St North
Sean Mac Dermott Street Lower
Buckingham St Lower
Killarney Street
Railway Street
Street
Seville
Oriel St Lwr
Place
Dominican Church
Dominick Place
Parnell Sq. West
Parnell Monument
Parnell
Cathal Brugha St
Dominick Street Lower
Dominick
O'Connell Upper
O'Connell St Upper
Marlborough Street
Gardiner Street Lower
Foley Street
Connolly
Connolly Station
Amiens
Sheriff Street Lower
Custom House Harbour
Sheriff Street Lower
King's Inns St
Parnell Street
Moore Street
27
29
St Mary's Pro-Cathedral
Department of Education
Talbot Street
Inner Dock
CUSTOMS HOUSE DOCKS
James Joyce
Earl St North
The Spire
Marlborough
Busaras
Store St
Busaras
Mayor
George's Dock
Mayor Square
Mayor Street Lower
Mayor Square
NCI
Samuel Beckett Bridge
Jervis Street
Mary Street
Henry Street
General Post Office
28
O'Connell-GPO
Abbey St
Abbey St Lower
Liberty Hall
26
Abbey Theatre
Beresford Pl.
Memorial Rd
Custom House
25
Custom
House
Quay
George's Dock
CHQ Shopping Centre
Commons St
Excise Walk
North Wall Quay
33
St Mary's
Liffey St. Upper
Jervis
Abbey Street Middle
Daniel O'Connell
Eden Quay
Rosie Hackett Bridge
Sean O'Casey Bridge
River Liffey
Abbey Street Upper
LUAS Tram (Red Line)
Liffey St Lower
Lotts
O'Connell Bridge
Burgh Quay
George's Quay
City Quay
City Quay
Strand Street Great
Bachelor's Walk
National Wax Museum
Poolbeg
St
Tara St Station
Moss Street
Gloucester St South
Tara Street
Creighton St
Ormond Quay Lower
14
Ha'penny Bridge
Aston Quay
West-moreland
D'Olier St
Millennium Bridge
Upper
Townsend
Street
Lime Street
Clarence Hotel
Wellington Quay
Temple Bar
Fleet Street
Temple Bar
13
Bank of Ireland
1
Westmoreland St
College St
Trinity
Chapel
Campanile
Pearse Street
Lombard St E.
Sandwith Street Lower
Hanover Street East
Grand Canal Dock
Essex St East
Gallery of Photography
Essex Q.
Parliament St
15
The Ark
Irish Film Institute
Olympia Theatre
The Irish Rock 'n' Roll Museum Experience
Dame St
College Green
Trinity College
2
Old Library
Examination Hall
COLLEGE PARK
Dublin Experience
Westland Row
Pearse Station
Pearse Street
Sandwith St Upper
Erne St Lower
Erne St Upper
16
City Hall
Dublin Castle
17
Werburgh
Suffolk St
Molly Malone
St Andrew's Church
Visit Dublin
Brown Thomas Department Store
Wicklow St
Nassau Street
Dawson
Boyne St
18
Chester Beatty Library
South Great George's St
Powerscourt Centre
3
St Theresa
Hodges Figgis
Duke St
LUAS Tram (Cross-City Line)
Leinster St South
Clare St
Oscar Wilde House
Fenian Street
Denzille Lane
Ship St Great
Drury Street
William St S.
Clarendon St
Bewley's Oriental Café
Phil Lynott
Grafton St
Dawson Street
Street
Molesworth St
Buswell's Hotel
7
National Library
National Gallery of Ireland
11
Hogan Place
Holles Street
Stephen St Upr
Stephen St Lower
Camden Lane
Gaiety Theatre
Anne St South
St Anne's
Royal Irish Academy
8
National Museum
6
Leinster House
Kildare St
Merrion Sq. West
Merrion Square North
Carmelite Church
Aungier Street
Wood St
Mercer St Lr
King St South
St Stephen's Green Shopping Centre
Stephen's Green
Little Museum of Dublin
9
Mansion House
Natural History Museum
MERRION SQUARE PARK
10
Grattan St
Peter Street
Peter Row
York Street
Royal College of Surgeons
St Stephen's Green North
Shelbourne Hotel
5
Government Buildings
Merrion St Upper
Merrion Square South
Merrion Square East
Mount St Lwr
Bishop Street
Mercer St Up.
St Stephen's Green West
ST STEPHEN'S GREEN
4
Merrion Row
Fitzwilliam Lane
Versch.Pl.
Stephen's Lane
New Bride Street
Kevin St Lower
Cuffe Street
Wexford St
Hume St
Ely Place
Baggot Street
Fitzwilliam St Lower
Number 29
Mount Street Upper
St Stephen
St Stephen's Green South
University Church
MoLI
Newman House
St Stephen's Green East
Pembroke St Lower
James's St East
James's Pl. East
Herbert Street
Camden Row
Montague Street
Harcourt Street
LUAS Tram (Green Line)
IVEAGH GARDENS
Iveagh House
Earlsfort Terrace
Leeson Street Lower
Quinn's Lane
West
North
12
FITZWILLIAM SQUARE
South
East
Fitzwilliam St Upper
Herbert Place
Pleasants Street
Camden St Lower
Camden Place
National Concert Hall
Pembroke St Upper
Fitzwilliam Place
Lad Lane
Pembroke Row
Lower
Bord Fáilte
Patrick Kavanagh Statue
Wilton Place
Wilton Terrace
Grand Canal
Mespil Rd
Heytesbury Street
Grantham Street
Shaw Birthplace
Harcourt
Hatch Street Upper
Hatch Street Lower

The O'Connell Monument.

DUBLIN

Dublin boxes above its diminutive size on every level, brimming with history, culture, wit and warmth, and the legendary hospitality locals extend to visitors has made this one of Europe's most popular city breaks.

With its vibrant mix of traditional pubs, hip bars, elegant Georgian architecture, cool shops and a colourful cultural scene to rival any European capital, Dublin bubbles with an infectious energy. The severe economic downturn that badly dented the city's confidence for five years after 2009 is largely in the rear-view mirror, and some parked elements of the docklands renewal project are now back on track. Dublin is a lively place to be, from the café-packed side streets around Grafton Street to the African and Asian stores that rub shoulders with traditional street traders on Moore Street. Culturally, the city is famous for its theatre, literature, art and music, which is no surprise considering that some of Europe's most prestigious writers and musicians including James Joyce, W.B. Yeats, Samuel Beckett, Brendan Behan, and U2 have all called Dublin home.

DUBLIN'S APPEAL

Dublin is a multi-layered place that charms visitors on many different levels. Some are drawn in by the echoes of history that resonate from every corner, from Viking-era areas, through the grand 18th-century Georgian town houses and the civic buildings that bear the marks of modern Irish history, which instil the city with depth, beauty and a certain solemnity. For others, it's a city of talkers, tales and laughter, pubs overflowing with ribald raconteurs, young and old, all clutching pints of porter. Some fall in love with the quiet, sophisticated urban parks of Merrion Square and the Iveagh Gardens, while others gorge on the city's collection of chic boutiques, lively street markets and the luxurious Brown Thomas department store.

Dublin delights in its superb setting. The city sits on a wide plain, beautifully bisected by the River Liffey, overlooked by hills and headlands and facing a

Main attractions

Trinity College
St Stephen's Green
National Museum
Temple Bar
Ha'Penny Bridge
Dublin Castle
Guinness Storehouse
Custom House
O'Connell Street
Phoenix Park

Maps on pages
114, ,137

The Ha'penny Bridge.

broad sweeping bay. Mountains are visible from the urban centre, which has changed dramatically during the last two decades. The city is now a mishmash of glorious architecture, old and new, which sits alongside dilapidated, sometimes derelict buildings, and tacky neon and plastic signage. But Dublin can still sparkle when it tries.

A DIVIDED CITY

Dublin is divided by the River Liffey, which flows through its centre, and also by the social differences, which the river delineates. In the early 18th century, the rich moved north across the river from the old medieval city with its teeming slums, to fine new terraces and squares, such as Henrietta Street and Mountjoy Square. But within decades they doubled back again to establish fashionable residences on the south side, around Merrion Square and Fitzwilliam Square, continuing in Victorian times through the suburbs of Ballsbridge and out along the coast to the attractive towns of DúnLaoghaire and Dalkey.

There are still middle-class enclaves on the Northside, but by and large Southsiders are better off, better dressed and (to their own ears) better spoken. Like any snobbery, of course, the north–south chauvinism works both ways, and just as many Southsiders look scornfully across the Liffey, Northsiders are inclined to judge the Southside as a wasteland of snobbery and pretension. Old prejudices are confirmed in modern developments: south of the river is the exquisite 2,100 seat Daniel Libeskind-designed Bord Gáis Energy Theatre (called the Grand Canal Theatre when it was built in 2010), home to opera and West End–style musicals, while north is the 14,000-seat 3Arena (originally the Point Depot, built in 2008) custom-designed for pop concerts and stadium rock.

BANK OF IRELAND AND AROUND

A good place to begin a walking tour is O'Connell Bridge. Retreat from the breadth and bustle of O'Connell Street and instead walk down Westmoreland

PARADOXES OF DUBLIN'S HISTORY

Dublin began by the banks of the Liffey, where Celtic settlements and churches existed at least from early Christian times, near a causeway crossing from which the city's Gaelic name, Baile Atha Cliath, 'The Town of the Hurdle Ford', is derived. But towns as such did not figure in the old Celtic way of things, and it is generally accepted that Dublin was founded in the 9th century, not by the Irish, but by the Vikings, who were plundering and colonising all the coasts of Northern Europe.

Dublin was soon a lucrative base for both raiding and trading, and the Danes clung on to it – despite persistent attacks by local chieftains and a great defeat at the Battle of Clontarf in 1014 – gradually intermarrying with the Irish and adopting Christianity. The Viking community began to turn into Gaels, and started to build places of worship for their new religion included the forerunner of the medieval Christ Church Cathedral, and St Michan's Church on the north bank of the Liffey. The Anglo-Normans arrived in the 12th century, and captured Dublin in 1170, ejecting the Vikings, who settled on the north bank of the Liffey. By the 14th century the Vikings had been completely assimilated into Irish and Anglo-Norman society. But, until Elizabethan times, direct English rule was restricted to a ribbon of land on the east coast known as 'the Pale', running roughly from Dundalk to the north to just south of Dublin. Territory outside of this area was regarded as wild and the people uncivilised, hence the expression 'beyond the pale'.

The colonisation by British landlords in the 17th and 18th centuries created Dublin's Golden Age, when many great buildings were erected, including the elegant Georgian squares lined by tall domestic dwellings.

Legislative independence was granted under the English Crown in 1782, but the Irish parliament in College Green was short-lived. After the rebellion of the United Irishmen in 1798, Britain brought Ireland under direct control again, instigating a long period of decline in Dublin.

The city was at the heart of the nationalist movements that led to the 1916 Rising, the subsequent War of Independence, the establishment of the Free State in 1921 and a brutal civil war. The next 40 years were a struggle.

Street into College Green, which contains two of Dublin's most impressive and historic buildings: the **Bank of Ireland** ❶ and **Trinity College**. The bank, with its curving, columnar, windowless facade, was built in 1729 to house the Irish Parliament. The colonnaded front was added in 1785 by James Gandon. Following the abolition of the Irish parliament, it became a bank in 1809. Visitors can explore the impressive, former House of Lords, with tapestries of the Battle of the Boyne (tel: 01-661 5933; guided tours Tues 10.30am; free).

Just north, on the corner of Westmoreland and D'Olier St, is the **National Wax Museum Plus** (www.waxmuseumplus.ie; charge) with myriad history exhibits and a chamber of horrors.

TRINITY COLLEGE

Opposite the Bank of Ireland, **Trinity College** ❷, whose sober facade is topped by a surprisingly bright blue clock, was founded in 1592 by Elizabeth I on the site of a confiscated monastery, but the frontage was built between 1755 and 1759. The porch inside the main gate leads to a spacious, cobbled quadrangle, on the right of which is the Examination Hall (1779–91), which contains a gilt oak chandelier from the old parliament and an organ said to have been taken from a Spanish ship at Vigo in 1702. On the left is the Chapel (1792) and beyond it the Dining Hall (1743). The 100ft (30-metre) campanile, which dominates the quadrangle was designed by Sir Charles Lanyon and erected in 1853 on a spot supposed to mark the centre of the medieval monastery church.

To the right of the second quadrangle is the **Old Library** (1712–32), where *the Book of Kells is housed*. This magnificently ornate 9th century manuscript copy of the gospels in Latin is put into context by an exhibition 'Turning Darkness into Light' and should not be missed. Purchase tickets online to bypass the queues (tel: 01-896 2320; www.tcd.ie/visitors/book-of-kells; charge). It is the greatest artefact of the flowering of Irish culture between the 7th and 9th centuries, the era when Ireland was

The Long Room library at Trinity College.

TRINITY COLLEGE

Set up exclusively for the Protestant Ascendancy class, Trinity College nourished many of Ireland's greatest writers, scientists and politicians.

Founded in 1591, Trinity covers 16 hectares (40 acres) in the centre of the city on land reclaimed from the Liffey estuary. It doesn't quite have the grandeur of the nearby Bank of Ireland and was described by James Joyce in *A Portrait of the Artist as a Young Man* as being 'set heavily in the city's ignorance like a dull stone set in a cumbrous ring'.

Trinity remained an exclusively Protestant university for most of its history, having been set up by Queen Elizabeth I to 'civilise' Dublin. The college has lost some, if not all, of its air of Ascendancy since the restriction on Catholic students was lifted in 1873. However, it is only since 1970 that they began attending in greater numbers, when the Catholic Church lifted its ban on studying at Trinity without prior special dispensation.

In academic circles, Oxford, Cambridge and Trinity were often mentioned in the same breath, and many English students who failed to make the first two ended up at 'Trinners'. Women students were admitted in 1903, earlier than in most British universities. Famous alumni include literary figures such as Jonathan Swift, Oscar Wilde, Samuel Beckett, Thomas Moore, Sheridan Le Fanu, John Millington Synge, Oliver St John Gogarty and Bram Stoker. Politicians, rebels and statesmen, among them Edward Carson, Douglas Hyde (Ireland's first president), Henry Grattan, Wolfe Tone, Robert Emmet and Leo Varadkar also made their mark.

DISTINGUISHED ALUMNI

Most of Trinity's buildings date from the 18th century. The entrance is flanked by statues of two of the university's many famous alumni, the historian and statesman Edmund Burke (1729–97) and the writer Oliver Goldsmith (1728–74).

The Berkeley Library, built in 1967, is named after Bishop George Berkeley, an 18th-century philosopher who came to study at Trinity in 1700 at the age of 15, and later served for a time as the college librarian. A proper polymath and the father of higher education in America (the university city of Berkeley, California, was named after him) Berkeley was born in Kilkenny, and was also a distinguished scientist, economist, psychologist and writer.

A figure from the 9th-century Book of Kells.

famed as 'the land of saints and scholars' and Irish monks re-Christianised Europe after the Dark Ages. Also in the library are the *Book of Durrow* (7th century), the *Book of Dimma* (8th century) and the *Book of Armagh* (c.807). Upstairs is the breathtaking Long Room, nearly 210ft (64 metres) in length and containing 200,000 of the college's oldest books. Temporary exhibitions highlight the library's fine collection.

GRAFTON STREET

Leaving Trinity by the main gate and turning left, you face the mouth of **Grafton Street,** the Southside's principal shopping thoroughfare, a pedestrianised street teeming with people and buskers. A buxom bronze statue of Molly Malone, the famous shellfish seller from the traditional song *In Dublin's Fair City*, once stood at the junction with Suffolk Street, but in 2013, to protect her from the building work on the LUAS Cross City Project, the 'the tart with the cart' (as Dubliners fondly refer to her) 'wheeled her wheelbarrow through streets broad and narrow' about 100 metres west, to the corner of Suffolk and St Andrew's Street, just outside St Andrew's Church. Near here you will also find the hi-tech **Visit Dublin** tourist office (3 Palace Street, Barnardo Square; year round Mon-Sat 9.30am-5.30pm, Sun 10.30-3pm; tel: 1850 230 330; www.visitdublin.com), an excellent place to pick up maps, free independent advice, accommodation advice and booking, and events, as well the **Dublin Pass** (https://gocity.com/dublin/en-us; charge; passes available for 1/2/3/4/5 days) with entry to over 25 top attractions. Children under 5 go free.

Head back to Grafton Street and turn right. Worth a visit for its luxurious atmosphere is **Brown Thomas** (www.brownthomas.com), a department store offering top international brands including Louis Vuitton, Chanel, Hermès, Prada and Tiffany & Co (remember to avail of tax-free shopping, if you are normally resident outside of the EU). The third-floor restaurant is an excellent spot for a little people watching

St Stephen's Green.

over a cup of coffee or a glass of wine. Alternatively, pop into Bewley's Oriental Café, Grafton Street's iconic coffee-and-cake stop, established in 1840.

Johnston's Court, a narrow alley off Grafton Street to the right, leads to the rear entrance of the **Powerscourt Centre** ❸, three storeys of stylish shops, antique galleries, cafés and a theatre, all under the roof of the former Powerscourt Townhouse, built in 1771–74 for Viscount Powerscourt.

ST STEPHEN'S GREEN

On returning to Grafton Street, a right turn and a short walk takes you to the corner of **St Stephen's Green** ❹, a large square with a delightful park bordered by some fine houses, and a landmark glass-domed shopping centre. The gardens, laid out as a public park in 1880, are a relaxing refuge from the traffic, contain several interesting sculptures and are crammed in summer with picnickers and sunbathers. The **Little Museum** of Dublin (15 St Stephen's Green; www.littlemuseum.ie; charge) on your left arriving from Grafton Street, occupies three storeys of a Georgian house. Owned by Dublin City Council, this museum allows the people to tell the story of their city and offers a fascinating insight into the everyday life of Dubliners over the years. Artefacts on display were donated by ordinary people and range from a signed U2 album to a facsimile of James Joyce's death mask. The curators' tours are rich in Dublin wit and high-grade gossip. There is no café but if you go across to *Tang* on Dawson Street you will receive a 10% discount on showing your ticket.

On the green's south side are two elegant Georgian houses: **Newman House**, numbers 85 and 86 (tel: 01-716 7422; charge; guided tours available) the original seat of the Catholic University of Ireland, which morphed into University College Dublin, where James Joyce, Flann O'Brien (Brian O'Nolan) and Gerard Manley Hopkins worked or studied. It has fine interior plasterwork. Also here is the Museum of Literature Ireland (MoLI) (www.moli.ie; charge)

Georgian splendour in Merrion Square.

with regular changing exhibitions. The Dedalus Library holds a wonderful collection of Joyce's works while the LitLab is a family-dedicated space. There is also the Common's Café, shop and Reader's Gardens to enjoy too. For more details of free literary events for adults and children city wide, visit www.dublincityofliterature.ie. Right beside it is **Iveagh House,** numbers 80 and 81, which was built for the Bishop of Cork, and once housed the Guinness family. It is now part of the Department of Foreign Affairs. The **University Church** (newman.nd.edu/university-church) was built in 1856 in colourful neo-Byzantine style.

On the north side of the green is the **Shelbourne Hotel** ❺. Built in 1824, the hotel has been an intrinsic part of Dublin's social and cultural life for over 180 years. It's now a grand, elegant and exceptionally sumptuous spot, which attracts well-heeled Dubliners and visitors to its bars and restaurants. In Earlsfort Terrace, which branches from the southeastern corner of the green, is the **National Concert Hall** (www.nch.ie). The building, beautifully renovated, has first-rate acoustics.

OFFICIAL DUBLIN

Back on the north side of St Stephen's Green, Kildare Street leads past the left-hand side of the Shelbourne Hotel and a block of modern state buildings to **Leinster House** ❻, built as a town house for the Duke of Leinster in 1746 and now home of Dáil Eireann (Irish parliament). It is flanked by two, nearly symmetrical, edifices with columnar entrance rotundas. These are the National Library and National Museum, both built in 1890.

Apart from more than 500,000 books, the **National Library** ❼ (www.nli.ie; free) has an extensive collection of old newspapers and periodicals and a gallery housing temporary exhibitions of its collection. There is also a genealogy advisory service. The enormous reading room in its rotunda is worth a look.

The **National Museum** ❽ (www.museum.ie; free) has exhibits ranging from prehistory through the early Christian period and the Vikings to the Independence struggle. Exhibits include such treasures as the Ardagh Chalice and the Tara Brooch, plus fine prehistoric gold artefacts.

Directly opposite Leinster House is Molesworth Street, and a few yards along it is **Buswell's Hotel,** a popular haunt among politicians and political journalists. At its far end, the street meets Dawson Street, location of Hodges Figgis, Dublin's oldest and best bookshop, dating back to 1768 and mentioned in James Joyce's Ulysses.

Turning left at the corner you find **St Ann's Church** (1720), a venue for concerts as well as religious services in the Anglican tradition. A few metres up the street is the **Mansion House** ❾ the residence since 1715 of the Lord Mayors of Dublin. A Queen Anne-style house, dating from 1705, it was decorated with stucco and cast iron in Victorian times.

Leinster House.

MERRION SQUARE

At the other end of Dawson Street (towards Trinity College), you can turn right along Nassau Street which quickly becomes Clare Street, past the Kilkenny shop and the entrance to the Millennium Wing of the National Gallery into **Merrion Square** ⑩, one of Dublin's finest parks. Laid out in 1762, it has had many distinguished inhabitants; Sir William and Lady 'Speranza' Wilde, surgeon and poetess, and parents of Oscar, lived at No. 1; Daniel O'Connell lived at No. 58; W.B. Yeats, who was born in the seaside suburb of Sandymount but grew up mainly in London, lived at No. 52 and later at No. 83; Sheridan Le Fanu, author of the seminal vampire story *Carmilla*, lived at No. 70. The Duke of Wellington, victor over Napoleon at the Battle of Waterloo, was born at No. 24 Merrion Street Upper, which runs off the southwest corner of the square towards Merrion Row and St Stephen's Green. The lush gardens make up a beautiful public park with a playground, inspired by the children's story *The Selfish Giant* by Oscar Wilde. Artists set up stall on weekends hanging their paintings on the wrought-iron railings.

The main entrance to the **National Gallery of Ireland** ⑪ (www.nationalgallery.ie; free, charge for exhibitions; free tours at weekends) is on Merrion Square West. Apart from a range of Irish work, the gallery has some Dutch masters and fine examples of the 17th-century French, Italian and Spanish schools. The Yeats Collection is a tribute to the artistic achievements of the Yeats family, especially Jack B. Yeats. The Millennium Wing houses temporary exhibitions, the gallery shop and the excellent, self-service Gallery Restaurant. Out front is a statue of George Bernard Shaw, who said he owed his education to the gallery and left it a third of his estate. This bequest increased significantly when his play *Pygmalion* was adapted in 1956 and became the enduringly popular musical *My Fair Lady*.

Leaving the gallery and turning right up Merrion Street Upper past the lawns of Leinster House, there is a fine view

The Natural History Museum.

THE MESSIAH'S BIRTH

Dublin's otherwise unprepossessing Fishamble Street is celebrated as the venue of the first performance of Handel's *Messiah*, conducted by the composer in 1742 in the Charitable Music Society's Hall, long since demolished. Because the hall was cramped and the attendance large, ladies were asked not to wear hooped petticoats and gentlemen not to wear their swords. *Messiah* was an instant success in Dublin, though London audiences remained cool towards it for several years. A hotel, named after the composer, stands beside the original site; the *Messiah's* birth is celebrated at this spot by a statue of the composer (in the nude), and at noon every 13 April by members of Our Lady's Choral Society (fully clothed), who sing a selection of choruses.

to your left along the south side of Merrion Square towards the distant cupola of **St Stephen**'s Church (1825), known locally as the 'Pepper Canister Church' and a popular venue for concerts.

Passing the **Natural History Museum** (www.museum.ie; free), on your right you reach the imposing gates of **Government Buildings**, which house the office of the Taoiseach (prime minister) and the Cabinet room. Tours are available on Saturdays from 10.30am–1.30pm; tickets (free) are available that morning from the National Gallery.

A left turn at the next intersection along Baggot Street, then a right up Pembroke Street leads to **Fitzwilliam Square** ⓬, the city's smallest, latest (1825) and best-preserved Georgian square. Jack B. Yeats lived at number 18, on the corner of Fitzwilliam Street, the longest Georgian street in Dublin. In an infamous piece of state vandalism, 26 houses on its eastern side were demolished in 1965 to make way for a new Electricity Supply Board headquarters. Perhaps out of shame, the ESB helped restore **Number 29,** (www.esb.ie/numbertwentynine) on Fitzwilliam Street Lower. Closed to visitors for the foreseeable future, you can virtually explore this Georgian House Museum, an elegant recreation of a middle-class house of the late 1700s, via the website.

Wander back now to Trinity College, a good starting point to begin exploring the oldest part of the city.

TEMPLE BAR

With your back to the facade of Trinity and the Bank of Ireland on your right, walk along Dame Street, passing on your right the imposing, layered structure of the modern Central Bank. The network of small streets between the Central Bank and the river quays, known as **Temple Bar** ⓭, is Dublin's 'Left Bank'. The area fell short of becoming a became a bus station as CIE, the state transport company, had bought up most of the buildings in the area and rented them out until it was ready to demolish them. Small shops and art galleries were among the renters, though, and

The quirky Temple Bar area.

an effective campaign was launched to build on their success and turn the area into a cultural quarter. It then gained an unsavoury reputation for bawdy hen and stag parties but has since regained its cultural credentials.

Temple Bar is a browser's paradise of cobbled streets, jam-packed with art galleries, second-hand bookshops, vintage clothes shops, designer consignment shops, record stores, pubs, clubs, cultural centres, restaurants and everything in between. Temple Bar Square is lively and buzzy with traditional music blaring out from the pubs. Meeting House Square is a cultural hub, with its Saturday food market and outdoor cinema events.

North of Temple Bar Square, Merchant's Arch – a favourite spot for buskers – leads to the river quay and the **Ha'penny Bridge** ⓮ (1816) – so-called because of the toll once charged for crossing it. This cast-iron pedestrian walkway across the Liffey has become one of the best-known symbols of the city. It is a convenient link to the Henry Street–Jervis Street shopping area across the river.

One of Temple Bar's most popular haunts.

The route from Temple Bar Square to Meeting House Square goes through **Curved Street,** which houses the Irish Rock 'N' Roll Museum Experience (http://irishrocknrollmuseum.com; charge). Entrance includes a behind the scenes visit to the **Button Factory** rock venue and the **Temple Lane Studios** recording studios. The **Gallery of Photography** on Meeting House Square shows both Irish and international work and has an interesting range of postcards and books (www.galleryofphotography.ie; free).

On Eustace Street, in a former Presbyterian Meeting House is the **Ark,** a cultural centre for children (www.ark.ie) with workshops, camps, film screenings and more. Further up the road is the **Irish Film Institute** – an arthouse cinema with a bookshop, café and bar (www.ifi.ie).

Continuing along Essex Street East, you pass the rear of **The Clarence** (www.theclarence.ie), which fronts onto the river quay and was bought by Bono and The Edge from the Dublin band U2 in 1992. Its art-deco Octagon Bar is a fashionable meeting place.

ANCIENT DUBLIN

Venture across Parliament Street and down Essex Street to the west of Temple Bar and you'll find a good collection of cutting edge interiors shops, retro treasure troves and small boutiques, as well as the stylish Cow's Lane Designer Mart market, on Saturdays.

Essex Street ends at its junction with **Fishamble Street,** the medieval 'fish shambles', or market, whose existence can be traced back to 1467 and which winds upwards from the quay alongside the Civic Offices.

Back on Dame Street, opposite City Hall, you see on your right the ornate Victorian doorway of the **Olympia Theatre** ⓯ (tel: 01-679 3323; www.olympia.ie). Despite its modest frontage, the Olympia has capacity for up to 1,600 concert-goers; its programme mixes plays, musicals and rock concerts.

CITY HALL

Dublin's medieval city once occupied the area between City Hall and Bridge Street, bordered by the riverbank to the north and defensive walls, which stretched as far as Bride Street in the south. **City Hall** 16 (www.dublincity.ie/dublincityhall; free) was designed in 1769 as the Royal Exchange by the London architect Thomas Cooley and taken over by the Corporation of Dublin in 1852. The entrance rotunda has a splendid, illuminated dome. The exhibition The Story of the Capital is housed in the restored vaults of City Hall, and tells the story of Dublin through the ages.

DUBLIN CASTLE

Dublin Castle 17 (www.dublincastle.ie; charge), just behind City Hall, was built between 1208 and 1220 on the site of an earlier Danish fortress and was the symbol of English rule in Ireland for almost eight centuries. The building as it now stands is mainly 18th-century; the largest visible remain of the Norman structure is the Record Tower, in the lower Castle Yard, which contains the **Garda (Police) Museum**. When Ireland holds the Presidency of the EU, and on other state occasions, the Castle is closed to the public.

Guided tours take in the Viking Excavation, the Chapel Royal and the castle's most impressive feature, the **State Apartments.** St Patrick's Hall, 82ft (25 metres) long and 40ft (12 metres) wide, with a high panelled and decorated ceiling, and handmade Donegal carpets is probably the grandest room in Ireland. Since 1938 it has been the scene of the inauguration of Irish presidents. The Gothic-style Church of the Most Holy Trinity was built as the Chapel Royal between 1807 and 1814 to a design by Francis Johnston; the exterior is decorated with more than 90 carved heads of English monarchs and other historical figures. Only the State Apartments and exhibitions can be explored on self-guided tours.

Grafton Street.

To the castle's rear, the Clock Tower building has been extended to accommodate the award-winning **Chester Beatty Library** ⓲ (www.cbl.ie; closed Mon Nov to Feb; free).

Sir Alfred Chester Beatty was born in New York in 1875 and became a successful mining engineer in Colorado. Having collected minerals and Chinese snuff bottles as a child, he became interested in Japanese and Chinese paintings. His knighthood was a reward for his help in supplying raw materials to the Allies in World War II. He moved to Ireland in 1950 and built a library to house his art collection. It has a fine collection of Chinese, Japanese, Persian, Indian and Middle Eastern manuscripts, paintings and ornaments. Audio-visual programmes provide background. It also houses the first-class **Silk Road Café** offering a taste of the Middle East.

Leaving the castle, head a short way down Dame Street towards Trinity College and turn right up busy South Great George's Street; on the left side is a Victorian shopping arcade worth a quick look.

The Chester Beatty Library.

Continue along Aungier Street, turn right into Bishop Street and cross New Bride Street into Kevin Street Upper and right again onto St Patrick's Close, where you find **Marsh's Library** ⓳ (www.marshlibrary.ie; charge), the oldest public library in Ireland, complete with original oak bookcases, named after its founder, Archbishop Narcissus Marsh (1638–1713). Among its 25,000 interesting items is Jonathan Swift's copy of *Clarendon's History of the Great Rebellion*, with Swift's pencilled notes. Historically, readers wishing to peruse valuable books were locked into elegant cages, which can still be seen.

THE LIBERTIES

The next junction marks the beginning of the **Liberties,** an area so named because it lay outside the jurisdiction of medieval Dublin. One of the city's most characterful working-class areas, it also had some of the worst 19th-century slum tenements. Turn right along Patrick Street to **St Patrick's Cathedral** ⓴ (www.stpatrickscathedral.ie). Dedicated in 1192, St Patrick's has been restored many times and, like Dublin's other cathedral, Christ Church, has belonged to the Church of Ireland since the Reformation. Jonathan Swift, Dean from 1713 to 1745, is buried in it, near his beloved 'Stella', Esther Johnson. A simple brass plate in the floor marks his grave.

Continue north to **Christ Church Cathedral** ㉑ (www.christchurchdublin.ie; charge). This prominent cathedral was founded by Sitric, the Danish King of Dublin, about 1040, and greatly expanded from 1172 onwards under the aegis of Strongbow (Richard de Clare) and St Laurence O'Toole. The central tower was built about 1600 after storm and fire damage to the original steeples. Lambert Simnel, 10-year-old pretender to the English throne, was crowned here by his supporters in 1487. The structure was greatly rebuilt in Gothic revival style in the 1870s. Two of the cathedral's many tombs are said to be those of Strongbow and his son, whom, according to legend, he executed for cowardice in battle.

Linked to the cathedral by a covered bridge is **Dublinia** ㉒ (www.dublinia.ie; last entry at 4pm) an exhibition, run by the non-profit Medieval Trust. State-of-the-art interactives and reconstructions give an insight into the medieval world of Dublin. There is also an archaeological lab and excavation site, and an exhibition of what life was like aboard a Viking warship. From the top of the 200ft (60-metre) St Michael's Tower, you can enjoy a panoramic view over the city.

ST AUDOEN'S CHURCH

High Street, which runs off the west side of Christchurch Place, was the backbone of medieval Dublin. Part of the old city wall and the only surviving city gate has been uncovered near the partially ruined **St Audoen's Church** ㉓ (tel: 01-677 0088; free). It was named by the Normans after St Ouen of Rouen. Its §aisle contains a font dating from 1194; the tower is 12th-century and three of its bells were cast in the early 15th century, making them the country's oldest.

On the other side of High Street, in Back Lane, is **Tailors' Hall,** the only surviving guildhall in Dublin, and now the offices of An Taisce, which works to preserve the country's natural and architectural heritage.

THE GUINNESS TOUR

One part of the national heritage which seems well able to look after itself is enshrined half-a-mile (1km) to the west along Thomas Street: **Guinness's Brewery,** the biggest in Europe, churning out 2.5 million pints of its celebrated black stout every day. The brewery doesn't admit visitors, but the **Guinness Storehouse** ㉔ (www.guinness-storehouse.com; last admission 5pm; charge) lets you explore – through sight, touch, taste and smell – the making and history of the world's most famous stout. The building also houses gallery and exhibition areas,

KEY TO THE STATUES

The statues lining the centre of Dublin's O'Connell Street are (from the bridge end): Daniel O'Connell (1775–1847), a great leader of constitutional nationalism; William Smith O'Brien (1803–64), leader of the Young Ireland Party; Sir John Gay (1816–75), proprietor of the *Freeman's Journal* (published 1763–1924) and organiser of the city's water supply; James Larkin (1876–1947), a famous trade union leader and co-founder of the Irish Labour Party; Father Theobald Mathew (1790–1856), the 'Apostle of Temperance'; and Charles Stewart Parnell (1846–91), inspiration of the Home Rule movement and a tragic victim of intolerance whose career was ruined by the tremendous public outcry over his union with Kitty O'Shea, who happened to be married to another Irish politician.

Christ Church Cathedral.

events venues, an archives room and the **Gravity Bar,** the highest bar in Dublin with an incredible panoramic view of the city. The admission ticket entitles you to a complimentary pint of the black stuff in the rooftop bar.

NORTH OF THE LIFFEY

O'Connell Bridge is once more your starting-point to explore Dublin's northern half, but before acquainting yourself with the main features of O'Connell Street, stay a little longer on the Southside, walking east along Burgh Quay and under the railway bridge for a view across the river to the **Custom House** 25, one of the masterpieces of James Gandon, the greatest architect of 18th-century Dublin. Although English, Gandon looked to the Continent for architectural models and it is easier to imagine the Custom House transposed to the banks of the Seine than to the Thames.

Finished in 1791, the building was extensively damaged in a fire started by Republicans to mark the Sinn Féin election victory in 1921 and has been largely rebuilt. The central copper dome, 120ft (38 metres) high, is topped by a statue of commerce by Edward Smyth. The keystones over the arched doorways flanking the Doric portico represent the Atlantic Ocean and 13 principal rivers of Ireland.

Gandon later designed Carlisle Bridge (widened and rebuilt in 1880 and renamed O'Connell Bridge), the Four Courts, the eastern portico of Parliament House (Bank of Ireland) and the King's Inns.

The gleaming building just downstream of the Custom House is the Irish Financial Services Centre (known as the IFSC). This is the gateway to Dublin's docklands development, a legacy of the optimistic boom years, spreading east from here on both sides of the Liffey. Those with an interest in contemporary architecture can follow a signposted walking trail.

THE ABBEY THEATRE

From the Custom House on the north bank of the Liffey, walk towards

A free pint at the end of the Guinness Storehouse tour.

O'Connell Bridge and turn into Marlborough Street, where you find the **Abbey Theatre** ㉖ home of Ireland's national theatre (www.abbeytheatre.ie). The present building was erected in 1966 to replace a predecessor, which was destroyed by fire.

The Abbey, founded in 1904 by W.B. Yeats, Lady Gregory and their collaborators, played a vital role in the cultural renaissance of the time and earned a world reputation through the great works of John Millington Synge and Sean O'Casey and for its players' naturalistic acting style. Performances were often turbulent: the most celebrated uproar was caused at a performance of Synge's *The Playboy of the Western World* by the use of the word 'shift' (petticoat). Downstairs in the Abbey its sister theatre, the **Peacock**, is used to showcase more experimental work.

O'CONNELL STREET

O'Connell Street ㉗ Broad and impressive, Dublin's main street was planned (as Sackville Street) in the mid-1700s by the first Viscount Mountjoy, Luke Gardiner, who widened the existing narrow roadway, and planted trees on a central mall.

O'Connell Street suffered from incongruous developments in the late 20th century, with plastic and neon signs and derelict sites disfiguring Dublin's main thoroughfare. The closure of the 160-year-old Clery's department store in 2015 didn't help, and the street suffered from a bad reputation as a hangout for drug users and pushers. Today, after years of extensive regeneration and renovation, including the newly working ornate gilded clock out front, the Clery's Quarter as it is now called is set to reopen its doors in summer 2023 with H&M and Flannels retail outlets, dedicated office space and Clery's Rooftop Restaurant (and bar).

Reaching for the stars is the **Spire of Dublin**, a 390ft (120-metre) stainless steel pillar, officially entitled the Monument of Light. Part of a beautification project to restore this once-elegant street to former glories, it shoots skyward from the spot where Nelson's Column (erected in 1815 to mark Nelson's victory over Napoleon) once stood, before republicans blew it up in 1966. An effigy of Anna Liva (the personification of the River Liffey) temporarily reclined in a fountain here before the spire was erected in 2003. Both installations were the subject of typical Dublin criticism and wit, with Anna Liva (who now lives closer to the river, on Wolfe Tone Quay) being branded the 'floozy in the Jacuzzi', and the spire sometimes referred to as the 'stiletto in the ghetto'.

Centrepiece of the street is the imposing Ionic portico of the **General Post Office** ㉘ (1815), epicentre of the 1916 Rising and the place where the rebels proclaimed the Irish Republic in ringing terms, to the initial horror of many Dubliners. Once the rising was put down and the executions began, with 15 captured leaders facing firing squads, public opinion altered rapidly; In Yeats'

The stainless-steel spire on O'Connell Street.

words: 'All changed, changed utterly, a terrible beauty is born'. The GPO's pillars are still pockmarked by bullets; although the building survived the fighting, much of the street was wrecked by British artillery and it suffered further in 1922 during the Civil War.

MOORE STREET MARKET

Off O'Connell Street, just past the GPO, Henry Street is the Northside's main shopping street. Its tributary to the north, **Moore Street,** is filled with fruit and vegetable stalls staffed by colourful and vociferous women. It is packed with a hive of ethnic food outlets and hair and beauty stores to cater for Dublin's burgeoning immigrant population. It's well worth visiting for a dose of down-to-earth Dublin, as well as Ireland's new multiculturalism, and there are some great no-frills Chinese restaurants hidden beneath Mandarin-scripted signs.

On the opposite side of O'Connell Street, walk down Earl Street and turn left into Marlborough Street to visit **St Mary's Pro-Cathedral** ㉙ (1816–25), the city's main Catholic Church. John Henry Newman first publicly professed Catholicism here in 1851. The area was once a notorious red-light district, known as 'Monto' (James Joyce's 'Nighttown'). A statue of Joyce stands nearby, on Earl Street North.

At the north end of O'Connell Street is the late 18th-century **Rotunda Room,** occupied by a cinema, a music venue and more recently by an exhibition centre. The **Rotunda Hospital** to the left (Europe's first maternity hospital) was financed by concerts in the Rooms. Built in conjunction with the hospital, the **Gate Theatre** (www.gate-theatre.ie) at the bottom of Parnell Square East was founded in 1928 by Micheál MacLiammóir and Hilton Edwards; the teenage Orson Welles made his first professional appearance here.

A few yards on past the Gate, the **Garden of Remembrance** (1966) commemorates Ireland's martyrs. The sculpture by Oisin Kelly, beyond the central lake, is based on the legend of

The Custom House.

the Children of Lir, who were purportedly turned into swans.

MODERN ART

On the north side of Parnell Square is the **Dublin City Gallery The Hugh Lane** 30 (www.hughlane.ie; free). Its nucleus is formed by the mainly Impressionist collection of Sir Hugh Lane, who died when the liner *Lusitania* was torpedoed in 1915. As a result of a wrangle over his will, the collection was split, each half being alternated every five years between Dublin and London's Tate Gallery. The gallery employed a team of archaeologists to painstakingly dismantle the London studio of Dublin-born artist Francis Bacon and faithfully reconstruct it here.

Parnell Street was always a bit of a rough-and-tumble type of spot with some dodgy pubs, but Dublin's growing Asian community has transformed the street into the city's Chinatown with annual Chinese New Year celebrations. If you are looking for cheap and authentic Asian cuisine, this is the place to go.

At Parnell Square East, turn left and then right into Great Denmark Street. On the left is **Belvedere College** 31, a fine 18th-century mansion, which has been a Jesuit secondary school for boys since 1841.

JAMES JOYCE CENTRE

Turn into North Great George's Street, where many grand Georgian houses have been saved from decades of decrepitude. At number 35 is the **James Joyce Centre** 32 (https://jamesjoyce.ie; tours must be pre-booked; charge), located in a beautifully restored late 18th-century townhouse, which features in *Ulysses* as the venue for dancing classes. The centre's most interesting exhibit is a set of biographies of real Dublin people fictionalised in Joyce's masterpiece. There are photographs and storyboards about Joyce's family and the many homes they inhabited. And, in a suitably Joycean collision of fact and fiction, you can view the front door of No. 7 Eccles Street, home of Leopold Bloom and his wife Molly, the central characters of *Ulysses* (the house itself was demolished). The centre's interior has splendid stucco ceilings.

Returning past The Hugh Lane Gallery to Parnell Square West, turn right, then left into Bolton bearing left into Capel Street. To the left in Mary Street is **St Mary's Church** 33, built from 1697 by Thomas Burgh, architect of Trinity College library. Here, in 1747, John Wesley preached his first sermon in Ireland. Theobald Wolfe Tone (1763–98), founder of the United Irishmen and father of Irish republicanism, was born nearby in a street now named after him.

ST MICHAN'S

To the other side of Capel Street, Mary Street leads via Mary's Lane to Church Street, where you find **St Michan's Church** 34, (Mon–Fri 12.30–3.30pm Nov to 16 March; 17 Mar to Oct Mon-Fri 10am–12.45pm/2–4.30pm and Sat year round 10am–12.45pm), founded in 1095 as a Viking parish church. The

The General Post Office (GPO), central to the 1916 Rising.

present structure dates from the late 1600s, but it was much restored in 1821 and again after the Civil War. Handel is said to have played on its organ.

In the vaults are 17th-century mummified bodies, preserved because the limestone walls absorb moisture from the air.

Leaving the church, turn down May Lane and left into Bow Street which will bring you to the **Old Jameson Distillery** (www.jamesonwhiskey.com; charge for guided tours), a museum is sited in the old warehouse of the 1791 whiskey factory.

THE FOUR COURTS

Return to the quays and turn left to end this section of the tour as you began it: with a look at a Gandon masterpiece. The **Four Courts** ㉟ (visitors can witness most court proceedings, Mon–Fri 10am–1pm, 2–4pm; free) was built between 1786 and 1802. The dominant lantern-dome is fronted by a six-columned Corinthian portico surmounted by the statues of Moses, Justice and Mercy, and flanked by two wings enclosing courtyards.

In 1922, after the building was barricaded by anti-Treaty republicans, Michael Collins' new government troops shelled it from across the river. In the ensuing fire, the Record Office was burnt, destroying priceless documents. Restoration was completed in 1932.

WEST DUBLIN

Board the westbound Red Line of LUAS at the rear of the Four Courts. After three quick stops, you'll be at Heuston Station.

From here it is only a five-minute walk west along St John's Road before turning north onto Military Road and the entrance to **Kilmainham Royal Hospital** (www.rhk.ie) founded by Charles II in 1680 'for the reception and entertainment of antient (sic) maimed, and infirm officers and soldiers'. It's a beautiful French-style building with exquisite grounds and now houses the **Irish Museum of Modern Art** ㊱ (www.imma.

The Four Courts.

ie; free, charge for special exhibitions), which combines Irish and international 20th-century art with various educational and community programmes. There's a nice café and beautiful formal gardens, lovely in summer.

KILMAINHAM GAOL

Exit the museum the way you came in, take a right turn onto Military Road and a right again onto Bow Bridge brings you to the South Circular Road and **Kilmainham Gaol** 37 (www.kilmainhamgaolmuseum.ie; charge), which has been intimately connected with Ireland's struggle for independence from its construction in the 1790s until it ceased to be a prison in the 1920s. Visitors are invited to browse in the museum, which explores 19th-century notions of crime, punishment and reform through a series of well-captioned displays. The upstairs section is devoted to the nationalist figures, some famous, some more obscure, who were imprisoned here, many awaiting execution.

After a bloody past, Dublin's Kilmainham Gaol became a popular film location. Interior scenes for the prison in which Noël Coward planned his heist in *The Italian Job* (1969) were shot here. So were scenes from *In the Name of the Father* (1993), *Michael Collins* (1996), *The Wind that Shakes the Barley* (2006) and execution scenes for the TV series *The Tudors* (2007). Scenes from *Paddington 2* (2017) and *The Young Indiana Jones Chronicles* TV series were also filmed here.

Upstairs visitors can see the '1916 corridor', containing the cells that housed the captured leaders of the Rising, and the stone-breakers' yard where 14 of them were shot between 3 and 12 May of that year. It is well worth a visit.

If you prefer a walk in the park to time in jail, turn left on Bow Lane from Military Road and left again on **Steeven's Lane**. Head past Heuston Station and cross the river to visit **Phoenix Park** 38 the southern boundary of which extends west on the Liffey's north bank

Kilmainham Gaol.

for about 3 miles (5km). At 1,760 acres (712 hectares), it is over five times as large as London's Hyde Park. Its name is a corruption of the Gaelic *fionn uisce* (clear water). You can rent bikes by the hour at the gatehouse of the Parkgate entrance, the best way to explore the huge open spaces of Dublins's Phoenix Park (www.phoenixparkbikes.com).

Among its features, all signposted, are: the Wellington Monument, an obelisk 197ft (60 metres) high, erected after Waterloo; **Dublin Zoo** (www.dublinzoo.ie), the third oldest public zoo in the world (1830), well known for the breeding of lions (it supplied the MGM announcer); the President's residence, **Aras an Uachtaráin**, formerly the Viceregal Lodge (1751–54); the US Ambassador's residence; and Farmleigh House and Estate (http://www.farmleigh.ie), once the home of the Guinness family and now in state ownership hosting cultural events and foreign dignitaries.

On the way back to the city, on the north side of the quays, is the former Collins Barracks, now the **National Museum of Decorative Arts and History** ❸❾ with displays of Irish silver, glass, furniture, Japanese art and a permanent exhibition on the Irish furniture designer and architect Eileen Gray (www.museum.ie; free).

Showing the Irish at war at the National Museum of Decorative Arts and History.

SOUTHSIDE SUBURBS

Most places mentioned in this section of the book are served by various buses departing from Eden Quay, beside O'Connell Bridge, and by the DART suburban trains.

Travelling out through Merrion Square North, along Northumberland Road past the squat, circular block of the **American Embassy** (1964), you reach the prestigious suburb of **Ballsbridge** ❹⓿ named after the bridge over the River Dodder. The large greystone buildings to the right on Merrion Road, just past the bridge, are the headquarters of the Royal Dublin Society (the RDS, www.rds.ie), the sponsor of improvements in agriculture and stockbreeding and the venue for the Dublin Horse Show (in August). The RDS's Simmonscourt Extension is used for exhibitions and concerts.

The main road south soon skirts the coast, affording fine views of the bay, and passes through **Blackrock** ❹❶, where Eamon de Valera studied and later taught at the prestigious boys' secondary school, Blackrock College.

DÚN LAOGHAIRE

A couple of miles further on is the town and port of **Dún Laoghaire** ❹❷ (pronounced 'dunleery'). The harbour, with its long, granite pier, was built between 1817 and 1859 and is exceptionally popular with walkers throughout the year. The pier is particularly beautiful on a summer's day when the sea twinkles and the views of craggy Howth are especially clear.

The next promontory, within easy walking distance, is that of **Sandycove**, with its Martello Tower where Joyce lived for a short time in 1904. He used it as the setting for the opening scene of *Ulysses* and it is now the **James Joyce Museum** ⓭ (www.joycetower.ie; free). **The Forty Foot** bathing place beside it was traditionally a place for gentlemen to swim in the nude, but these days both male and female swimmers of all ages come to plunge into the very cold waters throughout the year – usually with togs on.

DALKEY

Just a 20-minute walk from Sandycove is the affluent and charming village of **Dalkey** 44. Dalkey is something of a celebrity hotspot, with lively pub and café scene. Bono, The Edge, Enya, Van Morrison, Neil Jordan are among its residents, as was the late Maeve Binchy. **Dalkey Castle** (www.dalkeycastle.com), a medieval tower house, has been restored and houses a heritage centre. Its battlements give excellent views of the surrounding land and seascape.

From nearby **Coliemore Harbour** there are summer boat trips (http://kentheferryman.com; daily; 10am–6pm) to **Dalkey Island**, a stone's throw offshore; it contains another Martello tower and the ruins of a Benedictine church. The island is a bird sanctuary and the waters are rich with seals.

You can enter **Killiney Hill Park** from Vico Road, which continues along the coast. At the summit of the park there are splendid views of the broad sweep of Killiney Bay (often likened to the Bay of Naples), Bray Head (the humpbacked promontory at its far side) and the two Sugar Loaf Mountains. DART travellers can continue on to **Bray** 45 as a seaside resort it has seen better days, but the seascapes en route are impressive and Bray Head offers bracing walks and fine views to the south.

NORTHERN SUBURBS

The attractions of the Northside are more diffuse. But it's worth visiting **Glasnevin** 46 (buses 13 and 19 from O'Connell Street) to see the beautifully arranged **Botanic Gardens** (www.botanicgardens.ie; free). Only 3 miles (5km) north of O'Connell Street, the gardens

make a tranquil contrast to urban sightseeing. The magnificent Victorian curvilinear glasshouses have been fully restored.

Glasnevin Museum and Cemetery Tour (www.glasnevinmuseum.ie; charge), the Republic's national burying ground contains the remains of Daniel O'Connell, Eamon de Valera, Michael Collins, Brendan Behan and many others. The striking museum (with shop and café) traces the history of Ireland through the lives of the 1.5 million people buried at Glasnevin. Tours are family friendly. Visitors can now climb the 55-metre O'Connell Tower and enjoy 360-degree views of Dublin, Wicklow and the coast.

CASINO MARINO

The coastal route northeast by the Custom House leads to the Casino at Marino (www.heritageireland.ie; charge) a small Palladian folly, that is a gem of its kind, with several unusual features: the roof urns are actually chimneys and the columns are hollow, serving as

Glasnevin Museum entrance.

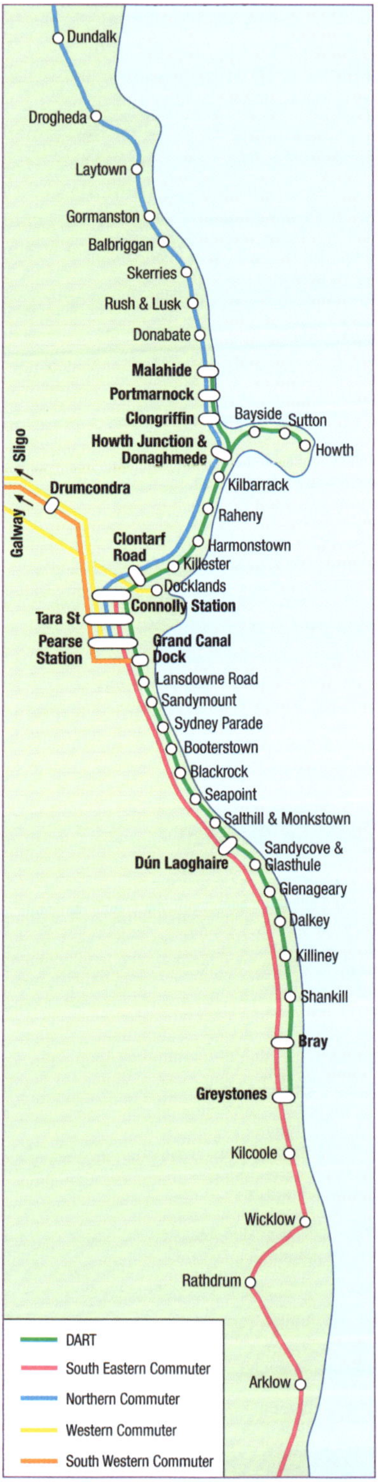

drains. It was originally part of the seaside estate of Lord Charlemont, whose town house is now the **Dublin City Gallery The Hugh Lane**.

Beyond Clontarf the coast road passes the **North Bull Island**, a huge sandbank growing from the North Wall of Dublin Port and containing two golf courses: St Anne's (www.stanneslinksgolf.com) and the famous Royal Dublin (www.theroyaldublingolfclub.com). It is also an important sanctuary for winter migrant birds.

HOWTH

Carrying on via the isthmus at the suburb of Sutton you reach **Howth Head** (also accessible by DART and bus), whose rugged brow overlooks the northern entrance to Dublin Bay. You can go directly to the village of **Howth** ㊼ or start instead at the Summit and walk to the village around the nose of the promontory by a splendidly scenic cliff path, which descends steeply to the fishing harbour. The novelist H.G. Wells called the view from the head 'one of the most beautiful in the world.' The offshore island of **Ireland's Eye** was the site of a 6th-century monastery and is now a bird sanctuary. Howth, along with Malahide, is the most fashionable place to live on the Northside, and it is easy to see why. The gardens at nearby **Howth Castle** (http://howthcastle.com; by appointment only) are beautiful, especially if you like rhododendrons.

Five miles (8km) north of Howth lies **Portmarnock** ㊽, which has fine beaches and a championship golf course (www.portmarnockgolfclub.ie). At **Malahide** ㊾ a pleasant resort and suburban town 7 miles (11km) north of Howth, is **Malahide Castle** (www.malahidecastleandgardens.ie; charge), inhabited by the Talbot family from 1185 for nearly 800 years, the castle, now publicly owned, is fully furnished with displays on the family's history. The 22 acres (9 hectares) of ornamental gardens contain over 5000 species, fully labelled. There is also a playground, pitch and putt and an Avoca café and shop.

Malahide Castle.

BLOOMSDAY

James Joyce's *Ulysses* takes place on a single day in 1904. Each year on that day, 16 June, the novel's events are re-enacted.

Countless literary critics have decreed *Ulysses* the greatest novel of the twentieth century, although, even in Dublin, it's probably more admired than read. With oblique thematic parallels to Homer's *Odyssey*, it documents a 24-hour period in the lives of an Irish Jew, Leopold Bloom, and a budding writer, Stephen Dedalus (the protagonist of Joyce's first novel A Portrait of the Artist as a Young Man), as they move around Dublin. The story reaches its climax when they meet.

The full novel was first published in 1922, in Paris. It was banned (for obscenity) in Britain and America – but never, curiously, in Ireland, although it was difficult to obtain here. The first Bloomsday celebrations took place in Dublin on 16 June 1954, the semicentennial of the events depicted in the novel. Initially they were designed to appeal mainly to academics, but after Joyce's centenary in 1982, Bloomsday became increasingly popular. People who boast that they have never opened a copy of Ulysses, happily dress up as Joycean characters and breakfast on kidneys to mark the occasion. Check www.bloomsdayfestival.ie for up-to-date information on Bloomsday celebrations.

Street performers strike a pose during Bloomsday celebrations in Dublin.

GORGONZOLA SANDWICH

Participants, wearing what approximates to 1904 garb, trace the paths of the book's characters. After a Bloomsday breakfast in Sandycove, they can listen to readings delivered by costumed actors, lunch on gorgonzola sandwiches and burgundy in Davy Byrne's pub, walk through the Northside, taking in Hardwicke Street, Eccles Street, Gardiner Street and Mountjoy Square, enjoy more readings at the Joyce Centre, and then discuss the book's finer points over a few pints of Guinness.

An actor recites his lines. The 265,222 words of Ulysses, packed with puns, parodies and allusions, formed some of the twentieth century's most experimental prose and is quite the feat to complete reading.

Celebrating Bloomsday with a pint of the black stuff and a well-loved copy of Ulysses.

Joyce was critical of the debilitating effects the priesthood had on Irish life. At one point he has the hero of Ulysses – Leopold Bloom, a Jew – praise psychological devices such as Confession.

Sculpture of Joyce beside his grave at Fluntern Cemetery in Zurich.

James Joyce (1882–1941)

One of ten children, James Augustine Aloysius Joyce was born in Rathgar, Dublin. He graduated from University College Dublin (UCD) in 1902 with a degree in modern languages.

In 1904, while living briefly in the Martello Tower at Sandycove, he met Nora Barnacle, a self-described 'country girl' from Galway, who worked as a hotel chambermaid. They moved abroad in October of that year, living first in Pola, then Trieste. While in Trieste, they had a son, Giorgio, and a daughter, Lucia (who was later diagnosed as schizophrenic), but did not marry until 1931. When war broke out in 1914, the family relocated to Zurich, where Joyce wrote much of Ulysses.

The Années Folles, brought them to Paris, and Joyce mixed with writers such as Ezra Pound, Scott Fitzgerald, T.S. Eliot and Ernest Hemingway. As a young man, the playwright Samuel Beckett acted as his secretary. When France fell in 1940, the Joyce's returned to Zurich. Joyce died a year later and was buried in Fluntern Cemetery. Nora lived out the remainder of her life in Zurich. She was buried alongside him in 1951.

Joyce said of Ulysses: 'I've put in so many enigmas and puzzles that it will keep the professors busy for centuries arguing over what I meant, and that's the only way of ensuring immortality.'

Joyce boasted that if Dublin disappeared it could be reconstructed out of the pages of Ulysses.

Powerscourt Gardens.

EXCURSIONS FROM DUBLIN

To the south lie the Wicklow Mountains, to the north the remarkable historical burial chambers of Newgrange and to the west some of the world's finest racehorse country.

Main attractions
- Blessington
- Glendalough
- Avondale
- Powerscourt House
- Hill of Tara
- Slane
- Newgrange
- Cooley Peninsula
- Celbridge
- Kildare

Map on page 144

Wicklow (www.visitwicklow.ie) is known as the 'garden of Ireland' and, while there are scenic spots galore (including some glorious gardens), the county also possesses a savage beauty that almost equals that of the west of the island. The Wicklow Mountains (www.wicklowmountainsnationalpark.ie), are a rugged mass of granite running from Dublin, through Wicklow and down into Wexford. Blanket bogs clothe the upper slopes, while peaty streams cascade swiftly downhill into deep lakes. The mountains run an impassable wedge through parts of the county, making it difficult to cover the whole area in one day – unless you drive at a non-stop clip, which would be silly in a place made to be savoured.

WEST WICKLOW

West Wicklow can be reached via the M50 and the N81. At **Blessington**, 19 miles (30km) from Dublin, the valley of the River Liffey was flooded in 1940, submerging 74 farmhouses and cottages to create a reservoir; a scenic drive skirts the perimeter. Less than 2 miles (3.2km) south is the grand, 18th-century, Palladian house, **Russborough** ❶. The house has an important collection of furnishings and paintings, including works by Goya, Gainsborough and Rubens. For family fun, there is a huge maze, a fairy trail and a playground (www.russborough.ie; charge).

Follow the N81 to **Hollywood** ❷, no relation to its Californian namesake, but coincidentally, a location for the films *Dancing at Lughnasa* (1998) and *Michael Collins* (1996). From here, a 15-mile (25km) drive on the R756 brings you across the bleakly beautiful Wicklow Gap to **Laragh** where, in summer, teas are served in the grassy village triangle.

A mile before Laragh is the turn to one of the most visited sites in the east of Ireland, **Glendalough**. Here, in the steep-sided valley between two lakes,

Powerscourt Waterfall.

St Kevin founded a monastic settlement in the 6th century. The ruins – a 110ft (33-metre) round tower and sacred structures – date from the 11th and 12th centuries (www.glendalough.ie; guided tours; ruins free, visitor centre charge).

Several roads meet in Laragh: take the R755 to the northeast, and after 6 miles (9km) you arrive in **Roundwood** ❸, purportedly the highest village in Ireland, 781ft (238 metres) above sea level. If you take the R155 6 miles (9km) to the northwest, you come to the gorgeous **Glenmacnass Waterfall**.

AVONDALE

Continuing south from Laragh, the R755 leads through the gently wooded Vale of Clara to **Rathdrum**, 7 miles (11km) away. **Avondale House and Forest Park** ❹ (tel: 0404-46111; www.coillte.ie/site/avondale-forest-park), the Georgian home of the great Irish politician, Charles Stewart Parnell (1846–91), is now a museum devoted to his memory and is surrounded by hundreds of acres of forest park with the wonderful **Beyond the Trees** experience (Thur-Mon 10am–4pm; charge; not open in bad weather), a walkway high in the canopy of the trees not for those afraid of heights that leads to a towering viewpoint 38m high with panoramic views. For the brave, a rapid slide down to ground level will get the blood pumping and save you retracing your steps back down along the gently spiralling walkway. There is also an airy restaurant overlooking a pretty courtyard garden and a great children's playground, as well as an exhibition space about the life and times of Parnell.

The picturesque village of **Avoca** ❺ with its multicoloured houses and working weaving mill is further south. Also at this end of the county is **Brittas Bay** (off the N11 at 'Jack White's Inn'), with its dunes and long stretch of sandy beach inviting visits all year-round.

Off the N11 at **Ashford**, are the world-renowned **Mount Usher Gardens** ❻, (www.mountushergardens.ie; Avoca Café open all year, gardens Mar–Oct; charge) Walk along the **Devil's Glen**, a mile or two northwest on the R764 and R765, through woodland to the Devil's Glen waterfall. Birdwatchers should head for the coast (off the R761) between Newcastle and Kilcoole, where migrant species often stop to feed.

POWERSCOURT

The village of **Enniskerry**, signposted off the N11 near Bray, has a lovely cut-stone clock tower at its centre. **Powerscourt House and Gardens** ❼ (www.powerscourt.ie) are about a mile to the south. The 18th-century stately home, gutted by fire in 1974, and restored in the mid-1990s, now houses upmarket shops, a garden centre and an Avoca restaurant. The grounds on one side are dominated by a golf course, but on the other, the heroic Italianate landscape designed by Daniel Robertson in the mid-19th century survives. Robertson, a martyr to gout and the sherry bottle, was said to have conducted operations from a wheelbarrow.

Powerscourt Waterfall, which has a separate entrance gate, is the highest waterfall in Ireland (398ft/121 metres).

EXCURSIONS NORTH

The countryside north of County Dublin is impressively larded with antiquities, and offers up well-preserved pre-Christian monuments, monastic sites and heritage towns. Some of the attractions, such as the megalithic passage graves in the Boyne Valley, can easily consume the best part of the day.

County Meath, which wraps around the northwest shoulder of Dublin, was the terrain of the pagan High Kings of Ireland and is known as the Royal County (www.meathtourism.ie). The ancient seat of the rulers was the **Hill of Tara** ❽, 28 miles (44km) from Dublin, off the M3, 7 miles (11km) beyond the village of Dunshaughlin. The limestone ridge commands fittingly regal views over the central plain of Ireland, smokily framed by distant mountain

Powerscourt House.

ranges. Ring forts, ruins and a standing stone mark the place that was the island's spiritual and cultural capital for millennia (http://hilloftara.org; access all year; guided tours, May–Sept).

The town of **Trim** ❾, 13 miles (21km) to the west, has Ireland's largest Anglo-Norman castle, **Trim Castle**, started by Hugh de Lacy in 1173 and used in the filming of Mel Gibson's *Braveheart* in 1994. The restored keep may be visited by guided tour, contact Trim Visitor Centre (046 943 7227) for details. Trim is well furnished with other historic structures, which are strung along the heritage trail that winds through the town and along the River Boyne. In fine weather, the riverbanks are the perfect place to picnic.

NAVAN

The Boyne drive takes you to the market town of **Navan** ❿, 9 miles (15km) away, with its fine Solstice Arts Centre (www.solsticeartscentre.com). Famous natives of the palindromic town include actor Pierce Brosnan, comedians Tommy Tiernan and Dylan Moran, and Francis Beaufort, who created the Beaufort wind force scale in 1805.

From Navan, a 7-mile (12km) drive on the N51 takes you to **Slane** ⓫, a beautiful 18th-century estate village above the River Boyne, and bedevilled by traffic travelling between Ireland's northwest and Dublin (it is 30 miles/50km from the capital on the N2).

The central crossroads contains a quartet of identical, three-storey, limestone Georgian houses, gazing implacably at each other across the square. The Gothic revival **Slane Castle** (www.slanecastle.ie) is the home of Lord Henry Conyngham, Earl of Mount Charles, and is a venue for monster rock concerts. Access to the castle is by tour only, with groups of 10 required to book in advance.

Less than a mile north of the village is the windswept **Hill of Slane** where in 433, St Patrick lit a Paschal fire to celebrate the arrival of Christianity in Ireland, much to the annoyance of the pagan high king, Laoghaire – who had decreed that no flames should be

Standing stone at the Hill of Tara.

visible from Tara during the festival of Feis Temro. The hill, which is open all year, contains the ruins of a 16th-century Franciscan friary, and has good views of the surrounding countryside.

NEWGRANGE

One of Europe's most important prehistoric clusters is just a few miles southeast of Slane: the neolithic burial mounds (a Unesco World Heritage site) at Newgrange, Knowth and Dowth.

Access to Newgrange and Knowth is solely by tour from the **Brú na Bóinne Visitor Centre** ⓬ near Donore (www.heritageireland.ie).

Dowth may be visited separately (signposted off the N51) and viewed from the outside. Its shaggy, unrestored mound makes a contrast to the renovated structures of Newgrange and Knowth. Newgrange (www.newgrange.com) is the only one of the monuments where access is allowed to the interior passage and chamber – the latter is aligned so that the rising sun sends in a shaft of light at the winter solstice (entry to the chamber for that occasion is by lottery). Built around 3200 BC, Newgrange is several hundred years older than the Pyramids, and 1,000 years more ancient than Stonehenge. The sites are busy in summer, and entry cannot be guaranteed. Go early in the day, and allow at least three hours.

About 5 miles (8km) north, in Louth, Ireland's smallest county (www.visitlouth.ie), stand the ruins of **Mellifont Abbey** ⓭ on the banks of the Mattock River. The first Cistercian abbey on the island, its earliest parts date from the 12th century. In 1690, the buildings were the headquarters of King William of Orange, who defeated James II at the Battle of the Boyne.

Not far from Mellifont is a modern monument that can be seen for miles, the **Boyne Suspension Bridge** at Drogheda. Completed in 2003, it has a main span of 555ft (170 metres) and a 310ft (95-metre) -high concrete pylon, from which 28 shimmering cables fan out like the work of a giant spider.

The busy town of **Drogheda** ⓮ is surrounded by rather utilitarian factories and retail outlets, but its core dates from Norman times, when it marked the northern boundary of the Pale. In 1649 the town was besieged and stormed by Oliver Cromwell and thousands of its citizens were killed, or transported to the Caribbean for slavery.

The **Millmount Museum** (www.millmount.net) is a fortified complex on a giant mound that includes a 19th-century Martello tower. The exhibits explore the town's industrial past. At **St Peter's Church** (www.saintoliverplunkett.com), in the town centre, a shrine protects the embalmed head of St Oliver Plunkett (1629–81), the Archbishop of Armagh. He was the last Catholic martyr to die in England – hanged, drawn and quartered. The 13th-century **St Laurence's Gate** is an exquisite remnant of the city's medieval walls.

A mile and a half (2km) west of Drogheda (off the Baltray Road) is

An interior passage at Newgrange.

Beaulieu House (www.beaulieuhouse.ie; guided tour), constructed in the 1660s in the Dutch style. The walled garden dates from the early 18th century. Half a dozen racing and rally cars from the 1960s and 1970s are on display in the car museum.

Six miles (10km) east of Drogheda, via the R150, is the seaside resort of **Bettystown**, where the intricate Tara Brooch (now housed in the National Museum of Ireland), was found in 1850. A couple of miles further south is **Laytown**, where an annual horse racing event takes place on the strand in early September (www.laytownstrandraces.ie).

Drogheda is just 30 miles (50km) from Dublin on the M1 motorway that moves quickly up to Belfast. **Dundalk** ⓯, 23 miles (37km) beyond Drogheda, is the last town before the border.

To the east is the scenic **Cooley Peninsula** (www.carlingford.ie), the mythical stomping ground of the brown bull of Cooley (Donn Cúailnge), who was the object of legendary Queen Medb's cattle raid in The Táin, a classic Celtic tale that introduces the hero Cú Chulainn. Dundalk Bay (on the south side of the peninsula) and Carlingford Lough (on the north) are both Special Protection Areas for wildlife, and are popular with birdwatchers.

The village of **Carlingford** ⓰ is an absolutely charming place where several stone-built medieval buildings nestle between the whitewashed houses on the narrow streets.

EXCURSIONS WEST

Kildare (www.visitkildare.ie), known for its stud farms and lush green pastures, has gradually taken on the additional role of a dormitory county for Dublin and it has many commuter apartment and housing developments. Yet the county still holds many attractions, including some of the best horses in the world, grand houses and demesnes, and a peaceful network of canals and towpaths that are popular with walkers.

Castletown House ⓱ (www.castletownhouse.ie) in **Celbridge** is 14 miles (22km) from Dublin, via the M4, taking the R449 Celbridge exit. Ireland's largest Palladian

The Barbican in Drogheda, also known as St Lawrence's Gate, was built in the 13th century as a gateway through the town walls.

THE M50

Dublin's ring road carries a massive volume of traffic, and often not very effectively. It was designed to cater for a maximum 45,000 vehicles per day, but now sees closer to 100,000. Note: this is the only toll road in Ireland where there are no booths and you have to pay online or ring a dedicated phone line before 8pm the following day or face a fine. Unfortunately, you cannot pay in advance of a journey either. Rental cars are usually covered in your car hire agreement but note that you will even receive fines through the post if you're driving in Ireland on UK or foreign plates to the address the car is registered to. See www.eflow.ie for more information. Morning rush hour is 7.30–10am; the afternoon rush starts at 4 or 4.30pm, with the road remaining busy until 6.30pm or later.

country house, it was constructed for the speaker of the Irish House of Commons, William Conolly in 1722.

Four miles (7km) to the southwest is **Straffan** with its Steam Museum (www.steam-museum.com) and pretty 18th-century walled garden at Lodge Park.

Head back north for 5 miles (8km) on the R403 and R406, and you come to the 18th-century university town of **Maynooth**, along the Royal Canal.

A few miles northwest (on the R148, R158 and R125) is **Larchill Arcadian Garden** ⑱, beyond **Kilcock** (www.larchhill.ie; charge). The restored ornamental landscape is a fine example of an 18th-century *ferme ornée*, with rare breeds and a large lake.

Head back to Kilcock and take the R407 to the rapidly expanding village of **Clane**. From there the R403 passes through **Prosperous**, one of the first towns where the United Irishmen rose in the 1798 rebellion. The road continues to **Allenwood**, from where the R414 travels through the Bog of Allen to the **Irish Peatland Conservation Council's Nature Centre** (www.ipcc.ie; charge) at Lullymore, about 3 miles (5km) before **Rathangan**. Here you may learn about bogs and peat, take guided walks and examine dozens of species of carnivorous plants from around the world.

KILDARE

From Rathangan it is 7 miles (11km) southeast to the town of **Kildare** ⑲ on the edge of the Curragh, the central plain of Ireland, which lies like a flat green blanket on the landscape. A mile outside the town, at Tully, is the famous **Irish National Stud** (www.irishnationalstud.ie; charge) with its charming Japanese Gardens and St Fiachra's Garden (see page 162). Tours of the stables and stud can be booked on admission.

Just over 7 miles (12km) to the east on the M7 and the R445 is **Newbridge**, home of Newbridge Silverware (www.newbridgesilverware.com), which you will come across in gift stores everywhere. From here, it is a 30-mile (50km) drive to Dublin via the R445, the N7, and the M50 (see page 148).

Castletown House.

HORSE CULTURE

Whether they're breeding them, racing them, exporting them or betting on them, the Irish have an extraordinary affinity with horses.

In 1809 *The History and Delineation of the Horse* recorded that 'the Irish are the highest and the steadiest leapers in the world.' They still are.

The pre-eminence of Irish-bred steeplechasers and hurdlers on the racecourses of Britain has been remarkable, and, given the legions of horses exported annually to trainers in England, it's even more remarkable that the greatest steeplechasers of the modern era were trained in Ireland. Perhaps the greatest of all was Arkle, who won the Cheltenham Gold Cup three years in succession in the 1960s. Had Arkle entered a referendum for the Irish presidency, the world might well have had its first equine statesman since Caligula.

The Irish prefer the reckless and often threadbare thrills of steeplechasing to its rich relation, racing 'on the flat'. Whereas top-class flat-racing throughout the world is dominated by the commercial requirements of the multi-million dollar bloodstock industry, this aspect is absent from racing 'over the sticks' because nearly all jumpers are geldings.

Ireland's prosperous bloodstock industry owes much to a 1969 government ruling that fees for the services of thoroughbred stallions would be exempt from tax.

Europe's only official race to be held on a beach takes place in July/August (depending on tides) at Laytown, an east-coast resort.

Many Irish people have a natural ability to understand and handle horses, which can still be seen in many small towns.

Bookmakers in Ireland have been slow to embrace online betting. Cynics claimed that's because the profit margins aren't so good.

Equine symbolism is frequently found in Ireland, as in this beast guarding the gates to the Powerscourt estate in County Wicklow.

Policemen on horseback.

Horses Through History

Until the 1990s the Garda Síochána was one of the major police forces that didn't have mounted police, but today a handful of Irish Draught Horses (a native breed, known for its versatility and good temperament) patrol the streets of Dublin.

Although horses have played a vital role in Ireland's economy over the centuries, it was the racing scene that inspired excitement. The Red Branch Knights of pre-Christian Ireland raced each other on horses, and horse racing was an essential part of public fairs in the early centuries AD.

In County Cork in the year 1752, a Mr Edmund Blake and a Mr O'Callaghan raced each other on horseback across the countryside from Buttevant Church to the spire of St Leger Church 4.5 miles (7km) away, jumping hedges, walls and ditches on the way. As a result, a new word, 'steeplechasing', entered the English language, and a new sport was created.

Steeplechasing was soon all the rage. Races were run, like the original, across open country from one point to another with the precise course left largely to the discretion of the riders. The tradition continues in its purest form during point-to-point races, informal meetings in which horses race around a track that has no railings.

The Curragh is the fashionable setting for all the Irish classic races: the 2,000 and 1,000 Guineas, the Derby, the Oaks and the St Leger. Prize money at the Derby now exceeds €1.5 million.

Galtee Mountains.

THE SOUTHEAST

In the sunny southeast you can find opera and national parks, pretty beaches, horse racing, medieval towns and ancient historical sites.

Main attractions
Irish National Heritage Park
Dungarvan
Lismore Castle
Ardmore
Ballymaloe
Kildare
Kilkenny
Jerpoint Abbey
Rock of Cashel

Map on page 154

The 'sunny Southeast', as it is popularly known, has one obvious advantage over the rest of Ireland: good weather. While tourists from overseas often head straight to Ireland's wild west, the Irish themselves habitually holiday in the southeast, which enjoys almost double the annual sunshine quota for other regions, and many Dubliners have holiday homes here. It can be busy in school holidays, but the beaches and backroads are ripe for exploration.

Geographically the region is quite distinct from the rest of the country, with undulating flat plains intersected by meandering river valleys producing some of the most fertile agricultural land in Tipperary, Kilkenny and Carlow. Unlike the rugged South and West, the Southeast has a relatively gentle coastal aspect of long sandy beaches, rocky bays and low cliffs along the Wicklow, Wexford and Waterford shorelines.

This chapter suggests two different routes for exploring – one coastal and one inland.

OPTION 1: DUBLIN TO CORK VIA THE COAST

The first tour travels from Dublin to Cork, through Wexford, Waterford, Dungarvan and Youghal. This route takes 4.5 hours – two hours longer than the main M7/M8 route, but it is far more scenic, with frequent sea views. Take a full day for the drive, or plan one or two overnight stops.

Leave Dublin on the N11 Bray road, and follow this to **Arklow** ❶. This is a small but lively fishing port and seaside resort on the estuary of the River Avoca known for boat building, and now a thriving commuter town with a population of 13,000. Sir Francis Chichester's yacht *Gypsy Moth III*, in which he won the transatlantic single-handed yacht race, was built at Tyrell's boatyard, as was the Irish Navy's late and much-lamented

Courtown Harbour, Co Wexford.

sail training vessel, the brigantine *Asgard II*, which sank in the Bay of Biscay in 2008. The **Arklow Maritime and Heritage Museum** (Bridgewater Centre, North Quay; www.arklowmaritimeheritage.ie; charge) contains a comprehensive display of artefacts and memorabilia tracing the maritime history of Arklow through the centuries. Its eclectic collection includes World War II mines and salvaged items from the wreck of the *Lusitania*, sunk by a German submarine in 1915.

Leave the M11 at interchange 23 for to R 472 to **Courtown** a pleasant alternative route to Wexford passing the first of several long sandy beaches.

The R742 leads to **Curracloe Strand**, 7 miles (11km) northeast of Wexford Harbour. The totally unspoilt strand is backed by dunes, and stretches for 6 miles (10km). It 'stood in' for the Normandy beaches when Steven Spielberg filmed *Saving Private Ryan* (1998). In winter it is home to numerous Canada geese. Information on the region's birds can be found at the **Wexford Wildfowl Reserve** (www.wexfordwildfowlreserve.ie; free), which is signposted off the R741 just outside Wexford at the quaintly

named North Slob, an area of mud flats at the mouth of the River Slaney. The harbour is partly silted up, and its mud flats attract a variety of ducks, geese and swans.

WEXFORD

Wexford ❷ (www.visitwexford.ie) is a small, easy-to-explore town consisting of a series of quays parallel to the water, with a compact network of smaller streets parallel to the quays. Crescent Quay is decorated with a large statue on a plinth of locally born Commodore John Barry (1745–1803). Walking tours leave from the nearby **Tourist Information Office** (The Quay Front; tel: 086 107 9497; daily 11am) visiting the remaining sections of the Norman town walls and the 13th-century Franciscan Friary.

Wexford, which has an interesting selection of small, old-fashioned shops and pubs, really shines in October during the two-week run of the **Wexford Festival Opera** (www.wexfordopera.com). Three full-length operas are performed at the fabulous **Wexford Opera House** with an international cast of up-and-coming stars. The tradition is to choose little-known works, with consistently interesting results. A series of fringe events guarantees musical entertainment from 11am to midnight.

The **Irish National Heritage Park** (www.inhp.com) at Ferrycarrig, 3 miles (5km) northwest of Wexford on the N11 Enniscorthy road, is an open-air museum on the banks of the River Slaney. A couple of hours among its life-size replicas of typical dwelling places will make you an expert on Irish history and architecture, from Stone Age man in 6000 BC, up to the 12th-century Norman settlements.

The 35-acre (14-hectare) museum includes a prehistoric homestead, a *crannóg* (lake dwelling), an early Christian fortified farm, a Christian monastery and a Norman castle. All the exhibits have guides dressed in the styles of the various periods.

Follow the N25 for 3 miles (5km) in the Rosslare direction to visit **Johnstown Castle Gardens** (www.johnstowncastle.ie). The grandiose grey stone

Wexford harbour.

Gothic building dating from the mid-19th century has grandiose rooms and subterranean passages to explore (check website for hours) The attractive landscaped gardens are open daily all year. Built for the Morgan family around 1810, the estate contains splendid plantings of Japanese cedars and Lawson cypresses, lakes, ornamental gardens, nature trails and a walled garden.

The **Irish Agricultural Museum** is in the courtyard. It has extensive displays of artefacts from Ireland's rural past, and a collection of Irish country furniture.

THE SCENIC ROUTE TO WATERFORD

The N25 travels to Waterford via New Ross, but we suggest this scenic alternative: Take the R730 and the N25 towards Rosslare, then turn right on the R730, going through Ballycogley to **Kilmore Quay** ❸. This quaint little fishing village of thatched, whitewashed cottages and friendly pubs is built between the dunes and a stone harbour wall, and looks out to the uninhabited **Saltee Islands**, one of Ireland's most important bird sanctuaries. In late spring to early summer, three million birds from 47 species stop here, and can be observed from local boats.

In mid-summer, the sea bird colonies on Gannet headland make for a memorable, and noisy, sight, with vast numbers of guillemots, fulmars and razorbills packing the cliff faces. Towards dusk, the sight of the puffins congregating in small groups near their nestling sites adds to the spectacle.

Heading west, the R736/R733 will take you to the **Hook Head Peninsula,** which forms the eastern side of Waterford harbour. At its extremity is the **Hook Lighthouse Visitor Centre** (www.hookheritage.ie; tours June–Aug). The original lighthouse tower was built by the Normans, 800 years ago, and can be visited on a guided tour. It is said to be the oldest operational lighthouse in the world and there are spectacular views from the balcony. On the east side of Waterford Harbour is **Ballyhack**, a picture-book pretty waterside village dominated by **Ballyhack Castle** (tel: 051-389 468 for viewings; free), a

The Irish National Heritage Park.

16th-century tower house. The castle is thought to have been built around 1450 by the Knights Hospitallers of St John, one of the two military orders founded in the 12th century at the time of the Crusades. A short car ferry hop (www.passageferry.ie) across the estuary from Ballyhack to Passage East provides a short-cut to Waterford City.

Alternatively, continue north on the R733 for 3 miles (5km) to **Dunbrody Abbey** (www.dunbrodyabbey.com), an impressive ruined Cistercian abbey dating from 1175.

The farmhouse near Dunganstown from which US President John F. Kennedy's grandfather emigrated to Boston is now the **Kennedy Homestead** (www.kennedyhomestead.ie). Displays for visitors (audio visual and photographic) are in the original farmyard, and include coverage of President John F. Kennedy's visit in 1963. The smallholding is still farmed by Kennedy descendants, and it is a touching experience to witness the humble origins of the great Irish-American dynasty.

WATERFORD

Waterford ❹ (www.visitwaterford.com), a city of 127,000 people, has a proud past as an important European port, but nowadays its wide, stone quays are mainly used for car parking. Its heyday was in the 18th century, when the famous glass-manufacturing industry was established.

The Tourist Office is on Parade Quay (tel: 051-875 823; Mon–Sat 9am–5.15pm). There is ample parking on the town's quays, and at the eastern extremity is the distinctive circular 'pepper pot' landmark, **Reginald's Tower** (The Mall, www.waterfordtreasures.ie), a massive, 12th-century cylindrical tower built by the Normans on a former Viking site. It is said that when the Norman Strongbow married the daughter of Dermot MacMurrough, part of a pact between the Norman invaders and the Irish king, the wedding took place here. It has subsequently been used as a mint, a prison and a military store. Today it houses The Viking Exhibition, original artefacts including 12th-century Viking jewellery, excavated during the

THE SOUTHEAST: GATEWAY FOR INVADERS

Given its close proximity to mainland Europe and Britain, the Southeast region was where new ideas and people inevitably landed in Ireland. St Declan, for example, who founded a monastery at Ardmore in 416, was preaching the Christian message long before the arrival of St Patrick, Ireland's patron saint. Other arrivals weren't so peaceful. The Vikings were the scourge of early Christian settlements at Ardmore, Lismore, Kilkenny and Cashel.

The beautiful illuminated manuscripts and precious metal implements fashioned by monks during the golden age of learning were prized booty sought by the Vikings. Irish round towers, tall, narrow stone buildings with a conical cap, and only one entrance high above the ground, were originally built at Irish monasteries with a dual purpose: as lookouts, and to provide a safe hiding place for Christian treasures in the event of a Viking raid. The Vikings persisted, though, and probably attracted by the relatively mild climate and fertile land, went on to found the cities of Waterford and Wexford in the 9th century.

The Anglo-Normans, led by the aptly named Strongbow, arrived in 1169. They came at the invitation of the then King of Leinster, Diarmait Mac Murchada (Dermot MacMurrough), as part of a complicated political alliance that would change the course of Irish history, ultimately allowing Henry II of England to gain a firm foothold for himself and his successors. Centuries later, at the behest of Henry VIII, Oliver Cromwell's bloody campaigns of 1650 destroyed many of the region's churches and monasteries. From the Middle Ages through to the 18th century, English influence in the Southeast was stronger than elsewhere in Ireland with many of the great estates of Russborough House, Kilkenny Castle, the Fitzgerald clan's headquarters Waterford Castle, and Johnstown Castle withstanding the political turbulence.

The 1798 Rebellion, when over 1,000 rebels armed with pitchforks and clubs died in a hail of cannon and rifle fire at Vinegar Hill in County Wexford was a defining moment. The United Irishmen's attempt to break free from British rule and form a republic, led by men like Wolfe Tone, failed but it lent momentum to later independence movements.

recent rebuilding of Waterford's shopping district nearby. Georgian Waterford starts behind Reginald's Tower, on **The Mall. City Hall** (office hours; free) is a neo-classical building dating from 1788, which contains some good examples of early Waterford crystal, including a huge chandelier. The same building contains the **Theatre Royal** (www.theatreroyal.ie), which has been tastefully restored, and is one of Ireland's few remaining 19th-century theatre interiors with three tiers of horseshoe-shaped balconies. Just beyond it is the **Bishop's Palace** (The Mall, www.waterfordtreasures.ie; free) originally an imposing town house. It now displays the **Waterford Treasures**, a collection of objects dating from 1700 to the present day. It illustrates Waterford's mid-18th-century heyday, and includes silverware, cut glass, and the sword of Thomas Francis Meagher, Irish patriot and hero of the American Civil War.

Behind the palace is **Christ Church Cathedral,** which replaced an older church in 1773. Designed by local architect John Roberts (1712–96), it is the only neoclassical Georgian cathedral in Ireland with trademark white stucco trim designs of florets and laurels and huge Corinthian columns. From here you can follow the crowds (heading left, that is, upriver) to explore Waterford's largely pedestrianised shopping centre.

The ruins of French Church on Greyfriar's Street to the right of the cathedral date back to an original 13th century Franciscan abbey. In 1695, it was given to a group of Huguenot refugees – hence the 'French' prefix. A splendid east window is all that now remains intact.

Opposite the City Hall, **The Waterford Crystal Experience** (The Mall; www.waterfordvisitorcentre.com) celebrates the city's long tradition of glassmaking, which dates back to 1783. The dramatic 50-minute tour features glass-blowing, before which the glass is heated to high temperatures in a blazing furnace, and cutting and engraving carried out by skilled master craftsmen.

The main N25 takes a fast inland route to Dungarvan. If you have time, take the coastal route leaving Waterford on the

Waterford city.

R684 for **Dunmore East.** This pretty cliff-side fishing village and holiday resort of thatched cottages is at the head of Waterford Harbour and has lots of nice restaurants and two sheltered beaches.

Tramore is a total contrast, with a long, flat sandy beach, a fun fair, caravan parks and other facilities aimed at the budget holiday market. The coast road continues through a series of villages with good beaches – **Annestown, Bunmahon** and **Clonea**. Known as Waterford's Copper Coast, the region was designated European Geopark status by Unesco in 2004 in recognition of its volcanic geology and its 19th-century copper mining heritage. Find out more at the Geopark Information Point (Bunmahon; www.coppercoastgeopark.com). Elsewhere in the sandstone cliffs secluded coves can be reached on foot. **Dungarvan** ❺, situated on Dungarvan Harbour and backed by wooded hills, is the county town of Waterford. It has some lively waterside pubs and is popular as a centre for watersport activity holidays.

If you're headed for Cork, skip to Ardmore below. Those heading west, or with time for a scenic detour into the Blackwater Valley, should pick up the N72 Cappoquin road outside Dungarvan.

VEE GAP: THE SCENIC ROUTE TO LISMORE CASTLE

Cappoquin ❻ is a quiet village nicely situated on a wooded hillside on the River Blackwater, a beautiful salmon and trout river. About 3 miles (5km) north of the village is **Mount Melleray** (www.mountmellerayabbey.org; free), a Cistercian (Trappist) abbey dating from the mid-19th century that welcomes visitors in search of solitude. The Vee Gap route is signposted form here, going north on the R669 into the Knockmealdown Mountains. There are a number of waymarked walking trails and places to stop on the side of the road. The Vee Gap is at the summit, from which you can see the Galtee Mountains in the northwest, and in good visibility the Rock of Cashel due north, rising out

At work at Waterford Crystal.

of the Tipperary Plain. Turn back here, and take the R668 to Lismore.

Lismore 7, a pretty wooded village of 900 inhabitants approached over a stone bridge, was an important monastic centre from the 7th to the 12th centuries, which is why the village has a cathedral. **St Carthage's** (1633) has some interesting effigies. More information on the village's past can be found at the **Lismore Heritage Centre** (tel: 058-54975; charge) opposite the castle car park. The village is dominated by the grey stone turrets of **Lismore Castle** (www.lismorecastlegardens.com; gardens and art gallery: 17 Mar–mid-Oct; charge). Built on a rock overhanging the river in the mid-18th century, the castle is a dramatic and imposing building. It is used as a summer residence by the Duke of Devonshire, and is not open to the public. The gardens include an 800-year-old yew walk. The Castle's west wing features a contemporary art gallery, and the gardens have a fine selection of contemporary sculpture by leading artists, entry is included in your ticket.

The structure, often described as the most spectacular castle in Ireland, dates back to 1753 and is situated in a panoramic position overlooking the Blackwater Valley with views over rolling, wooded hills to the Knockmealdown Mountains beyond. Private groups of up to 23 guests can rent the castle when the Duke is not in residence, and they are looked after by his personal staff.

Lismore Castle.

ARDMORE

Heading back south, beyond Dungarvan the main tour joins the N25, which climbs the **Drum Hills** giving good views back across Dungarvan harbour. **Ardmore** involves a 5-mile (8km) detour, but is worth the effort. St Declan established a monastery here in the 5th century (freely accessible). Today the remains of a medieval cathedral and round tower stand on a cliff top with stunning views over Ardmore Bay. The 12th-century cathedral with its sturdy, rounded arches is a prime example of the Hiberno-Romanesque style, while the slender round tower with its conical roof is an elegant contrast. There are also interesting stone carvings. The tiny village at the bottom of the cliff has good sandy beaches and there are some great places to eat in the village itself and in the swanky Cliff House Hotel.

Youghal 8 (pronounced 'yawl'), famous for its long sandy beaches and historic town centre, found fame in 1956 when John Huston filmed the New Bedford scenes of *Moby Dick* here. Photos of Gregory Peck and other cast members on location can be seen in Paddy Linehan's Bar on the quay. Also on the waterfront, the quayside **Youghal Tourist Office** (Market Square; www.youghal.ie) houses a heritage centre, and is the starting point for walking tours of the town's historic centre. Built in 1776 as a jail, the Clock Tower is a distinctive landmark that straddles the road in the town centre. The steps beside it lead to a street with excellent harbour views, and to the 13th-century St Mary's Collegiate Church. Sir Walter Raleigh (*c*.1552–1618) lived next door, where he smoked the first tobacco and planted the first the potato plant in Ireland – a claim disputed by several other places. The sensational sandy beaches which have made Youghal a favourite holiday destination are outside the town on the Cork side, and extend for 3 miles (5km).

QUAKER CONNECTIONS

Turn left off the N25 in Castlemartyr for **Shanagarry** ❾, a tidy village built of grey stone, with many Quaker connections. The famous hotel, **Ballymaloe House** is to the east of the village. **Ballymaloe Cookery School, Farm Shop and Gardens** have a geometric potager (kitchen garden), a formal fruit garden and a shell house. **Shanagarry Design Centre** (tel: 021-464 5838) beside the parish church, is a large craft shop with a good café, run by the Kilkenny Shop, stocking ceramics by artists including Stephen Pearce. **Shanagarry House** where William Penn, the founder of Pennsylvania, spent time as a teenager, is opposite the Design Centre.

Ballycotton, 3 miles (5km) beyond Shanagarry is a fishing village built on a cliff top overlooking a small island and lighthouse. There are good cliff walks, and numerous nesting sea birds can be seen in early summer. The brightly coloured fishing fleet supplies much of Cork city's fish.

Midleton ❿, an ever-expanding but pleasant market town, is the home of Ireland's largest distillery. A new distilling complex was built in 1966, and the **Old Midleton Distillery** (www.jamesonwhiskey.com) now houses an audio-visual display and an optional guided tour that explains the distilling process of Irish whiskey. You can sample a drop of the famous product in a traditional Irish pub. Admirers of industrial architecture will enjoy the carefully restored 11-acre (4.5-hectare) 18th-century site. Most of the buildings are of cut stone, and the original waterwheel still functions. The N25 continues for 15 miles (24km) into Cork city.

Idyllic Ballycotton, Cork.

OPTION 2: KILDARE TO CASHEL VIA KILKENNY

This alternative, inland route from Dublin to Cork takes in some of the Southeast's most interesting historical sites. Kildare, with its Japanese Gardens and National Stud, has a Cathedral and a 12th-century Round Tower associated with St Brigid. The historic medieval town of Kilkenny, famous for its black marble, lies 23 miles (37km) south of Kildare, and the magnificently restored castle is a must-see.

You can linger in the Kilkenny area exploring the pretty riverside villages of the Nore and the Barrow, or continue to Clonmel, a compact market town on the River Suir, and head into the Nire Valley for a taste of unspoilt hill and bog land. Both options lead to Tipperary, and the spectacular ecclesiastical ruins on the Rock of Cashel.

At Cahir, there is a massive castle to visit, and quiet woodland walks through the relatively unfrequented Glen of Aherlow.

Leave Dublin on the main N7 Limerick motorway, taking the Kildare exit.

The Dubai Duty Free Irish Derby Festival takes place at the Curragh Racecourse.

The road cuts through **The Curragh** ⓫ (www.curragh.ie) a broad plain of 6,000 acres (2,400 hectares). The **Curragh Racecourse** is the heart of the Irish horseracing world, and the Irish Derby is held here every June. If you are lucky, you might see a string of racehorses galloping by. Otherwise, the plain is used for exercises by the Irish Army which has a large camp here.

St Brigid founded a religious settlement in **Kildare** ⓬ in the 5th century. The present Cathedral dates partly from the late 17th century and partly from the 19th century. The 108ft (33-metre) **Round Tower** beside the cathedral belongs to a 12th-century monastery. If you're feeling lively, you can climb to the top for excellent views of the surrounding countryside.

THE NATIONAL STUD

Horses have been in southeast Ireland for seven centuries, but the first stud farm was not established until 1900. Its founder, a Scottish colonel, William Hall Walker, who later became Lord Wavertree, presented it to the British government in 1916 with the aim of founding a British National Stud. It was bought by the Irish government in 1943.

Today, the most prestigious of all of Kildare's many studs, the **National Stud** (www.irish-national-stud.ie) is where top-class breeding stallions are stabled. Admission also allows you to visit the **Irish Horse Museum** and the **Japanese Gardens**, laid out between 1906 and 1910 by Japanese landscape artist Tassa Eida and his son Minoru, which have been carefully preserved as one of the country's horticultural gems.

Also in the National Stud grounds is **St Fiachra's Garden**, created to celebrate the millennium with 4 acres (1.6 hectares) of woodland and lakeside walks.

MEDIEVAL KILKENNY

Kilkenny ⓭ was founded as a monastic settlement by St Canice in the 6th century. In 1641 a Catholic parliament, the Confederation of Kilkenny, tried to organise resistance to the persecution of Catholics. Cromwell's destructive 1650 campaign put a brutal end to such aspirations. While **Kilkenny** likes to promote itself as 'Ireland's medieval capital', its rich heritage is not immediately obvious. Start at the Tourist Information Office in **Shee Alms House** (Rose Inn Street; tel: 056-775 1500; free), where you can equip yourself with free maps. This charming stone house with mullioned windows was built in the mid-17th century as a hospital for the poor. Frequent walking tours leave from here daily.

The sites of medieval Kilkenny start with St Canice's Cathedral at one extreme and end with the Castle at the other. Between them is a **Tholsel** (town hall) dating from 1761, the ruins of a 13th-century friary, the **Black Abbey**, and **Rothe House** (www.rothehouse.com), a 16th-century merchant's town house. Built by John Rothe around 1594, it is a fine example of a merchant's house of the Tudor period. Owned by the Kilkenny Archaeological Society, it contains a collection of Bronze Age artefacts, period costumes and Ogham stones. Rothe House also has a genealogical centre for tracing ancestors.

Kilkenny Castle (www.kilkennycastle.ie; charge, access to castle grounds and art gallery free) has been sumptuously restored. The grey stone, turreted landmark towers over the River Barrow, which serves as its moat. The original castle was built by the Butler family and dates from 1659. It has since been rebuilt several times.

The ornate Georgian stable yard of the castle across the main road is occupied by the Kilkenny Design Centre (Castle Yard; kilkennydesign.com), which has a big display of local and national crafts and several workshops.

While walking along Kilkenny's main street to reach St Canice's Cathedral note the narrow, covered passageways on either side of the road that lead to cobbled alleyways lined by small houses, many with attractive floral displays. Known as 'slips', these are

The Japanese Gardens at the Irish National Stud, County. Kildare.

a particular feature of Kilkenny, and a reminder of its medieval past.

St Canice's Cathedral (www.stcanicescathedral.ie), dating from the 13th century, is built in the Early English style. The Gothic interior is remarkable for its wealth of medieval monuments and life-size effigies, many carved from a locally quarried black marble. Amidst the many Norman memorials, be sure to view the female effigy in the south aisle wearing a Kinsale cloak, and St Ciaran's Chair, in the north transept, made of black marble with designs from the 13th century.

The 6th-century **Round Tower** in the Cathedral grounds is the only remnant of St Canice's monastery. You can climb its 167 steps, and enjoy an astounding view. In rainy weather it is closed to visitors for safety reasons.

Kytler's Inn (Kieran Street; www.kytelersinn.com) dates back to 1324 when Dame Alice Kytler, 'the sorceress of Kilkenny', was accused of poisoning her four husbands, and of being a witch and brothel keeper. (She fled to England and stayed there.) The restaurant retains a medieval air with exposed beams and 14th-century stonework.

RIVERSIDE VILLAGES

If you have time for a day-long drive around the Kilkenny area, explore one of the pretty villages on the rivers **Nore** and **Barrow**. The rivers meander through rich countryside with gently sloping wooded hills dotted with old villages of grey stone buildings, until they meet in New Ross and flow into the sea at Waterford.

Leave Kilkenny on the R700 south for **Bennettsbridge** ⓮. Some of Kilkenny's best craft artisans live and work in this village, which straddles the River Nore, and have created their own craft trail (www.madeinkilkenny.ie). You can visit **Nicholas Mosse Pottery** (http://nicholasmosse.com), for its lovely pottery, shop and excellent café. Candle makers Moth to a Flame (www.mothtoaflame.ie) is also worth a look.

Thomastown is a small town with an arty vibe, a couple of pubs and

Kilkenny Castle.

cafés, including the Blackberry Café – great for lunch and afternoon tea – and restaurant Tabu Tapas (https://taburestaurant.ie). Pop into Brid Lyons Ceramics (www.bridlyonsceramics.com) or Bernard Kavanagh (Tel: 086 082 1251), both in the town centre, for local pottery. In the 13th century the town was walled and fortified, and the 18th-century stone-arched bridge over the River Nore indicates its former importance.

The other side of the bridge brings you to the **Grennan Mill Craft School** (www.grennanmillcraftschool.com) which has annual exhibitions over Kilkenny Arts Festival, and beside it is a pleasant outdoor swimming area patrolled by lifeguards in summer. Wattie's seasonal ice cream shack is a short stroll down the road. Carrying on up the Waterford Road (1.5 miles/3km) brings you to **Jerpoint Abbey** (http://jerpointpark.com), one of the most attractive monastic sites in Ireland. The ruined Cistercian monastery is 12th-century. The church, with its Romanesque details, dates from this period. In the transept chapels the visitor can see 13th- to 16th-century tomb sculpture. The tower and cloister date from the 15th century. Another Kilkenny artisanal favourite is **Jerpoint Glass** (www.jerpointglass.com; free), where you can watch uncut glass being blown. It is just two miles up from the abbey, take the right turn off the main road signposted for **Mount Juliet** and it's just after the Mount Juliet entrance on your left. Eoin Leadbetter Woodturner is also here and along the same road is Karen Morgan pottery.

Return to Thomastown and cross the Nore again to reach **Inistioge**. The village is on a bend of the river and has a picturesque tree-lined square beside a 10-arched stone bridge. Its narrow, sloping streets of small stone houses, village pubs, cute café, and antique store make it a popular location for filming period movies, such as *Circle of Friends* (1995), based on a novel by Maeve Binchy which starred Colin Firth and Minnie Driver. **Woodstock Gardens and Arboretum** (www.woodstock.ie) which was laid out in the 19th century with interesting trees

SELLING THE AULD SOD

When the Irish emigrated to America, it's said, they brought their churches, schools and music, but the only thing they couldn't bring was the soil. That omission was rectified in 2006 when the Auld Sod Export Company began selling 12oz (340 grams) plastic bags of 'Official Irish Dirt' from a field in the village of Cahir, County Tipperary, to a warehouse in Speonk, New York. At US$5 a bag (including a packet of shamrock seeds) it wasn't exactly dirt cheap, but the company piled up $2 million of sales in its first four months.

Auld Sod advised the 40 million Americans who admit to Irish ancestry that they could use the soil to grow an Irish rose for their sweetheart or scatter it over the casket or grave of the dearly departed (http://auldsod.software-development.ie).

Nicholas Mosse Pottery Store, Bennettsbridge.

and shrubs from the Far East, is open to the public and has tea rooms in a cast-iron conservatory, but the house itself was burnt down in 1922.

Seven miles (11km) south of Inistioge, turn left off the N700 to The **Rower**. This little village marks the start of an especially scenic stretch of road, with views over the River Barrow on the right-hand side, and the Blackstairs Mountains beyond the river.

Graiguenamanagh (The Hamlet of the Monks) ⓯ was an important commercial centre in the 19th century, when the River Barrow was used to transport coal and grain. Nowadays herons fish along its weir, and one of its stone-built warehouses is now a stylish waterside B&B and restaurant.

There is a genuinely nostalgic stretch of old-fashioned pubs on the hill to the west of the bridge, in whose dark interiors you can buy groceries as well as pints. At the top of this hill on the right is **Duiske Abbey** (tel: 059 972 4238), a Cistercian Abbey founded in 1204. The exterior is pebble-dashed and does not look very promising. However, the main nave of the abbey was adapted in 1983 to serve as the parish church. Its combination of modern and ancient features is much praised by some, and lamented by others. Whatever your opinion, its light-filled interior is certainly worth a look. Try and spot the Knight of Duiske, an effigy in chain mail, the hammerbeam roof in Irish oak and the magnificent Romanesque processional door in the south transept.

St Patrick's Cathedral on the Rock of Cashel.

Both the R705 from Graiguenamanagh and the R700 Thomastown–Inistioge road lead to **New Ross** ⓰ where the River Nore and the Barrow form a long estuary before reaching the sea. The town, which is in County Wexford, was built on a steep hill overlooking the River Barrow at a strategically important river crossing. On the river bank you will see the tall masts of the **Dunbrody Famine Ship** (www.dunbrody.com), docked to the east of the river, a full-scale replica of a sailing ship built in 1845 to transport emigrants to North America. On board, actors tell the stories of the passengers, who travelled on 'coffin-ships' in order to escape the Great Famine. It is both an entertaining and a sobering reminder of the ordeal suffered by over a million people who emigrated from Ireland.

CLONMEL

From New Ross, follow the N25 and N24 west to **Clonmel** ⓱, a busy County Tipperary market town on the River Suir. The area to the north and east of the town is known for its apple orchards, and Clonmel is the centre of the Irish cider-making industry. However, travel to the south, and you will find another kind of scenery altogether.

The **Nire Valley Drive** is a sign-posted circular route of about 23 miles (37km) that travels along the edge of the **Comeragh Mountains to Ballymacarbry**, and the **Nire Valley**, returning to Clonmel through **Clogheen**. This is not for the faint-hearted; the roads are narrow, sometimes steep, and there are several hairpin bends, but the forest and bogland scenery is magnificent. Ballymacarbry is a good base from where to follow the various waymarked trails in the area.

THE ROCK OF CASHEL

From Clonmel, head northwest on the R688 to **Cashel** ⓲. A cluster of romantic-looking, grey, turreted buildings stands on a limestone outcrop rising (200ft) 60 metres above the Tipperary plain, and absolutely every tour bus stops here. Try to avoid the crowds by visiting at lunchtime or in the late afternoon.

The **Rock of Cashel** (www.cashel.ie) was probably once a centre of Druidic worship. By the 4th century AD, Cashel was the ceremonial centre of the Kings of Munster. It was here, legend has it, that St Patrick baptised King Aengus.

The largest building on the rock, the shell of **St Patrick's Cathedral,** built in the Gothic style, was in use from the 13th to the mid-16th centuries when it was desecrated in Oliver Cromwell's campaign. **Cormac's Chapel** is a simpler building dating from 1127, before the Norman invasion, with a high, corbelled roof similar to those found in early saints' cells in Glendalough and Dingle. Cormac's Chapel is generally considered one of the greatest achievements of native Irish church architecture. The entry archway is a fine example of the Hiberno-Romanesque style of architecture. The broken sarcophagus within the chapel is believed to be Cormac's final resting place. Don't miss the medieval paintings in the old plasterwork.

After enjoying the memorable views of the surrounding countryside at the rock, take a wander down to the luxury **Cashel Palace Hotel** (www.cashelpalacehotel.ie) just below, a red-brick, Queen Anne–style bishop's palace built in 1730. It's worth staying over here with its charming Guinness Bar which lists the names of many famous people who have visited, Michelin-starred Bishop's Buttery, and spa. Note also the well-preserved wooden Victorian shop fronts across the road.

Cahir ⓳ (pronounced *'care'*) situated on a hill above the River Suir, has

Jerpoint Abbey.

a certain faded charm, due chiefly to the well-proportioned Georgian houses in its main street and square. It is best known for its antique shops and its castle. **Cahir Castle** (tel: 052-744 1011) is a massive limestone fortress dating from the mid-12th century set on a rock in the River Suir. There is an informative guided tour, but avoid the audio-visual display. Walk up the hill beside the castle to the attractive main square. About a mile outside Cahir on the Clonmel road (also accessible by footpath from the castle car park) is the **Swiss Cottage** (tel: 052-744 1144; closed mid-Nov–Mar), a thatched *cottage orné* built in 1810 to amuse the Earls of Glengall. It allowed its lordly aristocrats to play make-believe as 'humble folk' for a day. To enhance the fantasy, hidden doorways were built to allow servants to bring food and drink without being seen.

Walkers might like to detour northwest on the N24 for 14 miles (22km) to **Bansha**, and on to Tipperary town and the **Glen of Aherlow** (www.aherlow.com), an excellent area for hiking, with marked trails of various lengths. The Glen, which is partly wooded and runs alongside the Aherlow River, has great views of the Galtee Mountains (sometimes spelt Galty), and is a good base for getting off the beaten track. The Glen of Aherlow leads to **Kilfinane** 20 at the heart of the Galtee and Ballyhoura mountains. Its main feature, the Kilfinane Moat, is an ancient, flat-top mound encircled by three ramparts.

THE BALLYHOURA WAY

The 56-mile (90km) **Ballyhoura Way** is a marked footpath through north Cork and County Limerick to Tipperary town. Some sections have been waymarked as loop walks varying in length from 2 miles (3km) to 12 miles (20km), with a map board at the starting point of each walk. This is beautiful, unspoilt countryside, a mixture of pasture and woodland, with medieval and megalithic monuments.

From Kilfinane, head west joining the N20 and turn south for Cork, or head south and join the N8 for Cork. Either way, Cork city is about an hour's drive.

Cahir Castle.

HORSE-DRAWN CARAVANS

Slow travel doesn't get much slower, but these holidays appeal to anyone, from students to retired executives, who are looking for relaxation.

Holidays in horse-drawn caravans have been available for the last 50 years. The caravans are of the type traditionally used by Travellers, since the 19th century – barrel-topped and brightly painted.

Operators offering these holidays at first bought caravans from the Travellers, and made modifications to them. That supply dried up, however, as the real 'travelling people' moved into modern caravans, towed by cars, or settled into houses. Today operators have the caravans made in the traditional style.

Today just a handful of operators in the Republic – in counties Mayo and Galway in the west, in Laois in the Midlands and Wicklow on the east coast – offer this kind of horse-drawn holiday. It can be a relaxing way of seeing a small area of the country. You clop along at a mile an hour, so you only travel about 10 to 15 miles each day and you see and smell everything around you – the birds and animals, the hedges and fields. Maps with descriptions of interesting features to look out for en route are supplied. It's more about the experience than packing it all in. The caravans usually sleep four people – some can fit an extra berth – and are well-equipped. Operators offer either fixed routes or will arrange alternatives in advance. Overnight stops are made at farms, pubs, guesthouses or hotels.

Holidaymakers are sent on their way after receiving instructions and practice in leading and driving the horse. The instructor will travel with them on the road until they feel confident and relaxed and will also meet up with them at their first overnight stop to help them unharness, and again the next morning before they head off. The horses used are quiet and are well-used to their line of work. There is a charge per night per caravan which covers grazing, showers, etc. Oats for the horse are supplied.

Taking it slowly through the countryside.

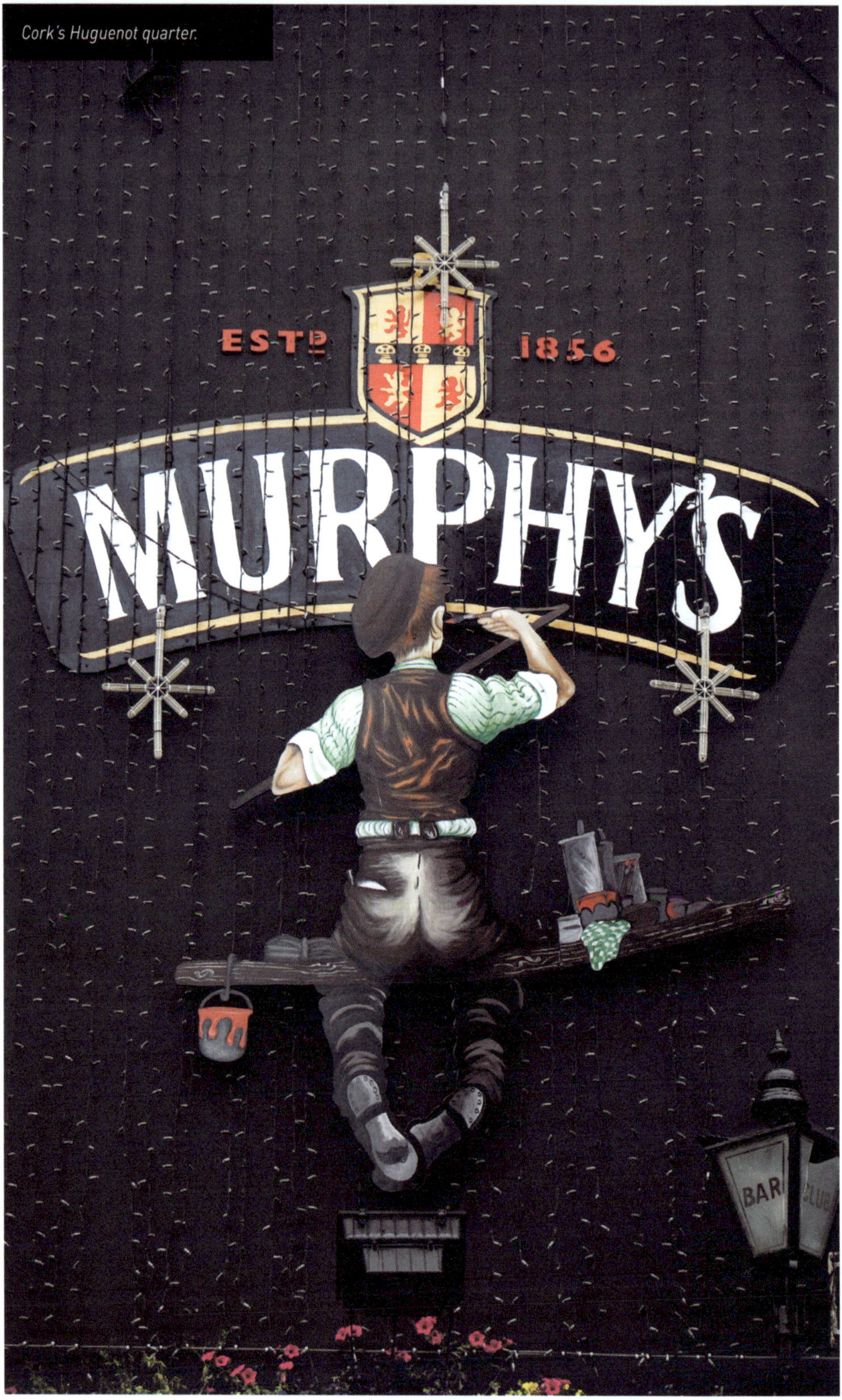

Cork's Huguenot quarter.

CORK AND SURROUNDINGS

After experiencing Cork's gentle charms, you can explore the port of Cobh, visit Fota Wildlife Park and get the gift of the gab at the Blarney Stone.

Pride of place runs deep amongst the natives of **Cork** ❶, an attitude ably underlined by its natives' repeated reference to their city as 'the real capital'. Renowned as much for the singsong lilt of their accent as for their traditional determination to usurp Dublin at commerce, culture and sport, the friendly population need little prompting to extol their proud birthright. The Cork catchphrase 'Up the Rebels!' – recalling the city's proud political past (Michael Collins was from Cork, although the county's tradition of rebellion long predates the 20th century) – is still used at sporting events.

SWELLING CORKING

With a population of over 125,000, metropolitan Cork has long-since lost its sleepy second-city status. Multinational companies such as Pfizer and Apple have business operations here, and there's a growing influx of immigrants from Europe, Africa and East Asia. The result is a cosmopolitan city bristling with tapas bars, busy restaurants and festivals, including the Cork Jazz Festival (www.guinnessjazzfestival.com) in October and International Choral Festival (www.corkchoral.ie) in May.

Lying at the mouth of the Lee, the city's historic centre is on an island created by two channels of the river. Easily walked end-to-end in a day, it allows the visitor easy access for sightseeing, shopping and idle strolling within convenient distance of any car park.

Founded by St Finbar in the 6th century, the name 'Cork' derives from the Irish *Corcach Mór Mumhan*, translated as the 'great marsh of Munster'. The place was prone to flooding and allowed early civilisation to flourish only on marshy islands joined by bridges.

Over the centuries, Cork, like much of Ireland, was invaded by Vikings, Normans and the English, and the Black

Main attractions
- St Finbar's Cathedral
- University College, Cork
- English Market
- Rory Gallagher Piazza
- Opera House
- St Anne's Church
- Cork City Gaol
- Blarney Castle
- Fota Wildlife Park
- Cobh

Maps on pages 172, 178

St Patrick's Quay.

Plague almost wiped out the city in 1349. The McCarthy's of Desmond, a native tribe who grasped power in the 12th century, are credited with constructing the first city walls, built in the present-day Shandon area. Over the centuries, these defensive structures were extended to make Cork one of the great walled cities of Ireland's medieval period.

Cork was most affluent in the 18th century, when its butter market was a source of vast wealth, and much of the best architecture – like the wide streetscapes of the South Mall, Grand Parade and the North Mall – dates from this period. In the 18th and 19th centuries, the era of the 'merchant princes', Cork's wealthiest citizens lived in its waterside suburbs or on the high ground north of the city to avoid the diseases endemic in its marshy centre, where slaughterhouses and tanneries proliferated. People still prefer to live outside the city, commuting from its pleasant hinterlands, and the city centre has a small population. However, some 400,000 people live within a 45-minute journey of Cork city, in attractive seaside locations such as Cobh and Kinsale, or satellite towns such as Midleton, Ballincollig and Carrigaline. The student population is large (around 35,000, University College and Cork Institute of Technology combined), as is evident in the city's bars and discos.

Cork's 2005 stint as European Capital of Culture prompted a redesign of St Patrick's Street and Grand Parade by Barcelona architect Beth Gallí, who gave the city a pedestrian-friendly focus with her pavements of polychromatic stone and futuristic street lights. The vibrant pedestrianised area between Patrick Street and the river, around Paul Street and Cornmarket, where there's a lively Saturday street market, boasts outdoor bars and café tables under awnings, where buskers abound.

Construction in Cork slowed when Ireland's fortunes nosedived after 2010, but now the tide has turned again, and over a billion euros' of development is taking place with luxury hotels and

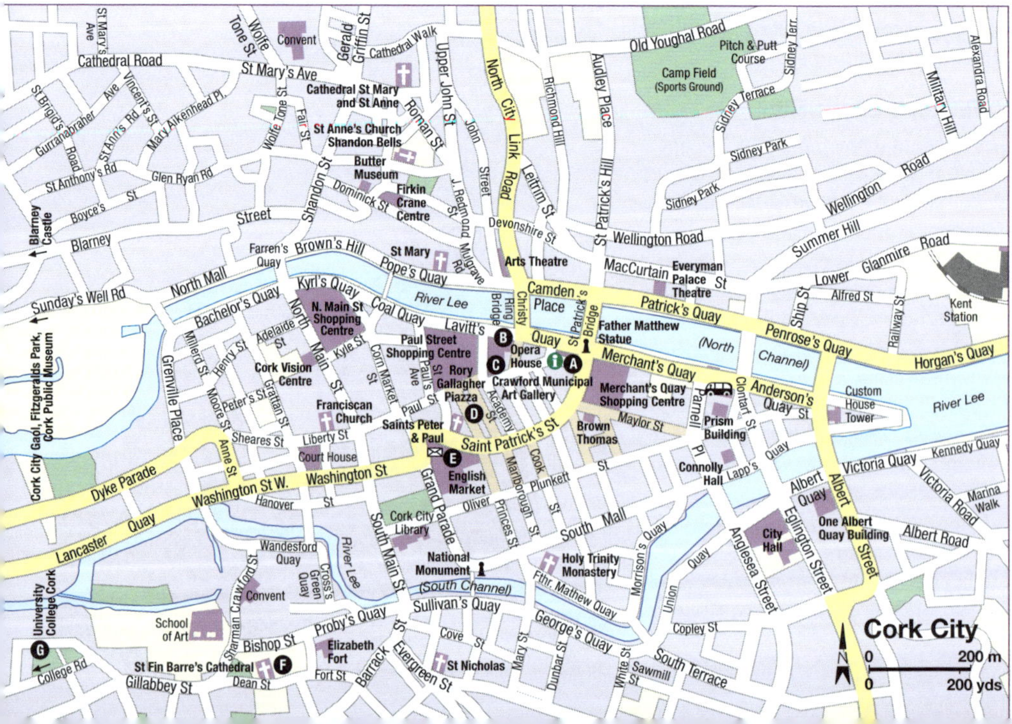

multi-storey skyscrapers. The €60m One Albert Quay complex, Penrose Quay and South Mall are all recent examples. A 15-storey, glass-fronted triangular office known as the Prism Building, inspired by New York's iconic Flatiron Building, is nearing completion on Clontarf Street, and the 34-storey Custom House Tower, complete with a cloud-tickling spire, in the Port of Cork is set to be Ireland's tallest building when complete.

THE CITY CENTRE

Cork's narrow lanes, half-hidden flights of steps and unexpected plazas lend themselves to lazy strolls or determined one-day sightseeing excursions. The city centre is often likened to Venice and Rome for its many bridges and steep hills, and – as in Venice or Rome – any geographical confusion can usually be resolved by walking a straight line to a major landmark.

Start at the **Tourist Information Office** Ⓐ (www.discoverireland.ie/Places-To-Go/Cork; free) Where Saint Patrick's Street meets the River Lee quays.

Walk west along Lavitt's Quay to The **Opera House** Ⓑ (www.corkoperahouse.ie), which dates from 1965, with its stylish facade and pedestrianised forecourt.

Turn left on to Emmett Place for the **Crawford Municipal Art Gallery** Ⓒ (www.crawfordartgallery.ie; free). It has an interesting permanent collection, in which most major 20th-century Irish artists are represented, and a good collection of topographical paintings of Cork in its 18th- and 19th-century prime. It also hosts touring exhibitions in an extension which wraps around the existing red-brick building.

Cross Academy Street and dog-leg (right turn, then left) to take Paul Street to the **Rory Gallagher Piazza** Ⓓ, a pedestrian square popular with buskers, named for the Cork-raised rock-and-blues guitarist who died in 1995 (a monument to Rory stands in the square). This area, known as the Huguenot Quarter, is the closest Cork gets to a 'left bank', with a cluster of design-conscious home furnishing stores, fashion and vintage clothing boutiques, and trendy cafés.

THE ENGLISH MARKET

Walk south along Carey's Lane, passing the back of Saints Peter and Paul's Church and the Huguenot Cemetery, to reach Saint Patrick's Street. Cross and continue along Princess Street, where you'll find an entrance to the **English Market** Ⓔ (www.englishmarket.ie; free), on your right. This huge indoor food market, with its ornate Victorian cast-iron frame, is one of the city's showpieces, trading since 1788. The market sprawls across a whole block to Grand Parade and houses over 150 stands, with artisan food makers, continental delis and organic farmers selling their wares alongside traditional fishmongers, beef, lamb and pork butchers and poulterers. There are a range of great oplaces to eat in here too. At the Princes Street end there's a top-lit

St Finn Bar's Cathedral.

piazza with a central fountain. Note the stall at the door with a display of tripe (cows' intestines) and *drisheen* (blood sausage), and the buttered eggs (the shells rubbed with butter to preserve their freshness) sold in the piazza.

Emerge onto **Grand Parade** and continue south, crossing Oliver Plunkett Street (look out for a terrace of three elegant Georgian houses with slate-hung, bow-fronted windows, typical of Cork's 18th-century prime) to the junction with South Mall. Prior to its 18th-century development (when it became a business area), 'The Mall' was a waterway where merchant ships moored – the flights of stone steps still visible on its north side recall its maritime past. Nowadays it's the city's legal and banking district.

To the southwest, across the south channel of the River Lee, you'll see the spires of **St Fin Barre's Cathedral** F (www.corkcathedral.webs.com; free. Pass the National Monument (unveiled on St Patrick's Day 1906, to commemorate the rebellions of 1798, 1803, 1848 and 1867), cross Nano Nagle footbridge and walk west along the quays to the ornate cathedral, sited where the city began as a monastic school in circa AD 650. The current church, completed in 1879, was designed by William Burges and built with white limestone. Burges also contributed the stained glass, sculptures, mosaics and metalwork for the Gothic Revival style interior. Check out the golden angel on top of the rotunda.

Further west, along Gillabbey Street and College Road, is the campus of **University College, Cork** G. The Visitor Centre (www.ucc.ie; free) is located in the north side of the 19th-century Tudor-Gothic style Quadrangle, adjacent to a display of ancient Ogham Stones – gravestone-like rock tablets etched with varying sequences of short lines, recording events and occasions in Ogham, an ancient language. Known locally as UCC, the college has 15,000 students. The campus has several interesting modern buildings too, notably the **Honan Chapel**, a Hiberno-Romanesque chapel dating from 1916, which showcases Celtic Revival arts

A river view in Cork.

and crafts, and the **Lewis Glucksman Gallery** (www.glucksman.org; free), a boldly designed art gallery with its top floor among the treetops, which has won several architectural awards. Professor George Boole – father of Boolean Logic, which formed the basis for modern computer science – spent much of his working life at UCC.

ST PATRICK'S STREET

Return to Grand Parade via **Washington Street** and follow the graceful curve into **St Patrick's Street**, Cork's main shopping boulevard. The major department store **Brown Thomas** has a good stock of Irish crystal. Look up, because above the modern shop fronts many of the buildings on Patrick Street (as it's generally called) have retained 18th- and 19th-century features. After lunch you'll hear a unique Cork phenomenon – cries of 'Eeeechooo!' from vendors of Cork's evening paper, the *Evening Echo*. A bronze statue of this quintessential Cork symbol, 'the Echo boy', stands at the junction of Patrick and Cook streets.

When you reach the Father Mathew Monument, dedicated to the clear memory of the 'Apostle of Abstinence', who served in Cork for most of his life, you're back at the tourist information office. Straight ahead is St Patrick's Bridge, and left is the modern Christy Ring Bridge. Both lead from the central island of Cork to the Northside.

Cross the Christy Ring Bridge, and climb the hill, taking Mulgrave Road then turning left on Dominick Street to reach the Shandon area, named for the bells of St Anne's Church. Here, on O'Connell Square, is the **Firkin Crane Centre** (www.firkincrane.ie; free) a classical rotunda attractively built in cut limestone, used for dance performances and lessons. In the 18th century much of Cork's wealth derived from the exporting of butter, packed in wooden barrels known as firkins, which were weighed by crane here in the Butter Exchange. You can learn more about this opposite at the **Cork Butter Museum** (www.thebuttermuseum.com; charge).

Shopping at Princes Street Market.

ST ANNE'S CHURCH

Across the road is Cork's iconic **St Anne's Church** (1722–26; free), topped by a large salmon-shaped weather vane above a four-sided clock, colloquially known as 'the four-faced liar' because quirks in its ancient machinery mean the times displayed on each side often don't agree. The steeple is of red sandstone faced with white limestone, a popular combination in local architecture, known as 'streaky bacon', from which the colours of the Cork hurling and football teams are taken. A climb to the belfry (www.shandonbells.ie) rewards visitors with the chance to play a tune on the famous Shandon Bells. Past the bell loft, stairs leads to the tower's terrace, with stunning views on all sides.

THE OLD PRISON

A 20-minute walk starting at the North Mall beside the river at the foot of Shandon Street, uphill into Sunday's Well Road leads to **Cork City Gaol** (www.corkcitygaol.com; charge), a 19th-century prison recreated with all its misery, featuring wax figures crouched in tiny cells and the sounds of dragging chains. The building also houses a fascinating **Radio Museum** in the former studio of Cork's first radio station, with numerous artefacts providing a history of the early days of radio broadcasting.

Walking back toward the city centre, cross the River Lee on Daly's Bridge, a pedestrian suspension structure known locally as 'the shaky bridge', to **Fitzgerald Park.** Set beside the river, the 18-acre (7-hectare) landscaped municipal park is a popular oasis. **Cork Public Museum** (tel: 021-427 0679; free) is housed in a Georgian house and contains historical artefacts relating to the city's history.

BLARNEY CASTLE

A visit to **Blarney Castle** 2 (www.blarneycastle.ie) makes a pleasant half-day outing. Don't be put off by Blarney's reputation as a tourist trap. The castle is surrounded by well-tended gardens, two rivers, a 'Druid' grotto and parkland (don't miss the lake), and the

Cork's Opera House.

THE CORK ACCENT

The singsong qualities of the Cork accent can often prove a tricky hurdle for the visitor to overcome, especially when combined with the speed of speech, which is generally acknowledged to be the fastest in the country. With a rich vein of slang running through daily discourse, the need for a polite 'pardon me?' will be frequent. Given the multiple waves of arrivals over the centuries – Viking, Norman, Elizabethan and Huguenot, to name but a few – Corkonians have assimilated a lexicon all of their own.

Cork Slang, Like (www.corkslang.com) by Seán Beecher, on sale at local bookshops, provides a good introduction. Thus you will learn that a *flah-bag* is a promiscuous woman, a *masher* is an attractive man, *langers* is drunk, *scauld* is tea and *meejum* is a measure of stout.

experience is humorously presented tongue-in-cheek as a load of Blarney.

The castle is not furnished, nor, like many castles of its age, is it a ruin. It is basically a 15th-century fortified home, and the staircase is narrow so that it can be defended by one man holding a sword. Kissing the **Blarney Stone** is supposed to bestow the gift of eloquence. The word Blarney has entered the English language to mean 'smoothly flattering or cajoling talk', but the origins of the strange tradition are obscure.

Having ascended the castle's many steps to the stunning vistas offered by the rooftop viewing point, those who would romance the stone are held by the waist while leaning over the battlements to offer puckered lips upon the legendary surface. There is no charge, but most people are so happy to survive the ordeal, they gladly pay for a souvenir photo at the exit.

FOTA WILDLIFE PARK

The east side of Cork Harbour is formed by three islands, **Little Island**, **Fota Island** and **Great Island**, all connected by causeways. The road from Cork to Cobh brings you past the walls of the 780-acre (315-hectare) **Fota Estate. Fota Wildlife Park** ❸ (www.fotawildlife.ie; charge) aims to breed certain species that are under threat in the wild. Giraffe, zebras, ostrich, oryx and antelope roam freely in grassland, monkeys swing through trees on lake islands, while kangaroos, wallabies, lemurs and peacocks have the complete freedom of the park. A baby rhino is one of the newest residents, the only one in the country. Fota is also the world's leading breeder of cheetahs, one of the few animals here that must be caged.

The freely accessible **Fota Arboretum** is beside the Wildlife Park, behind Fota House (www.fotahouse.com; charge for tours). The house, built as a shooting lodge, was enlarged in 1820 to a symmetrical neoclassical design. The arboretum has a beautiful collection of mature trees. Many of these specimens were introduced from Asia, Australia and the Americas during the 19th century.

There is no dignified way to kiss the Blarney Stone.

THE COVE OF CORK

Cobh ❹ (pronounced 'cove') was a small fishing village, referred to as the Cove of Cork. It grew in importance as a British naval base during the 18th and 19th centuries thanks to its natural deep-water harbour. The fine cut-stone buildings on the two main islands in its harbour were built by the British Navy during the Napoleonic Wars (1792–1815). In Victorian times Cove became Queenstown, and after Independence reverted to its original name in Irish transliteration.

Cobh is attractively located on a steep slope with a Victorian-style promenade of colourfully painted houses, and panoramic south-facing views of Cork harbour. It is a popular commuter town, linked by rail to the city. Visitors are attracted by its maritime history as the last – and first – European port of call for transatlantic shipping. Between 1848 and 1950 about 2.5 million adults and children emigrated through the port. Their transport ranged from convict transports and the 'coffin ships' of the famine years, overcrowded and unseaworthy, to the luxury of White Star and Cunard liners.

Cobh was the last port of call of the ill-fated *Titanic* in 1912, and it was to Cobh that most of the bodies recovered from the torpedoing of the *Lusitania* in 1915 were brought. The Titanic Experience Cobh (www.titanicexperiencecobh.ie occupies the former offices of the White Star Line, and is an interactive exhibition leading to the actual dock from which passengers embarked on the tenders that carried them out to the liners. The old railway station is now the Cobh Heritage Centre (www.cobhheritage.com; free). The history of emigration from Cobh is covered in **The Queenstown Story**, an imaginative audio-visual exhibition. Allow at least an hour.

A large, Gothic-revival church, **St Colman's Cathedral**, was built in granite between 1868 and 1915. From its parapet you can see Roches Point in the south, which marks the harbour entrance, and the open sea beyond.

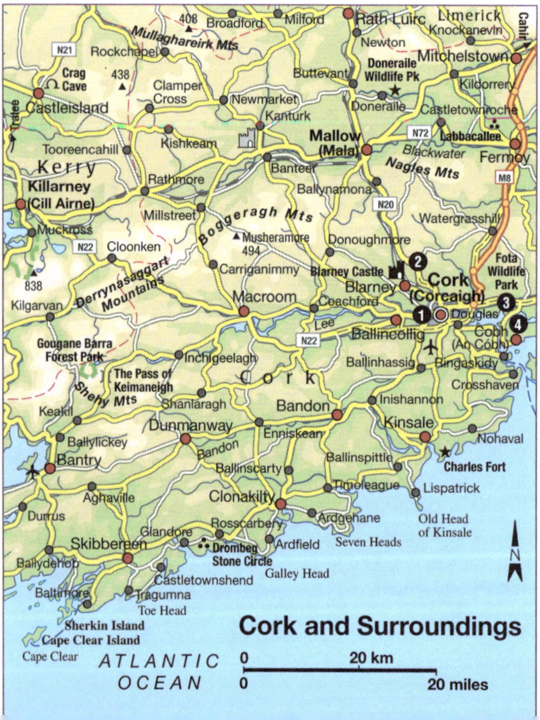

Cheetah family at Fota Wildlife Park.

Memorial to emigration.

The Ring of Kerry.

THE SOUTHWEST

This is where the Atlantic Ocean first touches Europe, and the mild climate enhances the spectacular scenery of the Wild Atlantic Way.

Counties Cork and Kerry, in Ireland's southwest corner, offer spectacular sea and mountain scenery, interspersed with lively small towns and villages – such as Kinsale, Clonakilty, Kenmare, Killarney and Dingle. Life moves at a slower pace in these parts, and old fashioned courtesies are alive and well: you'll notice, for example, on the smaller back roads, passing cars and pedestrians will wave and it is the norm to return the gesture. Refreshingly, people find it quite natural to strike up a conversation simply because you happen to be in the same place at the same time, and overall, friendly informality prevails.

TOURING THE SOUTHWEST

Bring strong walking shoes and waterproof jackets. The further west you go, the more likely you are to encounter rain, as the clouds scud in from the Atlantic, but it is seldom continuous heavy rain, and the showery weather typical of Killarney and Dingle often alternates with sunshine, creating some magical light effects, including numerous rainbows.

The rich farming country on the fertile plains of the Rivers Lee and Bandon give way to more rugged, hilly land, the closer you get to the coast. More than 600 miles (1,000km) of coastline include impressive slate and sandstone cliffs, long sandy beaches and rocky inlets, and easily accessible offshore islands, with abundant wildlife. This is part of the Wild Atlantic Way, a 1600 mile (2600 km) route that stretches up as far as the northern headlands. Because of the proximity of the Gulf Stream, parts of the coast of west Cork and Kerry, including Glengarriff, Killarney and Sneem, are frost-free year round, and have lush, sub-tropical vegetation.

An added bonus throughout the region is the high quality of its natural produce – farmhouse cheeses made

Main attractions

- Kinsale
- Glandore
- Mizen Head
- Bantry Bay
- Glengarriff
- Killarney
- Ring of Kerry
- Valentia Island
- Dingle
- Tralee

Maps on pages 182, 192

Riding the Atlantic waves.

from the milk of cows grazing on fertile green fields, locally reared beef, pork and lamb, freshly caught fish and shellfish, local honey, home-grown potatoes, salads and vegetables (increasingly organic) will impress foodies with their flavour and freshness. All can be found in shops, on the farm gate and at markets, and all are sourced for the best local restaurants.

The pleasures of the southwest are chiefly rural. Most people who visit the area come for the outdoors and the scenery. The lakes and mountains of Killarney can compete with the wildest (if not the highest) Europe has to offer, while the **Ring of Kerry** presents a succession of spectacular seascapes. The less-frequented **Beara Peninsula** is preferred by walkers and cyclists who enjoy the relative lack of traffic and the simple B&B accommodation available. The West Cork coast also has its champions: relatively small scale cliffs and hills, miles of fuchsia hedges dripping with dark red, honey-scented flowers, clashing exuberantly with swathes of sprawling purple heather.

The most popular part of the west among visitors is the extreme tip of

the Dingle Peninsula, a largely Irish-speaking area rich in prehistoric and early Christian remains, with some of the world's best coastal scenery and the country's best traditional music.

KINSALE

Kinsale ❶ (www.kinsale.ie), 12 miles (19km) south of Cork Airport on the R600, is the big success story of Irish tourism. Once a run-down fishing port, it is now a wealthy resort with so many restaurants that it's known as 'the gourmet capital of Ireland'. It is situated at the top of a fjord-like harbour where the River Bandon runs into the sea. Craft shops, galleries, restaurants and antique shops abound. While the south-facing slopes of the inner harbour have been marred by up-market housing developments, including a series of large apartment blocks known locally as 'Heineken Heights', the outer harbour is mercifully unspoilt.

The **Old Courthouse** in Market Square dates from 1600. In 1706 a Dutch-style gabled frontage and octagonal clock tower were added. The Courthouse contains the **Kinsale Regional Museum** (tel: 021-477 7930; free), with exhibits including mementoes of the *Lusitania*, sunk 14 miles (23km) off the coast by a German submarine in 1915. The inquest into the sinking was held here.

Also of interest nearby are the 12th-century **St Multose Church** and the 16th-century restored **Desmond Castle** (tel: 021-477 4855; charge), which houses the International Museum of Wine. (Many emigrant Irish families from the 17th century onwards got involved with the wine trade in Europe, Australia and the US.) Originally built as a custom house, from the mid-18th century Desmond Castle was used as a prison, and it is known locally as the French Prison after a tragic fire in which 54 prisoners, mainly French sailors, died. **Charles Fort** (tel: 021-477 2263; charge), a five-minute drive down Kinsale Harbour, is a star-shaped fort built in 1677, enclosing 9 acres (3.5 hectares) of ground. Because it is overlooked by high ground,

Kinsale.

it was never a great success militarily, and its working life as a recruit training centre ended in 1921 when the IRA burnt it down. There is good cut-stone work on many buildings, and wonderful sea views. On the outer harbour side of the fort an attractive footpath runs along beside the sea towards the harbour mouth for about 1 mile (2km; free).

COURTMACSHERRY ESTUARY

Leave Kinsale by crossing the River Bandon to the west. The R600 runs along the edge of the **Courtmacsherry Estuary**, which, in winter months is home to great flocks of plover, oyster catchers and curlew. In the summer, cormorants, egrets and herons should be easy to spot.

The distant view of **Timoleague** ❷ is dominated by the grey stone ruins of the waterside 12th-century **Timoleague Franciscan Friary** (www.timoleague.ie). Until the 16th century the monks here were wine importers. The ruins are freely accessible. There are some garish modern graves inside, but the tall Gothic windows framing views of the estuary offer an irresistible photo opportunity. The interior walls of Timoleague's tiny 19th-century **Church of Ireland** are entirely covered by a mosaic mural in the decorative style favoured by the Oxford Movement. The 20th-century Hiberno-Romanesque-style **Church of Our Lady's Nativity** contains some fine stained-glass windows by the acclaimed Dublin artist, Harry Clarke (1889–1931).

CLONAKILTY AND ENVIRONS

Arriving at **Clonakilty** ❸, take the bypass and park in one of the designated areas to explore the colourful and compact town centre on foot. **Emmet Square** is lined by tall Georgian houses. The **General Post Office** is in a small 19th-century church. Note the hand-painted shop signs above wooden shop fronts, which have been revived in recent years. The **West Cork Model Railway Village** (www.modelvillage.ie) in the old railway station at the east end of town is a 1:24 scale model of the towns of Bandon, Kinsale, Clonakilty and Dunmanway, as they were in the

Drombeg Stone Circle.

1940s, and of the long closed West Cork Railway. Historians will like the eclectic **West Cork Regional Museum** (Old Methodist School, Western Road; tel: 023-883 3115; May–Oct), which has memorabilia of the West Cork patriot Michael Collins (see page 50) among its extensive collection. Collins' birthplace, a dignified memorial featuring the walls of the family farmhouse and a bronze statue, is signposted 6 miles (9km) west of Clonakilty, just beyond **Lissavaird**.

The **Michael Collins Centre** (www.michaelcollinscentre.com) is 2 miles/3km outside Clonakilty off the R600 Timoleague road. It offers an audio-visual display, photo and militaria exhibition featuring the local hero, and can organise guided tours (in your own car, or tour bus) of the somewhat scattered sites associated with Collins. Lectures and other events mark the anniversary of his death on 22 August 1922, in an ambush at **Béal na Blath**, 17 miles (27km) north of Clonakilty.

Continuing west on the N71, the road crosses a wide sea inlet at **Rosscarbery** ❹. This was an important monastic centre from the 6th to the 12th centuries. The protestant Cathedral Church of St Fachtna (1612) is the smallest cathedral in Ireland and has been attractively renovated. The pretty village square, on a hill above the main road, with craft shops, bars and cafés is worth exploring.

Turn left just beyond Rosscarbery on to the R597 Glandore road. From June to September this little road, and many others like it around west Cork, are lined by tall hedges of *Fuchsia magellanica*, a shrub with bright red bell-shaped flowers imported from Chile in the 19th century. It has adapted so well to the climate that it grows wild in profusion.

About 2 miles (3.5km) along is the road to the **Drombeg Stone Circle** (free), one of the most complete and most impressively situated of the region's early Iron Age remains. The circle is oriented to the winter solstice; if it's cloudless on 21 December, it is an impressive sight as the last rays of the sun travel through a cut in the distant mountains and land on the flat stone at the far side of the circle.

FUCHSIA BRANDING

A green logo featuring a fuchsia flower and the words 'A place apart – West Cork' is part of a regional branding exercise designed to enhance the area's reputation for high-quality food, accommodation and craft products. Those sanctioned to use the fuchsia logo must adhere to strict quality criteria, and reflect local characteristics including environmental quality, and an awareness of the richness and diversity of local heritage. The fuchsia sign on a menu guarantees the best regional ingredients. Producers include Castletownbere's Shellfish de la Mer, luxury cakes from Coolmore Foods, wild smoked salmon from Ummera Smoked Products, West Cork Bakery's handmade bread, Skeaghanore Duck from Ballydehob (very flavoursome) and Follain Teo's high-fruit preserves, relishes and marmalade.

A bronze statue of Michael Collins in Clonakilty.

In winter, **Glandore** ❺, a tiny village built on the south-facing slope of a protected harbour, with a year-round population well below 100, will be virtually empty, while in summer it will be teeming with wealthy visitors and their yachts. This lovely spot is known locally as Millionaire's Row. **Union Hall,** on the opposite side of Glandore Harbour, is a small fishing village. Skipper Colin Barnes (Tel. 086-3850568; www.corkwhalewatch.com runs boat trips from Reen Pier in Union Hall, with regular sightings of dolphins, seals and fin, humpback and minke whales. Trips leave daily at 10am and 3pm, weather permitting, from May to September, and there's one trip a day October to April at 10.30am. The brightly painted trawlers moor nearby at **Keelbeg Pier**. Note the characteristic multicoloured houses: it's said this tradition began when fishermen used whatever was left over from the annual painting of their boats to brighten up their houses. The custom has been enthusiastically adopted by developers of new holiday homes, but you will quickly learn to distinguish the real thing.

CASTLETOWNSHEND

Castletownshend (www.castle-townshend.com) is signposted from Union Hall on an attractive backroad, which passes through **Rineen**. Castletownshend is one of the prettiest, and most unusual villages in west Cork, with a history tightly tethered to the Townshend family ever since English soldier and politician Richard Townsend built a castle there in the 17th century. Wander along its two streets, noting its large, well-designed three- and four-storey houses, often stone-built and neoclassical.

A wall plaque in **St Barrahane's Church** enlarges on the history. Behind the church are the graves of Edith Somerville (1858–1949) and her writing partner, Violet Martin (1862–1915). As Somerville and Ross, they are best known for a series of comic sketches of Irish country life, *Some Experiences of an Irish RM* (Resident Magistrate). They also wrote a well-received novel,

A hotel in Skibbereen.

The Real Charlotte. There's a wonderful view of the sheltered anchorage from their graves.

SKIBBEREEN

Skibbereen ❻ is a market town built in a solid bourgeois style in the 19th and early 20th centuries. Symptomatic of the changes that have taken place in rural Ireland since the economic boom, it now has a tiny (but very welcome) bypass, in the form of a ring road studded with supermarkets and DIY warehouses.

The **Skibbereen Heritage Centre** (www.skibbheritage.com; closed winter; charge), on Upper Bridge Street explains the causes of the Great Famine of 1845–7 that took the lives of over 10,000 people in the area.

Baltimore, 8 miles (13km) south of Skibbereen, is a popular sailing and holiday village on **Roaringwater Bay.** The bay covers an area between Mizen Head in the west and Baltimore in the east, which is known for its numerous rocks and islands. In good visibility, the **Fastnet Rock Lighthouse**, can be seen on the horizon some 14 miles (23km) to the south.

Baltimore is also the base for the mail boats and ferries servicing Roaringwater Bay's two largest inhabited islands, Cape Clear and Sherkin. A quick hop by ferry, **Sherkin Island** (http://sherkinisland.eu) boasts the ruins of a 15th-century Franciscan friary, just beside the pier. The island is 3 miles long and 1.5 miles wide (5km by 2.4km) with several pleasant sandy beaches, and good peaceful walking on its quiet, almost traffic-free roads. It's popular for day trips.

BIRDWATCHING CENTRE

With a population of 120, **Cape Clear Island** is an Irish-speaking island about 3 miles long by 1 mile (5km by 2km) wide. It is reached via a thrilling 45-minute boat ride through the rocks of Roaringwater Bay. Weather permitting there are several daily services, see the website for details: (www.capeclearferries.com). The island has three pubs, a youth hostel, a campsite, a bird observatory, a heritage centre and plenty of simple

The Baltimore Beacon warns ships of the treacherous coast.

BALTIMORE'S BOATING TRADITION

From May to September, Baltimore's fleet of gaff-rigged wooden sailing boats can be seen in the harbour. A group of enthusiasts rescued the bones of an old sailing ship rotting in the mud, and used it as a template to revive the area's traditional mackerel boats. These were built for speed, to get the catch back into port ahead of the pack, and provide exciting sailing. The boats, which were in use up to the 1950s, are built in a traditional yard at Oldcourt (just outside Baltimore) by Liam Hegarty and Fachtna O'Sullivan, whose families have been building boats here for generations.

There are now about 40 sailing vessels in the fleet, of various designs, and several canoe-like currachs, traditionally built of tarred canvas on a wooden frame. The smaller 'towelsail' yawls were used for crab fishing in inland waters, and are designed to navigate shallow rocky coves. The 'towelsail' was a sail hung over the body of the boat to create a tent (*teabhal* in the local Irish dialect, pronounced 'towel') for the crab fishermen who spent many nights aboard.

The season begins each year on the last weekend in May with mussel eating and net mending competitions in the Baltimore Seafood and Wooden Boats Festivals (www.baltimorewoodenboatfestival.com). In summer the fleet travels to regattas along the Cork coast.

accommodation, and it hosts a storytelling festival every September. Cape Clear's Bird Observatory often reports landings of rare migratory birds, and the appearance of large flocks. The ferry also serves Fastnet Rock Lighthouse.

The N71 west leaves Skibbereen beside the banks of the **River Ilen**. Keep an eye out to the left for your first panoramic view of Roaringwater Bay and its numerous islands.

Ballydehob ❼ is a lively, brightly painted village built on a hillside, apparently in the middle of nowhere. There is a pleasant walk along its disused railway viaduct, a relic of the short-lived West Cork Railway. The village is a popular retreat for city folk – English, Dutch, German and even Irish – seeking a better quality of life.

Continue on the R592 towards Schull. In good weather you will see **Mount Gabriel** (1335ft/407 metres) on your right. The two white balls on its summit guide transatlantic air traffic. While Ballydehob has a reputation for being arty, **Schull**, 3 miles (5km) down the R592, is the heart of fashionable west Cork, a summer resort for wealthy Dubliners. Walk down to the pier for another look at Roaringwater Bay, and then explore its one main street, checking out its restaurants, bookshops and craft boutiques.

Glengarriff.

MIZEN HEAD

Leave Schull on the R592 to travel to the tip of the **Mizen Peninsula**. The road passes rocky, rugged bits of low-lying coast. About 4 miles (7km) west at **Altar**, there is a megalithic tomb on the left, known locally as the Altar Rock. The **Mizen Head** is a dramatic spot with wild Atlantic waves pounding the rocks even in the calmest weather. The lighthouse signal has been automatic, and the station unstaffed since 1993. The **Mizen Head Visitor Centre** (www.mizenhead.net) is located in the lighthouse keeper's house on an island at the tip of the peninsula. To reach it you must cross a concrete suspension bridge while the waves swirl around 150ft (45 metres) below. It's worth bringing a camera.

The **Sheep's Head Peninsula** is a thin finger of land dividing Dunmanus Bay from Bantry Bay to the north. From Goleen or Schull, follow the R591 to Durrus, and follow signs for the Sheep's Head Drive (50 miles/80km), which leads to the N71, and Bantry town. The peninsula is small and sparsely populated, with most people living in scattered farmhouses. There is a timeless air about the gorse and heather of the heathland, and the rough fields divided by grey stonewalls. The marked Sheep's Head Way (www.thesheepsheadway.ie), a walking trail of over 60 miles (100km), has been designed with loop walks of one to two hours; maps are available locally. The views to the north and south are superb. Stop at the Tin Pub in Ahakista to experience old-style hospitality, then explore the nearby megalithic stone circle, signposted as part of the waking trail. Near Kilcrohane is a plaque commemorating the novelist J.G. Farrell *(Troubles, The Siege of*

Krishnapur) who was swept out to sea while fishing from the rocks in 1978, shortly after moving to live in the area.

THE SHORES OF BANTRY BAY

The town of **Bantry** ❽ is distinguished only by its setting on the shores of **Bantry Bay**. **Bantry House and Gardens** (www.bantryhouse.com), a short walk from the town centre, is a large, mid-18th century mansion with a magnificent setting overlooking the famous bay (which is 4 miles/6.4km wide). The gardens have been reinvigorated over the years to striking effect, including an ancient wisteria artfully trained onto a circular trellis and the interesting selection of pots and statues decorating the pathways, collected on travels over the years.

Inside, there is a fine collection of treasures, including Aubusson carpets, Gobelin tapestries, Russian icons, Chinese lacquer and a mixture of French and Irish 18th-century furniture.

Head inland from Bantry via **Kealkil** to visit **Gougane Barra**, a deep tarn which is the source of the River Lee. The lake is surrounded on three sides by steep precipices, which run with cataracts after heavy rain. **St Finbar's Oratory**, a small stone-built chapel (a 20th-century replica) on an island in the lake, can be reached by a causeway. This is believed to be where St Finbar lived in the 6th century before founding his monastery in Cork city. A pilgrimage is still held on the first Sunday after St Finbar's Feast Day, 25 September. There's something quite special about this place, particularly if you can appreciate it early, before the daytrippers arrive.

GLENGARRIFF

The N71 climbs above Bantry Bay into open, more rugged country, offering ever-changing views across the bay. **Glengarriff** ❾, a wooded glen with a sheltered harbour warmed by the Gulf Stream, has an especially mild climate, with an average annual temperature of 52°F (11°C). Azaleas, rhododendrons, magnolia and camellias grow in abundance. **Glengarriff Bamboo Park** (www.bamboo-park.com; charge) has walks through over 30 different species of bamboo and palm trees with superb sea views.

Glengarriff village is teeming with craft shops, serving coaches en route to Killarney. Take a ferry from the pier to **Ilnacullin Gardens** (www.harbourqueenferry.com) on **Garnish Island**, five minutes offshore. Allow about an hour and a half. Don't miss the formal Italian Garden, with colonnades and a terrace heightening the contrast between the classical man-made beauty of the garden and the wild mountain scenery that surrounds it. Alternatively, you can take a boat trip around the harbour without landing on the island. Except in very bad weather, you will see families of basking seals on the rocks between the mainland and the island.

THE RING OF BEARA

The **Ring of Beara** (www.ringofbeara.com) is less well known than its neighbour

Bantry House.

to the north, the Ring of Kerry, yet it also offers impressive scenery. It is a favourite haunt of walkers, cyclists, birdwatchers and people who enjoy natural beauty. Although the drive covers only about 68 miles (110km), much of it is on narrow, winding roads, so allow a full day.

The **Beara Peninsula** stretches for about 30 miles (48km) southwest from Glengarriff, forming the north side of Bantry Bay. The **Caha** and **Slieve Miskish** mountains run down the centre of the peninsula, and the road around it is mainly on a narrow coastal plain.

A shorter route to Kenmare, avoiding the Ring of Beara, can be taken at Adrigole, about 12 miles (19km) beyond Glengarriff. The R574 climbs north across the peninsula in a series of small but sharp hairpin bends, leading to the **Healy Pass** (1,083ft/330 metres). Stop here to enjoy a panoramic view of Bantry Bay to the south, with the Kenmare River and the MacGillycuddy's Reeks in the north. Turn right at Lauragh on to the R571 Kenmare road.

The Ring of Kerry.

Many would consider **Castletownbere** ⑩, with a population of about 850, little more than a village, but it is a busy working port, home to Ireland's largest white fish trawling fleet. Get a feel for the place by walking along the quays and admiring the brightly coloured fishing fleet. The film director Neil Jordan, who has a house nearby, is one of several international celebrities to have fallen for the charms of this remote spot. **McCarthy's Bar** in the main square will be familiar to readers of Pete McCarthy's humorous travel book of the same name: he is pictured on its cover having a pint with a nun. It is a traditional bar-cum-grocery shop, and still does a roaring trade supplying victuals to the town's many trawlers.

Leave town on the R575 for **Allihies**. After about 5 miles (8km) a sign on the left indicates the Dzogchen Beara Retreat Centre (www.dzogchenbeara.org), a Buddhist mediation centre with hostel, and in summer a café. Visitors are welcome to join daily meditation at their cliff top centre, or simply enjoy the gardens and sea view.

Allihies village is a straggling line of brightly coloured cottages set between sea and hills (now augmented by replica cottages, mainly second homes), and was built for the copper miners working in the hills behind it. The sandy beach at **Ballydonegan** was formed of spoil from the mines. The **Allihies Copper Mine Museum** (www.acmm.ie) complete with café, explains the history of mining in the area, from the Iron Age to the arrival of Cornish miners in the 19th century, and the subsequent departure of many miners for Butte, Montana when the mines closed in the 1950s. Walk up to the abandoned mines (marked by tall brick chimneys) and enjoy the views of sea and wild hillside. You can walk from here to the next village, **Eyeries** (7 miles/11km), on a grassy footpath that forms part of the Beara Way. Even if you only walk a few miles of it, the peace and isolation will be memorable.

The road between Allihies and Eyeries, another village of small, brightly coloured houses, is one of the highlights of the Ring of Beara. In good weather the **Iveragh Peninsula** isclearly visible to the north, across the **Kenmare River**, as are the conical shaped **Skellig Islands** off its tip. You will get a closer look at these rocky islands from the Ring of Kerry.

Derreen Gardens (www.derreengarden.com; charge) were planted 100 years ago beside Kilmakilloge Harbour, a sheltered inlet on the south shore of the Kenmare River. The woodland gardens run down to the water's edge and contain many azaleas and rhododendrons, massive stands of bamboo and groves of New Zealand tree ferns – all of which thrive in the mild air warmed by the Gulf Stream.

Kenmare ⓫, an attractive little town backed by hills, has a good selection of shops and restaurants. Guided boat trips of the Bay are run from Kenmare Pier by Seafari Seal and Eagle Watching Cruises (www.seafariireland.com). The **Kenmare Heritage Centre** (tel: 064-6641233; Apr–Sept) explores themes of local interest, including lacemaking. Sheep are still traded from makeshift pens at the traditional Friday market.

KILLARNEY

Killarney ⓬ (www.killarney.ie) may be the most commercialised area in the Southwest, but it is still possible to avoid the crowds and enjoy the lakes and hills. The romantic scenery of boulder-strewn, heather-clad mountains, deep blue lakes dotted with wooded islands and wild woodland has been preserved within a large national park. Avoid the town by day. Killarney isn't a great place to shop for crafts, as it caters chiefly for the first-time visitor, but it is always useful to visit the Tourist Information Office beside the central car park for details of special events, festivals, guided walks, and Gaelic Games (hurling and football).

Enjoying a visit to Killarney is largely a matter of attitude. You won't appreciate it from the inside of a car. One great pleasure here is the damp woodland aroma that permeates the mild air. As in the rest of Kerry, it is important not to be put off by rain. Any weather, good or bad, tends not to last long around here. In fact, the lakes of Killarney look especially good when seen through a light drizzle.

Arriving from Kenmare, you may decide to stop on the N71 as it passes through Killarney National Park, to climb the path beside the **Torc Waterfall** and enjoy the view.

KILLARNEY NATIONAL PARK

A nice contrast to the wildness of Torc can be found across the road in **Muckross Park**, a neatly trimmed lakeside area with gravel paths that forms the nucleus of the **Killarney National Park** Ⓐ (www.killarneynationalpark.ie). This is a car-free zone, and it is a good place to take a ride on one of Killarney's famous jaunting cars (open horse-drawn carriages). The drivers (jarveys) are traditionally great talkers. Don't

The path to Ross Castle.

be surprised if you hear a phone ring during your quaint ride; the jarveys use their mobile phones to line up their next customer. Jarveys are now obliged to use 'dung catchers' on their horses when driving through Muckross Park.

Muckross House **B** (www.muckross-house.ie; charge), built in the 19th century in the Elizabethan style, houses a folklore and farming museum. You can admire the rhododendrons and azaleas in the formal gardens free of charge.

Muckross Traditional Farms **C** (optional joint ticket with Muckross House) is a largely outdoor attraction with a healthy walk between three different-sized farms, all inhabited by chatty, well-informed guides (disguised as farmers), illustrating farming methods before electricity and the internal combustion engine. This may be your only chance to get up close to a pair of Irish wolfhounds: huge but gentle creatures that live on the middle farm.

Ross Castle **D** (tel: 064-663 5851; Apr–Oct; free) is a 14th-century castle keep that has been fully restored and furnished. You can hire a rowing boat here, and take a picnic over to **Innisfallen Island** **E** about 1 mile (1.6km) offshore. The wooded island has the remains of an abbey founded about 600AD, which is famous for the *Annals of Innisfallen*, a chronicle of world and Irish history written in this remote and beautiful spot up to 1320 by a succession of monastic scribes.

Consider taking an organised half-day coach-horse-and-boat trip through the **Gap of Dunloe** **F**, a narrow mountain pass formed by glacial action. The organised trip has the advantage of allowing you to travel through the Gap on foot or horseback and then go back to town by boat without having to retrieve your car.

The Gap itself is an unpaved path that stretches for 4 miles (6.4km) between the **MacGillycuddy's Reeks** and the **Purple Mountain** **G**, which gets its name from the heather that covers it in the autumn. There is no motor traffic, but in summer there is a constant stream of ponies, jaunting cars and

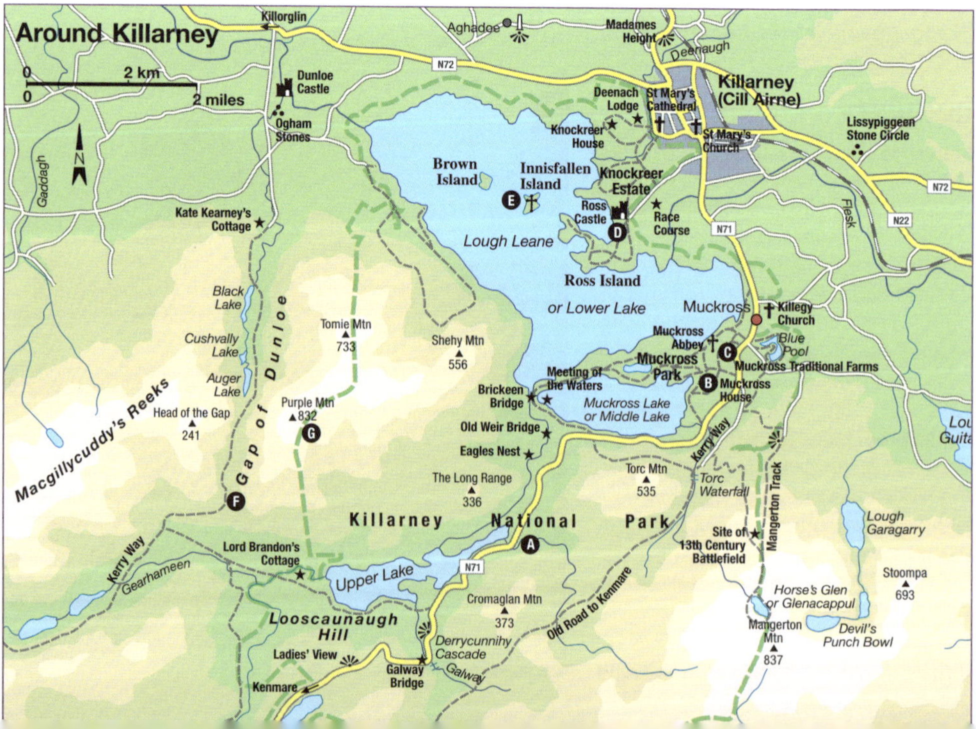

pedestrians. The scenery is first-rate, with a chain of five small lakes beside the road, and massive glacial boulders, but don't expect solitude.

THE RING OF KERRY

You can drive non-stop around the 112 miles (180km) of the Ring of Kerry (www.theringofkerry.com) in under four hours, but allow a full day as you will want to make several stops. The Ring of Kerry is justifiably famous for its combination of lush, sub-tropical vegetation and rugged seascapes. In July and August the narrow two-lane road can be clogged by a slow procession of tour buses (Kenmare Coach and Cab, www.kenmarecoachandcab.com; and O'Connor Autotours, Killarney, www.oconnorautotours.ie are two good options) and RVs. A less congested option is to do the Ring of Beara instead or to make your way straight to Dingle.

Killorglin ⓭ is a busy village which makes the most of its strategic position on the road between Killarney and Dingle. Its focal point is now a modern square at the top of the town. It is famous for the Puck Fair – Ireland's oldest fair, dating back to pagan times, held annually from 10–12 August. On the first day, a mountain goat is crowned King Puck, garlanded with ribbon, and installed on a tall throne overlooking the town, where it stays until the evening of the third day. Horse trading in the traditional manner is still a feature, along with plentiful free entertainment. There are good walks nearby in Glenbeigh Woods and on Rossbeigh, 3-mile (5km) long sandy beach.

Cahersiveen ⓮ (pronounced 'cah-her-sigh-*veen*') is the chief market town for the Iveragh peninsula. Don't expect a buzzing metropolis, but the revamped 56-bed Skellig Star hotel in town is a sign of Ireland's improving fortunes (helped along by Star Wars tourism in recent years).

The Barracks (www.theoldbarrackscahersiveen.com) is a community-led heritage centre occupying an exotic-looking, white-turreted building. The story goes that it should have been built in India, on the Northwest Frontier, but the plans

Red deer in Killarney National Park.

were mistakenly sent to Ireland. In fact, its architect, Enoch Trevor Owen, habitually built in what he called the Schloss style, and looked at from another angle, his design suits the hill-backed location very well. But why spoil a good story? Nowadays it houses an amusing and informative series of exhibitions.

Follow the sign outside The Barracks to the pier. The prettiest part of Cahersiveen is its backside, which overlooks the wide estuary of the River Ferta and the green hills beyond.

VALENTIA ISLAND

Look out for signs to the Valentia Island car ferry (April–Sept daily 8.15am–10pm) about 3 miles (5km) west of Cahersiveen. This lands you in **Knightstown** at the eastern tip of **Valentia**, a sleepy place that is eerily quiet with just a couple of bars. The island is 6.75 miles (11km) long and 1.7 miles (3km) broad, with a population of about 700. It takes its name from the channel between the island and the mainland, Beale Inse, and has nothing to do with Spain. The relative lack of traffic here and wonderful sea views make it a good destination for walkers; maps are available locally; don't miss the Tetrapod footprints near the Slate Quarry, made by a precursor of the dinosaur. The original transatlantic cable connecting Europe with Newfoundland was laid from here between 1857 and 1865. Valentia is connected to the mainland by a causeway at **Portmagee**. The **Skellig Experience** (www.skelligexperience.com; Apr–Oct), beside the causeway, offers visitors a remote look at the islands, but for the real deal, opt instead for a boat trip (www.skelligsrock.com; Apr–early Oct). There are two types of tour, with the more expensive one landing on Skellig Michael. Note: the water can be rough, and bad weather leads to cancellations, sometimes for several days.

Skellig Michael, the largest of the three islands, was inhabited by monks from the 7th until the 12th centuries. It rises in a cone shape to a double peak 712ft (217 metres) high. A flight of 600 steps lead to the monastery, built of dry stone with no mortar. Enthusiastic

Dingle harbour.

guides, all trained archaeologists, live on the island June–August, to supervise visitors and tell them the island's history. The popularity of this super remote craggy outcrop has soared since the latest instalment of the *Star Wars* saga hit the big screens, with shooting for key scenes in *Episode VII* (*The Force Awakens*), and *Episode VIII* (*The Last Jedi*) taking place on Skellig Michael.

A SCENIC DRIVE

If the weather is good, take the scenic road from Portmagee to Waterville through **Ballynahow**, along an impressive arc of coast and mountains with great views of the Skelligs.

Rejoin the main Ring road just before **Waterville** ⓯, a popular base for golfers, and anglers who have a choice of deep-sea fishing in Ballinskelligs Bay or angling on Lough Currane, half-a-mile inland.

The next stretch of road is one of the most scenic stretches, winding along the edge of **Ballinskelligs Bay** through rocky coastline backed by rugged green hills. **Derrynane House** (www.derrynanehouse.ie; charge) is a mile beyond **Caherdaniel**. The house belonged to national hero Daniel O'Connell (1775–1847), remembered for championing Catholic Emancipation (securing civil and voting rights for Catholics), finally achieved in 1829. The 320 acres (130 hectares) of woods surrounding the house (year-round; free) have pleasant walks and access to an attractive sandy beach.

Castlecove is a small, friendly place with good sandy beaches. A narrow lane beyond the church climbs 1.75 miles (3km) to **Staigue Fort**. This is a well-preserved example of a prehistoric stone fortress, dating from 1500 BC. It consists of a circular dry-stone wall, 115ft (35 metres) in diameter, varying in thickness from 13ft to 5ft (4 to 1.5 metres). A series of steps in the walls lead to a platform with good sea views. The landowner requests a small donation.

Sneem ⓰ is another pretty village, laid out English-style around a village green beneath a semi-circle of low mountains. Some of the charm has been lost following over-intensive development of holiday homes. Turn your back on these and walk down the road beside the Blue Bull (signposted 'Pier') past an attractive communal garden. Looking back through the reeds you can appreciate Sneem's sheltered location between the sea and the hills.

Sneem marks the start of the most sheltered part of the Ring of Kerry's coast. Here you will see lush, subtropical growth – wild rhododendrons, azaleas, camellias and bamboo – evidence of the benign effect of the Gulf Stream. The N70 continues past Parknasilla, a large hotel resort with pleasant walks in its wooded waterside grounds, on to Kenmare, where the N71 leads to either Killarney or Glengarriff.

THE DINGLE PENINSULA

The weather can make or break a visit to **Dingle** ⓱ (also signposted as An Daingean, its original, official, name);

Beehive stone huts on Skellig Michael.

see page 197). If the sea mist is down, consider postponing your trip. At Killorglin take the N70 to Castlemaine, and in Castlemaine take the R561, which gives good views across the bay of the coast of the Iveragh peninsula. **Inch** has 4 miles (6.5km) of sandy beach backed by dunes. There is safe swimming and the surf is suitable for beginners. The beach is also popular with shore anglers and walkers. There is free parking, and a couple of simple cafés.

Dingle has a population of about 1,500, which can treble in summer. Its tourism was boosted by the filming of *Ryan's Daughter* in 1969. In the years following 1985, a wild dolphin, Fungi, made the area its home much to the delight of locals and tourists and a bronze statue commemorates it on the pier. Skippers tout for business, offering 'money-back if no dolphin sightings' deals.

Dingle, where you will hear the Irish language spoken in everyday dealings, is very popular with visitors, and offers good restaurants and lively music pubs. A triangular 10-minute walk from the pier area, up Green Street (the best place for craft shops), down Main Street and back along the Mall to the pier takes you past most of the shops, pubs and restaurants.

An Diseart (Green Street; www.diseart.ie; grounds free) is a huge 19th-century convent, converted into an Institute of Spirituality and Celtic Culture. Its walled gardens and graveyard create an oasis in the town centre, and the building has beautiful stained-glass windows in pre-Raphaelite style.

Continue west on the R559. Between **Ventry** and Slea Head there are over 400 *clocháns* ('beehive' huts). The farmers charge you a nominal sum to visit them. These small conical huts of unmortared stone are not prehistoric, as the farmers claim; the oldest date from the early Christian period, the 5th to 8th centuries, and were used by hermit monks. Others were built within the past 100 years or less to house farm implements: there is little timber in these parts, so it is cheaper to build with stone. Dunbeg Fort, just beyond Ventry, is an excavated

Slea Head.

Iron Age promontory fort dating from about AD 800, built on a cliff edge – too close, perhaps, as the site and adjacent visitor centre were forced to close due to coastal erosion in 2018. The *clocháns* half a mile further on, which look out to the Skellig Rocks, are worth visiting. The road then climbs westward around Eagle Mountain to **Slea Head,** and has good panoramas.

THE BLASKET ISLANDS

The group of seven rocky islands offshore are the **Blasket Islands**. The **Great Blasket,** the largest one, is about 4 miles (7km) long and 0.75 mile (1.5km) wide. It was inhabited until 1953. The islanders were great storytellers and have made a lasting contribution to Irish literature. **The Great Blasket Centre** (www.blasket.ie; closed Nov–Mar) tells their story using many old records and photographs. Below Mount Eagle is the village of **Dunquin**, a scattered settlement whose harbour was once the landing point for the islanders. Stop at Dunquin Pier, and walk down the steep, concrete path.

At the time of writing, the Blasket Islands ferry is not operational (check for updates www.blasketislands.ie), but half- and full-day eco boat tours visit the island regularly when weather permits (www.marinetours.ie), leaving from Ventry.

ON TOWARDS TRALEE

Gallarus Oratory (well signposted) is an extraordinary little building of unmortared 'dry' stone, which probably dates from the 8th century. It is in the shape of an inverted boat, with a door at the west and a window in the east wall. It remains as dry and solid as the day it was built, and is very dark inside.

Avoid the **Conor Pass** in bad weather – take the N78 through Annascaul instead. The drive is hair-raising in all weathers as you climb steeply to 1,496ft (456 metres) above sea level.

Both roads meet at Camp on the N86 Tralee road.

Tralee ⓲ (pop. 23,750) is the county town of Kerry, but don't expect a lot. While it may seem like a booming metropolis after a few days in Dingle,

Summer comes to Ventry Strand.

DINGLE'S FIGHT TO SAVE ITS NAME

A new law in 2005 decreed that all Irish-speaking places must use the Irish-language version of their place name, and that only the Irish-language version can appear on legal documents, maps and signposts. The Dingle Peninsula is known as Corca Dhuibhne (pronounced *'corka ghivnah'*) in Irish, but Irish is spoken only at the far western tip of the peninsula, which is where the new legislation comes into effect. But the people of Dingle Town, officially within the Irish-speaking area, are reluctant to lose a name that they consider is effectively an international brand name, worth millions to its thriving tourist industry. Many refused to call their town An Daingean.

A local plebiscite was held in 2006. It favoured the bilingual name Dingle Daingean uí Chúis (the fortress of O'Cush – pronounced *'dangan ee quish'*), but the central government argued that complex legislation would be needed to create an exception to the rule protecting Irish-language place names. Meanwhile, the name 'Dingle' was used by most local businesses, and the same government's tourist publications, while the legal arguments continued in Dublin. The Irish-language sign for An Daingean at the town's entrance was defaced by graffiti to read DINGLE. Finally, in 2013, the long-running (and bad-tempered) debate was settled, with bilingual road signs erected.

Tralee is essentially a quiet market town. In August it comes to life briefly for the **Rose of Tralee Festival** (www.roseoftralee.ie), a beauty and personality pageant. The town's most attractive area is near the museum: the **Town Park** and **Denny Street,** with its nicely proportioned Georgian houses. The park is the headquarters of **Siamsa Tíre** (www.siamsatire.com), Ireland's national folk theatre, which stages nightly performances in summer.

The enjoyable **Kerry County Museum** (http://kerrymuseum.ie) is in a neoclassical building at the top of Denny Street. The country to the north of Tralee is the flatter, more sheltered part of Kerry. Take the R551 north from Tralee to **Ardfert**, a small village with the impressive ruins of a large 12th-century cathedral (tel: 066-713 4711; May–Sept; ruins: free).

Access to the long sandy beach at **Banna Strand** and a monument commemorating Roger Casement's landing from a German submarine in 1916 can be had about 2 miles (3km) north of Ardfert.

BALLYBUNION

The road continues to **Ballybunion**, a small seaside resort famous for its championship golf course, dramatic cliff walk and sandy beaches. Beside **Lady's Strand** is Ballybunion Seaweed Baths (tel: 068-27469; Jun–Sep), where farmers came to ease their aching bones after harvest time A warm seawater bath is still a great tonic, especially on a rainy day.

Listowel, a quiet little place, with a large main square, is known for **Listowel Writers' Week** (http://writersweek.ie) which takes place every June. The remaining 15.3m-tall towers of its 13th century Listowel Castle (tel: 086-385 7201; June–Aug, guided tour only; free) can be climbed by an external staircase, giving views of the River Feale and the town square below. There is an attractive walk along the riverside. From **Tarbert** on the banks of the Shannon Estuary a car ferry runs to Killimer in Co. Clare (www.shannonferries.com), providing a scenic alternative to a long detour through Limerick.

Festival time in Tralee.

THE IRISH LANGUAGE

Even though the most famous Irish writers wrote in English, Irish is the Republic's official language. But how many people can speak it fluently?

From the foundation of the Irish Free State back in 1922, enormous efforts were made to encourage everyone to learn and use the language – including making it compulsory at school and awarding extra marks for answering in Irish in examinations.

THE GAELTACHT

The new Irish State also designated geographical areas, most along the western seaboard, as the Gaeltacht. Within them, people use Irish all the time, and residents receive grants from the government to promote the language and cultural heritage. There are sizeable Gaeltacht areas in counties Donegal, Mayo, Galway and Kerry as well as smaller parts of counties Cork, Waterford and, the only inland area: Meath. Generations of Irish teenagers have spent part of their summer on subsidised holidays in these areas – sent home if they speak English.

Visitors from overseas can also spend their holidays in Gaeltacht areas, learn some Irish, and enjoy pubs with traditional music sessions and *céilís* (literally translated as 'dance gatherings'). Check out www.oideasgael.ie.

Such is human nature that compulsory Irish at school had the opposite effect to its intent on the general population of the Republic. While everyone educated here has some knowledge of the language, until recent decades they usually denied they did, while using some words in conversation: *craic* (fun) probably the most commonly heard.

Attitudes to the language have changed over the last two decades, particularly in the Republic. A grassroots movement developed to increase the number of all-Irish schools – *gaelscoileanna* – where all subjects are taught through that language. Since the 1980s the number of schools has steadily grown into the hundreds across the country for both primary and secondary level with over 50,000 students.

IRISH-LANGUAGE MEDIA

There's been an Irish language radio station since 1972, Raidió na Gaeltachta, run by State broadcaster RTÉ, joined by the television service TG4 in 1996. There's also the Dublin community radio station Raidió na Life, and BBC Northern Ireland provides about 40 hours a week of radio in Irish. The 2016 Census revealed that use of the language had dropped in Gaeltacht areas, from 96,090 people, down from 96,628. It also showed that among the general population aged 3 and up, 39.8 percent use it daily correlating to over 1.7 million. How well these people speak it is another matter.

The growth of all-Irish schools and the increased viewing share for TG4 year on year, despite huge competition from overseas channels, show that an enthusiasm for the language survives. And on road signs in the Republic it shares equal billing with English.

The popular slogan 'Guinness is good for you' in Irish.

Dunguaire Castle.

LIMERICK AND THE SHANNON REGION

Just beyond Limerick is a landscape of ruined castles and wonderful caves, the dramatic coastline a stark contrast to the moonlike landscape of the Burren.

Main attractions
King John's Castle
St Mary's Cathedral
Bunratty Castle
Ennis
Lahinch
Cliffs of Moher
Doolin
Lisdoonvarna
The Burren

Maps on pages 202, 208

The counties of Clare and Limerick constitute most of this region where golfing, fishing, walking and surfing are all popular activities. The Cliffs of Moher rise almost vertically out of the sea and north of them lies the mysterious Burren, a bleak, seemingly endless expanse of land that is almost moonscape in its appearance, peppered with pretty Alpine and Mediterranean wildflowers.

LIMERICK CITY

Limerick ❶ is a modern city (urban population 94,000) with a medieval core on King's Island. It is more than 1,000 years since Viking traders established a sheltered seaport at the head of the Shannon estuary. But even today the city is full of historical reminders.

The bulk of the city lies to the east of the River Shannon, and footpaths give access to the wide, fast-flowing Shannon, its best asset. For decades, the city's high levels of crime (magnified by feuds and drug wars), has been a thorn in the side of the tourist authorities, but an active regeneration programme is making headway in changing the city's outlook.

An attractive riverside path, the Spokane Walk, skirts the Shannon and leads from the Tourist Information Office at Arthurs Quay Park, and over a steel footbridge to King John's Castle, so that the entire medieval quarter can comfortably be visited on foot while enjoying riverside views. Pubs and cafés with outdoor tables and a thriving weekend farmers' market add to the lively ambience.

The **Tourist Information Centre** Ⓐ (20 O'Connell St; tel: 061-317 522; www.limerick.ie; Mon–Sat 9am–5pm; free) offers details of historical guided city tours, including *Angela's Ashes* walking tours of locations in Frank McCourt's memoir.

The Curragower Bar, Clancy's Strand.

KING JOHN'S CASTLE

To get a feel for the history of the place it's best to start in the medieval quarter. The top attraction here is the 13th-century **King John's Castle** B on King's Island (https://kingjohnscastle.ie). The castle is one of Ireland's most impressively sited Norman fortresses, with curtain walls and drum towers surviving. Climb one of the round towers for an excellent view of both river and town. An interactive display recounts Limerick's history from its foundation by the Vikings in 992 AD and there are fun medieval games and exhibitions for kids.

Look into the elegant **Bishop's Palace** C (Church Street, King's Island www.limerickcivictrust.ie), the former Palace occupied by the Church of Ireland Bishops from 1661 to 1784. Walking tours of Georgian Limerick depart from here; phone for details. The Palladian-style Palace houses a Hall of Fame Room comprising portrait drawings of 23 local people honoured for their outstanding achievements. One of these is the late Richard Harris, a rugby star turned actor, who enjoyed a cinema career spanning 50 years, including a starring role in the *Harry Potter* films.

A short walk across Thomond Bridge takes you to the **Treaty Stone** Ⓓ, a rough-hewn limestone block raised on a pedestal. Tradition has it that on this rock the Treaty of Limerick was signed in 1691 marking the surrender of the city to William of Orange. The treaty promised that the government would respect Catholicism, but it was rejected by the English and Irish Parliaments, and Limerick was thus dubbed the 'City of the Broken Treaty'. The Latin inscription on the stone is taken from Virgil's description of Troy: 'It was an ancient city, well versed in the arts of war.'

Back across the river, in Castle Lane, the **Limerick City Museum** Ⓔ is based in a granary-style building housing more than 60,000 objects illustrating historical aspects of the city and surrounding areas (www.limerick.ie; free).

LIMERICK'S CATHEDRAL

A short distance along Nicholas Street is what many regard as the *pièce de résistance* of the city's sights – **St Mary's Church of Ireland Cathedral** Ⓕ (www.cathedral.limerick.anglican.org; charge). Founded by King Donal Mór O'Brien on the site of his palace, it is the oldest building in constant use in Limerick and there is at least one daily service. Built in the form of a cross, it incorporates both Romanesque and Gothic styles.

The Romanesque West Door is magnificent, the black oak misericorde (mercy) choir stalls are carved with animal features, and there's a pre-Reformation altarstone, a leper squint window, and stained-glass windows. The Cathedral hosts many civic and musical events and has an unbroken tradition of choral music for more than 800 years.

HUNT MUSEUM

From the Cathedral, cross over the Matthew Bridge and on Rutland Street you will come immediately to the former Custom House, now the **Hunt Museum** Ⓖ (www.huntmuseum.com). This superb private collection contains 2,000 original works of art and antiquity. They

George's Quay and the Locke Bar.

range from the 9th-century enamel Antrim Cross, to Egyptian, Roman and Etruscan pieces, Chinese porcelain, works by Picasso, Renoir and the great Irish artists Jack B. Yeats and Roderic O'Conor. The collection was assembled by John Hunt, a medievalist, and his wife Gertrude, and left to the nation on his death in 1976.

Limerick is full of delightful architectural surprises. From Rutland Street, a brisk 20-minute walk through the main shopping area (allow more time for window shopping) along O'Connell Street leads to the spacious streets of the Georgian area, a district known as **Newtown Pery**. Turn a corner in this area with its well-ordered geometry and you'll be enchanted by a church, a square or a terrace of houses with brightly painted doors and semi-circular fanlights.

THE CRESCENT AND ST JOHN'S SQUARE

The Crescent Ⓗ consists of elegant four-storey houses and has been well restored. Now mostly offices, they are occupied by accountants, solicitors and the like. From here Barrington Street leads to Pery Square and the **People's Park** Ⓘ where workers bask on the grass at lunchtime with their sandwiches. No. 1 Pery Square, one of a fine terrace of houses built around 1830 overlooking the park, has been restored and is now a boutique hotel with a popular bar and bistro. Another, the **Georgian House and Garden** can be visited on the Limerick Civic Trust's walking tour, or by appointment (www.limerickcivictrust.ie/walking-tours).

Make a short detour down Parnell Street and along Upper and Lower Gerald Griffin streets to take in the exquisite **St John's Square** Ⓙ. This 'square' is in fact a three-sided terrace of houses with a basement and three bays. The mid-18th-century houses are the earliest Georgian development in Limerick and were originally occupied by the gentry as town houses during the winter.

St Mary's Church of Ireland Cathedral.

ART GALLERIES

Music and the arts are flourishing in Limerick. The **Belltable Arts Hub** Ⓚ (69 O'Connell Street, www.limetreetheatre.ie) boasts a 220-seater venue and three rehearsal spaces. The **Limerick City Gallery of Art** Ⓛ (http://gallery.limerick.ie; free) in Pery Square was once a Carnegie Library. Its permanent collection of Irish art ranges from the 18th century to the 21st, and it has a nice contemporary art selection, too. Zest coffee shop is on site to stop for refreshments. The gallery is the focal point of a city-wide Biennial of Contemporary Art – EVA (www.eva.ie) – a major event on Ireland's visual arts calendar.

THE UNIVERSITY

The **University of Limerick** (www.ul.ie) Ⓜ in the suburbs at Plassey, north of the Dublin Road, has established a reputation as Ireland's leading university in industry-led research. It is a showcase for contemporary Irish architecture and sculpture, and hosts concerts and musical events ranging from pop to classical.

Apart from its vibrant artistic side, the city is renowned for its passion for sport and one game in particular. For more than 100 years rugby has been part of the lifeblood of Limerick, played by all sections of the population. Some wags joke that the city has three cathedrals: St Mary's, St John's and Thomond Park, the 'cathedral' of rugby fans, not just in Limerick, but throughout the entire Province of Munster.

Rugby is the game of the people, stirring passionate support and local loyalties. The oldest senior club, Garryowen, has even given its name to the game's international vocabulary – the Garryowen, called after the traditional attacking ploy: the 'up and under'.

SHOPPING CENTRE

Many familiar chain stores have branches in Limerick. The liveliest part of the shopping district is the pedestrianised Cruise's Street area, off O'Connell Street. At numerous cafés, many with outdoor tables you can choose from the usual range of espressos, mochas, cappuccinos or lattes. You will also stumble across antique dealers, barbers, victuallers and saddlers, and Fox's Bow, an alleyway with quirky shops. The restored **Milk Market** N (www.milkmarketlimerick.ie), at Corn Market Row, comes alive every Friday, Saturday (the busiest day, open from 8am–3pm) and Sunday. A great range of food is on offer: cheeses, fish, seaweed, sausages, jams, chutney and breads, as well as organic farm produce. Sunday is the day for antiques, books, CDs, and vintage clothing. A canopy provides protection against the weather.

SOUTH OF LIMERICK CITY

Attractions to the south include museums, visitor centres and charming villages. **Lough Gur** 2 (www.loughgur.com), 12 miles (19km) south of Limerick on the N24-R514 near Bruff, is one of Europe's most complete Stone Age and Bronze Age sites. It has a

Milk Market.

A MELTING POT

In Limerick you are likely to hear Polish, Russian or Estonian spoken as much as you will hear English. It is home to Ireland's second largest Polish community after Dublin, with an estimated 10,000 living and working in the city. There are numerous shops selling Polish food, drink, newspapers and magazines. The Polish in Limerick have their own website, http://PolskiLimerick.com.pl, and the local newspaper, the *Limerick Leader*, runs a weekly column in Polish. A Polish Arts Festival (www.polishartsfestival.ie) takes place every year, too.

There is also a large African community, from Nigeria, Ghana, Somalia, the Congo and elsewhere. The churches established by African Christians hold lively Sunday services, which is a welcome new component of the city's culture.

horseshoe-shaped lake, rich in birdlife. The **Grange Stone Circle** is 150ft (45 metres) across and contains about 100 boulders. More than 20 other stone circles, tombs, hut foundations, lakeside dwellings and ring forts have been excavated beside Lough Gur.

An interpretative centre built in the form of Neolithic huts houses a collection of artefacts and has an audiovisual presentation introducing the site. Guided walks can be booked in advance.

Adare ❸, 10 miles (17km) southwest of Limerick, is one of Ireland's prettiest villages. Several of its stone-built cottages are thatched, and they all have colourful front gardens. Adare is noted for its antique dealers, but don't expect bargains.

The **Adare Heritage Centre** (www.adareheritagecentre.ie; free, charge for exhibition) has a Tourist Information Centre (tel: 061-396 255) with free maps of the village, and a helpful history display. The 14-arch bridge over the River Maigue dates from medieval times and leads to the Augustinian Friary built in 1315, and now Adare's Anglican church. The cloisters were converted into a mausoleum for the Earl of Dunraven in 1826 and the church was restored in 1852. A metal stile beside the church leads to a charming riverside walk of about a mile, which loops back to the village centre down Station Road.

Opposite the Augustinian Friary is the entrance to the lovely **Adare Manor and Golf Resort**, now a luxury hotel. It is steeped in history and has been painstakingly maintained. It also has one of Ireland's finest parkland courses and regularly hosts Irish and international golf tournaments. Entry is restricted to guests and golfers only.

Adare Manor was the seat of the Earls of Dunraven, who built the picturesque, thatched cottages that line the village for their workers. The original 18th-century manor was enlarged in the Gothic Revival style in the mid-19th century. In its grounds are the ruins of the 14th-century **Desmond Castle** and of a 1464 Franciscan Friary, accessible by a separate entrance.

Lough Gur.

CITY OF SIEGES

Limerick was besieged three times in the 17th century as Britain strove to subdue the Irish. The first blockade, in 1651, was led by Oliver Cromwell as part of a merciless campaign after the execution of Charles I. By the time the citizens surrendered five months later, 5,000 had died of disease or starvation.

The other two sieges, in 1690 and 1691, were linked to William of Orange's campaign to secure the English throne against the Catholic James II. After James fled to France, many of his supporters holed up in Limerick. William's first siege failed to dislodge them. The following year a more determined siege sapped the citizens' morale and they signed the Treaty of Limerick, which promised religious liberty and restoration of property but was not honoured.

FLYING MUSEUM

On the south bank of the Shannon Estuary, **Foynes** ❹ played an important part in aviation history. In the late 1930s flying boats would land on the sheltered stretch of the Shannon between Foynes Island and the shore, having made the transatlantic crossing from Newfoundland. The award-winning **Foynes Flying Boat Museum** (www.flyingboatmuseum.com) commemorates those days with models and photographs, and includes the original terminal building, radio room and weather forecasting equipment – the only such museum in the world. It was during this time that Irish Coffee – a mix of coffee and whiskey topped with whipped cream – was invented by barman Joe Sheridan, who wanted to cheer up a group of cold, travel-weary passengers who had been forced back by bad weather.

SHANNON CROSSING

There is a pleasant drive along the flat wooded shores of the wide Shannon estuary to **Tarbert** ❺, where a car ferry will take you across the Shannon Estuary in 20 minutes to County Clare. The ferry is often accompanied by a pod of about 100 bottlenose dolphins, whose presence will be announced over the loudspeakers.

NORTH OF LIMERICK CITY

This is castle country, with ruined stumps of crumbling tower houses dotted around the place. There were once more than 420 tower houses in the Shannon area. Few are as imposing or as carefully restored as Bunratty whose rectangular 15th-century keep is surrounded by four corner turrets, each topped with battlements and a set of flags.

Bunratty Castle and Folk Park ❻ (tel: 061-361 511; daily 10am–5pm) is strategically placed on the road between Shannon Airport and Limerick city. It contains furniture and paintings from the 15th and 16th centuries. The Folk Park behind it consists of 25 acres (10 hectares) of reconstructed and fully furnished farmhouses, cottages and shops, as they would have appeared to

Adare Manor.

a visitor to mid-western Ireland in the late 19th century. There is even a village street with blacksmith, pub, drapery, print works and post office. **Durty Nelly's**, an old-world Irish pub next door to the village, has been copied all over the world.

Another corny but enjoyable experience is the medieval Irish banquet, a purely tourist-oriented but good-natured event – essentially a meal with Irish cabaret during which the guests are serenaded by Irish colleens – which takes place twice nightly at Bunratty and at the nearby **Knappogue Castle** (tel: 061-360 788) at Quin, to the north of Bunratty. Knappogue is a 15th-century Macnamara stronghold, also restored and furnished in period.

THE CRAGGAUNOWEN PROJECT

The **Craggaunowen Project** ❼ (www.shannonheritage.com/Craggaunowen) is built in the grounds of another castle, a 16th-century tower house. The project has reconstructed authentic replicas of dwelling places in prehistoric and pre-Christian Ireland. On an island in the lake, reached by means of a footbridge, is a *crannóg*, a fortified dwelling of clay and wattle. A small ring fort, which shows how a farmer would have lived in the 5th or 6th centuries, has been built. Also at Craggaunowen is the traditionally built boat in which the writer and adventurer Tim Severin sailed to Nova Scotia in 1976, retracing the legendary 6th-century voyage of St Brendan, and making a plausible case for its historical reality.

To escape from the beaten path of the castle trail, consider an outing to **Scarriff** ❽, a quiet little town set on high ground overlooking Lough Derg. It is a rural backwater, popular with visitors in summer and sleepy in winter, which has a reputation for traditional music. **Drewsborough House** near **Tuamgraney**, to the south of Scarriff, is the birthplace of the novelist Edna O'Brien who has written scathing descriptions of the inhabitants of this area, which was considered remote 50 years ago.

Both Scarriff and Tuamgraney are on the scenic drive that goes all the way around **Lough Derg** ❾, a wide, almost sea-like part of the Shannon River, which is popular with watersports enthusiasts. It is worth taking in at least the 5-mile (8km) stretch northeast to **Mountshannon**, a neat 18th-century village. Offshore you can visit **Holy Island**, an uninhabited 49-acre (20-hectare) island that had a 7th-century Christian settlement. There are the remains of five churches and a 79ft (24-metre) high round tower. **St Conran's Church** in Tuamgraney is based in a 10th-century church that is the oldest church in continuous use in Ireland.

ENNIS

Ennis, a busy market town 23 miles (37km) west of Lough Derg, has an inviting cosiness, partly due to its size and human scale but also because a bypass has diverted much of the traffic. Ennis prides itself as being 'Ireland's friendliest town'. The Tourist Information Office (www.visitennis.com) is on Arthur's Row, off O'Connell Street.

The same building is shared with the library and **Clare Museum** (www.clarelibrary.ie/eolas/claremuseum; free), which tells the story of 6,000 years of history through the *Riches of Clare* exhibition.

Ennis Friary (www.heritageireland.ie) is a Franciscan Friary founded by the O'Brien Kings of Thomond in the 13th century. The well-preserved ruins consist of a nave, chancel, belfry and cloister.

Ennis is known as a centre for traditional Irish music and dance. Performers and students (many of them youngsters) flock to the Fleadh Nua (www.fleadhnua.com) a competitive festival for musicians and dancers held annually at the end of May. Traditional musicians gather in the local pubs and hold impromptu music sessions year-round too, all of which can be enjoyed for the price of a drink – ask locally where to go. More formal, ticketed events, and the finals of the Fleadh Nua are held at **Glór Theatre** (Friar's Walk; www.glor.ie; free). The striking modern building hosts well-known touring acts on the Irish music scene, locally produced drama, and there is a craft gallery and coffee shop onsite, too.

KILRUSH

Moving down to the coast, **Kilrush** ❿ is 5.5 miles (9km) west of Killimer where the car ferry from north Kerry docks. Kilrush, with a population of 3,290, is the biggest town on the coast of west Clare. It was designed by a local landlord in the 18th century to complement his estate.

The style chosen for the town is pleasantly neoclassical, with wide streets and a main square big enough to accommodate horse fairs. Traditional livestock fairs (mainly horses, donkeys and sheep, with side stalls) are held in the square on the first Thursday of March, June and October.

The ruins of the Vandeleur family mansion, which was destroyed by fire in 1897, are at the centre of the

Bunratty Castle.

420-acre (170-hectare) Kilrush Forest Park. The **Vandeleur Walled Garden** (Vandeleur Demesne, Killimer Road; www.vandeleurwalledgarden.ie) is enclosed behind old stone walls at the centre of a woodland estate, and has a courtyard with a coffee shop and a Victorian-style glasshouse displaying unusual and tender plants.

A 15-minute boat ride from Kilrush Creek Marina (Griffin Boat Hire; tel: 065-905 1327; Apr–Oct daily) will take you to **Scattery Island** which has a 6th-century monastery founded by St Senan, the remains of five churches and a round tower. The monastery was plundered by Vikings before being recaptured by Brian Ború. There is a Visitor Centre on the island, and guided tours are available free. Dolphin-watching cruises run by the **Shannon Dolphin and Wildlife Foundation** (Kilrush Creek Marina; www.shannondolphins.ie; June–Sept) operate daily in summer, weather permitting, to watch families of bottle-nose dolphins playing in the estuary. Another firm, Dolphin Discovery (www.discoverdolphins.ie) also operates from Kilrush Marina in the summer.

Kilkee ⓫, 8.5 miles (13km) to the west, is on the Atlantic coast of Clare, as opposed to the banks of the Shannon Estuary, and has a sandy beach. The village has been rather overwhelmed by bland developments of holiday homes (it is traditionally a favourite weekend spot for Limerick City people), but its centre retains an old-world charm. There is a scenic drive south to Loop Head lighthouse, a round trip of about 34 miles (55km). At **Carrigaholt** ⓬ a 16th-century tower house stands beside the pier with good views from its top floor across the Shannon Estuary to north Kerry.

LAHINCH

The west-facing beaches, where long rolling waves break on the sand after their Atlantic crossing, are popular with water sport enthusiasts all the way up the coast to **Lahinch** ⓭ (sometimes spelt Lehinch) also famous for its golf links. This part of the west Clare coast

A sandy beach in Lahinch.

has become the haunt of some of the world's leading surfers because of the immense size of its waves. A 'new' wave, Aill na Searrach (the leap of the foals) or Aileens to its friends, was first successfully surfed in 2005, and has attracted many of the world's leading surfers. Aileens is hidden at the base of cliffs and rises to epic proportions of up to almost 40ft (12 metres). Those hoping to conquer it do so with the help of a jet-ski. The Clare waves suit surfers of all abilities when conditions are right and it is the country's fastest-growing sport. For an updated daily surf report visit www.lahinchsurfshop.com; for general information on surfing in Ireland contact the Irish Surfing Association; www.irishsurfing.ie.

From Lahinch, **Ennistymon** ⓮, 2.5 miles (4km) inland is a charming, old-fashioned resort town on the Cullenagh River, which has retained many original wooden shop fronts and some friendly pubs. The river has a series of waterfalls visible from its seven-arched bridge.

THE CLIFFS OF MOHER

Towering to 650ft (214 metres) high and stretching for 5 miles (8km), the **Cliffs of Moher** ⓯ on the west coast of Clare have always been a popular destination. But with upwards of 1 million visitors a year tramping across them, erosion began to set in calling for an extension of old paths, elevated viewing platforms, more seating and the ecological reconstruction of the cliff wall and grass.

For those who wish to keep dry and warm, the whole experience can now be enjoyed in the sparkling New Visitor Experience (www.cliffsofmoher.ie; charge). The centre was 17 years in the planning and cost more than €31 million. It is largely hidden from view as it has been subsumed into the contours of the landscape and covered by a hillside. As you approach, the building appears to be in darkness – the idea being to create a dimly lit cave-like effect. Parking is included in entry (much cheaper if booked online), and there are ATM facilities.

DOOLIN CAVE

Just over 3 miles (5km) away you come to an experience that should feature on the itinerary of every tourist to County Clare: **Doolin Cave**, Pol an Ionáin 'the ivy cave' (www.doolincave.ie). One of the world's biggest freestanding stalactites, 'The Great Stalactite', opened in 2006 after a 15-year battle over planning permission. The stalactite – it's more than 600,000 years old – was discovered by two English cavers in 1952 and is an extremely popular draw.

A minibus driver brings you the short distance to the entrance where you are given a hard hat and torch before descending 125 steps to experience a stunning subterranean world and a memorable sight. The visitor is plunged into darkness and then in a flash the subtly lit stalactite appears before you in the main chamber. The stalactite

The Cliffs of Moher.

THE CLIFFS OF MOHER

The Visitor Experience exhibition will teach you all about the ridged Cliffs of Moher, a protected haven for many species of seabirds.

Formed by layers of siltstone, shale and sandstone, the Cliffs of Moher have long been recognised and protected. In 1988 the area around them was designated as a Refuge for Fauna and the following year became a Special Protection Area for birds. The layering of rock has led to the development of narrow horizontal ledges that provide nest sites for seabirds including fulmars, guillemots, razorbills and puffins. The area is Ireland's most accessible breeding site of puffins, and hundreds of pairs of these comic-looking birds nest there. The designation includes the cliffs, cliff-top maritime grass and heath, and a 200-metre zone of open water.

MOHER RANGER TOURS

For the real elemental experience and to properly feel the gustiness of the wind on your face and see the waves booming below, you should walk up to the edge.

The sheer cliffs are what make this coastline so beautiful.

With binoculars you can look across to Liscannor Bay or pick out the Aran Islands. Friendly and knowledgeable 'Moher Rangers' will guide you round and explain the significance of the site, taking you up to O'Brien's Tower built in 1835 by Cornelius O'Brien, a descendant of Brian Ború, the High King of Ireland. The best time to spot the sea birds is at the height of the breeding season from early May to the end of July. You should have fine views of puffins wheeling in to land and be able to pick out rows of guillemots and kittiwakes crouched precariously on ledges.

INTERPRETIVE CENTRE

The Visitor Experience's exhibition area features the Atlantic Edge (an optional multimedia exhibition) incorporating the themed zones of ocean, rock, nature and man. It includes the Ledge, computer-generated images of life above and below water that lets you see close-up the natural world from a bird's-eye perspective. You can also take a Clare journey with a high-definition cinematic aerial tour of varied landscapes tracked on a map of the county.

A touch screen displays the changing earth over geological time; there are views of cave interiors and explanations of Clare's underground rivers. The human history of life has not been neglected and a rich fund of legends from the area are told through taped interviews and displays. It's a long way from the 1950s when a local guide, Dinney McMahon, realised he could make a living from trading to tourists at the cliffs. He sold postcards, tin whistles and *shillelaghs* (a traditional knotty walking stick/weapon with a large knob at the end, made out of wood, also known as blackthorn sticks), and charmed visitors with stories of local gods as well as the habits of the birds. He died of a heart attack at 80 while making his way to his stand on the cliffs; a memorial stone marks the spot.

One of Europe's busiest tourist attractions, the cliffs are worth a half-day visit. If you enjoy walking, follow the 5-mile (8km) waymarked trail from Doolin (part of the Burren Way), and experience the cliffs in the old-fashioned, pre Visitor Centre mode. This is one of Ireland's most popular locations, as the numerous clips on YouTube confirm, and always manages to stir something within the imagination. In high season, get there early before the crowds.

hangs more than 20ft (7 metres) from the ceiling and weighs in at 10 tons – and it is still developing. The cave tour takes one hour and numbers are limited to 20.

DOOLIN

Doolin ⓰ (also called Roadford on some maps) consists of a long straggle of B&Bs, hostels and hotels, several restaurants, craft shops and three pubs. The pubs are renowned for traditional music. Some young musicians spend the whole summer camping here, learning from their elders.

Doolin Ferries (www.doolinferries.com) and The Cliffs of Moher Cruises (www.mohercruises.com; Apr–Oct) both run a service from Doolin Pier to the three Aran Islands (Easter–Oct), and also offers a tour of the Cliffs of Moher.

LISDOONVARNA

Moving inland to **Lisdoonvarna** ⓱, if you visit the Burren Smokehouse (www.burrensmokehouse.ie) you will be shown an exhibition kiln and smoke box with a short audio-visual presentation of the smoking process in action. The town developed as a spa centre for tourists due to the healing properties of its sulphurous spring water (the baths, alas, are no more). Today its main claim to fame is its **Matchmaking Festival** in September when shy farmers meet women under the direction of Willie Daly, a third-generation matchmaker, horse whisperer and publican (his bar is at 1 Main Street, Ennistymon). The festival now offers a matchmaking website and speed dating (www.matchmakerireland.com).

Music is a permanent soundtrack to the lives of the people of Clare. The next village on the southern fringe of the Burren, **Kilfenora** ⓲ is famous for the Kilfenora Ceilí Band (www.kilfenoraceiliband.com), a group of local traditional musicians which celebrated its 100th anniversary in 2009, and tours throughout Ireland and to the UK and USA. It is also the home of the **Burren Centre** (www.theburrencentre.ie; charge to exhibition). A multi-dimensional

Doolin coastline.

exhibition tells the story of the Burren and there is an informative video presentation. The centre also houses a tourist information point, exhibition area, craft shop and tea rooms.

Next door to the centre it is well worth a look at the 12th-century **St Fachtnan's Cathedral** with its fine collection of medieval High Crosses. A sloping glass roof has been installed on the north chapel to protect the crosses from the elements. Information panels outline the details of the crosses, the most famous being the impressive Doorty Cross with its bishop holding his hand up in blessing.

THE BURREN

Travelling east from Kilfenora you come to the beautifully proportioned ruin of **Leamaneh Castle** where you turn north, entering the hauntingly magical kingdom that is the **Burren** ⓳.

This is botanical holy ground of a high order, a meeting place of plants from the Arctic, the Alps and the Mediterranean. Over 70 percent of Ireland's native flora is found here, including 24 species of orchid and 25 types of fern. The best-known flower in this wild rock garden is the spring gentian *(Gentiana verna)* a dazzling small blue plant that can be seen in April and May. Search hard and you will find it growing alongside brightly coloured magenta geraniums, early purple-orchids and swathes of creamy mountain avens all sprouting from the grykes (vertical crevices that lie between the pavement). The clints are the glacially polished horizontal surfaces that you walk across and which occasionally wobble.

The Burren is renowned as a place of geological and archaeological wonder. Miles of gunmetal grey ancient stone walls thread in all directions. Everywhere there are giant boulders – glacial erratics – that were dropped by the glacier. These rock refugees are part of the topographical outdoor decor of the place and have stood for 15,000 years.

Spend just a short time here and you will quickly realise why the Burren means 'rocky place'. It is a Karst landscape hewed from stone: stone monuments, stone cottages, stone fields, pavement, rocks and walls. With a patina all its own, it is unlike anywhere else in Ireland.

Irish dancing sculpture in Lisdoonvarna.

CARRON

Follow the road from Leamaneh Castle to **Carron** where you will see a *polje*, a geological term for a depression in the limestone and where a turlough, or seasonal lake (full of fresh water in winter and entirely dry in the summer) is to be found. Carron has the **Michael Cusack Centre** (www.michaelcusack.ie). Cusack (1847–1906) was the founder of the world's largest amateur sporting organisation, the Gaelic Athletic Association. The 19th century herdsman's cottage where Cusask grew up has been fully restored. The centre tells the story of his life from his humble origins in Carron through his travels and careers. Nearby, the Burren Perfumery & Floral

Centre (www.burrenperfumery.com; free) highlights the sensory side of the Burren and has a café serving delicious home baking and other organic food.

Now retrace your route back to the main road and you will come to **Caherconnell Visitor Centre** (www.burrenforts.ie). This centre explains the circular and walled farmsteads found throughout the Burren that are known locally as 'Cahers'. There are more than 500 of them, including the spectacular Cahercummaun. The best preserved is found at Caherconnell.

POULNABRONE

A short distance north you will see from the road what is unquestionably Ireland's best known, most-visited and most-photographed megalithic burial tomb, the **Poulnabrone** (the pool of the sorrows) portal dolmen with its huge capstone. Ancient, baffling, yet strangely familiar as its image is reproduced all around you on postcards, T-shirts, book covers and holiday brochures; it was built about 4,500 years ago.

Each day numerous tour coaches stop at this dolmen, which, although now roped off for protection, is in its natural state. A timeline on a signboard interprets its significance and puts it in context with information on the surrounding flora.

The dolmen was excavated in 1986 and the remains of 22 bodies – 16 adults and six children, male and female – were discovered. The bodies were reckoned to be at least 1,500 years old.

AILLWEE CAVE

Follow a twisting road with hairpin bends down Ballyallaban Hill for 3 miles (5km) and you come to another underworld adventure, **Aillwee Cave** (www.aillweecave.ie), discovered around 1940 by a herdsman. Guides accompany you on a 35-minute tour through caverns, over bridged chasms, under weird formations, past pale threads of straw stalactites hanging down alongside waterfalls. The Burren Birds of Prey Centre (same contact details) is

The Burren.

located at the cave, and puts on flying displays of falcons, hawks and owls.

BALLYVAUGHAN

Picturesquely sited **Ballyvaughan** ⑳ (pop. 220) is the best base for exploring this unique landscape. The village has two hotels, pubs and cafés and a bicycle hire business – one of the best ways of appreciating the Burren is on two wheels.

Each May, Ballyvaughan hosts **Burren in Bloom** (www.burreninbloom.com), a month-long programme of talks and tours. Illustrated talks on the flora, birdlife, archaeology and geology as well as history and folklore tours, ghost tours of Aillwee Cave, workshops, concerts and traditional music nights are all on the packed itinerary.

Before heading north out of the Burren it's worth a short detour off the main road to explore the well-preserved ruins of **Corcomroe Abbey**. Now roofless, this Cistercian abbey was built shortly after 1195 in a serene valley near Bell Harbour. According to legend, the stonemasons who built it were executed when they had finished their work to prevent them building a more beautiful church elsewhere.

KINVARRA

There is a pleasant scenic drive along the south shore of Galway Bay to **Kinvarra** ㉑, a charming fishing village at the head of Galway Bay with a grassy quayside and an alternative spelling of Kinvara. It is popular with visitors who enjoy its old-fashioned pubs and modern restaurants. The highlight of the year is the annual Cruinniú na mBád in mid-August, 'the gathering of the boats'. In this festive regatta, traditional Connemara sailing craft – the brown-sailed Galway Hookers, which were once used to carry turf across the bay – race against each other in a grand spectacle.

In spring, the Fleadh na gCuach, 'the cuckoo festival', a traditional Irish music event, attracts large crowds.

The floodlit **Dunguaire Castle** (tel: 061-360 788; May–Oct) is a four-storey tower house built by the shore in 1520.

Kinvarra.

At night this lonely sentinel is used for medieval banqueting, hence the floodlighting. A recent addition to Kinvarra is **Murphy Store,** (tel: 091-637 760) a 200-year-old listed building on the quayside that has been restored from dereliction. Originally used as a grain store, it is now a coffee and craft shop specialising in seaweed-based products from Ireland's west coast. The work of local artists and potters is also on display.

In the centre of Kinvarra, it's well worth visiting a small café and gallery run by **Burrenbeo** (www.burrenbeo.com), an information and education resource, with a good selection of books on the Burren.

YEATS ASSOCIATIONS

The final leg of a Shannon journey takes the visitor to **Gort**, a pleasant market town with a large main square, on the main road from Ennis to Galway. It is known locally as 'Brazil', as it has a large community of Brazilian residents, mostly from the same area in northeast Brazil, who came to Ireland originally to work in the meat-processing industry. Gort Forge is mentioned by the poet W.B. Yeats, who restored the nearby castle, **Thoor Ballylee** ㉒ (www.yeatsthoorballylee.org; May–Sept and for special events) a 16th-century tower house that was the summer home of the Nobel prize-winning poet from 1917 to 1928. Follow the signposts from the N18 for 3 miles (5km) to enjoy this secluded location in a wooded area beside a stream.

The tower house, which Yeats bought for £28, was discovered for the poet by his benefactor, Lady Gregory (1852–1932), herself a playwright and collector of folklore. Her house at **Coole Park** ㉓ (Coole Park Visitor Centre; www.coolepark.ie; grounds free), 2 miles (3km) northwest of Gort was demolished in 1947, but its grounds are now a nature reserve.

In the walled garden stands a great copper beech tree, the famous 'Autograph Tree' on which Lady Gregory's guests – Yeats, the playwrights George Bernard Shaw, J.M. Synge and Sean O'Casey, the poet John Masefield and the painter Augustus John – carved their initials.

Dunguaire Castle.

THE BURREN

North Clare contains a strange landscape, a treeless limestone plateau that's a place of pilgrimage for botanists and geologists.

A frustrated general serving Oliver Cromwell, one of the many ruthless invaders from across the Irish Sea, famously condemned this bleak place as having 'not enough wood to hang a man, not enough water to drown him, not enough clay to cover his corpse.' The view probably hasn't changed much in 350 years, but now the Burren (meaning great rock) is a national park. It covers 200 sq miles (500 sq km) of lunar-like limestone formation with delicate flora and fauna of Arctic, Alpine and Mediterranean origin, brought to the area by migrating birds. Here you will find, in seasonal abundance – but protected by the State – orchids, the purple bloody cranesbill and azaleas. The Burren is also an area of potholes, seasonal lakes, caves and streams.

THE VIEW FROM CORKSCREW HILL

Properly appreciating the extraordinary nature of the place requires some study. The Burren Experience (www.burren.ie), on the northside of Ballyvaughan village, on the Kinvarra road, gives an introduction, but a finer overview can be had at the original Burren Centre (www.theburrencentre.ie), to the south in Kilfenora village. A good overall view of this 'stony district' can be had from the so-called 'Corkscrew' Hill on the road linking Ballyvaughan with Lisdoonvarna, but by far the best way to explore the fissured terrain is on foot.

Scattered throughout the region are tombs, chambers and dolmens of the Stone Age – notably, near Corkscrew Hill, the famous Poulnabrone Dolmen, dating from 2,500 BC.

The origin of this bleak limestone terrain lies 70 million years ago. Shells of marine animals were compacted on the seabed and later pushed above the waves by geological shifts. A soft rock, the limestone has been eroded by wind and rain, creating cracks and crevices which both drain off rainwater and provide shelter for the remarkable variety of fauna.

The Burren is home to many plants which flourish in its apparently inhospitable landscape. They are nurtured by a unique combination of soil, heat and moisture.

Carron, east of the Burren, means the Cairn and has yielded up useful archaeological evidence of Bronze Age life. The stones that today form walls to keep the wind at bay were then used to construct a great cairn 8ft high and 50ft in diameter (2.4 by 15 metres) which protected the bodies in the burial mound. At Kilnaboy, in the upland part of the Burren, is the great stone fort of Cahercommaun (7th–10th centuries).

Poulnabrone Dolmen.

The Tombs that have defied time

Poulnabrone Dolmen dates from 2,500 BC and is a striking example of the many ancient monuments which are particularly common in this part of Ireland because of the ready availability of limestone slabs. Its name means 'pool of sorrows'. Because its massive capstone is set at an angle, it has been fancifully been called a launching pad for a Stone Age missile.

Such single-chambered portal graves were originally covered with a mound of earth and stones, testament to the great reverence the Neolithic people had for their dead.

Passage-graves, in which the burial chamber was reached through a passage, reveal sophisticated building techniques and often-intricate abstract carvings. Some of Europe's most spectacular examples can be seen at Newgrange, west of Drogheda in County Louth.

Stone circles, which served as prehistoric temples, are probably related to the megalithic tombs. Some of the most impressive can be found at Lough Gur in County Limerick and near Hollywood in County Wicklow.

The most commons monument is the ring fort – about 30,000 survive. These were circular stone defences surrounding dwellings or royal seats.

It's surprising to find small green fields in such a stony landscape. But sheep farmers know how to survive the bleak winters in the west of Ireland. Animal farming flourishes due to the Burren's mineral wealth, which has especially helped horse breeding.

On the road through the Burren from Kinvarra lies the ruined Corcomroe Abbey, founded by Cistercian monks around 1195. Although Henry VIII dissolved the monasteries in 1554, the abbey's remoteness allowed the monks to remain for many years.

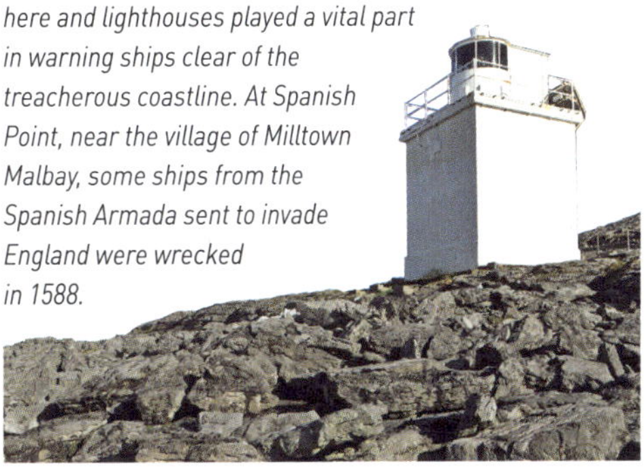

Co. Clare is very much part of the western seaboard, from its natural boundary of the Shannon estuary to its northern border with Galway. The full force of the Atlantic can be felt here and lighthouses played a vital part in warning ships clear of the treacherous coastline. At Spanish Point, near the village of Milltown Malbay, some ships from the Spanish Armada sent to invade England were wrecked in 1588.

Pretty Galway Bay.

GALWAY AND THE WEST

Beyond the liveliness of Galway city lies Connemara's wild, evocative landscape. Here Irish is still spoken and the beauty of the rural countryside, with its vast skies and empty hillsides, is spellbinding.

Main attractions
- Eyre Square
- Lynch's Castle
- Galway Races
- Lough Corrib
- Aran Islands
- Clifden
- Kylemore Abbey
- Westport
- Achill Island

Maps on pages 222, 226

The short-lived boom in the Irish economy led to rapid development in many parts of the west of Ireland, including Galway, which had long been a quiet backwater. These days Galway city, with a population of 80,000 is surrounded by a dual-carriageway ring road, which boasts 16 roundabouts and is frequently grid-locked. But as most people live in new suburbs, the city's historic centre and docks remain relatively unscathed.

Galway ❶ has developed a unique personality, combining a strongly Irish identity with cosmopolitan influences, epitomised by the broad cultural mix of the Galway Arts Festival (www.giaf.ie). Being a compact city with quaint shops and numerous pubs in a largely pedestrianised historic centre, Galway has become a popular party destination. The party often starts on the train, with beer and card games, as those who arrive by rail will notice. Spanish teenagers, Irish hen parties and couples on a city break all enjoy the unique atmosphere. Seafarers also like Galway, and it has twice been the final port of call for the Volvo Ocean Race, a 39,000-mile (62,800km) ocean-racing marathon that ends in a massive party.

THE MEDIEVAL CITY

The city lies on the northeastern shore of **Galway Bay**. Unlike Dublin, it wasn't conquered by the Vikings but was invaded by the Anglo-Normans in the 13th century. It developed strong trading links with France and Spain, rather than England and Wales, which has contributed to its unique character.

The medieval city grew up on the eastern bank of the River Corrib, inside the stone walls between 1232 and 1243, developing as a thriving port for wine, spices and fish. It became known as the 'City of the Tribes' because of the influence of 14 wealthy Anglo-Norman merchant families who ruled it as an

A Galway hooker in the bay.

independent city-state. These families held power in the town and county for many centuries. Each family had its own street and mansion with stone-faced designs. Remnants of the buildings and the stonework can be seen on a walk around the city.

THE MODERN CITY

The logical starting point, and the place where people travelling by bus and train arrive, is **Eyre Square**. The square, Galway's focal point and main public park, was presented to the city in 1710 by Mayor Edward Eyre. In 1963 it was where the US president John F. Kennedy made a speech after receiving freedom of the city, and it is sometimes referred to as John F. Kennedy Memorial Park. The square has been re-landscaped in a €10 million project, with a sweeping walkway, giving the city's iconic central point a much-needed facelift.

Fourteen flags, each one representing one of the Tribes, now fly along one side of the square. The adjacent **Quincentennial Fountain** Ⓐ, was erected in 1984 to celebrate the 500th anniversary of Galway becoming a city. The fountain is composed of sheets of iron depicting the area's distinctive sailing boat, the Galway hooker. Nearby is a newly restored statue of Pádraic Ó Conaire, a local author who wrote in Irish – the original of which was beheaded by vandals in 1999.

Browne's Gateway Ⓑ, the entrance to the town house of a merchant family originally built in 1617, is a cut-stone doorway and window, and stands beside the flags.

The **Fáilte Ireland Tourist Information Centre** Ⓒ (Forster Street tel: 091-537 700; www.galwaytourism.ie; Mon–Sat 9am–5pm) just off the eastern corner of Eyre Square on Forster Street, is well stocked with booklets, maps, postcards and gifts.

Galway is compact enough to not lose your bearings. The most notable ecclesiastical building is the Anglican Cathedral, the **Collegiate Church of St Nicholas** Ⓓ (www.stnicholas.ie). Built around 1320, it is the largest parish church of the medieval period in Ireland. Christopher Columbus is reputed

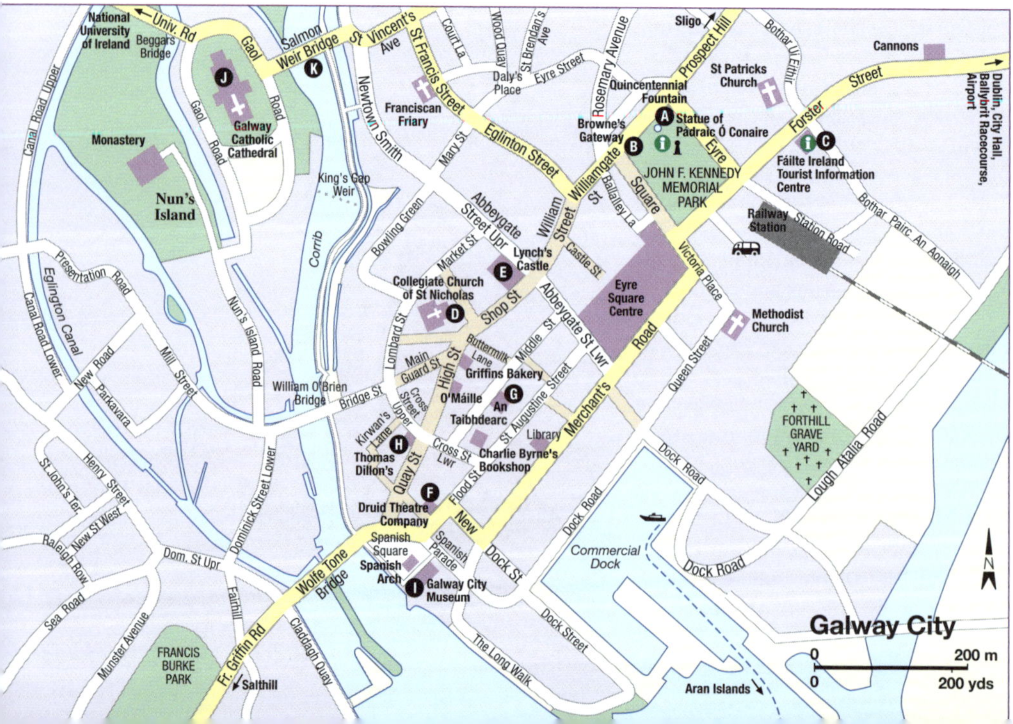

to have prayed here in 1477 before setting off on his voyage of discovery.

Outstanding features of interest inside the church include the Crusader's Tomb dating from the 13th or early 14th century with an inscription in Norman French, and a carved Baptismal Font of the late 16th or early 17th century. The **farmers' market** (www.galwaymarket.com; Sat 8am–6pm, also open Sun, bank holidays 12-6pm, Fri July–Aug & every day during Galway Arts Festival) beside the Collegiate Church of St Nicholas is not to be missed. It is one of the liveliest in the country, with organic vegetable growers from Connemara sharing space with sushi-makers, purveyors of Indian street food, flower sellers, wood turners and knitwear stalls, while buskers entertain with juggling and music.

LYNCH'S CASTLE

Another historic building is **Lynch's Castle** Ⓔ in Shop Street. This was the town house of the premier Tribe and is now a bank displaying in its foyer a series of wall panels telling the story of the castle. The castle – in fact a fortified town house – dates from the 15th century. The imposing smooth stone facade is decorated with carved panels and stonework, as well as gruesome gargoyles that include a lion devouring another animal, and a monkey and child. Inside, a reproduction of a 1651 map shows the symmetrical yet simple layout of the streets.

TRADITIONAL SHOPS

A stroll around Galway's streets is an assault on the senses. The streets that coalesce – **William, Shop, High** and **Quay streets** (the latter leading down to the Spanish Arch) are lined with dozens of restaurants and pubs, many with outdoor tables.

The survival of smaller independently owned businesses is part of the appeal. In Galway the usual corporate giants sit cheek by jowl with traditional, family run shops: drapery stores, cheesemongers, bakers, barbers, bespoke tailors and shops selling shooting and fishing tackle.

For more than 60 years, for example, the family-run **Ó'Máille's** (16 High Street; www.omaille.com) has specialised in handwoven tweed, including hand-knitted Aran sweaters. Its claim to fame is that it produced the costumes for John Ford's classic 1952 film *The Quiet Man*, filmed in the village of Cong, about an hour's drive north of Galway (see page 28).

Charlie Byrne's (The Cornstore, Middle Street; https://charliebyrne.ie) is a sprawling shop that stocks a huge selection of new and old books.

The centre of the city also buzzes with chic cafés, bakeries and bustling pubs. Two popular places include **Goyas Bakery** (2-3 Kirwan's Lane; https://goyas.ie) and Le Petit Delice (7 Mainguard Street; www.lepetitdelicegalway.com).

THE ARTS

Galway has a strong artistic and literary tradition, as evidenced by its rash

Open-air chess.

of festivals. The city's most celebrated drama group, the **Druid Theatre Company** **F** (www.druid.ie) on Flood Street, presents work by Irish playwrights and has built up an international reputation. The National Irish Language Theatre, **An Taibhdhearc** **G** (pronounced 'thive-arc'), is based in Middle Street, and holds summer shows and traditional singing and drama. For details of forthcoming events, visit www.antaibhdhearc.com.

THE GALWAY RACES

The Arts Festival is closely followed by the **Galway Races** (www.galwayraces.com), a week-long extravaganza running from late July to early August that brings thousands of people to the city in search of *craic*: after a day at the races the tradition is to party all night. Accommodation at this time is scarce, and prices shoot up: if you're not a racing fan, avoid Galway in race week. The races are held at **Ballybrit Racecourse** 3 miles (5km) to the east of the city near Galway Airport.

Gargoyle at Lynch's Castle.

THE CLADDAGH RING

Across the Corrib River, opposite the city, was the **Claddagh**, the original Irish settlement situated outside the city walls. There's little trace of the old, thatched cabins in the area's current modest housing, but the fishing village gave its name to the **Claddagh Ring.** This was a traditional ring with two hands holding a heart that wears a crown. The heart represents love, the crown is loyalty and the hands symbolize friendship. According to tradition, the rings were handed down from mother to daughter.

One of Galway city's oldest shops, **Thomas Dillon's** **H** (1 Quay Street; https://claddaghring.ie), established in 1750, sells fine gold and sterling silver examples of the ring. At the back of the shop, the small **Claddagh Museum** tells the story of this ring that is now a much sought-after fashion accessory and a symbol of romance.

GALWAY CITY MUSEUM

Galway City Museum **I** (Spanish Parade; www.galwaycitymuseum.ie; free),

FESTIVAL FEVER

The Galway Arts Festival (www.giaf.ie), is held during the last two weeks in July. This dynamic mixture of drama, music, poetry and dance showcasing local and national culture kicks off with a parade led by the flamboyant street theatre company, Macnas, whose name means 'joyful abandonment'. While the Cúirt International Festival of Literature (www.cuirt.ie), in late April, offers a cross-section of contemporary writing. It has hosted an impressive array of international talent including the Nobel Prize winners J.M. Coetzee, Nadine Gordimer, Derek Walcott and Seamus Heaney. Galway's compact city centre practically guarantees that you will be rubbing shoulders – or sharing a bar counter – with other festival goers and the big names, giving the experience an extra edge.

a fine building on the city side of the Spanish Arch that was another product of the boom years. The ground floor covers the contemporary city, emphasising the arts scene, and two upper floors focus on medieval and post-Famine Galway.

THE SPANISH ARCH

The only remaining gate of the Norman walls that surrounded the ancient city, the sturdy **Spanish Arch** was built in the late 16th century and still stands beside the **Fishmarket.** It took its name from the former trade with Spain and leads through to the **Long Walk** where small ships and boats are berthed and where you may sometimes come across a flotilla of swans.

The Fishmarket is an outdoor area used 100 years ago to load kelp on to carts to be sold as fertiliser. Nowadays this grassy open space with welcoming benches is a popular place for tourists to rest and young people to congregate, often entertained by the city's ubiquitous buskers.

THE CATHOLIC CATHEDRAL

From the Spanish Arch a pleasant riverside path will take you to **Galway's Catholic Cathedral** ❶ (www.galwaycathedral.ie) – or, to give it its full magisterial title, the **Cathedral of Our Lady Assumed into Heaven and St Nicholas.** Built between 1959 and 1965, the Cathedral with its copper dome has an impressive variety of interior art. The last great building to be built of natural stone in Ireland, its stained-glass windows depict John F. Kennedy, Christ rising from the dead and the Irish patriot Padraig Pearse, leader of the 1916 Easter Uprising.

A sight not to be missed on the river beside the cathedral is the **Salmon Weir Bridge** Ⓚ built in 1819. Lying north of the Church of St Nicholas, it is the last bridge upstream before the waters of the **Corrib River** open out into the lough. At the right time of year (generally early spring but sometimes later) hundreds of fish wait under the shadow of the bridge before making their way upstream to spawn in Lough Corrib.

Galway Arts Festival exhibition.

The West
0 10 km
0 10 miles
N
Stags of Broad Haven
Benwee Head
Portacloy
Downpatrick Head
Sligo Bay
Erris Head
Broad Haven
The Arches
305 Glinsk
Belderrig
15
Céide Fields
Ballycastle
Rathlackan
Lenadoon Point
Easky
Aughris Head
Doonamo Fort
Annagh Head
Knocknalina
Belmullet
Barnatra
Glenamoy
Benmore 351
Creevagh
Kilcummin
Killala Bay
Rathlee
Templeboy
Sligo
Corraun Point
Bunnahowen
Slieve Fyagh 331
Killala
Owenbeg
Knockalongy 543
Enniscrone
Mullet Peninsula
Drumreagh
Carrowmore Lake
Moyne Abbey
Rosserk Friary
Corbally
Inishkea North
Bangor Erris
Doobehy
Belville
512
Sligo
Inishkea South
Fallmore
Tristia
Ballina (Béal an Átha)
16
Bunnyconnellan
416
Masshill
Bellacorick
Eskeragh
Crossmolina
Slieve Gamph or Ox Mts
Doohooma
Slieve Car 720
Tobercurry
Blacksod Bay
Shranamanragh Br.
Keenagh
Errew Abbey
Mullany's Cross
Ridge Point
Nephin Beg 628
N26
Slievemore 671
Dugort
Nephin Beg Range
Nephin 804
Lough Conn
Corlee
N17
Croaghaun 667
Deserted Village
Castlehill
Derreen
Moy
Achill Head
Keel
628 Glennamong
698 Birreencorragh
Glen Nephin
Pontoon
Lough Cullin
Foxford
Callow
Charlestown
Dooagh
14
Srahmore
Lough Feeagh
Furnace Lough
Beltra Lough
Longford
Achill Island
Cashel
Achill
Beltra
Swinford
Dooega
Corraun Peninsula
Mulrany
Rockfleet Castle
Burrishoole Abbey
429 Croaghmoyle
Ross West
Strade
N5
Ireland West Airport Knock
Ashleam Bay
Carrickkildavnet Castle
521 Corraun Hill
Newport
Castlebar (Caisleán an Bharraigh)
18
Turlough
National Museum of Country Life
Mayo
Cloghmore
Newport Bay
Bruff Cross Roads
Bolinglanna
Clew Bay
Kiltamagh
Westport House
Balla
N17
Clare Island
Ballytoohy
Westport Bay
Westport
N5
Cloonkeen
17
Knock
12
461
Murrisk Abbey
11
13
Ballyhaunis
Kilsallagh
Murrisk
Louisburgh
Croagh Patrick 763
Ballintubber Abbey
Plains of Mayo
Ballynastangford
Roonah Quay
Emlagh Point
Kilgeever Abbey
Knappagh
Killavalley
Lough Carra
Claremorris
Brickeens
Inishturk
Cregganbaun
Carrowkennedy
Partry
Moore Hall
Ballygarries
Kinnadoohy
Mweelrea Mts
Sheeffry Hills
Doo Lough
761
Partry Mountains
Ballindine
Cloonfad
Tonakeera Point
Hollymount
Inishbofin
Bofin
Oceans Alive Visitor Centre
Delphi
Killary Harbour
Tourmakeady
Lough
Milltown
Aasleagh
Devil's Mother
Ballinrobe
Dunmore
Salrock
Mask
Foxhall
Cashleen
Kylemore Abbey
648
Kilmaine
N17
Ballynakill Harbour
10
Leenone
Maumtrasna
Neale
Carrowntanlis
Cleggan
Letterfrack
Bennacunneen 578
Cong
6
Ashford Castle
Aughrus More
Connemara National Park
Maumturk Mts
Clonbur
Cong Abbey
Shrule
Tuam
Streamstown
728
Finnisglin
Maum
Lough
Kingstown
Clifden
The Twelve Pins
Caggan
Bunnafollistran
Ross Abbey
Caherlistrane
8
9
Connemara
Leckavrea Mt 612
5
Corrib
Mannin Bay
Connemara Heritage & History Centre-Dan O'Hara Homestead
Recess (Sraith Salach)
Curraun
Greenfield
Headford
Moneen
Knockmoy Abbey
Clare
Toombeola
Maam Cross
Oughterard
Aughnanure Castle
Ballyconneely
Cashel
Shannawona 346
Knockferry
Ardrasodan
Slyne Head
Errisbeg
4
300
Roundstone
N83
Callow
Derryrush
Gortmore
Screeb
Rosscahill
Ballyconneely Bay
Glinsk
Tullokyne
Cloonboo
Turloughmore
Pearse's Cottage
Rosmuck
Claregalway
Mace Head
Carna
Kinvarra
Galway
Moycullen
M17
Ballybrit Racecourse
Carnmore
Athenry
Kilkieran
Bealadangan
St Macdara's Island
Mweenish Island
Lettermore Island
Costelloe
Corrib
M6
Casheen Bay
Salthill
1
Lettercallow
Rossaveal
3
2
Galway (Gaillimh)
Oranmore
Carraroe
Inverin
Barna (Bearna)
Clarinbridge
Lettermullan
Cashla Bay
Ballynahown
Spiddal
Gorumna Island
Carrowmore
Kilcolgan
North Sound
Galway Bay
Aughinish
Inishmore
Onaght
Oghil Church
Dunguaire Castle
Ardrahan
ATLANTIC OCEAN
Dún Aengus Fort
Oghil
Kilronan
Black Head
Corcomroe
Kinvara
Fanore
Bealaclugga
Coole Park
Temple Benen
Killeany
Ballyvaughan
Aillwee Cave
Thoor Ballylee
Aran
Inishmaan
Foul Sound
Slieve Elva 345
Gort
7
Islands
Inisheer
The Burren
Poulnabrone
Fardurris Point
Lisdoonvarna
Caherconnell
Lough Cutra
Leamaneh Castle
Boston
M18
Doolin
Burren National Park
Doolin Cave
Tubber
South Sound
Clare
Kilfenora
Killeen
Limerick

SALTHILL

Galway's small neighbour **Salthill** ❷ is just 2 miles (3km) along the coast, and offers an escape from the city streets as well as tremendous views of the wide expanse of **Galway Bay.** This resort was built in the early years of the 19th century. The walk from the city to the end of the promenade, where you must kick the rock before turning back, is a traditional, often bracing, Sunday afternoon activity for Galway residents.

As befits such a place, it has its quota of amusement arcades, discos and a fairground. **Leisureland** (Salthill Road Lower; www.leisureland.ie; free) is a family entertainment and amusement complex with three swimming pools and a waterslide. It is also used for concerts, exhibitions and conferences.

Atlantaquaria (Toft Park, Salthill; www.nationalaquarium.ie; charge), the country's national aquarium, is a good place to spend an hour on a rainy day and get acquainted with some of the 170 species of marine and freshwater life including seahorses, stingrays and the angel shark. The estuary exhibit shows the fish that make the mouth of the Corrib River their home.

CONNEMARA

Connemara, Galway City's hinterland, is full of lakes, bogs and mountains, but almost empty of people. Traditionally, its farming and fishing communities clustered around the coast, while its interior was inhabited chiefly by sheep farmers. Until Clifden was built in the mid-19th century, Connemara did not even have a town. It has always attracted visitors, especially painters who have found inspiration in the light and landscape. Two extensive ranges of mountains, the **Twelve Pins** (also known as **Twelve Bens**) and the **Maumturks**, dominate the views and attract walkers.

The visitor does not have to travel far from the city before entering the Irish-speaking area known as the **Gaeltacht.** The road signs are in Irish only. One of the first places you will come to is **Bearna** (Barna), which has a lively

Entertainment at the King's Head pub, Galway.

hotel, The Twelve, and a golf club with an 18-hole championship course. Much new housing, most of it architecturally undistinguished, has been built along this stretch of coast, which is now a commuter belt; if such developments offend, take the inland N59 road via Oughterard, turning off for Roundstone west of Recess. The coast road wends its way around bays and inlets and through a series of former fishing villages which become more picturesque the further you get from the city, including **An Spidéal** (Spiddal), **Casla** (Costelloe), **Scrib** *(Screeb)*, **Cill Chiarain** (Kilkieran), **Caiseal** (Cashel) and eventually **Roundstone**. The latter is a pretty holiday resort with a sheltered harbour for fishing and sailing boats, a little gem of a place, which has attracted many artists and writers. Here you re-enter the non-Gaeltacht part of Connemara before completing the journey to Clifden, the 'capital of Connemara'.

In both **Spiddal** ❸ and **Roundstone** ❹ local crafts thrive. **Spiddal Craft & Design Studios** (www.spiddalcrafts.com; free) offers visitors the chance to see artisan craftworkers putting their skills on display and to buy directly from them. Workshops include candle-making, leather work, pottery, screen printing, weaving and wood turning.

In a former Franciscan Monastery in Roundstone, a bodhrán-making business, **Roundstone Music, Craft & Fashion** (www.bodhran.com; daily; free) is a popular attraction.

LOUGH CORRIB AND CONG

If you chose the inland route (N59) to Roundstone via Oughterard, you will have distant views of **Lough Corrib** ❺, the Republic of Ireland's largest lake. Renowned for its salmon and brown trout, it also has a number of islands. You can take a day or evening cruise from Oughterard to **Cong** ❻ on the Mayo side of the lake, and sample its tranquillity from the water (www.corribcruises.com).

To reach Cong by car, drive around the lake via Maam Cross and Clonbur, a scenic hour's drive of 48km (30

Galway Cathedral.

miles). While Cong is best known for its associations with John Ford's film *The Quiet Man*, it is also a tranquil lakeside village surrounded by a wealth of archaeological remains including stone circles and burial mounds. There are also the remains of a 12th-century Augustinian abbey (village centre, freely accessible) with fine cloisters and a stone fishing hut. You can walk the mile from the abbey to Ashford Castle (www.ashfordcastle.com), one of Ireland's great castle hotels, on a lakeside path. The original building dates from the 12th century, but the existing castle, a splendid turreted affair, was built by the Guinness family in 1857 as a holiday home.

THE ARAN ISLANDS

During a holiday in Connemara, a side trip to the **Aran Islands** ❼ is regarded as *de rigueur*. Aran Island Ferries (www.aranislandferries.com), operates daily services from **Ros a' Mhil** (Rossaveal) on the Connemara coast, with a bus link to Galway City. An air taxi service to the three islands is run by Aer Arann Islands (www.aerarannislands.ie) from Connemara Regional Airport, a 45-minute drive east of Galway city. The flight takes less than 10 minutes; the ferry journey to Inisheer (the furthest island) is one hour. The three Aran Islands – **Inishmore, Inishmaan** and **Inisheer** – contain many pre-Christian and early-Christian remains. Visitors should carry waterproof clothes and wear shoes suitable for uneven terrain.

Inishmaan and Inisheer are small enough to walk. The best option on Inishmore, the biggest island, is to hire a bicycle in **Kilronan,** the main village: you can even opt for an electric bike if the hilly terrain is daunting (www.aranislandsbikehire.com). You can leave your luggage at the Inishmore Tourist Information Office (Kilronan, tel: 099-61263), which can also help you find B&B accommodation.

Fishing is still important to the islanders, but tourism has been growing significantly. As many as 2,000 day-trippers a day in peak season can visit

Connemara is characterised by lakes, bogs and mountains.

Inishmore, which has a permanent population of 900.

You can cycle or take a minibus to **Dún Aengus** stone fort on Inishmore, one of Europe's finest prehistoric monuments. Perched on the edge of a vertical 200ft (60-metre) cliff, it consists of four semi-circular defensive walls. The experts have failed to date Dún Aengus with any accuracy: some say 4,000 BC and others 1,000 BC. But, apart from its historic interest, the view from its ramparts is one of the most striking imaginable. On a clear day the sweep of coastline from Kerry and Clare to the south, as well as the length of Galway to the western extremity of Connemara is visible.

CLIFDEN

Back on dry land, **Clifden** ❽ the region's principal town, is a lively spot with a good choice of hotels, B&B accommodation and restaurants, and is one of the best places to buy traditional tweed. In August the town hosts the Connemara Pony Show, an annual highlight based around these small sturdy local ponies.

Clifden.

CONNEMARA NATIONAL PARK

Connemara National Park (Letterfrack; www.connemaranationalpark.ie; daily, visitor centre charge, park freely accessible) is an unfenced nature reserve covering 5,000 acres (2,000 hectares) and is rich in wildlife. A series of summer programmes serves up an enticing choice of walks, talks and special events.

Nearby, hidden away in the hillside beneath the Twelve Pins, is the restored cottage of Dan O'Hara, a tenant farmer evicted because he was unable to pay his rent and who has been immortalised in song and story. The cottage is now part of **Connemara Heritage & History Centre** ❾ (Lettershea; www.connemaraheritage.com; free) and gives visitors an insight into the life of a farmer in the west of Ireland just before the 1845 potato famine. The centre provides an audio-visual tour of Connemara through the ages with reconstructions of a *crannóg*

INSPIRED BY ARAN

The Aran Islands have long attracted artists, novelists, poets, philologists, and filmmakers. Robert Flaherty's 1934 film *Man of Aran* made the islands known worldwide and the playwright John Millington Synge wrote his book *The Aran Islands* while living on Inishmaan. It also inspired the plot of *The Playboy of the Western World*. Liam O'Flaherty, born on Innishmore is famous for his nature stories and as author of the novel *The Informer* (filmed by director John Ford in 1935 and starring Victor McLaglen).

Tourism to the islands was boosted in the 1990s by the British TV comedy series *Father Ted*, which featured the exploits of three priests on the fictional Craggy Island. An annual festival, 'Tedfest', is held on Inishmore in March. See www.tedfest.org.

Irish is the daily language of the people on Aran, but most are fluent in English.

(prehistoric artificial island home) ring fort and *clochán* (a dry-stone hut).

KYLEMORE ABBEY

The road between Letterfrack and Leenane features one of Ireland's most photographed buildings – the dramatically sited **Kylemore Abbey** ⑩. This late 19th-century limestone and granite building was erected by a Liverpool merchant as a gift to his son, and, until 2009 was run by the Benedictine nuns as a boarding school for girls. The miniature Gothic chapel, craft shop and restaurant are all open to the public (www.kylemoreabbey.com; charge).

The next village is **Leenane,** situated dramatically at the mouth of **Killary Harbour,** Ireland's only fjord, and marking the separation of counties Galway and Mayo. Its **Sheep & Wool Centre** (www.sheepandwoolcentre.com; charge) has live breeds, demonstrations of spinning and weaving, a multilingual historical video and, of course, a gift shop.

A choice of roads here will take you up to **Westport,** either via the spectacular **Doo Lough Pass** to **Louisburgh** or directly along the N59.

CROAGH PATRICK

Looming ahead you will see the unmistakable cone of **Croagh Patrick** ⑪, Ireland's holy mountain. The Reek, as it is known, is climbed in honour of St Patrick by more than 30,000 pilgrims – many of them barefoot – on the last Sunday in July. Some set out before dawn and many are still descending as darkness falls. The Visitor Information Centre (Murrisk; www.croagh-patrick.com; free) at the base of the mountain contains fascinating information about the archaeological discoveries on the summit. The remains of a dry-stone oratory were carbon-dated to between 430 AD and 890 AD. Across the road from Croagh Patrick, on the banks of Clew Bay, are the ruins of **Murrisk Abbey** (1456).

CLARE ISLAND

Clare Island ⑫ is well worth visiting to learn the seafaring exploits of Grace

The much photographed Kylemore Abbey.

O'Malley, or Granuaile (1530–1603), a pirate queen who preyed on cargo vessels; late in her life she audaciously journeyed to London to do a deal with Queen Elizabeth I, negotiating in their only common language, Latin. Clare Island has a population of about 350 and holds much interest for the botanist. It measures 3.5 by 1.5 miles (5.5km by 2.5km) and has a small hotel and some B&Bs. There is a ferry service (www.clareislandferry.com) that takes 15 minutes from Roonagh Harbour, Louisburgh.

WESTPORT

Picturesquely situated on the Carrowbeg River, **Westport** ⓭ a busy market town with colourful shop fronts, that attractively combines the old and the new, is designated as one of Ireland's heritage towns. Voted 'Best Place to Live in Ireland' by readers of *The Irish Times* it boasts a tree-lined riverside mall, fine Georgian buildings, an octagon, and myriad lovely pubs, including Matt Molloy's (www.mattmolloy.com) – owned by a famous flautist of the same name, who is a member of the Chieftains – where you can hear traditional Irish music most nights of the week. The town's quays, a ten-minute walk from its centre, are on Clew Bay, and the old warehouses have been nicely developed as tourist accommodation. This is the place for spectacular sunsets, to be watched, perhaps, from the terrace of one of the two waterside pubs. Don't miss **Clew Bay Heritage Centre** (www.museumsofmayo.com; free) at The Quay for a look back at the way people once lived.

One of Ireland's most historic homes, **Westport House & Country Park** (The Demesne, Westport; www.westporthouse.ie) is set in magnificent parkland on the outskirts of Westport and has attractions for children of all ages. It is owned by direct descendants of Grace O'Malley.

ACHILL ISLAND

In 1910 the Belfast artist Paul Henry set out for **Achill Island** ⓮ for two weeks.

View of Croagh Patrick.

He was immediately captivated by its beauty, tore up his return train ticket, and stayed nine years. Henry described it as 'a windswept island at the back of beyond'. But he felt it 'talked' to him and that he had been carried there 'on the currents of life'.

Top to bottom, Achill Island measures just 15 miles (24km) by 12 miles (18km). It is joined to the mainland by a causeway built in 1888 but once you cross **Achill Sound** a feeling of isolation and otherworldliness persists in the stark landscape. The island is largely shaped by the wet Atlantic climate and it rains with a grim persistence. About 2,500 people live on the island. In the winter the caravan parks, B&Bs, craft and coffee shops are closed, the scattered villages deserted, the numerous clusters of new holiday homes empty, and the long sandy beaches at **Keel, Dooagh, Trawmore,** as well as the silver and golden strands in the remote north side are deserted apart from wading birds. This is the best time to visit when you share the tranquil beaches with sanderlings, oystercatchers and golden plovers.

To get a feel for the past, take the narrow single-track road signposted to the **Deserted Village** on **Slievemore Mountain.** More than 70 roofless stone houses are all that remain of this village that in 1837 was the largest human settlement on the island. A single grassed-over street runs between the houses and even today there is a feeling of desolation about it.

The most scenic route on Achill is the **Atlantic Drive** that loops round the south of the island and takes in **Carrickkildavnet Castle,** a 15th-century tower house.

For more information, contact Achill Tourism (www.achilltourism.com) in Achill Sound.

THE MAYO COAST

Crossing back to the mainland again, continue along the remote north Mayo coast road and you will be startled by a pyramid-shaped building. This is the remarkable **Céide Fields** ⓯

HEINRICH BÖLL

Achill Island has long had a magnetic pulling power for writers, poets and painters. The German writer Heinrich Böll, who won the Nobel Prize for Literature in 1972, spent 35 summers on Achill, visiting the island right up until his death, aged 67, in 1985.

Böll lived in a cottage in Dugort (*Dubh gort*, meaning black field and pronounced with a heavy local emphasis on the second syllable sounding like 'du-gort'). The cottage, where most of his novels were written, is now a residential retreat for international and Irish artists and writers. When he first came to Achill, Böll said he felt like he was 'playing truant from Europe'. His *Irish Journal, A Traveller's Portrait of Ireland* (1957) shows a warm affection for the area as well as the country itself.

Achill Island beach.

(pronounced 'kay-jey') Visitor Centre (Ballycastle; tel: 096-43325). An extensive stone-age monument, the site includes field systems, dwelling area and megalithic tombs dating back 5,000 years. The bog's rare wild flowers and the spectacular cliffs opposite the centre attract botanists, geologists and birdwatchers.

The neighbouring towns, **Killala** and **Ballina** ⓰, have their own particular charms for the visitor. Killala rises above a small harbour, its skyline dominated by a pencil-thin 10th-century round tower and the spire of the Church of Ireland. Ballina, with its streets sloping down to the River Moy, is the largest town in Mayo and is internationally renowned for salmon angling. The area attracts large numbers of visiting fishermen and women for both game and coarse angling.

KNOCK

An inland detour takes you to **Knock** ⓱ where in 1879 several people reportedly saw the Blessed Virgin silhouetted on the gable of the local church. The story is told by **Knock Folk Museum** (www.knockshrine.ie; Basilica: all year; main pilgrimage season from the last Sun in Apr to the 2nd Sun in Oct; free).

The village is thronged year-round with tourists and pilgrims and is brimming with shops selling souvenirs and religious artefacts. Holy water is offered free on tap: you'll need to bring your own bottle. One of Ireland's most popular pilgrimage places, it is visited by over 1 million people each year.

To end your cultural tour of the west with a reflective look at what life in rural Ireland used to be like, turn off the N5 to visit the award-winning **National Museum of Country Life** ⓲ (www.museum.ie/Country-Life; free) at Turlough Park, 5 miles (8km) from **Castlebar,** County Mayo's capital. The museum, the first branch of the National Museum to open outside of Dublin, houses the National Folklife Collection detailing the domestic lives of people who lived in rural Ireland between 1850 and 1950.

National Museum of Country Life.

Ballina's cathedral at sunset.

Birr Castle.

INLAND IRELAND

Bogs, lakes and rivers dominate the countryside of these oft-overlooked counties in the middle of the country. Fishing and boating are the big attractions here, and the landscapes are seductive.

Geography classes for Irish primary school children traditionally reduced their country to a common item of domestic tableware – a saucer. With the outer rim representing the ragged, mountainous coastal regions, the Midlands were credited with the dubious honour of being Ireland's flat centre.

In a region marked by the relative absence of physical drama, where bog land and lake account for much of the terrain, the counties of Longford, Laois, Offaly, Westmeath, Roscommon, Cavan and Monaghan have long played second fiddle to the more popular tourist regions of the South and West.

However, bisected by the River Shannon, the region is rich in varied recreation options, from fishing on the many lakes, walking the Slieve Bloom hills, to exploring the slower pace of life in its sleepy towns and villages.

ECHOES OF THE PAST

Perceived by many, including the Irish, as a rather dull part of the country, the Midlands are, in fact, one of the last remaining regions where the pace of life harks back to an Ireland of 30 years ago. The attendant bustle and ubiquitous traffic jams are happily still absent. Life here is still unhurried and friendly.

The inland counties offer much for the visitor – especially Clonmacnoise, Ireland's most important and atmospheric monastic site. Grand mansions and castles pepper the region, and farmers' markets and espresso bars sit comfortably with centuries-old pubs and grocery shops as new blood mixes happily with old, unchanged ways.

FROM BALLINASLOE TO CLONMACNOISE

Ballinasloe ❶, the chief town of east County Galway, has long been an important crossing place of the **River Suck**, and marks a kind of border,

Main attractions
- Clonmacnoise
- Birr Castle
- Lough Derg
- Emo Court
- Mullingar
- Strokestown Park House and Famine Museum
- Athlone
- Bellamont House
- Castle Leslie
- Patrick Kavanagh Centre

Map on page 238

Clonmacnoise monastic site.

Inland Ireland
10 km
10 miles
Manorhamilton
Lough Macnean Upper
Belcoo
Enniskillen
Maguiresbridge
Parke's Castle
Glenfarne
Blacklion
L. Macnean Lower
Florence Court
Marble Arch Caves
Florence Court Forest Park
Drumcard
NORTHREN IRELAND
Lisnaskea
Scotstown
Omagh
Castle Leslie Hotel
Glaslough
Middletown
Monaghan (Muineachán)
Rossmore Forest Park
Scotch Corner
Creaghanroe
L. Gill
Dromahair
Tiltinbane 592
Cuilcagh 665
Leitrim
Dowra
Glangevlin
Swanlinbar
Derrylin
Upper Lough Erne
Newtownbutler
Clones
Derrynawilt
Smithborough
Newbliss
Swan's Cross Roads
Castleblayney
Ballintogher
Drumkeeran
Ballinagleragh
Derrynacreeve
Teemore
Wattle Bridge
Tyrone Guthrie Centre/ Annaghmakerrig House
Rockcorry
Patrick Kavanagh Centre
496
Benbrack
Source of the Shannon
Slieve Rushen 405
Lough Allen
Iron Mts
519 Bencroy or Gubnaveagh
Ballyconnell
Belturbet
Scotshouse
Monaghan
Heapstown Cairn
Geevagh
Arigna
Slieve Anierin 586
Milltown
Drumlane Abbey
Garadice Lough
Butlersbridge
Cootehill
Bellamont House
Shantonagh
Sligo
Lough Arrow
Corrigeenroe
Drumshanbo
Ballinamore
Doogary
Killashandra
Bellanacargy
Moyduff
Shercock
Ballinafad
Lough Key
Knockvicar
Shannon
REPUBLIC OF IRELAND
Cloughoughter Castle
Killykeen Forest Park
Lough Oughter
Cavan (An Cabhán)
Canningstown
Dún A Rí Forest Park
Carrickmacross
Boyle
Lough Key Forest Park
Leitrim
Carrick-on-Shannon
Garvagh
Carrigallen
Cornafean
Bellananagh
Cavan
Kingscourt
Bailieborough
Drumsna
Cloone Grange
Arvagh
Erne
Cross Keys
Billis Bridge
Croghan
Mohill
Rinn Lough
Hill Street
Lough Boderg
Dromod
Ballyjamesduff
Virginia
Ballyroddy
Lough Bofin
Drumlish
Lough Gowna
Kilcogy
Lough Sheelin
Lough Ramor
Mullagh
Moynalty
Roscommon
Roosky
Rathcroghan
Strokestown
Lough Forbes
Ballinalee
Granard
Finnea
Oldcastle
Tulsk
Scramoge
Longford
Carriglas Manor
Strokestown Park House & Famine Museum
Termonbarry
Lisryan
Loughcrew Passage Grave
Crossakeel
Ceanannus Mór (Kells)
Castleplunket
Longford (An Longfort)
Mostrim (Edgeworthstown)
Coole
Four Mile House
Tullynally Castle
Castlepollard
Cross Keys
Meath
Runnabackan
Coolshaghtena
Killashee
Lough Lene
Clonmellon
Lanesborough
Lough Derravaragh
Collinstown
Rathowen
Corlea Trackway Visitor Centre
Keenagh
Carrickboy
Multyfarnham
Roscommon
Suck
Crookedwood
Delvin
Athboy
Newtown Cashel
Lough
Ballynacarrigy
Lough Owel
Trim
Mullingar (An Muileann gCearr)
Athleague
Knockcroghery
Ballymahon
Ballivor
Skeagh
Ballygar
Rahara
Ree
The Downs
Raharney
Four Roads
Galway
The Pigeons
Westmeath
Lough Ennel
Rathmoylan
Curraghboy
Ballymore
Longhanavally
Belvedere House & Gardens
Kinnegad
Kiltoom
Glasson
Dublin
Brideswell
Ballykeeran
Moyvoughly
Ballynagore
Milltownpass
Enfield
Rochfortbridge
Kilglass
Athlone (Baile Átha Luain)
Moate
Horseleap
Castlejordan
Johnstown Bridge
Carrowreagh
Corraree
Tyrrellspass
Edenderry
Kilbeggan
Rhode
Cornafulla
Ballynahown
Clara
Carbury
Ballydangan
Grogan
Kiltober
Grand Canal
Bog of Allen
Clonmacnoise
Clonfinloughstone
Tullamore (Tulach Mhór)
Rathvilla
Ballinasloe (Béal Átha na Sluaighe)
Daingean
Kildare
Aughrim
Shannonbridge
Charleville Forest Castle
Brackagh
Clonbullogue
Allen
Crossconnell
Ferbane
Geashill
Rathangan
River Suck
Laurencetown
Cloghan
Killeigh
Bracknagh
Hill of Allen
Galway
Shannon Harbour
Blue Ball
Newbridge
Drumatober
Banagher
Offaly
Clonygowan
Portarlington
Kildare
Killimor
Taylor's Cross
Kilcormac
Cloghan Castle
Clonaslee
Mountmellick
Monasterevin
National Stud & Japanese Gardens
Fivealley
Rosenallis
Shannon
Pike
Cadamstown
Emo Court
Nurney
Portumna
Birr
Slieve Bloom Mts
The Cut 411
Coolbanagher Church
New Inn
Fontstown
Abbey
Kinnitty
Vicarstown
Portumna Castle
Carrigahorig
Laois
Woodford
Drimmo
Portlaoise (Port Laoise)
Rock of Dunamase
Athy (Baile Átha)
Lough Derg
Terryglass
Aderin 527
Sharavogue
Ballinderry
Boheraphuca
Mountrath
Stradbally
Gorteeny
Ballingarry
Mount St Joseph's Abbey
Borrisokane
Camross
R. Barrow
Coolbawn
Tipperary
Shinrone
Pike of Rush Hall
Cromoge
317
Ballylynan
Cloghjordan
Roscrea (Ros Cré)
Timahoe
Dromineer
Abbeyleix
Castledermot
Dunkerrin
Garrykennedy
Ballybrophy
Nenagh (An tAonach)
Moneygall
Durrow
Limerick
Toomyvara
Cork
Rathdowney
N16
A4
N2
N3
N4
N5
N52
N80
M6
M4
M7
N77
M8
1
2
3
4
5
6
7
8
9
10
11
12
13
14
15
16
17
18
19
20

more psychological than physical, between the west of Ireland and the Midlands. Every year during the first week of October Europe's oldest horse fair takes place here. Between Ballinasloe and Loughrea, off the M6, is the **Dartfield Horse Museum and Heritage Centre** (www.dartfield.com; free). The museum occupies a courtyard of the original Dartfield House. As well as an exhibition on the history of Irish horses and Connemara ponies, together with farm machinery and carriages, there are 350 acres to enjoy, and a walking tour to see a variety of animals including horses, deer and sheep. Horse riding is also available.

From Ballinasloe take the R357 to **Shannonbridge** ❷. This is the point where county Galway meets counties Offaly and Roscommon, and the River Suck flows into the River Shannon. There's a lot of bog in the Midlands, in various stages of development. The state-run Irish Peat Board, Bord Na Móna, who run the Blackwater Power Station, closed the passenger railway line in November 2008 but they are working closely with the Irish Tourist Board (Fáilte Ireland) to develop eco-tourism in the bog land.

Clonmacnoise ❸ (tel: 090-967 4195; www.heritageireland.ie; daily) is one of Ireland's most important monastic sites, superbly located on a bend in the River Shannon. It was built on an esker, or natural gravel ridge, that overlooks a large marshy area. The monastery was founded in AD 545 by St Kieran and was the burial place of the Kings of Connaught and Tara. While it may appear remote today, in earlier centuries transport for pilgrims was easier by water than over land.

The earliest of the surviving ruins dates from the 9th century. The monastery was plundered from then onwards by the Irish, the Vikings and the Anglo-Normans until it was destroyed in the Elizabethan wars of the mid-16th century by the English garrison from Athlone. Yet there's still plenty to be seen. The Visitor Centre has a collection of carved grave slabs dating from the 9th to the 12th centuries, as well as a helpful audio-visual presentation.

Among the older surviving buildings of the complex are the shell of a small cathedral, two round towers, the remains of eight smaller churches and several High Crosses. There are various doorways and chancel arches in the Irish Romanesque style. One of the churches, Temple Connor, was restored by the Church of Ireland in 1911 and is used for services.

AROUND LOUGH DERG

Head south for **Shannon Harbour**, the junction of the Grand Canal and the River Shannon, which is a popular mooring place for river cruisers. About 5 miles (8km) further south is **Banagher** ❹, another popular boating centre with a marina. This pretty, one-street village will be eerie and empty in winter, and bustling with river enthusiasts in summer.

Lough Derg.

The town has two notable literary connections, the first of which is Anthony Trollope, who worked in the area as a land surveyor in 1841 and penned his first novel, *The Macdermots of Ballycloran*, here. Charlotte Brontë spent her honeymoon in the area. A common Irish exclamation: 'That beats Banagher!' dates back to a period during the 19th century when the town was ruled by corrupt officials and gave rise to this definition of poor standards still in popular currency.

Signposted from the centre of the village and lying a mile or so outside it is the lovingly restored **Cloghan Castle** (www.cloughancastle.ie; private hire only).

BIRR

Birr ❺ is an attractive Georgian town, more or less in the centre of Ireland, dominated by **Birr Castle and Demesne** (www.birrcastle.com; charge).

As an estate town that grew in tandem with the castle, Birr is a good example of Georgian town planning, with many original entrance fanlights, door panelling and iron railings still intact.The gardens of Birr Castle cover 100 acres (40 hectares) and have more than 1,000 species of trees and shrubs with an especially strong Chinese and Himalayan collection. In spring, magnolias, crab apples and cherries will be in flower; in the autumn, maples, chestnut and weeping beech supply colour. The box hedges subdividing the formal gardens are the highest in the world.

The 17th-century castle is private, but its stable block now houses a **Historic Science Centre** (www.birrcastle.com/science). The owners of Birr Castle, the Parsons family, later ennobled as the Earls of Rosse, have manifested a scientific bent for several generations. In the 1840s the 3rd Earl of Rosse built the Great Telescope which enabled him to see further into space than any of his contemporaries. The telescope, which has a 56ft (17-metre) tube and a 6ft (1.8-metre) mirror, was in use until 1908 and has been restored to working order.

Walk into town along **Oxmanton Mall**, a tree-lined thoroughfare that leads from the castle gates past a row of elegant

The gardens at Birr Castle and Demesne.

Georgian houses. **Emmet Square** in the town centre is the location of one-time coaching inn **Dooly's Hotel** (dating from 1747; www.doolyshotel.com), which gave its name to the Galway Blazers when they set fire to it after a Hunt Ball in 1809, almost destroying the building.

LOUGH DERG

From Birr, head to **Borrisokane** and the eastern shores of **Lough Derg** ❻. At Lough Derg the Shannon widens into a 50 sq mile (130 sq km) lake that is about 10 miles (16km) across at its widest point. This side is in County Tipperary and the west of the lake is in County Clare. The circular **Lough Derg Drive** (about 50 miles/90km) passes through a succession of pretty villages, but the lake itself is not always visible. The villages on this side of Lough Derg are peaceful, out-of-the-way places to stay that have been steadily gaining in popularity. Most visitors either have a boat of some kind or are interested in fishing – mainly coarse angling – on the lake. Others enjoy walking around the lake.

Terryglass is one of the prettiest villages near Lough Derg, although you have to leave the main road to find the lake. **Dromineer** on the other hand is right on the water, and has a ruined castle on its pier. Many of the people you meet in the pubs will be temporarily living on river cruisers, which they own or have hired.

The Slieve Bloom Mountains (www.slievebloom.ie) are a very accessible range of hills perfect for either leisurely strolling or steep hiking on waymarked trails. The Slieve Bloom Way is a 20-mile (32km) circular trail through mostly uninhabited landscape and hidden vistas. You can dip in and out of the trail at many points, but the villages of Cadamstown and Kinnity are ideal starting points.

NENAGH

Nenagh ❼ is a Tipperary market town, bypassed by the busy Dublin–Limerick main road. All that remains of the original Norman settlement is the **Nenagh Castle Keep**, or 'donjon', with walls 20ft (6 metres) thick. It reaches to a height of 100ft (30 metres). Across the road in the **Governor's House** of the old town gaol is the **Nenagh Heritage Centre** (tel: 067-33850; www.nenagh.ie; free), which includes the condemned cells and execution room of the gaol, and a museum of rural life.

Roscrea ❽, is an attractive little town, rich in heritage, bisected by the main road from Thurles to Athlone that cuts through the west facade of the 12th-century St Cronan's Abbey, which is all that remains, with a round-arched doorway containing a moulded figure of St Cronan.

Roscrea's 13th-century castle is a polygonal structure with two D-shaped towers. The gatehouse is topped by 18th-century gables and chimneys. It now houses the **Roscrea Heritage Centre** (tel: 0505-21850; www.heritageireland.ie; daily Apr–mid-Sept; charge also includes Damer House).

Roscrea Castle.

Damer House (Wed–Sun 11am–5pm), which stands inside the castle walls, is an elegant, 18th-century, three-storied house with a plain, symmetrical facade and a handsome pine staircase. It was completed in the 1720s and became a Bishop's Palace before being converted to a military barracks in 1798. It was very nearly demolished in the 1970s to make room for a car park but was saved through the vigilance of the Irish Georgian Society.

EMO COURT

Travel east again, bypassing **Portlaoise**, to visit **Emo Court** 9 (www.emocourt.ie). This fine Georgian mansion was built in 1792 for the Earl of Portarlington in the Classical style by James Gandon, best known for Dublin's Four Courts and Custom House. It was restored and donated to the nation in 1996 by a private benefactor.

Approached via an avenue of splendid giant sequoia trees, the house is certainly worth a visit. Built over a 70-year period as a result of the first Earl's fluctuating financial fortunes, the house is the only large-scale domestic example of Gandon's work apart from the Custom House. Pride of place goes to the domed rotunda, designed by Gandon's successor, William Caldbeck, a mix of marble pilasters with gilded Corinthian capitals supporting the enormous blue painted dome which was inspired by Rome's Pantheon.

The gardens were created in two parts. The Clucker, named because it was once the site of the nun's quarters of an ancient abbey, is planted with azaleas, rhododendrons and Japanese maples. The Grapery is planted with trees and shrubs and leads down to the peaceful lakeside walk. Inside the house is a nice coffee shop and gift shop.

Nearby is **Coolbanagher Church,** also designed by Gandon, within which are the original 1795 architectural plans. An intricate 15th-century font from an earlier church has been incorporated. Close by is Gandon's mausoleum for Lord Portarlington.

Walking the Slieve Bloom Way.

CHARLEVILLE FOREST CASTLE

There is another interesting house in an entirely different style to the north near Tullamore, **Charleville Forest Castle** ⑩ (www.charlevillecastle.ie). The castle is gradually being restored by volunteers, and hosts music and arts events.

Designed by Francis Johnson, the architect responsible for many of Dublin's Georgian houses, this fine example of Gothic Revival style was commissioned by Baron Tullamore in 1812. With its flag tower and castellated turrets rising high over an estate of pleasant woodland walks and gardens, the house is built of grey limestone with an internal gallery complete with some intricate plasterwork running the entire length of the garden front.

Five avenues lined by Irish yew trees radiate from the house. The grounds contain many impressive trees including an oak believed to be 700 years old. Tullamore is also where Irish Mist and Tullamore Dew liqueurs are made. The drinks' histories and traditional distilling methods are explained in the **Tullamore Dew Heritage Centre** (tel: 057-932 5016; daily; charge for tasting tours).

AROUND LOUGH ENNEL

Follow the N52 from Tullamore for 7.5 miles (12km) north to **Kilbeggan** ⑪. **Locke's Distillery** (www.kilbeggandistillery.com; daily; charge for tasting tours), advertised for miles around, is on the banks of the River Brosna, which is fed by springs from nearby Lough Ennel. It claims to have been the world's oldest pot-still distillery. After closing in 1957, it was reopened as a museum in 1987.

It is said that all good whiskey depends on the water that goes into the distillation process. The distillery was in use from 1757 to 1953 and much of the original equipment is still in place. There are enticing smells of malt and oak as you view the equipment, and a tasting.

The low-lying **Lough Ennel** can be seen from the N52 between Kilbeggan and Mullingar. It is a popular place for swimming, boating and fishing. The restored **Belvedere House and Gardens** (www.belvedere-house.ie; daily) is remarkable for its beautiful setting, with terraced gardens descending in three stages to the shores of the lake.

Mullingar ⑫, the chief town of County Westmeath, is an important cattle-dealing centre with a pleasant, old-world ambience which is also popular with anglers. The Cathedral of Christ the King (Mary Street; tel: 044-934 8338; free) was completed in 1939 with a finely carved facade in the Renaissance style. Inside are mosaics by the Russian artist Boris Anrep. Tours are available from May–Sept; phone for details.

AROUND LOUGH DERRAVARAGH

Tullynally Castle ⑬ (www.tullynallycastle.com; charge), to the north of Mullingar, just beyond **Castlepollard**, used to be known as Pakenham Hall. This massive, grey stone, turreted house overlooking **Lough Derravaragh** has been the seat of the Pakenham family, now the Earls

Locke's Distillery, the last remaining example of a small pot-still whiskey distillery in Ireland.

of Longford, since 1655. The current family includes the children of the late British peer Lord Longford: his historian son Thomas, and his daughters, biographer Antonia Fraser and novelist Rachel Billington. The castle is the private home of Thomas Pakenham, and the interior is only open to the public by prior arrangement (see website).

The original fort was converted into a two-storey house in the 18th century. A Gothic facade was added in the early 19th century, and in the mid-19th century Sir Richard Morrison designed the central tower and two wings. The landscaped gardens, which include a grotto, have spectacular views of Lough Derravaragh.

Multyfarnham, a 2-mile (3km) detour off the N4 Longford road, is a one-street town with a few good old-fashioned pubs. Multyfarnham's **Cistercian monastery**, founded in 1306, has an attractive slender tower 88ft (27 metres) high. The abbey was restored by the Franciscans in 1973. Its stained-glass windows show the legend of the Children of Lir who were turned into swans and lived nearby on Lough Derravaragh. The Franciscans have built a life-size Stations of the Cross in a grove of evergreens beside a fast-flowing stream.

Lough Ree.

To the south of Longford off the R397, the **Corlea Trackway Visitor Centre** at Kenagh (www.heritageireland.ie; free) interprets an Iron Age Bog Road dating from 148 BC – the largest of its kind ever to be uncovered in Europe.

FAMINE MUSEUM

If you can only visit one stately home in the Midlands, then follow the N5 for 25 miles (40km) west of Longford to **Strokestown Park House and Famine Museum** ⓮ (www.strokestownpark.ie; charge). The village leads to an imposing Georgian-Gothic arch, which leads to the house. The village, with its exceptionally broad main street, was laid out in the early 19th century to complement the new entrance. The house itself is a fine Palladian mansion designed by Sir Richard Cassels in the 1730s. The central block was the family's residence while the wings either side contained the stables and the kitchen areas. The kitchen is especially interesting. A gallery runs above it from which the lady of the house could oversee the staff without entering the kitchen itself. Each Monday morning she would drop a menu with instructions for the week's meals. Tunnels to hide the movements of tradesmen and servants link the main block of the house to the kitchens and stables. The walled garden has also been restored in line with horticultural practices of the 18th century.

The house, accessible by guided tour only (40 minutes), was at the centre of a large estate. It stayed in the Mahon family until 1979 when it was bought and resztored by a local businessman. Allow another hour for the **Famine Museum**, housed in the stable yard (see page 245).

West of Strokestown where the N5 crosses the R367 lies **Tulsk** and the

Cruachan Aí Visitors Centre (www.rathcroghan.ie; charge), which explores the archaeological, historical and mythological aspects of Cruachan, burial place of the Kings of Connacht.

ROSCOMMON

Roscommon ⓯, to the south of Tulsk, is a pleasant market town built on a low hill in the midst of rich cattle and sheep country. **Roscommon Castle** (freely accessible), to the north of the town, is an impressive ruin on a green field site. It was originally a 13th-century Norman stronghold. It has massive walls defended by round bastions at each corner, and the mullioned windows can still be seen in some of the remaining walls.

Adjacent to the town are the remains of the 12th-century **Roscommon Abbey** founded by Felim O'Conor, king of Connacht, who was buried there himself in 1265. Eight sculpted figures represent the 'gallowglass' – professional soldiers for hire used extensively during the period. Much of the remaining structure dates from the 13th century.

RECALLING THE FAMINE

The Famine Museum at Strokestown Park House presents a vivid display tracing the history of the family and the estate and links this to the national events in 1845–50 which led to Ireland's Great Famine and the resulting mass emigration or death of more than 2 million people – almost one-quarter of the population.

It balances the history of the big house with the experiences of the peasants who worked the land there. Moving documents record the pleas made to the Mahon family by tenants starving to death as a result of a devastating potato blight, together with the response they received. The museum also aims to raise awareness of contemporary famine by demonstrating the link between the causes of the Great Irish Famine and that of famine in the developing world.

AROUND LOUGH REE

Thanks to the ring road around Athlone, it is possible to drive from Roscommon to **Glasson,** which is about 6 miles (10km) outside Athlone, without fighting Athlone's traffic. Glasson is one of a series of pretty villages on the eastern shore of **Lough Ree** ⓰, part of the River Shannon. There are good amenities for water sports, attractive country pubs and restaurants, and a series of lake shore and forest walks. The poet and dramatist Oliver Goldsmith (1730–74), best known for his 1773 comedy *She Stoops to Conquer*, is associated with this area.

The play's central device, by which a traveller mistakes a private home for a country inn, supposedly happened to Goldsmith at Ardagh House in Ardagh, which is now a school. The house where he grew up, Lissoy Parsonage, is now in ruins. The **Three Jolly Pigeons** pub (tel: 090-648 5162) on the Ballymahon road, is the headquarters of the annual Oliver Goldsmith Summer School. Though he rarely returned to his childhood county,

Tullynally Castle.

his recollections of Longford are also thought to have influenced his epic poem *The Deserted Village.*

ATHLONE

Athlone ⓱, which straddles the River Shannon at an important strategic point to the south of Lough Ree, has the distinction of being half in County Westmeath and half in County Roscommon. It is an important commercial centre, and the busiest town in the Midlands (www.athlone.ie).

Athlone Castle (www.athlonecastle.ie; charge) is a squat, 13th-century building, which was badly damaged in 1690 when the Irish made a stand here against the advance of Cromwell's forces. The castle has been beautifully restored and now has a €4.3m visitor centre on its long history, the highlight being the Siege of Athlone in 1690–1. The area behind the castle is being promoted as Athlone's 'Left Bank'. There are some nice town houses dating from the 18th and 19th centuries, several good restaurants and bars.

Cavan town.

You will notice that even relatively modest restaurants in Athlone tend to have trilingual menus. This is because the town is very popular with holidaymakers on Shannon cruisers, most of whom eat ashore as often as they can. The nicest thing to do in Athlone is to take a boat trip up the Shannon to Lough Ree. Viking Tours Ireland (www.vikingtoursireland.ie) have a replica Viking longboat, comfortably equipped with snack bar on board, that leaves regularly between Easter and August for a 90-minute cruise from the quay beside Athlone Castle.

CAVAN'S CRUISING

Across the border to the south of Enniskillen, landlocked County Cavan, emptied by emigration, bridges the two Irelands by providing the source of two great rivers: the **Shannon,** which flows south to the Atlantic, and the **Erne**, which flows north into Fermanagh's magnificent lakes. Both rivers are ideal for cruising. Most of the county's scattered towns and villages have small hotels, which cater for visiting fishermen. The Ballinamore–Ballyconnell canal linking the two river systems has been reopened and pleasure trips along the canal are in demand (Inland Waterways Association of Ireland; www.iwai.ie).

Cavan ⓲, a busy market town and a popular destination for anglers, is a pleasant place to explore on foot with many unspoilt old pubs. It is the site of a 14th-century Franciscan friary, of which only a belfry tower remains. The Roman Catholic Cathedral, in contrast, dates from 1942.

St Feithlimidh's Cathedral (tel: 049-433 7168; guided tours on request; free) at Kilmore is just off the main Cavan-Crossdoney road, 3 miles (5km) west of Cavan town. It has been a place of worship for up to 15 centuries. The cathedral dates mainly from the 19th-century and is built in the Early Decorated or Middle Pointed style with a central tower that is finished by a distinctive four-sided pyramidal roof. Its Romanesque doorway dates from the early 13th century and came from a nearby priory on Trinity Island in Lough Oughter.

Killykeen Forest Park (www.coillte.ie/site/killykeen-forest-park; free) 5 miles (8km) from Cavan town, covers 600 acres (240 hectares) of mixed woodland overlooking Lough Oughter on the Erne river system and offering a picturesque landscape of lakes, islands and woodland. It is especially popular with fishing enthusiasts, as well as walkers and cyclists, thanks to its forest paths and trails.

A bit further north just off the R201 near Milltown is Drumlane Abbey (www.drumlane.ie), located in a peaceful setting on the Erne River. The Augustinian St Mary's Priory was founded here in the 12th century, although the buildings possibly date back to the sixth century. There are remains of the round tower minus its roof, a church, graveyard and stone crosses.

VILLAGE IRELAND TOURS

A circular tour going west and north from Cavan would take in 17th-century **Cloughoughter Castle** on an island in Lough Oughter and nearby **Killeshandra**, a popular spot for anglers; **Arvagh**, a peaceful village 14 miles (22km) southwest on the R198 by Lough Garty; **Dowra**, to the northwest on the R200 near the Black Pig's Dyke, thought to be an ancient frontier earthwork; **Swanlinbar on the N87**, with its faded, once-a-spa charms, on the Border; **Blacklion**, on Lough Macnean 33 miles (52km) northwest on the N3/R200, a hamlet surrounded by many prehistoric ringforts and cairns including a beehive-shaped sweat house, a Celtic form of Turkish bath; and **Butlersbridge**, 4 miles (6km) north on the N3 near which Ballyhaise House, now an agricultural college, has a rare 1733 oval saloon and two storeys vaulted over in brick.

A tour going east and south would cover: **Cootehill**, 16 miles (26km) northeast on the R118 which has a splendid 1730 Palladian house, **Bellamont**

Athlone.

House, built for the Coote family in Bellamont Forest. Often hailed as Ireland's loveliest 18th-century house, it was built by Sir Edward Lovett Pearce and inspired by Italy's Palladian villas. One of its most famous owners, Charles Coote, Earl of Bellamont, was known as 'the Hibernian seducer' because of his extramarital activities. He was eventually shot in the groin by Lord Townshend. A portrait by Sir Joshua Reynolds hangs in the National Gallery of Ireland. The house is privately owned but there are walking trails open to the public in Bellamont Forest.

Southeast 13 miles (21km) on the R192 to **Shercock**, is where the playwright Richard Brinsley Sheridan once lived; **Kingscourt**, where the Catholic church has some renowned stained glass; **Bailieborough**, on the R165, which has a fine main street; **Virginia**, 19 miles (33km) southwest on the N3, planned as a garrison town in 1610 and now a handsome, peaceful place with Cuilcagh House, owned by playwright Tom McIntyre (private), where Dean Swift began *Gulliver's Travels*, 3 miles (5km) east; and **Ballyjamesduff**, where the award-winning Cavan County Museum in Virginia Road (www.cavanmuseum.ie; free) houses a collection of pre-Christian and medieval artefacts including the 1,000-year-old Lough Errol dugout boat and Lavey Sheela-na-gigs.

Church in County Monaghan.

THE CAVAN WAY

The Cavan Way provides a pleasant hill and valley walking connection between the Leitrim Way at Dowra and the Ulster Way at Blacklion village. The walk follows quiet valley and river-sided landscapes to the enclosed uplands of the river's source at the mystical Shannon 'Pot' (from the Irish *Lag na Sionna*, meaning 'hollow of the Shannon').

Walkers enjoy the upland section between the 'Pot' and Blacklion, which includes the forested Burren area and its cemetery of ancient tombs, stone megaliths and monuments. For more information, Cavan Tourism can be found in Farnham Street, Cavan town (tel: 049-433 1942; www.cavantourism.com).

MILD MONAGHAN

To the northeast, in Monaghan, is the small agricultural town of **Clones** ⓳ (pronounced 'clone-ess'), whose most famous son is Barry McGuigan, the 'Clones cyclone' who became world featherweight boxing champion in 1985. The town's commercial centre is Fermanagh Street, signalling the town's former significance for the farmers of south Fermanagh.

But, just as partition destroyed its role as an important railway hub, so the Troubles initially hit trade as northerners became reluctant to cross the border. However, the two tills on most shop counters hint that the two different currencies – the British pound in Northern Ireland and the euro in the South – have encouraged a great deal of cross-border price comparing, especially on diesel and petrol.

The writer Patrick McCabe was born in Clones. His popular novels include *The Butcher Boy* and *Breakfast on Pluto*, both filmed by Neil Jordan.

Clones has an ancient lineage. The remains of a 12th-century Augustinian abbey (known as '**the Wee Abbey**') can be seen in Abbey Street. An ancient cross in the marketplace shows scenes from the Bible, such as The Fall of Adam and Eve and The Adoration of the Magi. The cemetery has a 9th-century **round tower**, 75ft (23 metres) high and rather dilapidated, and an early Christian carved **sarcophagus**, thought to be the grave of the founder, St Tiarnoch, the key to which can be obtained from nearby Patton's pub.

Several Georgian houses are a reminder of the town's 18th-century prosperity. Another sign of the vanished 'Ascendancy' era are the 'big houses', once the homes of the well-to-do Anglo-Irish, many of which have fallen into disrepair.

Monaghan is a quiet, trim county of snug farmhouses and tranquil market towns, and lakes and rivers that draw fishermen. Its administrative centre, **Monaghan** ⓴, 12 miles (19km) northeast of Clones, has a **Market House** dating from 1792, an imposing 19th-century Gothic Revival cathedral (**St Macartan's**) and a good **County Museum** (www.monaghan.ie; free) highlighting prehistoric relics and local arts and crafts. The **Garage Theatre** (www.garagetheatre.com), located in a disused ward of a psychiatric hospital, mounts excellent touring productions. The tourist office is located at Monaghan County Council, The Glen, Monaghan town (tel: 047-73718).

Rossmore Forest Park, 2 miles (3km) southwest of Monaghan town on the R189 to Newbliss, has several forest walks, a nature trail and a yew walk. The ruins of the 16th-century **Rossmore Castle** provide a viewing point to the surrounding countryside. The park contains examples of a wedge tomb and a court tomb dating 3,000 to 1,800 BC. The landscape has many drumlins (low rounded hills), laid down during the Ice Age over 10,000 years ago when

Cloughouter Castle, Cavan.

boulder clay was deposited as small hillocks by moving ice.

CASTLE LESLIE

To the north, 5 miles (8km) on the R185, by Glaslough, is the reputedly haunted **Castle Leslie** (www.castleleslie.com), home of the literary Leslie family and now a hotel with a thriving equestrian centre. Set on an estate of 1,000 acres (400 hectares), Castle Leslie is rich in Victorian splendour, both in its furniture and family portraits. Winston Churchill, a first cousin of the family, best known for its writers and eccentrics, was a regular guest.

To the south, east of **Newbliss**, 10 miles (16km) on the R188, at **Annamakerrig House** is the **Tyrone Guthrie Centre** (www.tyroneguthrie.ie), an international haven for professional artists in all art forms. Six miles (10km) east is **Rockcorry**, where John Gregg invented Gregg's Shorthand, America's favourite.

Continuing along the R183 to **Castleblayney**, a town so steeped in the tradition of country music it has been called the Nashville of Ireland. It's a good centre for walking, fishing and golf, and is situated by the attractive Lough Muckno. Hope Castle (tel: 042-974 9450; free), built on the site of Blayney Castle in the 18th century, is now a leisure park.

Poet and novelist Patrick Kavanagh grew up 10 miles (16km) east of attractive **Carrickmacross**, at tiny Inishkeen, where a riverside museum, the **Patrick Kavanagh Centre** (www.patrickkavanaghcountry.com; free) run by local volunteers, celebrates his work. While he spent most of his life in Dublin, the harsh isolation of his native county informed much of his work during his life. Mocked by the Dublin literary community of the time, Kavanagh, an irascible character, claimed, perhaps justifiably, that he was hated. When *The Irish Times* surveyed 'the nation's favourite poems', 10 of Kavanagh's poems were in the first 50.

Traditional local lace is still made and sold in Carrickmacross (www.carrickmacrosslace.ie).

The 18th-century Hope Castle.

RURAL BUNGALOWS

Ireland's legendary green countryside is defaced by a rash of houses built with unsuitable materials and painted with more exuberance than taste.

Promotional photos of Ireland could lead visitors to believe that the majority of the rural population lives in small, two-room cottages nestling in the landscape. On the contrary, most country people have given up their dark, cramped accommodation in favour of something more commodious – and visible. From the 1960s, new homes began to appear, often next door to the old cottage. The preferred design was, at first, a modest bungalow, with larger windows, decent plumbing and perhaps an extra bedroom or two. Their owners, seized by fits of individuality, often painted the walls in colours that were unexpectedly cheerful (sometimes garish), or added panels of stone cladding.

QUIRKY PASTICHE

Over the years, rural homes have become larger and more embellished – although many retain the one-storey format. Some are garnished with Georgian porticoes and balustrades; others loop off into Spanish-arched verandas, while still others sprout eagle-topped gateposts and gold-tipped wrought-iron gates. Tyrolean bargeboards, Victorian lamp stands and fairytale wishing wells have likewise found a place in the Irish countryside. The more exuberant homeowners have gone for a jolly *mixum gatherum* of the whole lot – causing architects and purists to despair.

Not only have many of the new houses turned their broad backs on the traditional designs, but they do not conform to the way that buildings have been placed in the Irish countryside since time immemorial. In the past cottages and farm structures were snuggled into the landscape unobtrusively – in the lee of a hill, in the fold between two fields, in the arm hold of a hedgerow. But the new residences are often displayed monumentally on the brow of a hill or dropped importantly into the middle of a plot, with little to no landscaping or thought to aesthetic appeal.

County council planning departments issue booklets on careful site selection and layout, and on appropriate design and materials, but this advice is blissfully ignored by many home builders. Indeed, the most famous catalyst for the new style residences was a pattern book called *Bungalow Bliss*, by Jack Fitzsimons, first published in 1971, and which ran to at least a dozen editions over 30 years. This and other pattern books include self-build designs that often pay no heed to traditional materials, form or scale.

BUNGALOW BLIGHT

Fitzsimons's book title has given rise to cries of 'bungalow blight' and 'bungalow blitz', in protest against the proliferation of single houses spreading ribbon-like along the rural roadsides of some counties. The National Trust for Ireland, An Taisce (www.antaisce.org), is in constant battle with local authorities over the granting of planning permission for such 'one-off' houses. But some county councillors are reluctant to veto the building projects of their constituents. There is a visceral desire among many Irish to have a house of their own, and this is hard to disregard. An Irishman's home is all-important. It is definitely his castle – and it may equally be his Spanish hacienda, Texan ranch or Tudor mansion - it just might not be quite as stylish or pleasing to the eye.

Lakeside bungalow with its own jetty Strangford Lough.

Slieve League Cliffs,
County Donegal.

THE NORTHWEST

The counties of Sligo, Leitrim and Donegal combine Stone-Age burial sites, a craggy coastline, quiet fishing villages and echoes of William Butler Yeats.

Southwestern Sligo, a land of bright lakes and dramatically carved valleys left behind when the last ice age retreated 10,000 years ago, wears its history on its sleeve. Huts from 2,000 BC cluster on a plateau high in the Bricklieve Mountains west of Lough Arrow.

To the west lie the passage tombs of Carrowkeel Cemetery where Stone Age farmers buried their dead. Cairn K catches the rising sun on the year's longest day, yet the main road to Dublin, the N4, is just a mile west. Across it and across Lough Arrow, south of Riverstown, is the 200ft (70-metre) unexcavated Heapstown Cairn. Almost every hilltop has a passage grave, every lake a defensive artificial island, a crannog, every river confluence a castle, a friary, a priory.

BALLYMOTE

Along the R295, and 5 miles (8km) northwest from Carrowkeel, Richard de Burgo, the Red Earl of Ulster, has left us the 10ft (3-metre) walls and six towers of his castle, built in 1300, in **Ballymote** ❶. The ruins beside it are of a Franciscan friary where, in 1391, priests wrote the 'Book of Ballymote', which enabled scholars to interpret Ireland's ancient Ogham (pronounced 'oh-am') script. At **Collooney**, north again 7.5 miles (12km) stands a castle, site of a great battle when the English fought off French troops supporting the 1798 rising.

Ireland's wild northwest coast is punctuated by seaside resorts, notably **Enniscrone** (or Innishcrone to some purists), on the shores of Killala Bay, at the southwestern end, and Bundoran in Donegal. Both have been revitalised by the sensational surf this Atlantic-facing coast enjoys, and the board-riding community it attracts. Recall the pre-wet-suit days by visiting the seaweed baths at Enniscrone **Kilcullen's Bath House** (www.kilcullenseaweedbaths.net).

Main attractions

- Sligo town
- Lake Isle of Innisfree
- Erne–Shannon Waterway
- Carrick-on-Shannon
- Bundoran
- Glencolumbkille
- Glenveagh National Park
- Inishowen Peninsula

Map on page 254

The dolmen at Carrowmore.

The Northwest
0
10 km
0
10 miles
N
ATLANTIC
OCEAN
Malin Head
Ballyhillin
Inishtrahull Sound
Urbalreagh
Doagh Island Famine Village
Malin
Pollan Bay
Ballyliffin
Carndonagh Cross
Gleneely
Dunaff Head
Fanad Head
Clonmany
Carndonagh
Castle Carry
Tory Island
West Town
Tory Sound
Melmore Head
Atlantic Drive
Glasmullan
Slieve Snaght
615
Horn Head
Sheep Haven
Downings
Rosapenna
Portsalon
Magherabane
Lough Swilly
Inishowen
Dunfanaghy
Carrickart
Inishbofin
Portnablagh
Illies
Bloody Foreland
Ards Forest Park
Cranford
Buncrana
White Castle
Greencastle
Magheroarty
Falcarragh
Doe Castle
Mulroy Bay
Glen Lough
Rathmullan
Muckish Mountain
670
Cresburgh
Scalp Mountain
483
Brinlack
Gortahork
Altan Lough
Milford
Burnfoot
Muff
Gola Island
Gweedore
Inch Island
Termon
Lough Fern
Earhart Centre
Owey Island
Bunbeg
Errigal
752
L. Beagh
Speenoge
Glenveagh National Park
St Colmcille Oratory
Ramelton
Gweedore
Grianán of Aileach
Derry
Torneady Point
Rosses Bay
Annagry
Dunlewey
Kilmacrenan
Ellistrin
River Swilly
N13
Ardmore
The Rosses
Loughanure
Gartan L.
Church Hill
Aran or Aranmore Island
Slieve Snacht
615
Derryveagh Mts
Glendowan Mts
Letterkenny (Leitir Ceanainn)
Belfast
Ballintra
Burtonport
Manorcunningham
New Buildings
A6
Dungloe
Commeen
St Johnstown
Claudy
Maghery
Rashedoge
N14
Crohy Head
Doocharry
Kingarrow
Cark Mountain
366
Foyle
Mountcastle
Gweebarra Bay
Fintown
Bellanamore
Raphoe
Rossgeir
Dunnamanagh
Drumnacross
Lettermacaward
Convoy
Beltany Stone Circle
Carnanreagh
L. Finn
Finn
Strabane
Portnoo
Nairn
Aghla Mt
596
Kilross
Lifford
Dawros Head
Dolmen Centre
Maas
Welchtown
Castlefinn
Commeen
N15
A5
Glenties
Ballybofey
Tangaveane
Cross Roads
Mourne
Plumbridge
Lavagh More
672
Donegal
Sion Mills
Scotch Town
Slievetooey
443
Ardara
Blue Stack Mts
Carnaween
521
Croaghnageer
547
Ardstraw
Port
Glengesh Pass
Castlederg
Gortin
Glen Bay
Folk Village Museum
Newtownstewart
Mullaghcarn
542
Glencolumbkille
Meentullynagarn
Lough Eske
Ulster American Folk Park
Gortin Glen Forest Park
Rossan Pt
Crove
Croagh
Letterbarra
Killen
Malin More
Slieve League
601
Carrick
Donegal
Killeter
Drumlegagh
Trabane Strand
Killybegs
Inver
Lough Derg
NORTHERN
One Man's Pass
Bruckless
Laghy
St Patrick's Purgatory
Omagh
Carrigan Head
Teelin
Kilcar
Mac Swyne's Bay
Fintragh Bay
Doorin Point
Tievemore
Tappaghan Mt
336
St John's Point
Rossnowlagh
Lack
IRELAND
Gortaclare
N15
Pettigo
Kesh
Dundalk
Donegal Bay
Ballyshannon
Erne
Castle Caldwell
Boa Island
White Island
Dromore
Fintona
A32
Belleek
Lower
Mullaghmore Head
Bundoran
Irvinestown
Mullaghmore
Cliffs of Magho
Lough
Kinlough
Killadeas
Kilskeery
Lough Navar Forest Park
Tully
Erne
Inishmurray
Cliffony
Lough Melvin
Garrison
Creevykeel Court Cairn
Monea
Devenish Island
Tempo
Streedagh Point
Grange
Rossinver
Slieve Beagh
371
Ben Bulben
526
Lissadell House
Leckanarainey
Ballyconnell
N15
Dartry Mts
Enniskillen
Castle Coole
Roskeeragh Point
Glencar L.
Leitrim
Lough Macnean Upper
A4
Raghly
Drumcliff
Manorhamilton
Belcoo
A4
Sligo Bay
Rosses Point
Maguiresbridge
Sligo (Sligeach)
L. Macnean Lower
Florence Court
Parke's Castle
N16
Aughris Head
Glenfarne
Marble Arch Caves
Lisnaskea
Strandhill
328
Lough Gill
Drumcard
Upper
Templeboy
Knocknarea
Inis Saimer
Innisfree
Dromahair
Florence Court Forest Park
Lough Erne
Derrynawilt
Dromard
Carrowmore
Tiltinbane
592
Derrylin
Ballysadare
Creevelea Abbey
Glangevlin
Cuilcagh
665
Newtownbutler
Clones
Enniscrone, Easky
Knockalongy
543
Coolaney
Ballintogher
Dowra
Swanlinbar
Teemore
Wattle Bridge
Slieve Gamph or Ox Mountains
Collooney
Drumkeeran
Ballinagleragh
Derrynacreeve
Slieve Rushen
405
Source of the Shannon
512
Sligo
Lough Allen
496
N4
Ropefield
Benbrack
Sligo Folk Park
Heapstown Cairn
Arigna Mining Experience
Iron Mts
519
Bencroy or Gubnaveagh
Ballyconnell
Belturbet
Scotshouse
Knocknashee
Templehouse Lake
N3
416
Masshill
Ballymote
Geevagh
Slieve Anierin
586
REPUBLIC
Castlebaldwin
Ballinamore
Bellanacargy
Carrowkeel Cemetery
Lough Arrow
Cavan
Mullany's Cross
321
Drumshanbo
Doogary
Bunnanaddan
Tobercurry
Corrigeenroe
Garadice Lough
Killashandra
Glenview Folk Museum
Ballinafad
R. Shannon
Lough Oughter
N17
Rooxsy
Lough Key
OF IRELAND
N3
Curlew Mts
Leitrim
Cavan (An Cabhán)
Gorteen
Moy
Knockvicar
Garvagh
Boyle
Carrigallen
Carrick-on-Shannon
Charlestown
Lough Gara
Lough Key Forest Park
Cornafean
Bellananagh
N4
Drumsna
Cloone Grange
Arvagh
Cross Keys
Mayo
Roscommon
Erne
Mohill
Killerdoo
Lough Rynn Castle
Ballaghaderreen
Roosky

From Enniscrone, follow the surfers' coast through **Easky** with its 15th-century Rosalee Castle and two Martello towers built to repel Napoleon in the early 19th century. Alternatively take the road south from Easky, past the sparkling waters of Easky Lough deep into the Ox Mountains before joining the N17 at Tobercurry. You may want to stop off at Lavagh, near Tobercurry, to explore the table top mountain **Knocknashee** ❷ (Cnoc na Sí; literally, Hill of the Fairies). The ruined 15th-century Franciscan friary at the foot of the mountain, Court Abbey, now picturesquely over-run by ivy, is also worth a visit.

CARROWMORE

At **Carrowmore** ❸, 5 miles (8km) southwest of Sligo town, the 6,000-year-old Bronze Age graves of Ireland's largest Megalithic cemetery (https://heritageireland.ie) are easily approached, scattered across the tussocky fields. Above them, on the western horizon, on top of 1,078ft (328-metre) Knocknarea, is the vast cairn, 200ft long by 35ft high (70 by 11 metres), consisting of 40,000 boulders. It is named Medb's (pronounced 'maeves') Cairn, supposedly for the 1st-century AD Medb of Connaught whose lust for glitz, baubles and fine clothes would put many a modern royal princess in the shade. The advised approach is from the south.

SLIGO TOWN

Sligo town ❹, best known for its associations with the poet, playwright and Abbey Theatre co-founder William Butler Yeats, is the county's tourist magnet. To the west lie miles of stretches of open beaches, and to the north mountains rise like jutting tablelands dominating the skyline.

Founded by the Normans in the 13th century, Sligo flourished into a prosperous town and has Catholic and Anglican Cathedrals. **Sligo Abbey** was built for the Dominicans in 1252 and was burned in a fire in 1414. It was rebuilt and damaged by fire during the 1641 rebellion and is the only surviving medieval building.

Today the town, with its diverting narrow streets and traditional shop fronts, is the business hub of the northwest of Ireland and with contemporary hotels it is an ideal base for exploring the region. Like so many Irish towns, the waterfront has been developed and along Rockwood Parade cafés, bars and restaurants offer alfresco dining, allowing you to watch swans struggling against the strong current of the River Garavogue. Hargadon's at 4–5 O'Connell Street (www.hargadons.com) is one of Ireland's most famous traditional pubs with much of its original wooden interior still in place. It also has an excellent restaurant and a wine shop.

Nobel Prize–winning poet, dramatist and writer W.B. Yeats (1865–1948), who spent most of his childhood holidays here, is Sligo's most famous literary connection, and his legacy is to be found all around. The **Yeats Memorial Building** (www.yeatssociety.com) in Hyde Bridge, is the venue for the

The Garavogue River in Sligo town.

Yeats International Summer School in August. A permanent Yeats photographic exhibition is on display and the River Café offers refreshment. A bronze statue portraying the poet stands across the bridge. The **Sligo County Museum** (www.sligolibrary.ie; free), housed in a former presbytery on Stephen Street contains Yeats's letters, a complete collection of his poems, photographs of his funeral, and his Nobel Prize citation.

The arts and theatre thrive in Sligo. The **Model**, home of the **Niland Collection** (The Mall; www.themodel.ie), was once an imaginatively extended Model School, and now a unique gallery featuring a nationally significant art collection with works by Jack Yeats (brother of William) and Paul Henry. The town supports two theatres. **Hawk's Well Theatre** (Temple Street; www.hawkswell.com) hosts visiting touring productions and shows by local companies. The **Blue Raincoat Theatre Company** (www.blueraincoat.com) is based at the Factory Performance Space on Lower Quay Street.

LISSADELL HOUSE

Head out of town and branch west, 4 miles (6km) along the northern shore of Drumcliff Bay to the extensively restored **Lissadell House** ❺, Ballinful (www.lissadellhouse.com; charge), visible from several vantage points.

Designed in the neoclassical Greek Revival style, it was built of local cut grey limestone for the Gore-Booths in 1833. By the end of the 20th century it had fallen into a dilapidated state, but even if the house were to crumble, Yeats has immortalised it: 'The light of evening, Lissadell, / Great windows open to the south, / Two girls in silk kimonos, both / Beautiful, one a gazelle.' The girls were Eva Gore-Booth and her sister Constance, later to become Countess Markievicz. Constance was court martialled and sentenced to death for her part in the 1916 Easter Rising but her sentence was commuted to penal servitude for life, however, she was released under the General Amnesty of 1917. She was the first woman to be elected to the British House of

Lissadell House.

Commons. She never took the seat, however, according to Sinn Féin's policy of abstentionism from participating in the UK Parliament. President Éamon de Valera read her funeral oration in 1927.

The neglect of the house was reversed in 2003 when the new custodians – Edward S. Walsh, a barrister from Dublin, and his wife, Constance Cassidy – bought the house for €4.55 million after the government declined to buy it on behalf of the Irish State. The property has been meticulously restored. Visitors can now visit the house (guided tours only) and gardens. For art lovers there are regular art talks and workshops.

LAKE ISLE OF INNISFREE

Southeast of Sligo town, the R286 follows a signposted 'Yeats Country Drive' along the north side of beautiful **Lough Gill** ❻ swinging south at the elegant 17th-century lakeside **Parke's Castle** (twww.parkescastle.com), and then joins the R288 to **Dromahair** and the 15th-century Creevelea Abbey ruins.

The final stage of the journey, a visit to Yeats's Lake Isle of Innisfree and a tour of Lough Gill, can be taken by boat (www.roseofinnisfree.com). Innisfree is a tiny island, just a mile square, and poor weather can make it difficult to replicate Yeats's vision.

The Yeats brothers spent their holidays at windswept **Rosses Point**, 4 miles (6km) northwest on the R291. The view across to Knocknarea is inspiring; mid-channel is a seafarer's marker, the Metal Man – according to Yeats 'the only Rosses Point man who never told a lie'.

North of Sligo, 5.5 miles (9km) on the N15 is tiny **Drumcliff** ❼ at the foot of the majestic cliffs of Ben Bulben. Although he died in France, Yeats by his own request was re-interred here in the dour little Church of Ireland graveyard, citing the spot in his poem which begins 'Under Ben Bulben's head' and finishes with the celebrated words inscribed on his tomb: 'Cast a cold eye/ On life, on death, / Horseman, pass by!' The adjoining church has been restored.

The adjoining round tower is evidence of St Columba's AD 575 monastery,

Drumcliff's Church of Ireland cemetery, resting place of W.B. Yeats.

whilst on the 10th-century High Cross it is just possible to make out the bible stories of Cain and Abel and Adam and Eve. Glencar Lough, east on the N16 and half in County Leitrim, has a dramatic setting. Earlier literary diversions may be contemplated at Cooldrumman, halfway between Drumcliff and Lissadell. Here, in the Battle of the Books, AD 561, it's claimed up to 3,000 monks and their supporters died in an argument as to whether St Finian was right in citing Derry's St Columba for breach of copyright.

Further north off the N15, turn west at Grange for superb **Streedagh Strand** with Carriag na Spáinneach (Spaniard's Rock), where three ships of the Spanish Armada foundered in 1588. Most of the shipwrecked, cold and starving were put to the sword. Some regrouped, joined the *La Girona*, only to suffer similar fates at Lacada Point, Dunluce, County Antrim. The little road east from Grange leads up Ben Bulben.

Mullaghmore 8 is a harbour village, a picture postcard from some perfect childhood holiday. The large sandstone castle built on a rock overlooking the harbour, Classiebawn, was inherited by Edwina, wife of Lord Louis Mountbatten. On 27 August 1979, Lord Mountbatten, his sister-in-law, the Dowager Lady Brabourne, his grandson Nicholas and a local boy, Paul Maxwell, were killed when a bomb containing 50lb (22.5kg) of gelignite exploded on their fishing boat. Three others were badly injured but survived. The IRA claimed responsibility; there was no local involvement.

The Blue Flag (EU-approved for quality) beach is golden; bright boats rock by the pier and waves splash on Mullaghmore Head.

Offshore is the low-lying uninhabited **Inishmurray Island**, 4 miles (6km) away with one of the most complete and visually exciting early Christian monastic settlements in Europe: the stunning remains of St Molaise's 6th-century monastery, and three churches within a 12ft (4-metre) dry-stone wall, are just about the only survivors of Viking raids in the 9th century. If the crossing from Mullaghmore, or Rosses Point, was

The beach at Mullaghmore.

rough enough, travellers might seek out the island's other curiosity, its cursing stones. Trips to the island can be arranged through Inishmurray Island Tours (www.inishmurrayislandtrips.com).

Sligo Folk Park ❾, (Coopershill, Riverstown; https://sligofolkpark.com) is worth a visit to see traditional craft demonstrations that include thatching, creel-making, butter-making and wood-turning, as well as a working forge. A museum is devoted to rural history with displays of farm implements.

LEITRIM: RESCUED BY WATER

North of Mullaghmore, Leitrim is allowed to just dip its toes into 2.5 miles (4km) of the Atlantic, before the shoreline reaches the **Drowse**, one of the best salmon rivers and the boundary with Donegal. Ten miles (16km) inland and Leitrim's border is with Fermanagh in Northern Ireland.

Another 20 miles (32km) east and its northern border is with Monaghan. At **Lough Allen** ❿ – its biggest lake, which divides the county into two topographical areas – there are scarcely 5 miles (8km) of Leitrim soil between north Monaghan and south Roscommon.

This tiny county of lakes and rushes, meandering rivers, bumpy roads, crumbling farmhouses, drumlins (low rounded hills) and neglected fields, often referred to as 'leaky Leitrim', once dismissed for its poverty, is now valued as a place that has retained the quiet charm of pre-Celtic Tiger Ireland. The Great Famine of 1845–49 hit the county hard, and emigration has continued ever since. The unflinching novels of John McGahern (1934–2006) who lived and farmed at Feenagh near **Mohill** ⓫, catch the air of rural desperation that pervaded.

McGahern was one of the most important Irish writers since Samuel Beckett. With his sparse and incisive lyrical style, he was the master of precise language. His stories, set deep in the poor Leitrim soil, tap into the social and economic realities of Irish life in the 1930s and 1940s. 'There is nothing dramatic about the Leitrim landscape,' he once wrote, 'but it is never dull.'

W.B. YEATS

The son and brother of artists, W.B. Yeats (1865–1939) studied art in Dublin and London but became interested in mysticism, the supernatural and Irish nationalism. With Lady Gregory, an Anglo-Irish aristocrat, he founded the Abbey Theatre in Dublin at the same time as his unrequited passion for Maud Gonne, an English-born revolutionary and actress, inspired his early poetry. At 52, he married the 25-year-old Georgie Hyde-Lees, who was deeply into mysticism.

The drama of the 1916 Easter Rising encouraged his interest in politics and he became a senator in the Irish Free State's government from 1922 to 1928, serving as chairman of a commission on coinage. He was awarded the Nobel Prize for Literature in 1923. His status as a major English-language poet is assured.

Looking towards Ben Bulben from Drumcliff churchyard.

His last published book, the painfully recollected *Memoir* (2005), illuminated much of the fiction that preceded it. The writer and commentator Fintan O'Toole summed up John McGahern's legacy thus: 'He changed Ireland, not by arguing about it, but by describing it.'

ERNE–SHANNON WATERWAY

That quiet countryside and unspoilt environment so powerfully described in McGahern's books is now attracting visitors. Leitrim has much going in its favour. A glance at the map shows a necklace of lakes linking the rivers Shannon and Erne via the Ballinamore–Ballyconnell Canal – more prosaically marketed as the **Erne–Shannon Waterway**. From spring to winter, the banks of the lakes and rivers – where cows drink hock-high amongst the flag irises – are dotted with the big green umbrellas of visiting anglers after bream, eel, perch, pike, roach and rudd. A licence is not required for fishing on the Shannon for pike, brown trout or coarse fish, but is necessary for the Erne and local fishery bylaws are strict. See www.fishinginireland.info.

Hired cruisers flying Austrian, British, Dutch, French and German ensigns ply the canal, their crews clinking their gin 'n' tonic glasses, their skippers nautical in caps, binoculars at the ready. Heron poise in the reed mace, great crested grebe dive before the bow wave. Amid the uncut water meadows, amateur botanists count sedges; birdwatchers tick off another species of warbler and cup their ear for the cry of corncrake and cuckoo.

Apart from the fishing, boating and birdwatching, tourists come for hill walking, horse riding, cycling and traditional music. The new money has brought music back to the pubs, turned old market houses into heritage centres and tourist offices, and refurbished town piers and lake fishing stands. The Organic Centre (www.theorganiccentre.ie) in **Rossinver** offers courses in subjects ranging from 'plant to plate' and 'growing in polytunnels'.

At the southern tip of Lough Allen, **Drumshanbo** ⓬ dances to the beat of the

Carrick-on-Shannon.

bodhrán and banjo as well as the piper and fiddler. Music seeps from the pubs at all times of the year but two highlights are An Tóstal (www.facebook.com/antostal), held each summer, and in mid-July a week-long annual festival of song and dance, the Joe Mooney Summer School (www.joemooneysummerschool.com).

Slieve Anierin (Sliabh an Iarainn; 'Mountain of Iron') lies northeast of Drumshanbo and the mountain takes its name from the fact that iron and coal were smelted from it. The mining on the nearby Arigna Mountains ended in 1990 but the memories are retained in the Arigna Mining Experience (www.arignaminingexperience.ie), which explains the social and mining traditions of the area. A 45-minute underground tour, led by ex-miners, shows what it was like to work in some of the narrowest coal seams in the western world. An exhibition area traces 400 years of mining history in the area and a DVD gives an insight into the mining process. A visit to the coffee shop is rewarded with stunning views of the natural surroundings.

CARRICK-ON-SHANNON

The county town, **Carrick-on-Shannon** ⓭, is a buzz of activity, much of it centred on the riverside and bustling marina with its opulent cruising boats, quality restaurants and luxury hotels. A walk around town with its attractive shop fronts is rewarding. Carrick boasts some striking architecture including the remarkable **Costello Memorial Church**, a tiny Catholic chapel on Bridge Street which is the smallest in Ireland and reputedly the second smallest in the world. The tourist office is based in the Old Barrel Store, at the Marina (www.leitrimtourism.com).

Drumsna, just southeast, where Anthony Trollope wrote his first novel, and Roosky 9 miles (14km) south again, have also found prosperity. **Lough Rynn Castle** (www.loughrynn.ie), once home to the earls of Leitrim, has now been converted into a luxury hotel where non-guests are welcome for afternoon tea and a stroll in the splendid gardens. It is 10 miles (16km) east of Carrick-on-Shannon. Ten miles (16km) to the northeast, **Carrigallen** has a flourishing theatre, the Corn Mill (www.cornmilltheatre.com).

The Leitrim Genealogy Centre (www.leitrimroots.com) on Main Street in **Ballinamore** ⓮ will help those interested in delving into their Irish past. The staff will compile a family history report.

For another take on the past, visit the **Glenview Folk Museum** (http://glenviewmuseum.ie; call to arrange a tour) just south of Ballinamore. The museum houses a private collection of 3,000 agricultural items from the 19th and 20th centuries. Nearby, fragments of the old Sligo Leitrim and Northern Counties Railway, whose initials were interpreted locally as 'Slow Late and Never Completely Reliable', can be traced.

DONEGAL

The Atlantic storms into Donegal's rocky coves, rumbling round white boulders up in banks beside the sheep-cropped

A necklace of lakes link the rivers Shannon and Erne.

grass. Rusty winches, skeletal memories of long-lost fishing enterprises, paint red the stone of crumbling piers. Dreamers and poets, and stressed-out business executives from mainland Europe, put thatch back on the roofs of old stone cottages, whilst the locals erect new bungalows, despoiling (for the tourist) the silent landscape of empty valleys, purple mountains, rushing streams and towering sea cliffs.

Donegal's people, like Leitrim's, will argue that they are hard done by. In Donegal, tenuously linked to the rest of the Republic by a slender isthmus, they say Dublin forgets them. Certainly, much of the county harks back to another age: tiny fields bound by drystone walls, the hay cut by scythe then tossed in cocks; a scattering of sheep, woolly dots on a distant, bare, impossibly steep, mountainside.

BUNDORAN

County Donegal contains seven Blue Flag beaches recognised for their safety as well as the quality and cleanliness of water and recycling facilities. The beaches start at **Bundoran** ⓯, which a few decades ago, was described in an architectural guide as 'a squalid place with little of interest'. In the intervening years the town has worked hard to clean up its act capitalising on its seaside location, marine wildlife and magnificent **Tullan Strand**. It is a popular centre for surfing, with many taking up the challenge offered by 'The Peak', a classic left-hander that runs to about 110 yards/metres and a bodyboarding wave known as three-D. Bundoran Surf School offers lessons (www.bundoransurfco.com). Regular sea angling and sightseeing trips with whale-, seal-, porpoise- and dolphin-watching cruises are available in the summer.

Good surfing at Bundoran.

Amongst the family attractions is **Waterworld** (Atlantic Way; www.waterworldbundoran.com), with its wave pools, water slides, seaweed baths, and sauna and steam rooms.

Rossnowlagh ⓰, Bundoran's smaller quieter cousin round the coast to the north, is a base for surfers. The extensive Blue Flag beach is very popular with families and there are lifeguards on duty during the summer months.

In the one-time garrison town of **Ballyshannon** ⓱, where the waters of the Erne are tamed to produce hydroelectricity, pretty Georgian houses survive and literary folk commemorate the town's most famous son, poet William Allingham (1824–89) remembered for his verse 'Up the airy mountain, / Down the rushy glen, / We daren't go a-hunting / For fear of little men'.

The more recent memory of another son of Ballyshannon, the rock musician Rory Gallagher (1948–95), is honoured at the annual **Rory Gallagher International Festival** (www.rorygallagherfestival.com) during the June Bank Holiday weekend, attracting up to 5,000 visitors to the town. Gallagher, who blazed a trail for rock guitarists, enjoyed a successful solo career selling millions of albums worldwide. His concerts have gone into the pantheon of rock history and his music is enjoying a resurgence of interest.

According to the 'Book of Invasions' ('Leabhar Gabhála'), Ireland's origin myth, Inis Saimer, the little island situated in the Erne Estuary, was were Ireland's first people settled.

THE COUNTY TOWN

Donegal ⓲, the lively county town, has a busy triangular 'Diamond' market square, congested with tourist traffic all summer. The town's history has a familiar ring. It has a notable **castle** (https://heritageireland.ie). Once an O'Donnell stronghold, it was redesigned, as was the town itself, by the Brookes, planters who took over the land after the so-called 'Flight of the Earls' in the early 1600s. In the now ruined O'Donnell-financed Franciscan abbey, south on the estuary of the Eske, monks compiled, in the 1630s, the medieval history known as *The Annals of the Four Masters*.

Complementary to tourism, the weaving and making up of tweeds is the main industry, and Magee's, the town's largest shop, is the industry's principal outlet. A mile south, **Donegal Craft Village** (www.donegalcraftvillage.com; free) established in 1985, demonstrates weaving and other craftworks.

Three miles (5km) south of Donegal town, at **Laghy**, the R232 runs southeast for Pettigo from where the R233 bears north 3 miles (5km) across desolate bog land to **Lough Derg** ⓳, with its tiny Station Island, focal point for a major act of pilgrimage, St Patrick's Purgatory (www.loughderg.org). The island, now covered with buildings, looks from a distance like a Canaletto painting, and the pilgrims commemorate the 40 days Ireland's saint spent on it, praying, fasting and expelling evil spirits. Many Irish Catholics, especially from the north and west, have spent the required three days of ritual there, walking barefoot, repeating prayers and consuming nothing but black tea and dry toast.

Pilgrims are increasingly coming for 'time', meaning time to pray, time to reflect, time for themselves and time away from the hectic everyday world.

DANIEL O'DONNELL

County Donegal's famous son Daniel O'Donnell is world renowned for his unique blend of country and Irish folk music. Born in Dungloe in 1961 and brought up in Kincasslagh, O'Donnell's success has been attributed to his close, friendly relationship with his huge fanbase, and his stage presence.

An initial career founded on a business studies degree was perhaps not the normal grounding for a music legend, but a portfolio of 20 UK Top 40 albums and 15 Top 40 singles unsurprisingly led to him receiving the award of an honorary MBE for services to the music industry in 2002. He has sold more than 10 million records and will forever be an icon in Irish culture.

Today, Daniel O'Donnell lives in his native county of Donegal.

A swan in Ballyshannon.

An increasing number of men are visiting the island, marking a change from the popular belief that the women came to the island to pray for the men. Lough Derg welcomes approximately 11,000 pilgrims a year – not only from Ireland but also from countries around the world.

KILLYBEGS

The road west from Donegal town runs past Bruckless, where there are live oysters and mussels for sale, then through the fishing port of **Killybegs** ⓴ (www.killybegs.ie), where hefty trawlermen, drinking amongst the Victorian villas, give the town a raffish, frontier air.

Kilcar, 7 miles (11km) on along the craggy, beautiful coastline, is another vacation, its traditional music and tweed centre is somewhat overshadowed by **Ardara** 20 miles (33km) to the northeast. It is rewarding to continue further west over the steep Glengesh Pass through quiet **Carrick**, then turning south for the precipitous drive past Teelin to Carrigan Head at the eastern end of 2,000ft (650-metre) **Slieve League** whose sheer cliffs – the highest marine cliffs in Europe – drop a scary 765ft (235 metres) into the indigo sea beyond. An alternative is to leave transport at Teelin, walking the signposted One Man's Pass in the same direction. The views from Amharc Mór are, when not shrouded in mists, spectacular – and vertiginous.

For those in need of a calming cup of coffee afterwards the **Slieve League Cultural Centre** (www.slieveleaguecliffs.ie) houses a tea shop and craft gallery, as well as archaeological, geological and tourist information.

GLENCOLUMBKILLE

Glencolumbkille ㉑, further west in the lowlands at the head of Glen Bay, represents a landmark in the development of a particular kind of Irish tourism. The idea was devised here that the draughty, cold traditional thatched whitewashed cottage could be upgraded, given central heating, pine furniture, a shower, television and fridge and clustered into a marketable group. Purists dismiss it,

Killybegs Harbour.

while its protagonists argue that it sustains life and employment in distressed rural communities. Four cottages in the **Folk Village Museum** (www.glenfolkvillage.com) present traditional life over the centuries; one cottage, the Shebeen, sells seaweed and fuchsia wine.

Tiny **Port,** hard to reach in the next valley north, demonstrates what happens when a village dies, but most travellers continue northeast for 16 miles (26km) to **Ardara** ㉒, where the Heritage Centre (www.ardara.ie) has a tourist information point, then to Glenties, both awash in season with Northern Ireland's holidaymakers buying Guinness, tweeds, Aran sweaters, salmon flies for the Owena and Owentocker rivers, and tapping their toes to fiddlers.

Drive north of Ardara to the gloriously soft sandy beach at **Nairn** (known as Tramore Strand) where sanderlings frequently perform like clockwork toys, and en route you will pass the wind turbine at the **Dolmen Centre** (Kilclooney, Portnoo; https://m.facebook.com/DolmenCentrePortnoo; free), the first eco-tourism centre in Ireland, which uses the latest in green energy.

North, the N56 continues to **Dungloe**, capital of the Rosses, a raggedly charming peninsula of islands, trout lakes and inlets. From **Burtonport**, 4 miles (6km) northwest, a 25-minute ferry service (www.arranmoreferry.com) runs to Arranmore Island, 3 miles (5km) offshore, with its dry-stone walls, holiday cottages and abundant wildlife. There are a number of activities to enjoy on the island including excellent lake and shore fishing. A brisk walk can be combined with a stop at one of the island's traditional Irish pubs renowned for their charming atmosphere. The west of the island has many marine caves and stacks carved from solid rock resulting in a spectacular cliff coastline, and there are great views of the mainland from Glen Head.

Ferries for bare and windswept **Tory Island** ㉓ (www.toryferry.com), a popular tourist destination, run the 15-mile (24km) sea journey regularly from Bunbeg. According to legend, the island was once home to Balor, the one-eyed

god of darkness. The word 'Tory' comes from the old Irish *Tóraidhe*, meaning 'outlaw' or 'bandit', and the last action of the 1798 United Irishmen Rebellion took place in the sea just off the island. The main village, West Town, has a 51ft (15-metre) round tower and the ruins of two churches. Corncrakes, almost extinct in the rest of Ireland, abound on Tory. This area, like Gweedore to the north, is traditionally Irish speaking.

The dramatic conical quartz mountain north of Dunlewey is **Errigal**, Donegal's highest at 2,466ft (752 metres). The peak south is Slieve Snaght, 2,017ft (615 metres). At the **Dunlewey Visitor Centre** (www.dunleweycentre.com; free) the traveller can step back in time into the mid-20th century within the preserved cottage of Manus Ferry, who was a renowned Donegal weaver. Boat cruises are available on the lake and visitors are entertained with tall tales of the ghost of the Green Lady.

DUNFANAGHY

Twenty-one miles (37km) north on the N56, **Dunfanaghy** ㉔ is a popular resort, especially with golfers, but also offers opportunities for walking, cycling and horse riding. **The Dunfanaghy Workhouse** (www.facebook.com/TheWorkhouse; free), where people fled from the distress of the Great Famine, was the scene of horrific suffering. Today, part of the building has been turned into an interpretative centre and exhibition gallery.

Right next door, the long-established **Art Gallery** (tel: 074-913 6224) has been attracting visitors for many years, its walls decorated with some of the most evocative and moody images of Donegal captured by contemporary Irish painters.

Round the coast, the **Falcarragh Visitor Centre** (An tSean Bheairic; www.falcarraghvisitorcentre.com; free), fuses culture, heritage, history and tourist information in a former police station.

From Falcarragh, travel southeast 8 miles (13km) along the R255 to walk through the 10,000 acres (400 hectares) of **Glenveagh National Park** ㉕ (www.glenveaghnationalpark.ie; charge for castle). The park was given to the nation

The castle at Glenveagh National Park.

by Henry McIlhenny whose family made their fortune from Tabasco Sauce.

With its castle and its formal French and Italian gardens mixing with the wild mountains, the park has a further surprise in the Regency-style **Glebe House Gallery** (www.facebook.com/TheGlebeHouseAndGallery), which displays paintings by Degas, Renoir, Picasso and the primitive painters of Tory Island. Much photographed is **Gartan Lough**, 3 miles (5km) south via a narrow bog road. On the shores of Gartan Lough, **Colmcille Heritage Centre** (Churchill; www.colmcilleheritagecentre.ie; charge) tells the story of the saint through an audiovisual display.

Letterkenny ㉖, the prosperous county town on the River Swilly 10 miles (16km) to the southwest, is useful as a base. Its most prominent landmark is the cathedral, built in modern Gothic style by local masons using Donegal stone.

A CHOICE OF ROUTES

The traveller could turn southeast from Letterkenny and head through little-visited east Donegal. If the mood takes you, a tour of the 18th-century courthouse and jail in **Lifford** (www.liffordoldcourthouse.com; booking essential; charge) will fill you in on the severe punishment meted out and the grim conditions endured by the inmates.

At **Raphoe,** a well-signposted 20-minute drive from Letterkenny off the N13, those interested in archaeology will want to inspect the impressive 64-stone **Beltany Stone Circle**, a Celtic ritual site (tel: 074-912 1160). Back on the N13 travelling south, the road transverses the rugged Barnesmore Gap, a scenic mountain pass that cuts through the Blue Stack Mountains. For centuries the gap has been a strategic gateway between northern and southern parts of County Donegal, hence, up to about 1800, it was the notorious haunt of brigands and highwaymen.

To the north of Letterkenny, a choice of routes presents itself. One option is to follow the N56 southeast from Dunfanaghy, then take the R245 north chasing the Atlantic Drive past the golfer's haven of Rosapenna around Mulroy Bay with its

Tory Island.

farmed mussel rafts and salmon cages. Continue around windswept Fanad Head, then south again to Rathmullan, from whence, in 1607, the leading clan chiefs took flight by ship for Spain.

Beyond, 7 miles (11km) southwest, is charmingly preserved, riverside **Ramelton**, where you can find your local roots – should you have any – via Donegal Ancestry (www.donegalancestry.com): thence to Letterkenny again. From here it's a tempting run northwest, for 16 miles (26km), to the 4,000-year-old **Grianán of Aileach**, a spectacular circular stone enclosure atop an 800ft (240-metre) mound. Its name is translated, controversially, as 'sun-palace'.

BUNCRANA

There are a number of cultural pit stops en route to Ireland's most northerly point, **Malin Head**, on the **Inishowen Peninsula**, a 40-mile (64km) -long drive. Tourism in the area has been boosted by the Foyle Ferry between Greencastle and Magilligan Point in County Derry. A shuttle service operates on the route, weather permitting, from mid-March to September (www.loughfoyleferry.com). In summer a regular ferry service also operates across Lough Swilly from Buncrana on the west side of Inishowen across to Rathmullan on the Fanad Peninsula. Both options avoid the long drive around the lough shores.

Along the shores of Lough Swilly, military historians will want to see Fort Dunree Military Museum (www.dunree.pro.ie; charge) near **Buncrana** ㉗ which has a heritage centre with an underground bunker and an extensive collection of military artefacts and memorabilia.

Near Ballyliffin, stop off at the **Doagh Island Famine Village** (www.doaghfaminevillage.com; charge). The entry fee includes a guided tour with tea and coffee, snacks and a sample of poitín.

The **Inishowen Maritime Museum and Planetarium** (www.inishowenmaritime.com) is drawing visitors to Greencastle. Astronomy is the focus and there are dazzling laser light shows in summer.

Most of Buncrana's many pubs have live music at weekends.

Malin Head.

Sailing on the Inishowen Peninsula.

Northern Ireland
0 10 km
0 10 miles
N
ATLANTIC OCEAN
Tory Island
West Town
Tory Sound
Inishbofin
Horn Head
Bloody Foreland
Magheroarty
Dunfanaghy
Portnablagh
Ards Forest Park
Falcarragh
Brinlack
Gortahork
Gweedore
Gola Island
Altan Lough
Muckish Mountain 670
Owey Island
Bunbeg
Gweedore
Errigal 752
Glenveagh National Park
L. Beagh
St Colmcille Oratory
Torneady Point
Rosses Bay
Annagry
The Rosses
Dunlewey
Gartan L.
Aran or Aranmore Island
Burtonport
Loughanure
Slieve Snaght 683
Ballintra
Derryveagh Mts
Glendowan Mts
Dungloe
Commeen
Maghery
Crohy Head
Doocharry
Kingarrow
Gweebarra Bay
Fintown
Lettermacaward
L. Finn
Finn
Aghla Mt 596
Portnoo
Nairn
Dawros Head
Dolmen Centre
Maas
Glenties
Tangaveane
Commeen
Lavagh More 672
Carnaween 521
Slievetooey 443
Ardara
Port
Glengesh Pass
Glencolumbkille
Crove
Meenfullynagarn
Croagh
Blue Stack Mts
Letterbarra
Donegal
Slieve League 601
Carrick
Killybegs
Inver
Teelin
Kilcar
Bruckless
Carrigan Head
Fintragh Bay
Mac Swyne's Bay
Doorin Point
St John's Point
Rossnowlagh
Donegal Bay
Ballyshannon
R. Erne
Mullaghmore Head
Mullaghmore
Bundoran
Kinlough
Inishmurray
Cliffony
Creevykeel Court Cairn
Streedagh Point
Grange
Benbulben 526
Dartry Mts
Lissadell House
Ballyconnell
N15
Glencar L.
Raghly
Drumcliff
Rosses Point
Sligo Bay
Sligo (Sligeach)
Parke's Castle
Strandhill
328
Knocknarea
Carrowmore
L. Gill
Innisfree
Dromahair
Ballysadare
Dromard
Coolaney
Collooney
Ballintogher
Drumkeeran
Sligo
Ropefield
N4
Sligo Folk Park
Heapstown Cairn
Geevagh
Templehouse Lake
Ballymote
Castlebaldwin
N17
Carrowkeel Cemetery
Tobercurry
Lough Arrow
Bunnanadden
321
Corrigeenroe
Ballinafad
Roscommon
Curlew Mts
Gorteen
Lough Key
Knockvicar
Boyle
Mayo
Lough Gara
Lough Key Forest Park
Melmore Head
Atlantic Drive
Sheep Haven
Downings
Carrickart
Fanad Head
Portsalon
Mulroy Bay
Doe Castle
Cranford
Glen Lough
Creeslough
Milford
Rathmullan
Lough Fern
Termon
Kilmacrenan
Ramelton
Church Hill
Letterkenny (Leitir Ceanainn)
Ellistrin
River Swilly
Rashedoge
Cark Mountain 366
Bellanamore
Drumnacross
Kilross
Convoy
Welchtown
Ballybofey
Raphoe
Donegal
Croaghnageer 547
Lough Eske
Laghy
Lough Derg
St Patrick's Purgatory
Tievemore
Pettigo
Castle Caldwell
Belleek
Boa Island
White Island
Castle Archdale Country Park
Cliff's of Magho
Lough Navar Forest Park
Tully
Lower Lough Erne
Lough Melvin
Garrison
Derrygonnelly
Rossinver
Leckanarainey
Leitrim
Monea
Devenish Island
Enniskillen
Castle Coole
Lough Macnean Upper
Manorhamilton
Belcoo
L. Macnean Lower
N16
Glenfarne
Marble Arch Caves
Florence Court
Tiltinbane 592
Cuilcagh 665
Glangevlin
Dowra
Ballinagleragh
Derrynacreeve
Source of the Shannon
Lough Allen
Iron Mts
496
Benbrack
519
Bencroy or Gubnaveagh
Slieve Anierin 586
Drumshanbo
R. Shannon
Leitrim
Carrick-on-Shannon
Drumsna
N4
Longford
Garvagh
Ballinamore
Garadice Lough
Malin Head
Ballyhillin
Inishtrahull Sound
Urbalreagh
Glengad Head
Culdaff Bay
Doagh Island Famine Village
Malin
Pollan Bay
Dunaff Head
Ballyliffin
Carndonagh Cross
Dunmore Head
Kinnagoe Bay
Clonmany
Carndonagh
Gleneely
Castle Carry
Glasmullan
Slieve Snaght 615
Greencastle
Magherabane
Moville
Lough Swilly
Inishowen
Illies
Lough Foyle
Buncrana
White Castle
Scalp Mountain 483
Burnfoot
Muff
Inch Island
Speenoge
Earhart Centre
Grianán of Aileach
Derry
Eglinton
Ballykelly
Glenhead
N13
New Buildings
Ardmore
Ness Wood
A6
Manorcunningham
St Johnston
Claudy
N14
Mountcastle
Rossgeir
R. Foyle
Park
Beltany Stone Circle
Dunnamanagh
Lifford
Strabane
Carnanreagh
Sperrin Mts
Woodrow Wilson Ancestral Home
Castlefinn
Dergalt
Mount Hamilton
N15
A5
Glenelly Valley
Sperrin Heritage Centre
Cross Roads
Sion Mills
Mourne
Plumbridge
Scotch Town
Ardstraw
Castlederg
Newtownstewart
Strule
Gortin
Mullaghcarn 542
Greencastle
Ulster American Folk Park
Gortin Glen Forest Park
A505
Killen
Drumlegagh
Kilwater
NORTHERN IRELAND
Omagh
Tappaghan Mt 336
Lack
Sixmilecross
Gortaclare
Kesh
A32
Dromore
Fintona
Garvaghy
Irvinestown
Augher
Killadeas
Kilskeery
Clogher
Aughnacloy
Fivemiletown
Tempo
Slieve Beagh 371
A4
A509
Maguiresbridge
Lisnaskea
Drumcard
Upper Lough Erne
Derrynawilt
Clones
Derrylin
Newtownbutler
Swanlinbar
Teemore
Wattle Bridge
Slieve Rushen 405
Belturbet
Scotshouse
Bellamont House
Ballyconnell
Cootehill
N3
Bellanacargy
Doogary
Killashandra
REPUBLIC OF
Cavan (An Cabhán)
Canningstown
Lough Oughter
Carrigallen
Cornafean
Bellananagh
Arvagh
R. Erne
Cloone
Grange
Cross Keys
Athlone

S. Carrine
Macharioch
Mull of Kintyre
Sanda Island
Cairnryan
Rathlin Island
Bull Point
Church Quarter
Rathlin Sound
Rue Point
Benbane Head
Giant's Causeway
Carrick-a-rede Rope Bridge
Ballycastle Bay
Benmore or Fair Head
Murlough Bay
The Skerries
Portrush
Dunluce Castle
Portstewart
Portbradden
Ballintoy
Bushmills
Ballycastle
Torr Head
Runabay Head
Moss-Side
Knocklayd 514
Castlerock
Coleraine
Dervock
Causeway Coastal Road
Cushendun
North Channel
Antrim Mountains
Ossian's Grave
Cushendall
Glenariff or Waterfoot
Mt Sandel Fort
Ballymoney
Armoy
Glens of Antrim
Garron Point
Garron Tower
Agivey
Killagan Bridge
Carnlough
Glenariff Forest Park
Carnlough Bay
R. Bann
Garvagh
Glarryford
Glenarm
Glenarm Castle
Causeway Coastal Road
Kilrea
The Sheddings
Carnalbanagh Sheddings
Balleygalley Head
Carntogher 462
Swatragh
Lislea
Arthur Ancestral Cottage
Broughshane
Ballygalley
Drains Bay
Stranraer
Glenshane Pass
Cullybackey
Sallagh Braes
Larne
Gracehill
Ballymena
Millbrook
Portmuck
Maghera
Moorfields
Island Magee
Gulladuff
Newferry
A36
Magheramorne
Gransha
Tobermore
Seamus Heaney Home
Bellaghy
Kildrum
Connor
Glenoe
Black Head
Lough Beg
Whitehead
Castledawson
Randalstown
Ballyclare
Magherafelt
Toome
Antrim
Patterson's Spade Mill
Carrickfergus
The Six Towns
Shane's Castle
Greenisland
Belfast Lough
Copeland
Waterworks
Ballyronan
Staffords-town
Muckamore
Templepatrick
Bangor
Groomsport
Moneymore
Springhill House
Belfast International Airport
Newtownabbey
Crawfordsburn
Holywood
Donaghadee
Kildress
Coagh
Ballinderry Bridge
George Best Belfast City Airport
Ulster Folk Museum, Ulster Transport Museum
Ballycopeland Windmill
Cookstown
Lough Neagh
Crumlin
BELFAST
Stormont
Newtownards
Ballyferis Point
Tullaghogue
Ardboe
Rams Island
Glenavy
Comber
Mount Stewart
Killycolpy
Drumbeg
Greyabbey
Enterprise Centre
Upper Ballinderry
Lisburn
Giant's Ring
Castle Espie Centre
Ards Peninsula
Lough Neagh Discovery Centre
Carryduff
Kircubbin
Coalisland
Charlestown
Lagan Valley
Ardmillan
Mahee I.
Ballyhalbert
Dungannon
Soldierstown
Strangford
Peatlands Park
The Temple
Kirkistown Circuit
Portavogie
Linen Green
The Argory
Hillsborough
Saintfield
Cloghy Bay
Lurgan
Rowallane Gardens
Killyleagh
Lough
Kearney Point
Moy
Ardress House
Craigavon
Annahilt
Benburb
Portadown
Dromore
Ballynahinch
Portaferry
Loughgall
Moyallan
Strangford
Blackwater
Blackskull
Dromara
Castle Ward House
Richhill
Banbridge
Inch Abbey
Kilclief
Navan Centre and Fort
Armagh
Tandragee
Slieve Croob 534
Scarva Visitor Centre
Leganannny Dolmen
Downpatrick
Struell Wells
Church Ballee
Killard Point
Gosford Forest Park
R. Bann
Moneyslane
Castlewellan Forest Park
Clough
Loughbrickland
Ardglass
Markethill
Killough
Lecale Peninsula
Middletown
Poyntz Pass
Bronte Homeland Interpretative Centre
Castlewellan
Dundrum
Dundrum Bay
St John's Point
Keady
Jerrettspass
Rathfriland
Kilcoo
Royal County Down
Newcastle
Tollymore Forest Park
Bessbrook
Hilltown
Newtownhamilton
Newry
Derrymore House
Mourne Mts
850 Slieve Donard
Creaghanroe
Killevy Churches
Mayobridge
Dunmore
573
Slieve Gullion
626
Attical
Ballybay
Castleblayney
Warrenpoint
Annalong
L. Major
Muckno Lake
Slieve Gullion Forest Park
Slieve Martin 486
Rostrevor
Creggan
Omeath
Carlingford Lough
Kilkeel
Crossmaglen
Forkill
509
Windy Gap
Greencastle
Broomfield
Proleek Dolmen
Carlingford
Cranfield Point
Irish Sea
Inniskeen
Dundalk (Dun Dealgan)
Ballagan Point
Shercock
IRELAND
Cooley Point
Carrickmacross
Fane River
Blackrock
Dundalk Bay
Louth
Dún Á Rí Forest Park
Reaghstown
Castlebellingham
Kingscourt
Louth
Dublin
Douglas, Liverpool

The Giant's Causeway.

NORTHERN IRELAND

Northern Ireland's traditional attractions are as alluring as ever with its gorgeous lakes and glens, stunning coastline and wealth of golf courses.

After three decades of the Troubles, the 1998 Good Friday Agreement ushered in a period of peace, encouraging many more travellers to explore this beautiful, rural part of Ireland, which boasts one of the British Isles' best coastlines. With soldiers no longer on the streets, the cities of Derry and Belfast have become more vibrant. And after the military checkpoints disappeared, the border became invisible – it's only when you notice post boxes are red, signs are in miles and prices are in pounds that you know you've crossed it. Of course, the fallout from Brexit could one day change all this.

THE BORDER QUESTION

The border snakes its way along 18th-century county boundaries, with farmland and even houses straddling it, taking little account of natural boundaries, such as rivers, or of the cultural differences that separate the Protestant and Catholic communities, with their respective unionist and republican leanings.

Northern Ireland (consisting of the six counties of Antrim, Armagh, Down, Fermanagh, Derry and Tyrone) was created on 3 May 1921 when the Government of Ireland Act of 1920 came into force (the fruit of the fourth Home Rule Bill). When the Anglo-Irish Treaty of 1921 came into effect on 6 December 1922 it effectively created two Irelands. A three-man Boundary Commission (representing the Irish Free State, Northern Ireland and the UK respectively) was tasked with revising the boundary in 1924. The Free State had envisioned the transfer of substantial territory (per the 'wishes of the inhabitants'), instead the finalised report found for a limited two-way transfer of territory (based on 'economic and geographic conditions'). Last-ditch diplomatic efforts in London were met with intransigence, and faced with territorial

Main attractions
- Derry City
- Ulster American Folk Park
- Enniskillen Castle
- Mourne Mountains
- Downpatrick
- Strangford Lough
- Mount Stewart
- Ulster Folk Museum
- Transport Museum
- Causeway Coastal Rd
- Giant's Causeway

Maps on pages 270, 274

Dual signage in Armagh.

concessions, the Free State dropped its demands for the transfer of nationalist areas in Northern Ireland, and the 1920 boundary was recognised.

It should be noted that the terms 'Ulster' and 'Northern Ireland' are not synonymous. Historically, the province of Ulster encompasses nine counties; Donegal, Cavan and Monaghan plus the six that constitute present-day Northern Ireland.

Donegal, Cavan and Monaghan, are still bound to the other six by firm family and trading ties. To many locals, therefore, the border is an abstraction, or perhaps an approximation. The states it divides don't even agree about its length, the Republic claiming it is 280 miles (448km) and Northern Ireland authorities adamant that it is 303 miles (485km).

The UK's decision to leave the EU in 2016 and pursuit of a hard Brexit has had Northern Ireland-specific ramifications as it shares a land border with an EU country. The Northern Ireland Protocol, which came into effect in 2021 (in effect Northern Ireland remains in the EU's single market for goods), continues to stroke tensions, and Stormont has been in limbo since February 2022. At the time of writing, British and Irish leaders were in the midst of talks and a compromise may be reached, but the future remains uncertain.

OLD DERRY'S WALLS

Across the border from Donegal, is the county of Londonderry and its famously friendly chief city, Northern Ireland's second, whose very name has long been a bone of contention for its main two communities. Catholics refer to Derry, for both county and city, while Protestants stick to Londonderry, with officialdom increasingly resorting to the clumsy **Derry-Londonderry** ❶ in a nervous effort to maintain neutrality. During its year as the inaugural UK City of Culture in 2013, it adopted the slogan 'Let's make it LegenDerry', but its official title was the hyphenated Derry-Londonderry. That year was also the 400th anniversary of the building of the 20ft walls that still surround the

city. Derry-Londonderry has undergone considerable development since the late '90s, and it reached its pinnacle in 2011 by the spectacular €14.5 million **Peace Bridge** Ⓐ, a graceful suspension bridge for cyclists and pedestrians. The beautiful structure over the River Foyle has transformed Derry's skyline, and is seen as a symbolic unification of all the communities that live there. Indeed, Derry's citizens take a matter-of-fact approach to its troubled history and will readily explain its complex loyalties to visitors.

There has been a renaissance in community activity, especially in the arts, and it has made great efforts to oblige the visitor with an annual calendar of attractions and festivals such as the massive Halloween Carnival (https://derryhalloween.com), and the City of Derry Jazz and Big Band Festival (www.cityofderryjazzfestival.com) in April/May. As with many border towns and cities in Northern Ireland, you'll find a general acceptance of euros if you're travelling from the Republic.

The city's growth was financed by London guilds, which in 1613 began creating the last walled city in Europe. Its purpose was mercantile success and you can still see traces of its former economic confidence in the ornamental facades of the old shirt-making factories, which provided the city with its livelihood for generations.

The **Derry City Walls** Ⓑ (www.thederrywalls.com; free access), 20ft (6 metres) thick and complete with watchtowers and cannon such as the 18-pounder **Roaring Meg** (dating from 1642), are marvellously intact.

THE BOGSIDE

Two 17th-century sieges failed to breach the walls, earning Derry the sobriquet 'maiden city'. Some say the city still has a siege mentality; a theory reinforced by the IRA's daubed slogan 'You are now entering Free Derry'. This was the name given to the **Bogside** Ⓒ, a densely populated Roman Catholic housing estate, when its inhabitants barricaded it against the police in 1969. Their grievances were old ones. After Ireland's partition in 1920s, the city's governing Unionists had fixed constituency boundaries to ensure a 'permanent' majority for themselves in what was a mainly nationalist area – an artificial majority that wasn't overturned until the mid-1970s. Feeling isolated from the prosperous eastern counties, and denied certain civil rights (including access to adequate housing), Derry's citizens built up both a wonderful community spirit and a resentment that led to marches and confrontation with the authorities. A good way to experience the political history of the Bogside is to visit **The Peoples' Gallery** (Rossville Street and Lecky Road; www.facebook.com/Gasmask69) in the centre of the area. Guided tours of all 12 murals by the artists can be booked in advance. For more on the civil rights movement – and the events of 30 January 1972, now known as Bloody Sunday, when British soldiers shot 28 unarmed civilians during a peaceful protest march – visit the Museum of Free Derry

Celtic, a Scottish football team, has a historic connection with the people of Ireland.

(www.museumoffreederry.org; charge), across Rossville Street from the Bloody Sunday Monument.

The most famous siege – which is still commemorated by Protestant marches every August – took place in 1689, when the Catholic forces of James II blockaded the Protestant supporters of William of Orange for 15 weeks, almost forcing them into submission. About 7,000 of the 30,000 people packed within the city's walls died of disease or starvation. One member of the besieged garrison chillingly recorded the selling prices of horseflesh, dogs' heads, cats and rats 'fattened by eating the bodies of the slain Irish'. To learn more, visit the new Siege Museum (13 Society Street; www.thesiegemuseum.org; charge).

The city's eventual relief is depicted on the siege memorial window of **St Columb's Cathedral** D (London Street; www.stcolumbscathedral.org; donation) a graceful 17th-century Anglican church built in Planter's Gothic style. The chapter house contains siege relics. Outside the walls, off Bishop Street Without, **St Columba's Long Tower Church** (tel: 028-7126 2301; free), built 1784, and known just as Long Tower Church, has a lavish interior.

The award-winning **Tower Museum** E (Union Hall Place; www.derrystrabane.com/towermuseum; charge) skilfully uses audiovisuals and photography to tell its story from both sides of the sectarian divide. There's also an exhibition on the recovery of a ship from the 1588 Spanish Armada, wrecked off Donegal's coast.

THE GUILDHALL

Streets from the city's original four gates (Shipquay, Ferryquay, Bishop's and Butcher's) converge on The Diamond, a perversely square-shaped market place at the top of Shipquay Street, the steepest main thoroughfare in Ireland. At the bottom of the street, the **Guildhall** F (Guildhall Square; https://guildhallderry.zcom; free), a Tudor-Gothic structures popular in Northern Ireland, clearly shows the influence of the London merchants. Behind the Guildhall is Derry Quay, celebrated in song by

Celebrating Halloween in downtown Derry.

thousands of emigrants who sailed down the Foyle from here, bound for a new life in America. Across the river is the old **Workhouse** (1840–1948), once home to 800 inmates.

There are now various tours to guide you around the city and its environs. The best place to enquire about these and all other tourist information is the **Derry Visitor and Convention Bureau** G (44 Foyle Street; www.visitderry.com; free), who also run their own walking tours of the city.

VOID (Patrick Street; www.derryvoid.com; free) showcases both established Irish and international artists in some eight exhibitions a year in its two galleries and six studios, while the **Verbal Arts Centre** (Stable Lane and Mall Wall, Bishop Street Within; www.verbalartscentre.co.uk) is the only centre in Ireland dedicated to storytelling, both verbal and written. Many in the city's resurgent arts community have links to the **Nerve Centre** (7–8 Magazine Street; www.nervecentre.org), which also stages live music and film festivals, and arts activities. A dynamic programme of events from drama and dance to comedy and musicals is hosted at the **Millennium Forum** (Newmarket Street; www.millenniumforum.co.uk) and the renovated **Playhouse** (Artillery Street; www.derryplayhouse.co.uk).

Shoppers will find plenty to keep them occupied but perhaps the most engaging destination is the Derry **Craft Village** H (Shipquay Street; tel: 028 7126 0329), a historic reconstruction of an 18th-century street and a 19th-century square with artisan craft shops, restaurants, bars, exhibitions and live music.

SMALL-TOWN TYRONE

Thirteen miles (21km) southwest of Derry city, in County Tyrone on the A5 is **Strabane** 2, a border town paired with Lifford on the Donegal side. In the 18th century Strabane was an important centre for publishing. John Dunlap, printer of America's Declaration of Independence, trained in **Gray's Printing Press** (49 Main Street; www.nationaltrust.org.uk/visit/northern-ireland/grays-printing-press). It's worth the effort

Peace Bridge, Derry.

if only for its intriguing display of ink, galleys, presses and the story of Dunlap's emigration. In Dergalt, 2 miles (3km) to the southeast, signposted off the B47, is a whitewashed cottage, the **Woodrow Wilson Ancestral Home** (tel: 028-7138 4444; free), where the 28th US president's grandfather once lived.

Sion Mills, 3 miles (5km) south of Strabane, is a village whose name betrays its origins. The linen-workers' old cottages are charming. The Parish Church of the Good Shepherd is a striking Italian-style edifice, contrasting with the modern architecture of St Teresa's Catholic Church, whose facade displays an image on slate of the Last Supper.

As you drive into **Omagh** ❸, the county town of Tyrone, 16 miles (25km) along the A5, the religious fragmentation of Northern Ireland is immediately apparent. On the right is the Presbyterian Church (Trinity); on the left, the Methodist Church; next, St Columba's Church of Ireland; then the Gothic spires of the Roman Catholic Church of the Sacred Heart, a poor man's Chartres Cathedral. There are many more. The joining of the rivers Camowen and Drumragh to form the Strule make the location pleasant enough, but Omagh is more a town for living (and praying) in than for visiting. Locals still recall the Saturday afternoon in August 1998 when a maroon Vauxhall Astra exploded in the town, killing 29 people. In its shops, alongside the usual linen souvenirs, are plaques and statuettes made of turf (peat). This is cut from the **Black Bog** between Omagh and Cookstown, 27 miles (43km) to the east.

AMERICAN CONNECTIONS

During tough times in the 1800s, the area's strong Scots-Presbyterian work ethic spurred many to seek their fortune in America. The results were remarkable and Northern Ireland claims that 11 US presidents have had roots in the province: Andrew Jackson, James Knox Polk, Andrew Johnson, James Buchanan, Ulysses S. Grant, Chester Alan Arthur, Grover Cleveland, Benjamin Harrison, William McKinley, Theodore Roosevelt

Ulster American Folk Park.

and Woodrow Wilson. Many Americans visit to seek out ancestral homes.

The Mellon banking family of Pittsburgh, having traced their roots to 4 miles (6km) north of Omagh, off the A5, endowed the **Ulster American Folk Park** ❹ (www.nmni.com/uafp; charge) on the site at Camphill as part of Northern Ireland's contribution to the bicentenary of America. To illuminate the transition made by the 18th-century emigrants, craftsmen's cottages, a schoolhouse, a blacksmith's forge and a Presbyterian meeting house from the Old World have been rebuilt on a peat bog alongside log cabins, a Pennsylvanian farmstead and a covered wagon from the New World. Peat is kept burning in the cottages, and there are demonstrations of candle-making, fish-salting and horse-shoeing as well as periodic 'living history' re-creations of battles between redcoats and Native Americans. An indoor exhibit recreates the main street of a century-old Ulster town, its hardware shop displaying foot warmers and lamp wicks. A replica of an emigrant ship links the continents. There's not a whiff of Disney, due to the attention to detail, though the American 'half' looks more prosperous than the original settlers found it. The award-winning park has a number of annual celebrations, including 4 July and an Appalachian and bluegrass festival.

A Centre for Migration Studies on the site has a reference library open to the public for research and staff will help with enquiries about migration history.

RELICS OF OLD INDUSTRIES

There's nothing Northern Ireland likes better than history, and almost every village in Tyrone – Castlederg, Donaghmore, Fivemiletown, Newtownstewart – has its heritage centre. One of the more interesting is along the A505 from Omagh. The An Creagan Visitor Centre in **Creggan** (www.an-creagan.com; free), at the foothills of the blue-tinged Sperrin Mountains, hosts an interpretative exhibition of the area, craft shop, bar/restaurant, self-catering cottages and regular cultural events.

The bluegrass festival at Ulster American Folk Park.

The Beaghmore complex features early Bronze Age stone circles and cairns.

DUNGANNON

In and around **Dungannon** ❺, 13 miles (21km) south of Cookstown and once the seat of the great O'Neill clan, there are several attractions. One of the more atmospheric places to shop here is the Linen Green (1 The Linen Green; www.thelinengreen.co.uk) in Moygashel, on the fringes of the town. Based in an old linen mill, it includes brands such as Jo and Co, La Jardin Spa and Newbridge Silverware. Less than 2 miles (3km) from Dungannon is the village of **Castlecaulfield**, created in the 17th century by Sir Toby Caulfield as part of the Ulster Plantation. It contains the remains of his mansion, where St Oliver Plunkett is said to have preached.

Signposted from the M1 motorway, exit 13, 7 miles (11km) east of Dungannon, is **Peatlands Park** (tel: 028-3839 9195), a preserved Irish bog with over 10 miles (16km) of marked pathways to explore.

Take the A45 from Dungannon and on the outskirts of Coalisland you will find the **Island Turf Crafts Gift Shop and Visitor Centre** (51 Dungannon Road; www.islandturfcrafts.com). There's an indoor bog, a museum exploring Ireland before and after the Ice Age and a shop selling turf crafts. Also at the Enterprise Centre is the **Irish World** genealogy centre (www.irish-world.com), which offers a range of services to people tracing ancestors in Tyrone and Fermanagh, and the **Craic Theatre Company** (www.craicartscentre.co.uk). Perhaps Northern Ireland's only (non-council-owned) community theatre, Craic stages everything from Shakespeare to musicals, plus visiting productions from the likes of DubbelJoint at its 200-seat theatre.

MAIN STREET COOKSTOWN

Twenty-five miles (40km) east of Omagh, **Cookstown** ❻, the exact middle of Northern Ireland, is renowned for its main street, 2 miles (3km) long and 160ft (50 metres) wide, and can be located from miles away by the 200ft (61-metre) spire of the Gothic-style Catholic church. The town has a strong tradition of nationalism, often refined

ANCIENT MONUMENTS

In most countries, a find such as the ancient Janus figure on Boa Island would have been turned into a major tourist attraction. Here, you have to keep a sharp eye out for the road sign pointing to 'Caldragh Cemetery' (free access), then tramp through cowpats down a farm lane until you come across a field full of overgrown, moss-covered gravestones, in the middle of which lurks the inscrutable figure. The lack of refurbishment makes the place feel splendidly eerie; you notice the figure's sexual arousal (east side of the figure, the west face is the female side) and the hollow in its head and wonder whether that hollow once held sacrificial blood.

A second Janus figure was discovered on the little island of Lusty Beg, near the small village of Kesh. There are holiday chalets for hire on this island.

in its many old-fashioned pubs. Local livestock sales give a good insight into the rough amiability of the rural Ulster character. Four miles (7km) west, the water-powered **Wellbrook Beetling Mill** (www.nationaltrust.org.uk/wellbrook-beetling-mill; see website for times; charge for non-members) has demonstrations of linen processing by costumed guides. Three miles north of Cookstown, at Moneymore, is a rare treat for lovers of historic costumes. Another National Trust property, the 17th-century **Springhill House** (www.nationaltrust.org.uk/springhill; see website for times; charge for non-members) has acquired an award-winning collection of costumes dating from 1690 to the 1930s. The impressive grounds, which house a children's adventure playground, are open year-round. Look out for the allegedly friendly ghost, Olivia Lenox-Conyngham, a one-time inhabitant of the house.

Many Neolithic graves and stone circles are sprinkled around both towns. The best are at **Beaghmore** (free access), 10 miles (16km) west of Cookstown, off the A505. Villages such as **Clogher** and **Coagh**, **Moneymore** and **Pomeroy** are noted for fine traditional musicians and a variety of ecclesiastical architecture. There's a run-down air about some, the result of chronic unemployment. But it's as well to remember writer John Broderick's advice in *The Pilgrimage*: 'The city dweller who passes through a country town and imagines it sleepy and apathetic is very far from the truth: it is watchful as the jungle.'

The poet Seamus Heaney is celebrated at **Seamus Heaney HomePlace** (45 Main Street, Bellaghy; https://seamusheaneyhome.com/about-homeplace; see website for exhibitions and events). Heaney's grew up on the family-farm at Mossbawn. Much of Heaney's poetry derives its imagery and colloquial language from his rural upbringing in this part of Northern Ireland.

ULSTER'S LAKELAND

To the southwest, **Fermanagh**, adjacent to Monaghan and Cavan, has many things in common with them, particularly

Uncrowded cruising on Fermanagh's lakes.

its tempo. Politically it is part of Northern Ireland and is the province's lakeland playground (a third of it is under water). But political divisions are less of a barrier these days: the restoration of the Ballinamore–Ballyconnell cross-border canal (Shannon–Erne Waterway) means that you can now travel all the way here from Limerick by inland waterway.

ENNISKILLEN

The county town, **Enniskillen ❼**, a Protestant stronghold since Tudor times, is built on an island between two channels of the River Erne as it flows from **Upper** to **Lower Lough Erne**. Waterbuses such the MV *Kestrel* run by Erne Tours (Round 'O' Jetty; www.ernetours.com) ply the lakes. Alternatively, visitors can charter day boats from Manor House Marine (Killadeas; www.manormarine.com).

The town's strategic importance is shown by **Enniskillen Castle** (www.enniskillencastle.co.uk; charge). The earliest parts date from the 15th century and the imposing water gate from the late 16th century. The castle houses two museums, one specialising in prehistory, the other in military relics.

Enniskillen is rich in small bakeries and butcher's shops, and there's a gossipy atmosphere as farmers mix with townsfolk in **Blakes of the Hollow** (http://blakesofthehollow.com), one of the North's finest pubs. Confusingly, the main street, best viewed from the head of the 108-step **Cole's Monument** (Forthill Park; tours every half hour; prebook via Enniskillen Castle) changes its name six times between the bridges at either end. One of the best-preserved towns in Northern Ireland, Enniskillen has several appealing areas, not least the **Buttermarket** (www.thebuttermarketenniskillen.com) in the centre, a restored 19th-century courtyard specialising in crafts and art galleries.

A true taste of the region's flavour can be gained by circling Lower Lough Erne by road or by boat. **Devenish Island ❽** is reached by ferry from Trory Point, signposted 3 miles (5km) north of the town at the A32/B82 junction. It is the best known of the lough's 97

Fishing by Enniskillen Castle.

islands because of its elaborate, well-preserved round tower, which you can climb by internal ladders. Close by are the decorative ruins of the 12th-century Augustinian abbey of St Mary.

Ten miles (16km) northwest of Enniskillen, **Castle Archdale Country Park** has pony trekking, boating and 230 acres (90 hectares) of lovely parkland with walks and cycle rides. The Archdale Centre is in the last remaining part of Archdale Manor House, the courtyard buildings. You can hire kayaks, canoes and powered boats from Castle Archdale Boat Hire & Watersports (Castle Archdale Park Marina; www.castlearchdaleboathire.com). **White Island**, with its 12th-century church, is fifteen minutes away by boat. The stone figures along the north wall pre-date the church and their origins baffles experts; some speculate that seven may represent the deadly sins.

A few miles on, past the village of **Kesh** is the strangest of all local stone figures: the two-faced Janus on **Boa Island** ❾, which is joined to the mainland by a bridge at each end.

Following the lough's shoreline, you reach **Pettigo**, an old plantation town once the railhead for pilgrims visiting the holy sites at **Lough Derg,** across the border in County Donegal. The River Termon, running through Pettigo, marks the border and is said to be stuffed full of bilingual trout. It is also said that when a man had his skull fatally cracked during a fist fight in the middle of the bridge a surveyor had to be called to determine whether he had died within the jurisdiction of the Northern police or the Republic's gardaí. An oak tree on one side of the bridge was planted in 1853 to mark the British victory at Sebastopol. A statue on the other side commemorates four IRA men who died fighting the British in 1922.

CASTLE CALDWELL

Castle Caldwell (tel: 028-6634 3165; daily dawn–dusk; free access), on the A47 4 miles (6km) east of Belleek, a ruined 17th-century castle by the lough-side nearby, has become the centrepiece of a working forest, popular with picnickers and birdwatchers. It's one of a number of areas where modern growth is being cut back and ancient woodland regenerated. A fiddler who, the worse for drink, fell off a barge and drowned is remembered on a fiddle-shaped monument with a cautionary verse that ends: 'On firm land only exercise your skill. / There you may play and safely drink your fill.'

The border touches the River Erne again at **Belleek** ❿, where anglers assure you that you can hook a salmon in the Republic and land it in Northern Ireland. It was after inheriting nearby Castle Caldwell estate in 1849 that John Caldwell Bloomfield discovered all the requisite ingredients to make pottery. He located his new company in Belleek in 1857, and despite many changes of ownership since, **Belleek Pottery** is still thriving. Today, the visitor centre (www.belleek.com/uk/belleek-visitors-centre; charge for tours) at the

The two-faced Janus carving on Boa Island.

distinctive 1893 factory building is one of Ireland's most popular attractions, with a museum, showroom, tearoom and audiovisual display.

You can take the scenic drive back to Enniskillen along the south side of the lough, stopping 5 miles (8km) northwest of Derrygonnelly on the A46 at **Lough Navar Forest Park** (tel: 028-6634 3165; free access), where a lookout point offers a panorama of five counties. Peregrine falcons and merlins are among various birds flying overhead, while plentiful deer herds graze. Two monuments here commemorate the crew of two American seaplanes that crashed locally during World War II. At **Tully**, off the A46, 3 miles (5km) north of the village, is one well-preserved 17th-century castle (Sun noon–4pm; free) whilst at **Monea**, 7 miles (11km) northwest of Enniskillen on the B81, is another with free access at all times.

MARBLE ARCH CAVES

'Over 300 million years of history' – impressive even by Irish standards – is the slogan used to promote **Marble Arch Caves** ⓫ (43 Marlbank Road, Florencecourt; www.marblearchcavesgeopark.com; see website for guided tours), a network of limestone chambers containing remarkable stalactites. The tour includes an underground boat journey and lasts roughly an hour and a quarter.

Located 12 miles (20km) southwest of Enniskillen, the caves are reached by following the A4 southwest for 3 miles (5km), then following signposts after branching off on the A32 towards Swanlinbar. The complex includes car parking, a souvenir shop and restaurant and you can get information on the nearby **Cuilcagh Mountain Park**, designated alongside Marble Arch Caves as a UNESCO Global Geopark.

CASTLE COOLE AND FLORENCE COURT

Two miles (3km) southeast of Enniskillen on the A4 is Ireland's finest classical mansion, **Castle Coole** (www.nationaltrust.org.uk/castle-coole; grounds daily 10am–dusk; see website for house

Marble Arch Caves.

opening times). Completed in 1798, it is a perfect example of late 18th-century Hellenism and has furniture dating from before 1830. A state bedroom is presented as it was for George IV. The park lake's graylag geese were established here 300 years ago.

Further south, **Florence Court** (www.nationaltrust.org.uk/florence-court; grounds daily dawn–dusk; see website for house opening times) is a beautiful 18th-century mansion 4 miles (6km) back. Contents include fine Rococo plasterwork and 18th-century furniture. The grounds include an ice house, a water-powered sawmill, a walled garden, extensive park and woodland and a yew tree reputed to be the parent of all Irish yew trees. You can sample home-made delights served in the Stable restaurant.

COUNTY ARMAGH

To the east is County Armagh, known as the Apple Orchard of Ireland, and during the 1980s and 1890s, its southern acres – thanks to terrorist activity near its border with the Republic – by the less-inviting sobriquet of Bandit Country.

Its county town of **Armagh** ⓬ (always called a city despite a population of just over 15,000) symbolises many of Northern Ireland's problems. Its two striking cathedrals – one Protestant, one Catholic, both called **St Patrick's** – sit on opposite hills like, someone once said, the horns of a dilemma. The two communities live mostly in separate parts of the city, with little interaction.

Armagh is known for its dignified Georgian architecture. At one end of an oval **Mall** – where cricket is played in summer – is a classical courthouse, at the other a jailhouse. The Ionic-pillared **Armagh County Museum** (The Mall; www.armagh.co.uk; free) contains many local artefacts, as well as records of Ireland's worst railway disaster, which happened in 1889 just outside Armagh; 80 Sunday School excursionists died when 10 uncoupled carriages ran down a steep incline into the path of a following train.

THE PLANETARIUM

Access is free into the gardens of the 1790 Observatory that accommodates Ireland's main **Planetarium** (www.armagh.space; pre-booking essential for shows). Astronomical shows have been enhanced by a major refurbishment to the Digital Theatre, including the world's most advanced digital projection system. There are interactive exhibitions and an outdoor Astropark with scale models of the planets, too and it also hosts regular activities.

Somehow the contemporary design of the **Market Place Theatre and Arts Centre** (Market Street; www.marketplacearmagh.com) sits comfortably within Armagh's historic centre. It is one of Northern Ireland's most important venues for drama, music and comedy and also has a popular bar and restaurant.

The Palace Demesne covers 70 acres of beautiful parkland, where the original palace building and stables, designed by Thomas Cooley in 1768, take centre stage. Today, it is a public park in the town centre that hosts many events.

St Patrick's Roman Catholic Cathedral, Armagh.

In the city centre is **St Patrick's Trian** (40 English Street; tel: 028-3752 1801). This explains St Patrick's connections with the city, including the 9th-century 'Book of Armagh' (see box) and also has an interesting craft shop.

Two miles (3km) west of the city, off the A28, is the high-tech **Navan Centre and Fort** (www.visitarmagh.com; charge), celebrating Emain Macha, Ulster's Camelot, dating to around 600 BC. Until restored, it was a neglected hilltop; now it comes complete with hands-on exhibits and audiovisual interpretation facilities.

ARMAGH'S VILLAGES

The city is surrounded by neat villages, reached through a network of pleasant lanes, some of which host the local sport of road bowling, culminating in the Ulster Finals (see page 93). In May, the countryside around **Loughgall** is radiant with apple blossom. In the village the **Dan Winter Ancestral Home** (9 The Diamond, Derryloughan Road; www.danwinterscottage.com; free) recounts the founding of the Orange Order. Lovers of art should investigate the quaint **Dispensary House Gallery** (88 Main Street; tel: 028-3889 2010; free).

Crossmaglen, a village at the heart of this fiercely republican area – known as Bandit Country during the Troubles – has a large market square, containing a striking bronze monument to the IRA; this village was in the frontline of many battles between the IRA and the security forces in the 1970s and 1980s. Remarkably, after enduring many sectarian murders, Crossmaglen has begun promoting tourism with some degree of success.

But it's the beauty of the Ring of Gullion (www.ringofgullion.org), and the mystical **Slieve Gullion**, source of myths like 'Deirdre of the Sorrows', which is the focus of modern tourism. There are fine walks and cycle rides around **Slieve Gullion Forest Park** (www.visitmournemountains.co.uk; free), where a forest drive winds up to two mountain-top Stone Age cairns.

Armagh Observatory.

Traditional music can be enjoyed at pubs, such as the Welcome Inn in **Forkhill**, on Tuesdays from 9pm.

PORTADOWN AND LURGAN

Between Armagh and Belfast is a chain of towns built on commerce. **Portadown** ⓭, 10 miles (16km) to the northeast, has found its role scaled down from that of a major railway junction to a prosperous market town noted for rose growing and coarse fishing. Linen manufacturing has diminished, as it has in **Lurgan**, 6 miles (10km) further along the A3. In the 1960s it was decided to link the two towns to form the 'lineal city' of **Craigavon**, thereby reducing congestion in Belfast; but the new city's population didn't arrive in the expected numbers and civic pride has kept the separate identities of Portadown and Lurgan very much alive despite the mushrooming between them of housing estates, schools and roundabouts.

Lough Neagh's wildlife is well explained in the **Lough Neagh Discovery Centre** (www.oxfordisland.com; free). The best way to explore the Lough is on board *The Maid of Antrim*, which departs from various points from April until October (www.facebook.com/MaidofAntrim; check sailing times).

Seven miles (11km) west of Portadown, off the B28 there are two National Trust mansions. The 17th-century **Ardress House** (Annaghmore; www.nationaltrust.org.uk/ardress-house; see website for opening times) has a fine collection of 18th-century furniture. Another National Trust property, the 19th-century **Argory** (144 Derrycaw Road, Moy; www.nationaltrust.org.uk/visit/northern-ireland/the-argory; see website for opening times) has been well refurbished, and has delightful grounds and a tearoom featuring great local baking.

BRONTË HOMELAND

Banbridge ⓮, 10 miles (16km) south of Lurgan, has a peculiar main street, bisected by an underpass taking through traffic, with sections of road on either side serving a collection of small shops. Just outside the town, off

Traditional crafts at the Navan Centre.

the dual carriageway, the Outlet shopping centre is among the biggest in Northern Ireland.

To its southeast, off the B10, is the '**Brontë Homeland Drive**', a confusingly signposted trail invented by the tourist authorities to capitalise on the fact that Patrick Brontë (alternatively, Brunty or Prunty), father of the novelists Charlotte, Emily and Ann, was born in a cottage at Emdale, 3 miles (5km) southeast of Loughbrickland. The family's fame was cemented in Yorkshire, not in Emdale, and there's nothing here to conjure up the claustrophobia of *Wuthering Heights* or *Jane Eyre*. But the drive through country lanes so narrow that the hedges almost meet is worth taking and, if you lose track of Patrick Brontë's trail on Ballynaskeagh Road, or Ballynafern or Lisnacroppin, it doesn't much matter.

The river valleys are peppered with the tall chimneys of disused linen mills so for access to the history and impact of what was the province's major industry go northwest along the Lagan valley to the impressive **Irish Linen Centre and Lisburn Museum** (www.lisburnmuseum.com; free) with its hand-loom weaving workshop. A range of damask table linen is sold in the museum shop with a flax flower pattern designed by the museum staff.

NEWRY

With its key location equidistant between Dublin and Belfast the newly appointed city of **Newry** ⓯, 19 miles (10km) to the southwest of Banbridge, was bound to prosper once the peace process began. Newry's two huge shopping centres, the Quays and Buttercrane, are the hubs of a city that attracts large numbers of cross-border shoppers hoping to make some savings due to the different tax systems. Newry and Mourne Museum and the tourist information centre are to be found in the restored 16th-century **Bagenal's Castle** (www.bagenalscastle.com; free) and its adjoining warehouse. Exhibitions explore the history of the area and building, and there is a café and shop too.

View of Lough Neagh.

From Newry you can drive 12 miles (19km) north on the A27, or walk or cycle along towpaths, to the **Scarva Visitor Centre** (tel: 028-3883 2163; free), which explains the building of the canal and its uses. Four miles (6km) west of Newry, on the A25, the thatched 18th-century **Derrymore House** (www.nationaltrust.org.uk/derrymore-house; grounds dawn–dusk) recalls a more sheltered world.

WARRENPOINT

From Newry it's 5 miles (8km) southeast to the pretty seaside resort of **Warrenpoint** ⓰, overlooking Carlingford Lough. Its Maiden of the Mourne Festival each August is a poor copy of the 'Rose of Tralee', but Warrenpoint's 'Blues in the Bay' (www.bluesonthebay.co.uk) held annually in late May is one of the best blues festivals in the UK. A few minutes around the coast, **Rostrevor**, sheltered by hills, is a smaller but prettier resort town with more of a Victorian atmosphere.

A steep half-mile walk up the slopes of **Slieve Martin** (1,595ft/486 metres) brings you to **Cloghmore**, a 'Big Stone' supposedly hurled by the Irish giant Fionn MacCool at a rival Scot. The geological explanation for this misplaced piece of granite is more mundane, having to do with glacial drift.

Skirting round the **Mourne Mountains**, past 14th-century **Greencastle**, takes you to the active fishing village of **Kilkeel**, capital of the so-called 'Kingdom of Mourne'. Despite its idyllic location between mountain and sea, there is little to recommend the charmless Kilkeel to the visitor, except perhaps Hanna's Close's traditional holiday cottages (www.mournecountrycottages.com) on the outskirts of town, an ideal base from which to explore the Mournes.

There's a choice here: you can proceed along the coast via **Annalong**, a smaller fishing village with old cottages as well as a **corn mill** and **harbour** (tel: 028-4175 2256; Apr–Oct 2–5pm) with a waterwheel dating from 1830, or you can turn inland into the Mournes. The Mourne Mountains meet the sea at Newcastle.

The Mourne Mountains.

THE MARCHING TRADITION

Parades and bunting, bands and bibles ... It's hard to escape these provocative rituals during July and August. What lies behind them?

Northern Ireland is unique in its flourishing popular culture: there are bands in every village and every housing estate, and nowhere else in the UK do normally discreet citizens sing and dance in the streets.

The main Orange procession, which celebrates the 1690 Battle of the Boyne in which William III (William of Orange) cemented the Protestant heritage, takes place on 12 July. On 13 July, the Black Men (the Orange Order's elite) dress up in period costume to re-enact 'King Billy's' routing of the Catholic King James II in the 'Sham Fight' at Scarva, County Down. On 12 August the Apprentice Boys march through Derry in memory of 13 apprentices who closed the city's gates against the forces of James II. While quiet church parades and processions occur throughout the year, this prolonged marching season throughout the summer can lead to provocation and an increase in sectarian violence.

THE GREEN ORANGEMEN

Lady's Day, in honour of the Madonna, Mary Mother of God, is held on 15 August by the Ancient Order of Hibernians, sometimes known as the Green Orangemen. (Green symbolises Catholic Ireland, orange Protestant Ulster.) Like their Orange counterparts, the Hibernians mix prayer with pageantry.

Now that the Troubles have ceased, such pageantry is slowly becoming less political and more of a tourist attraction. Traditionally, it appeared to Catholics to be a sign of 'triumphalism' and to Protestants as another nationalist provocation.

A BIG INVESTMENT

Flautist James Galway started his career in a Belfast band, and there can be few parts of Europe where such a high percentage of the population plays an instrument. In late spring and early summer, motorists driving through the leafy lanes of Ulster must be prepared to round a corner to find the road blocked by columns of men in bowler hats solemnly drumming and tootling their way to a local band contest. Scottish and Gaelic pipers compete with ecumenical harmony, at their own expense and 'for the glory of it', in villages and towns throughout summer. With a set of pipes costing £1,500 or so, there may be £2.5 million worth of pipes keening at a typical contest.

Battle of the Boyne parade, Belfast.

MEANDERING IN THE MOURNES

The Mournes are 'young' mountains (like the Alps) and their chameleon qualities attract walkers. One moment the granite is grey, the next pink. You walk by an isolated farmhouse, and within moments are in the middle of a wilderness. One minute, the Mournes justify all the songs written about them; the next, they become plain scrubland and unexceptional hills. The weather has a lot to do with it.

Off the B27, the remote **Silent Valley Mountain Park** (daily 10am–dusk) cradles a large dam, which supplies Belfast and County Down with water. In the heart of the Mournes, this beautiful and tranquil spot is ideal for picnics and hiking, and there is an innovative exhibition in the modern information centre.

Slieve Donard, the highest peak at 2,796ft (850 metres), has exhilarating panoramic views.

As you reach the foothills of the Mournes, turn right just before Hilltown towards **Newcastle** ⓱. This is east Down's main resort, with a fine, sandy beach, an inordinate number of cake shops and the celebrated Royal County Down Golf Club, one of the world's top 10 links courses. Home to the famous Slieve Donard Hotel and adjacent to the tranquil Murlough National Nature Reserve, Newcastle has undergone a serious makeover, including a smart promenade, but even that can't quite remove its old-fashioned seaside resort atmosphere.

Several forest parks – **Donard, Tollymore, and Castlewellan** – are good for riding (by pony or bicycle). This is an area that invites you to unwind, that doesn't understand people in a hurry.

Five miles (8km) inland from Newcastle, **Castlewellan** is a picturesque village with a wide main street. Nine miles (14km) to the west, **Rathfriland** is a steep plantation town with livestock sales and views of the Mournes.

As an alternative to heading into the Mournes from Newcastle, one can continue round the coast, via **Dundrum** (home of Ireland's finest Anglo-Norman

Castlewellan Castle.

castle) to **Ardglass**, where several smaller, ruined castles hint at its strategic importance in the Middle Ages to unwelcome kings visiting from Britain. A source of wonderful local seafood, Dundrum has two excellent restaurants to enjoy it, the Buck's Head and Mourne Seafood Bar.

DOWNPATRICK

Seven miles (11km) inland to the northwest is **Downpatrick** ⓲, which has a Georgian air and a cathedral supposedly built on the site of St Patrick's first stone church. The saint himself is said by some to be buried here. You can follow Patrick's story in a high-tech interactive exhibition with audiovisual film at the **St Patrick Centre** (St Patrick's Square; www.saintpatrickcentre.com), itself the hub of Downpatrick's famous week of celebrations around St Patrick's Day, 17 March. A hundred yards or so away the atmospheric **Downpatrick and County Down Steam Railway** (www.downrail.co.uk) runs weekends between June and September and special holidays.

Down County Museum (The Mall; www.downcountymuseum.com; charge for tour) housed in an old gaol, explores the local heritage. The Christian theme continues, off the A7 a mile northwest at riverside Cistercian **Inch Abbey** (028-9082 3207). The **Struell Wells** (free access), off the B1, 1.5miles (2.5km) east of the town, are evidence of pagan worshippers long before Christianity.

North of the town there begins a prosperous commuter belt, populated by well-spoken professionals who put their money into making their homes ever more comfortable. The source of their prosperity and the commercial magnet to which they are drawn each working day lies to the north: Belfast.

COMBER

Comber ⓳, 17 miles (27km) to the north at the head of Strangford Lough, was a linen town and still has a working mill. The town centre retains its old character, despite the developers, with cottage shops and a square. **Castle Espie** (Wildfowl and Wetlands Trust;

St Patrick's grave in Down Cathedral – though the saint's last resting place is a matter of dispute.

www.wwt.org.uk/wetland-centres/castle-espie; nature reserve daily 10.30am–4.30pm), on the shores of Strangford Lough, is the base for Ireland's largest collection of ducks, geese and swans.

The conservation area of **Strangford Lough** is noted for its myriad islands, most of which are sunken drumlins (low rounded hills), the smooth glacial hillocks that characterise County Down's landscape. There are rocky shores on this side of the lough at places like **Whiterock Bay**. **Mahee Island,** accessible by bridge, has a golf course and the remains of **Nendrum Abbey** (tel: 028-9082 3207; grounds open access; free), an early monastery.

THE ARDS PENINSULA

You can reach the **Ards Peninsula**, a 23-mile (37km) -long finger dotted with villages and beaches, by means of a regular car ferry that chugs a slanted course from **Strangford** ⓴, 8 miles (13km) from Downpatrick, across to Portaferry. The Vikings are said to have had a trading post at Strangford in the 9th century. Nearby is **Castle Ward House** (www.nationaltrust.org.uk/castle-ward), an 18th-century Georgian mansion. Overlooking the lough, the house has two 'fronts' in differing styles (classical and Gothic) because the Lord and his Lady had diverging tastes. There are wildfowl in the 700-acre (280-hectare) grounds, and the **Strangford Lough Wildlife Centre** (www.strangfordlough.org) is located at the water's edge. There's also a Victorian laundry, two small 15th-century castles and an adventure playground for children.

The ferry across the mouth of the lough deposits you at Portaferry, where the sunsets are as fine a sight as anywhere in the world and where the local lobster and the **Exploris** (Castle Street; www.exploris.org.uk), Northern Ireland's only sea aquarium, are not to be missed.

Nine miles (14km) north of Portaferry along the A20 is the one-street town of **Kircubbin**, a boating centre with a small pier jutting into Strangford Lough. Two miles (3km) inland takes you to the **Kirkistown Circuit**, a

Strangford Lough.

wartime airport and the home of car racing in Northern Ireland. Motor sport has a keen following in Northern Ireland; motorcycle racing and rallying can take place on public roads closed by Act of Parliament for the events.

Four miles (6km) further north on the A20 in the pretty village of **Greyabbey** is the site, with 'physic garden', of a Cistercian abbey dated 1193, and one of the most complete of its type in Ireland (www.greyabbeyhouse.com; by appointment).

Two miles (3km) north of the village is another National Trust treasure, **Mount Stewart** (www.nationaltrust.org.uk/mount-stewart; see website for times). It is an 18th-century house, which has several fine gardens and a mild microclimate that fosters delicate plants untypical of the area. The rhododendrons are particularly fine, and the gardens contain a variety of statues of griffins, satyrs, lions and the like. The **Temple of the Winds**, an 18th-century folly in the grounds, was built by James Stewart, a rival of Robert Adam, and is modelled on another in Athens. It offers a splendid view of the lough.

NEWTOWNARDS

Newtownards ㉑, a sprawling commuter town at the head of Strangford Lough, belies its name; it's an old town, dating back to the 17th century. It was an old market town and still is a bustling shopping centre with a blend of traditional shops and a covered shopping centre. There is a fine sandstone town hall and other buildings of historical interest include **Movilla Abbey** on the site of a 6th-century monastery about 1 mile (1.6km) to the east of the town.

The **Somme Museum** (233 Bangor Road, www.sommeassociation.com/visit/somme-museum; see website for opening times) reconstructs elements of the 1916 battle in which many Ulstermen died.

Overlooking the town is **Scrabo Tower** (Scrabo Country Park; tel: 028-9181 1491), a 19th-century memorial to Charles Vane, the 3rd marquess

Donaghadee.

of Londonderry, offering vistas of the lough and the soft-hilled countryside and good walks in the nearby **Killynether Wood**.

Donaghadee 22, 8 miles (13km) to the east, is notable for its much-painted harbour and lighthouse, and summer boat trips (Nelson's Boats; tel: 028-9188 3403) up Belfast Lough and to **Copeland Island** (a bird sanctuary), just offshore. The twisting road passes 18th century **Ballycopeland Windmill** (Millisle; www.ballycopelandwindmill.com; guided tours available; charge) and quiet beaches at **Ballywalter** and **Ballyhalbert**, and the fishing port of **Portavogie**, which has occasional evening quayside fish auctions.

BANGOR

Bangor 23 was originally a small seaside resort, noted for its abbey. The expensively rejuvenated seafront still has to gentrify some of its fast-food bars and souvenir shops to do justice to the marina packed with yachts and cruisers. Rowing around the bay in hired punts and fishing trips from the pier are evergreen attractions. The town has a leisure centre with heated swimming and diving pools. For some reason, perhaps the bracing sea air, Bangor is favoured by evangelists who trawl for souls along the sea wall by the little harbour.

The **North Down Heritage Centre** (Town Hall, Castle Park Avenue; www.northdownmuseum.com; free) Housed in the converted stables and laundry of Bangor Castle it contains some interesting treasures ranging from ancient manuscripts to a display on locally born songwriter and artist, Percy French (1854–1920), who wrote 'The Mountains of Mourne' among other famous songs.

The old Bangor has been overgrown by acres of housing developments and shopping centres, many of them inhabited by people who work in Belfast. It is a busy town with a weekly open-air market, plenty of pubs and eating places, and parkland. The best beach is nearby **Ballyholme Bay**, a sandy arc which can become very crowded.

Ulster Folk Museum and Ulster Transport Museum.

If you leave Bangor by the A2, a detour to the right will take in the beaches of **Helen's Bay**, the nearby wooded **Crawfordsburn Country Park** (tel: 028-9185 3621; free) and the picturesque village of **Crawfordsburn** with its charming **Old Inn**. Such havens are unusual so close to a city the size of Belfast.

THE GOLD COAST

The A2 from Bangor to Belfast runs through what locals enviously describe as the **'Gold Coast'**. This is stockbroker country, where lush lawns meet mature woodland. Hillside sites, overlooking the shipping lanes, have traditionally lured the well-heeled. **Cultra,** 6 miles (10km) from Bangor, has leafy lanes and the resplendent **Culloden Estate & Spa**. They go in for yachting, golf and horse riding around here.

Holywood, an ancient religious settlement a mile further on, enjoys a quiet prosperity since it was bypassed. Nothing much happens here, apart from summer jazz and rumours of the odd dance around the Maypole, but it has pleasant craft shops and art galleries, and good pubs and restaurants.

Nearby, at Cultra Manor are the award-winning **Ulster Folk Museum and Ulster Transport Museum** ㉔ (http://nmni.com/uftm; charge). The Ulster Folk Museum brings social history to life. Farmhouses, cottages, churches and mills have been painstakingly reconstructed – often brick by brick from their original locations. Freshly made soda bread, a local speciality, is sometimes baked over a traditional peat fire. On another part of the site the Ulster Transport Museum is also fascinating; exhibits range from horse-drawn chariots right up to a prototype of the ill-fated Belfast-built DeLorean sports car. There is a *Titanic* exhibition and a state-of-the-art X2 Flight exhibition, where you can simulate flying.

From here it's a straight run into Belfast (see next chapter).

NORTH OF BELFAST

If you aren't in the mood for city life, however, a good ring-road system will

Carrickfergus Castle.

take you through the city to the north shore of Belfast Lough and the suburbs of **Whiteabbey** and **Greenisland**, with some opulent housing.

Carrickfergus ㉕, 12 miles (19km) north from Belfast along the A2, is yet another market and dormitory town. Its big synthetic-fibre plants are empty now – a contemporary monument to its industrial past. The imposing 12th-century Norman **Carrickfergus Castle** (Marine Highway; tel: 028-9335 1273) beside the harbour, scene of gunrunning exploits early in the 20th century, still attracts attention for its authenticity. It is a real castle in every sense, with a portcullis, ramparts, chilling dungeons, cannons and a regimental museum in the keep. Looking to the new age of leisure, the town's **marina** has 300 berths. The parish church of St Nicholas (with stained-glass windows to Santa Claus) is 12th-century.

In Antrim Street, **Carrickfergus Museum & Civic Centre** (www.midandeastantrim.gov.uk/things-to-do/museums-arts; free) displays treasures excavated in Carrickfergus and provides general historical information about the town.

A mile to the east at Boneybefore, the **Andrew Jackson Cottage and US Rangers Centre** (www.midandeastantrim.gov.uk/things-to-do/museums-arts) is a reconstruction of the thatched cottage home of Andrew Jackson, the seventh president of the United States. There is a museum dedicated to the elite US Rangers army unit in the grounds.

The countryside north of Carrickfergus becomes rich meadowland, with the sleepy seaside town of **Whitehead**, base for the Railway Preservation Society of Ireland on Castleview Road, from where occasional steam excursions run. The town nestles at the mouth of the lough, with a seashore walk to the Black Head lighthouse.

Beyond this begins the peninsula of **Island Magee**, with unspoilt beaches and caves, which wraps around Larne Lough. From here, the road runs into unlovely **Larne** ㉖, a port with frequent ferries to and from Stranraer in Scotland (an hour and ten minutes away).

Cushendun.

THE CAUSEWAY COASTAL ROAD

The rewards of continuing along the coast are spectacular views of brown moorlands, white limestone, black basalt, red sandstone and blue sea along the **Causeway Coastal Road**. A notable engineering achievement, it is explained in the Larne Tourist Information Centre (www.midandeastantrim.gov.uk; free). The road, designed in 1834 by Sir Charles Lanyon as a work of famine relief, opened up an area whose inhabitants had previously found it easier to travel by sea to Scotland than overland to the rest of Ireland.

At various points, you can turn into one or other of Antrim's celebrated nine glens – **Glenarm**, **Glencloy**, **Glenariff**, **Glenballyeamon**, **Glenaan**, **Glencorp**, **Glendun**, **Glenshesk** and **Glentaisie** – and into another world. It's a world of weather-beaten farmers in tweeds; a world of sheep sales conducted by auctioneers who talk like machine guns; a world with a baffling dialect that turns a ewe into a 'yow' and six into 'sex'; a world where poteen, the 'mountain dew', is distilled in lonely places. It's not hard to track down this illicit (and potentially lethal) alcohol. 'It's floating about,' they'll tell you. 'In fact, it's practically running down the streets.'

Ballygalley ㉗, at the start of the famous scenic drive, has a 1625 fortified manor house (now a hotel) and, inland from the coast road, a well-preserved old mill and pottery. **White Bay** is a picnic area around which small fossils can be found. **Glenarm** has a beautiful park adjoining a fussy castle, home of the earls of Antrim. **Carnlough** has a fine harbour and, running over its main street, a white bridge built in 1854 to carry limestone from the quarries to waiting boats. The Londonderry Arms hotel (also 1854) retains the charms of an old coaching inn. An eponymous literary summer school at **Garron Tower**, 5 miles (8km) north, celebrates John Hewitt, an acerbic dissenter poet.

The village of **Waterfoot** is the entrance to **Glenariff Glen**, a deep wooded gorge dubbed by Thackeray 'Switzerland in miniature'. Wildflowers

Carrick-a-Rede Rope Bridge.

carpet the upper glen in spring and early summer, and rustic footbridges carry walkers over the Glenariff River, past postcard-pretty waterfalls.

About 1.5 miles (2km) to the north, **Cushendall**, 'capital of the glens', was created largely by a wealthy 19th-century landowner, Francis Turnly. His most striking structure was the four-storey red sandstone **Curfew Tower**, built as 'a place of confinement for idlers and rioters'. The village has a good beach and is a popular sailing centre. Just to the north is **Layde Old Church**, dating back to the 13th century and containing some ancient vaults. Six miles (10km) further on, **Cushendun** ㉘ is a village of Cornish-style white cottages, graceful old houses and friendly pubs, has been captured on countless canvases and is protected by the National Trust (www.nationaltrust.org.uk/cushendun).

THE NORTHERN COAST

Crossing the towering **Glendun Viaduct** (1839), just before arriving at Ballycastle, one passes the ruins of **Bonamargy Friary**, founded around 1500. A vault contains the massive coffins of several MacDonnell chieftains who stood out successfully against the forces of England's Queen Elizabeth I.

The best time to visit **Ballycastle** ㉙ is during the **Auld Lammas Fair**, held on the last Monday and Tuesday of August. Then this unspoiled town turns into one throbbing marketplace as farmers with impenetrable accents bring their livestock in from the glens and hundreds of stalls sell souvenirs, bric-a-brac, dulse (dried, edible seaweed) and yellowman (a sweet confectionery). It's great fun – an authentic folk event that owes nothing to the manipulations of tourist boards.

The **Ballycastle Museum** (www.causewaycoastandglens.gov.uk/see-do/arts_museums; free) concentrates on the folk and social history of the glens. It is housed in an 18th-century courthouse and market building.

RATHLIN ISLAND

A seafront memorial marks the spot where, in 1898, Guglielmo Marconi first

ROPE BRIDGE

A highlight of the Antrim coast is just west of Ballycastle. The Carrick-a-Rede Rope Bridge, a pedestrian suspension bridge over an 18-yard/metre channel, leads to Carrick Island, and an Atlantic salmon fishery. With a wooden floor, the bridge bounces as it swings in high winds, causing shrieks from thrill-seekers. Spare a thought for the salmon fishermen who traversed this chasm daily in the course of their work on a far flimsier structure than today's bridge.

Fortunately, no accident ever occurred on the bridge and old photographs show people performing stunts, such as riding a bicycle across and doing handstands on a chair.

Once across on Carrick Island the view is fantastic and complemented by an array of diverse seabirds.

The Giant's Causeway.

seriously tested wireless telegraphy. He made his historic transmission between here and **Rathlin Island** ㉚, 8 miles (13km) off the coast towards Scotland's Mull of Kintyre. The boomerang-shaped island, whose population has slumped from 2,000 to 75 since 1850, makes its living from farming and fishing and attracts geologists, botanists and bird-watchers; the reserve (tel: 028-2076 3948) managed by the Royal Society for the Protection of Birds, is home to an estimated 250,000 birds of 175 species.

Five miles (8km) west, off the A2, is the **Carrick-a-Rede Rope Bridge** (www.nationaltrust.org.uk/carrick-a-rede; pre-booking required; charge), 65ft (20 metres) wide swinging over a 80ft (24-metre) chasm to an island salmon fishery (see page 299).

THE GIANT'S CAUSEWAY

The **Giant's Causeway** ㉛ , is an astonishing assembly of more than 40,000 basalt columns, mostly perfect hexagons formed by the cooling of molten lava. Nowadays it attracts some 750,000 visitors a year. Dr Samuel Johnson, when asked by his biographer James Boswell whether this wonder of the world was worth seeing, gave the immortal reply: 'Worth seeing? yes; but not worth going to see.' It was a shrewd judgment in the 1770s when roads in the region were primitive enough to turn a journey into an expedition; indeed, the existence of the Causeway hadn't been known at all to the outside world until a gadabout bishop of Derry stumbled upon them in 1692.

Today this geological curiosity disappoints some visitors, who expect the columns to be bigger – the tallest, in the **Giant's Organ**, are about 39ft (12 metres) or who find their regularity diminishes their magnificence. Northern Ireland's only UNESCO World Heritage Site is managed by the National Trust (www.nationaltrust.org.uk/visit/northern-ireland/giants-causeway). Despite misleading signage, the site itself is actually free to enter, with public footpaths running through it, but parking isn't cheap and you need to pay to

Dunluce Castle.

enter the new **Giant's Causeway Visitor Centre** (44 Causeway Road; www.giantscausewayofficialguide.com; charge), located 2 miles (3km) north of Bushmills on the B146. At busy times of the year, book an entry time online in advance of your visit. From the centre it is a 20-minute downhill walk to the Causeway; minibuses are available – a popular option on the way back up. Admission includes a one-hour guided tour of the spectacular exhibition on all aspects of the Causeway. There is a park-and-ride service from Bushmills, with discounted entry.

One of the most pleasant ways to reach the Giant's Causeway from Bushmills is on the Giant's Causeway and Bushmills Railway **steam train**, which operates daily July, August and Easter (https://giantscausewayrailway.webs.com).

BUSHMILLS DISTILLERY

The Old **Bushmills Distillery** 32 (Distillery Road; www.bushmills.com; see website for guided tours; charge), a couple of miles away, boasts the world's oldest whiskey-making licence (1608). Old Bushmills, Black Bush and Bushmills Malt, made from local barley and the water that flows by in St Columb's Rill, can be tasted after a tour. Connoisseurs tend to prefer the classic Black Bush to the more touted (and expensive) malt. The main difference between Scotch whisky and Irish whiskey, apart from the spelling, is that Scotch is distilled twice and Irish three times.

About 2 miles (3km) along the coast road are the romantic remains of **Dunluce Castle** (tel: 028-2073 1938; charge). Poised on a rocky headland besides sheer cliffs, the 14th-century stronghold is huge and dramatic. It was abandoned in 1641, two years after part of the kitchen collapsed into the sea during a storm, carrying many servants to their death. In the graveyard of the adjacent ruined church are buried sailors from the Spanish Armada galleass *Girona*, which was wrecked on nearby rocks in 1588 with 1,300 men on board and was located on the seabed in 1967. Many of the *Girona*'s treasures are in Belfast's Ulster Museum.

PORTRUSH AND PORTSTEWART

Next along the coast are two seaside resorts. **Portrush** 33 is the brasher, tackier, offering amusement arcades, burger bars, karaoke pubs, souvenir shops, guesthouses, a children's adventure play park, boats trips for sea fishing and viewing the Causeway and two championship golf courses. **Portrush Coastal Zone** (8 Bath Road; tel: 028-7082 3600; free) has rock pool animals in a touch tank.

Portstewart, the quieter of the two resorts, is a tidy Victorian town with a huge strand, popular with anglers for its fine beach casting.

Nearby **Coleraine** is a busy market town, enlivened by also being home to the North Coast campus of the University of Ulster, a striking modern campus in 312 acres of landscaped parkland, with over 5,200 full-time students.

Bushmills Distillery.

A CHOICE OF ROUTES

Here, you can either continue westwards towards Derry or south towards the international airport and Belfast.

Along the first choice, the A2 towards Derry, on a windswept headland is **Downhill Demesne** ㉞ (www.nationaltrust.org.uk/downhill-demesne-and-hezlett-house; grounds dawn–dusk; see website for house and temple opening hours), concealing the ruins of Downhill Castle and Hezlett House, and Mussenden Temple, perched precariously on a cliff, which housed an eccentric bishop's library and possibly his mistress; it was inspired by the temples of Vesta at Tivoli and Rome. Downhill Forest has lovely walks, a fish pond and waterfalls.

The alternative route is southwards through the relatively prosperous farming country 'east of the **Bann**'. This long, under-used river, which flows from the southeast of the province through Lough Neagh and into the Atlantic near Portstewart, is a rough and ready political dividing line between the western counties of Londonderry and Tyrone, with their preponderance of nationalists and Roman Catholics, and the eastern counties of Antrim and Down, with their unionist/Protestant majority.

In a thriving market town like **Ballymoney** ㉟, 17 miles (27km) southwest of Ballycastle, archaic words that would have been familiar to Shakespeare crop up in conversation – a legacy of the Scots Presbyterians who settled in the 1800s.

As elsewhere in Ulster, churches loom large. There's one on each of the four roads leading into a small village like **Dervock**, for instance, 4 miles (6km) north of Ballymoney, the ancestral home of America's President William McKinley (assassinated in 1901). **Ballymena** ㊱, 19 miles (30km) southeast of Ballymoney, is the staunchly Protestant business centre of the county. The county town, **Antrim** ㊲, 11 miles (18km) to the southeast, offers more to see. There's an almost perfectly preserved round tower, more than 1,000 years old, in **Steeple Park**, with the area earmarked for works.

The Mussenden Temple.

The **Antrim Castle Gardens,** (tel: 028-9448 1338; free) are laid out like a miniature Versailles and run down to the shore of Lough Neagh. The Garden Heritage Exhibition in the restored Clotworthy House explains the history of the gardens and the family who created them. Don't miss the Garden Coffee Shop and the garden-themed Visitor Shop.

LOUGH NEAGH

Lough Neagh (pronounced *'Nay'*), 17 miles long and 11 miles broad (27 by 18km) is the largest inland sheet of water in the British Isles. Legend has it that the warrior giant Fionn McCool created the lake by scooping up a mighty handful of earth to fling at a rival Scottish giant (he missed, and the rock and clay fell into the Irish Sea to create the Isle of Man). Due to the lough's marshy edges, it has few access points – a reason, perhaps, why it is still one of Western Europe's most important bird habitats.

The **Lough Neagh Discovery Centre** on Oxford Island (see page 287) runs audiovisual shows about the wildlife and has a gift shop and café. There is sailing and water-skiing, with marinas at **Oxford Island** (south shore) and **Ballyronan** (west shore).

A large eel fishing industry is based at **Toome**. Until it became a fishermen's cooperative, gun battles used to take place on Lough Neagh between the police's patrol boats and the vessels of organised poachers.

The atmospheric, **Patterson's Spade Mill** (751 Antrim Road, Templepatrick; www.nationaltrust.org.uk/pattersons-spade-mill; at the time of writing the mill was closed to public tours for maintenance, see website for updates) is the last working water-powered spade mill in the British Isles. Thanks to Northern Ireland's troubled past, even such a common garden tool as the spade has a politicised story, with Catholics still sometimes derogatorily described as left-footers or people who 'dig with the other foot' – a reference to the days when one-sided spades were still made.

Oxford Island.

Parliament Buildings, Stormont.

BELFAST

A popular short break destination, this is a city of unexpected charms, mixing splendid Victorian architecture with genuine hospitality.

Belfast's dominant Victorian and Edwardian architecture is reminiscent of a northern English city, such as Leeds or Liverpool, a far cry from the Georgian elegance of Dublin, just a hundred miles south. But Northern Ireland's capital has other attributes. A low-rise, open city, framed between lofty green Cave Hill and the great blue bowl of Belfast Lough, dotted with charming parks and open spaces and, for a major city, it is surprisingly easy to get around and out of, into the beginning of Northern Ireland's beautiful rural hinterland.

Above all, it's the people of Belfast who remain its great attraction. Despite preconceptions to the contrary, Belfast people remain among the friendliest you will meet, with an easy and down-to-earth sense of humour. And, ironically, it is precisely that synthesis of Ulster Scots and native Irish, so long a source of division, that gives the people of Belfast their distinct personality.

Belfast sells itself today as the birthplace of the legendary RMS *Titanic*, whose luxurious embellishment symbolised the apex of Belfast's Edwardian heyday as one of the world's greatest shipbuilding ports, and whose watery fate prefigured Belfast's own long industrial and manufacturing decline. Now the city, rejuvenated with the help of huge investment from the UK government, has been enjoying a renaissance as a short-break destination.

THE CITY CENTRE

The city radiates out from City Hall and the magnificent Victorian streetscape of Donegall Square. North of the square is a largely pedestrianised shopping area, leading to the Cathedral Quarter, Belfast's cultural district. Frequent bus services (Metro Bus Nos 26, 26a, 26b or 26c) and a signposted footpath

Main attractions

- City Hall
- Crown Liquor Saloon
- Albert Memorial Clock
- Titanic Belfast
- Royal Botanic Gardens
- Ulster Museum

Maps on pages 306, 319

Ulster Hall.

Belfast City
0
500 m
0
500 yds
N
39 Belfast Castle
Crumlin Road Goal
37
Crumlin Road
Crown Courthouse
Mater Infirmorum Hospital
Flax International Arts Centre
Antrim Road
CEMETERY
Clifton House
Carlisle Circus
Hopewell Ave
Clifton St
Yorkgate Shopping Centre
Cinema
Black Box
Henry St
Queen Street
York Street A2
Dock St
Garmoyle St
Corry Rd
St Joseph's
Pilot St
M 2
Titanic Slipway
Olympic Slipway
Titanic Belfast 20
TITANIC QUARTER
SS Nomadic
Queens Road
Titanic Studios
River Lagan
Clarendon Dock
Clarendon Road
Abercorn Basin
Great Georges Street
North
Hopewell Cres.
Denmark St
Hopewell
Parade
Malvern St
Shankhill
St Matthews
36
St Patrick's Cathedral 32
Frederick St
Little
Patrick St
Nelson St
Sinclair Seamen's Presb. Church
38
Harbour Office
Corporation Sq.
Ferry Terminals
Public Record Office of Northern Ireland
SSE Arena 19
Sydenham
Old Road
Channel Rd
George Best Airport
Shankill Rd
Peters Hill
Westlink
Carrick Hill
Donegall St
Library St
Kent St
Union St
Academy St
Ulster University 31
MAC
Home Front Exhibition
30
St Anne's Cath.
Talbot St
York Gr. Patrick St
Dunbar Link
Corporation St
General Post Office
15 Belfast Central Library
Duke of York
The Black Box
Custom House
18 Donegall Quay
Big Fish
Albert Memorial Clock
17
Northern Ireland Tourist Board
M 3
Conway Mill, Clonard Monastery, Peace Wall, Cultúrlann McAdam Ó Fiaich, Belfast City Cemetery, Milltown Cemetery
Dover St
North St
Smithfield Market
Millfield
Gresham St
Exchange and Assembly Rooms 29
Waring St
33
Merchant Hotel (Ulster Bank)
McHugh's
Malmaison
Belfast Hotel
Queen Elizabeth II Bridge
Middlepath St
Bridge End
Wilson St
CastleCourt Shopping Centre
First Presbyterian 14
Kelly's Cellars
R'mary St
13
Royal Ave
Bank St
St Mary's
High St
16
St George's
23
Ann St
Queen's Bridge
Short Strand
Falls Road
Divis Street
Castle St
Morning Star
Church La.
St Peter's Cathedral 35
Barrack St
Old Museum Arts Centre
College Ave
Queen St
Fountain St
Donegall Pl.
Castle La.
Masonic Bldg
Corn Market
Ann St
Victoria Square
Victoria Sq
Bittles Bar
Kitchen Bar
Belfast County Court
Oxford Street
Belfast Waterfront Hall 21
Montpottinger Rd
Arran St
Milford St
Albert St
Cullingtree Road
College Sq N
College St
Belfast Welcome Centre 1
Arthur St
Linen Hall Lib. 12
Donegall
Chichester
Street
Victoria Street
Royal Courts of Justice
Laganbank Rd
Wellington Pl.
College Sq E
Durham St
7 Royal Belfast Academical Institution
City Hall 2
Titanic Memorial
Well'ton St
Deanes Meat Locker
Square
May Street
22 St George's Market
Lanyon Pl.
East Bridge Street
34 Parliament Buildings, East Belfast
Grand Opera House
3 Ten Square Hotel
Grosvenor Road
Grosvenor Hall 8
Europa Hotel
James St
Franklin St
5 Royal Ulster Rifles Museum
Bedford St
Friendly Street
Central Station
Maysfield Leisure Centre
Glengall St
10
9 Crown Liquor Saloon
4 Ulster Hall
Joy St
St Malachy's 6
Cromac Street
Great Victoria Street Station
Boyne Bridge
Great Victoria St
Deanes Deli and Vin Café
BBC
Linenhall St
Adelaide St
Alfred Street
Lwr Stanfield St
Stewart Street
Ravenhill Road
Linfield Rd
Bruce St
Ormeau Ave
Bankmore St
Westlink
Sandy Row
Dublin Road
Ulster Bank Bronze Figures
Maryville St
Apsley St
Lindsay St
Cromac Place
Blythe Street
11
Shaftesbury Square
Reformed Presbyterian
Donegall Pass
Elm Street
Walnut St
Ulster Television
Indoor Tennis Centre
River Ter.
Lagan
Donegall Road
Laverys
Bradbury Pl.
Botanic Ave
Botanic St
Vernon Street
City Hospital Station
Crescent Arts Centre 28
Lwr Cres.
Cameron St
McClure St
Cooke St
Ormeau Road
KING WILLIAM PARK
CRESCENT GDNS
House Belfast
The Other Place and No Alibis
Cromwell Rd
Shaftesbury Ave
Balfour Avenue
Ormeau Embankment
Belfast City Hospital
Jubilee Road
Crescent Church
Villa Italia
Mt Charles
Camden St
Seamus Heaney Centre
Queen's Film Theatre
University Street
Hatfield St
Farnham St
Rutland St
ORMEAU PARK
Dunluce Ave
Fitzwilliam St
University Sq.
Union Theological College
Fitzroy Ave
Dudley St
Ulsterville Ave
Lisburn Road
Elmwood Ave
College Pk
University Avenue
Rugby Avenue
Elmwood Hall
College Gardens
Queen's University 24
Rugby Rd
College Pk. Ave.
Carmel St
Deanes at Queens
University Road
Palm House
Agincourt Avenue
Rugby Road
Wellesley Avenue
Lord Kelvin
BOTANIC GARDENS 25
Wellington Park
26 Ulster Museum
Eglantine Avenue
Malone Avenue
Elaine St
Pretoria St
Colenso Par.
Queen's University Sports Complex
Stranmillis Embankment
Annadale Embankment
Delhi St
Candahar St
Burmah St
Ava Avenue
Ormeau Road
Park Road
North Parade
South Parade
Windsor Avenue
Malone Road
Chlorine Gdns
Stranmillis Road
Derryvolgie Ave
Windsor Park
Ridgeway St
Lyric Theatre 27
King's Bridge
Sunnyside St
Haywood Ave
Adelaide Pk

lead east across the River Lagan to the Titanic Quarter. To the south of Donegall Square, Great Victoria Street has several notable buildings, and leads to Shaftesbury Square, gateway to the University Quarter (also known as Queen's Quarter).

The **Visit Belfast Welcome Centre** ❶ (9 Donegall Square; http://visitbelfast.com; free) is a good place to pick up information leaflets and the multilingual staff can advise on everything from attractions and events to restaurants and bars and accommodation, not just for Belfast but Northern Ireland as a whole.

Around the corner is the **City Hall** ❷ (Donegall Square; www.belfastcity.gov.uk/cityhall; free). Built between 1898 and 1906, it is dubbed a 'Wrenaissance' building due to its shameless borrowing from Sir Christopher Wren's St Paul's Cathedral in London. Its plush Council Chamber has resounded to some of the liveliest debate in the history of public affairs. The portraits of the lord mayors in the corridors tell their own story of Belfast's divided history, a long line of formally dressed unionists eventually reaching the first nationalist (and Catholic) lord mayor in 1997. The current lord mayor is Sinn Féin's Christina Black.

There is a coffee shop and an exhibition area. The surrounding gardens are a favourite summer lunchtime spot, and the venue for many annual events. Additionally, they hold a number of monuments, notably Thomas Brock's frumpy statue of **Queen Victoria** and his marble figure of **Thane**, and a monument commemorating the lives lost in the *Titanic* disaster of 1912. On the east side of City Hall, in the **Titanic Memorial Gardens** – opened on the centenary of the tragedy – an immense plinth is inscribed with the names of all 1,512 victims.

City Hall occupies the former site of White Linen Hall (demolished in 1896; its library was relocated to Donegall Square North) and on its south side you'll find several building dating to Belfast's linen era.

LANYON'S LEGACY

Charles Lanyon (1813–89), an English architect, carpetbagger and engineer, conferred on Belfast's new bank buildings the majestic solidity of the palazzi of northern Italy. He understood the essence of the architectural faddishness and caught the spirit of early Victorian righteousness.

His neoclassical Crumlin Road Gaol promises unbridled retribution. Queen's University's faux Elizabethan design unashamedly appropriates Oxford's Magdalen. His Doric facade of the Union Theological College promises dour Presbyterianism. His Palladian Custom House intimidates. He was also responsible for 14 churches. Although a philanderer who openly bought election votes, Lanyon was knighted, became the city's mayor and was also one of its Conservative MPs.

City Hall in winter.

BELFAST'S TURBULENT HISTORY

The history of Ireland's only industrial city is brief by European standards, but it is a stormy one of power struggles in factories and politics.

Belfast could barely be said to have existed before the arrival of Arthur Chichester in 1599. Appointed lord deputy of Ireland by James I in 1604, and tasked with the anglicisation of the fiercely Irish province of Ulster, Chichester was instrumental in the plantations that followed in the wake of the 'flight of the earls' in 1607 and changed the nature of Ulster forever.

Chichester built a striking timber castle in 1611 (which later burnt down) and developed a small 'towne of good forme' around it. For almost two centuries, Belfast grew slowly, handicapped by a corrupt and incompetent corporation. Despite a growing importance as a trading port, the town did not register its first major shipbuilder until the arrival of William Ritchie (whose first dry dock, dating from 1796, can be seen near Clarendon Dock).

Queen's University, 1890s engraving.

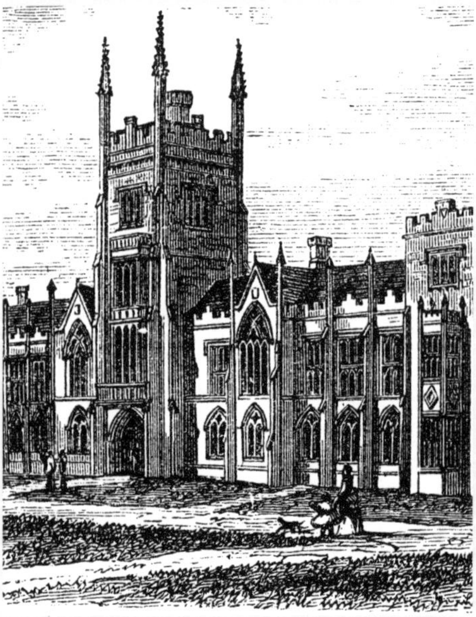

During the Industrial Revolution, Belfast added world-leading roles in shipbuilding, engineering and various kinds of manufacturing to its existing pre-eminence in the linen industry, and the by now populous town hit its stride. It was over this period that the buildings that dominate Belfast today began to take shape as the great industrialists and entrepreneurs turned to architects such as Sir Charles Lanyon to reflect the town's increasing prestige in a more permanent way. Lanyon himself was responsible for many of Belfast's most iconic buildings (see page 307), including Queen's University, the Union Theological College and Crumlin Road Gaol.

UNIONIST POWER BASE

Despite a growing Catholic population, with many thousands having flocked to the linen mills of West Belfast during the 19th century, a strong Protestant bias prevailed in Belfast (a power base later locked in by the partition of Ireland in 1921).

By the 1870s, a young William Pirrie had added his insatiable ambition and extraordinary abilities as a salesman to the firm of Edward Harland and Gustav Wolff, who were on their way to becoming the world's greatest shipbuilders from their fast-expanding base at Queen's Island. But the workplace was bitterly divided by sectarianism. The shipyards were strongly Protestant, and in the 1920s, Catholic workers were expelled from them altogether.

Following Queen Victoria's conferring of city status on Belfast in 1888, Belfast Corporation invited designs for a new city hall to be built on the site of the old White Linen Hall. The competition was won by Alfred Brumwell Thomas, an Englishman who happily admitted his debt to Christopher Wren and St Paul's Cathedral. Similarly clad in finest Portland stone, City Hall was adorned with marble from the same quarry that supplied Classical Rome and no expense was spared to impress. When the building opened in 1906 critics of its budget-busting extravagance were silenced and the ambition of the new city, now with a population of 450,000, appeared to have no limit. In fact, Belfast was already nearing the apex of its prestige.

Today, tourism chiefs have divided Belfast into a series of quarters, and though boundaries tend to be vague, each has a distinct personality.

THE LINEN QUARTER

The oldest extant building on Donegal Square South is Yorkshire House on the corner of Linenhall Street. Formerly, a linen warehouse it is now occupied by the chic hotel **Ten Square** ❸ (www.tensquare.co.uk). Its exterior boasts an eclectic collection of carved roundels with sculpted portrait heads.

Celebrated architect Charles Lanyon (see page 307) left his mark at **35–37 Linenhall Street**.

Running parallel on the west side is Bedford Street, home to the distinguished Italianate **Ulster Hall** ❹ (No. 30; www.ulsterhall.co.uk). Designed by Lanyon's rival, W.J. Barre, and purpose-built as a music hall in 1862, it now hosts rock and classical concerts, and cultural events; restored to its Victorian splendour, it has become home of the Ulster Orchestra.

Next-door neighbour, the **Royal Ulster Rifles Museum** ❺ (No. 28; www.royal-irish.com/museums/royal-ulster-rifles-museum), with its extensive collection of regimental memorabilia, is well worth visiting. The building itself, another Barre design, is an excellent example of Belfast's warehouse architecture.

Around the corner at No. 24 **Alfred Street** is the Catholic **St Malachy's Church** ❻ (www.saintmalachysparish.com), noted for its redbrick Tudor-style exterior and delightful fan-vaulted ceiling, famously described as an upside down wedding cake. The church, dating from 1844 underwent an extensive restoration in 2009.

GRAND BELFAST

Despite damage from bombs and planners, **Great Victoria Street**, which runs south from the city centre to Shaftesbury Square, contains several of Belfast's best-known buildings. Before heading south, walk north to College Square East for a view of the beautifully proportioned classical facade of one of the city's finest buildings, Sir John Soane's dignified redbrick **Royal Belfast Academical Institution** ❼, a prestigious non-denominational grammar school for boys, commonly known

The Crown Liquor Saloon, preserved by the National Trust.

as 'Inst'. The Baroque Portland stone building to the north, now part of **Belfast Metropolitan College**, has one of the last working steam-engine-powered ventilating and heating systems.

The street's highlights start at the corner with Howard Street, with the twin-domed **Grand Opera House** ❽ (www.goh.co.uk) designed by theatre architect Frank Matcham. The building – with its plush brass and velvet, gilded elephant heads supporting the boxes, and excellent acoustics – was extensively refurbished and extended in 2006. Thanks to its now extended wing space, the venue where Luciano Pavarotti made his UK debut and Sarah Bernhardt, Orson Welles and Laurel and Hardy all appeared, can now house the grandest West End productions.

Diagonally opposite the Opera House, you can't help but notice the Tudor Gothic bulk of the **Presbyterian Assembly Rooms** now given over to an elegant shopping centre, the Spires Mall. Also on this side of the road, it's worth taking time to enjoy Guinness and oysters at one of the world's most beautiful Victorian pubs, the **Crown Liquor Saloon** ❾, (www.nicholsonspubs.co.uk), which was elegantly restored by the National Trust on the advice of John Betjeman. Its tiling and stained-glass windows were the work of some of Italy's finest craftsmen, in Belfast to work on Catholic churches and the White Star liners, in the 1880s.

Across the road from the Crown Liquor Saloon is a landmark familiar to the many journalists who visited Belfast during the Troubles: the **Europa Hotel** ❿. Belfast's first luxury hotel – built to a grand scale on the site of the Great Northern Railway Station – opened in 1971. Targeted by the IRA an estimated 33 times it was once known as the 'most bombed hotel in Europe'. A photographic timeline was installed to mark the hotel's 40th anniversary. The Italian marble lobby dates from a refurbishment in 2008. Nowadays the Lobby Bar and the Piano Lounge are atmospheric spots for a drink or afternoon tea and champagne.

Titanic Belfast.

Great Victoria Street meets the Dublin Road, which runs parallel to it, at **Shaftesbury Square ⓫**, gateway to the university district. The Dublin Road, like many student neighbourhoods, is well endowed with small ethnic restaurants, fast food outlets and cheerful, noisy pubs.

LINEN HALL LIBRARY

Back in the city centre, walking east along **Wellington Place**, is the **Linen Hall Library ⓬** (17 Donegall Square North; www.linenhall.com; free). It is Ireland's last public subscription library. As well as the definitive collections – the Troubles, Northern Ireland theatrical material, C.S. Lewis and Irish studies – it also has a pleasant café and literary-themed shop. See website for upcoming events.

To the north is Donegall Place, with its streetscape of British chain stores. Off it, past Castle Junction, west down Bank Street, is **Kelly's Cellars ⓭** (Nos 30–32; https://kellyscellars.co.uk), dating from 1720. Though considerably refurbished, the bars retain much of the charm, which appealed to Henry Joy McCracken and other Protestant leaders of the United Irishmen as they plotted here in 1798. It is also known for excellent Irish traditional music sessions held Monday to Thursday evenings.

Across High Street, you can take two routes. The first, north, brings you to **Rosemary Street**. **No. 33** is the birthplace of William Drennan, founder of the Society of United Irishmen, and **No. 41** is the 1783 **First Presbyterian Church ⓮** (www.firstchurchbelfast.org), the oldest place of worship within the city – its congregation once included RMS *Titanic* designer Thomas Andrews, no doubt attracted by its charming boat-like interior. One of Belfast's oldest thoroughfares, Rosemary Street also hosts that shrine to freemasonry, the **Provincial Grand Lodge**. A plaque on the wall commemorates radical Belfast Presbyterian Henry Joy McCracken who worshipped in the church that once stood here.

ARISTOCRAT OWNERS

The industrial revolution was facilitated by a change in land ownership. Until the mid-19th century, Belfast was the only Irish town to be run as a private fiefdom by a single family, lying as it did within the Donegall estate in County Antrim, owned by the descendants of the one-time lord deputy of Ireland, Arthur Chichester, with the head of the family being the marquis of Donegall. This barony withered several times, when the erstwhile holder died childless, but was repeatedly revived.

Over the years, some peers contributed to the construction and upkeep of public buildings in Belfast, but others squandered the family fortunes, and by 1855 virtually the whole town had been sold to tenants or rich speculators. The family's legacy lives on in the number of Belfast streets named after them.

Festival time at the Albert Memorial Clock.

Further up Royal Avenue the red sandstone **Belfast Central Library** ⑮ (www.librariesni.org.uk/libraries/greater-belfast/belfast-central-library; free) is a good place to start for those wishing to research Belfast or Northern Irish history and culture, with extensive collections and a wide range of periodicals and newspapers going back to the 19th century.

HIGH STREET

The second route takes you up High Street from the junction with Victoria. At **No. 105** is the striking portico of the magnificent 1816 **St George's Church** ⑯ (http://stgeorges.connor.anglican.org; free), which was transported by canal from the house of the eccentric Frederick Augustus Hervey. At Queen's Square, across Victoria Street, the **Albert Memorial Clock** ⑰ was, until its restoration, *threatening* to rival the Leaning Tower of Pisa, while the renovated **McHugh's Bar** (www.mchughsbar.com) claims to date to 1711, which if true, would make it Belfast's oldest surviving building.

Around the corner, Lanyon's glorious **Custom House**, where Anthony Trollope once worked, looks over what is now Belfast's premier public space. Since its transformation in 2005, **Custom House Square** has become a premier outdoor venue, used for all kinds of events from carnivals to live music.

TITANIC QUARTER

Donegall Quay ⑱ is the place to see local sculptor John Kindness's now famous **Big Fish**, a 32ft (9.8-metre) salmon whose ceramic 'skin' tells the history of Belfast.

Across the River Lagan, at the gateway to the Titanic Quarter, the **SSE Arena** ⑲ (Queen's Quay; www.ssearenabelfast.com) is home to the Belfast Giants ice hockey team and is a venue for sporting events and pop concerts. The Odyssey Pavilion (www.odysseypavilion.co.uk) hosts the interactive discovery centre for family fun, **W5** (www.w5online.co.uk; see website for opening hours; charge) with nearly 200 interactive exhibits. There is also a bowling alley,

Waterfront Hall.

cinemas, and a number of cafés, bars, restaurants and nightclubs.

The city's most popular attraction (book online to avoid queues) is of course the **Titanic Belfast** ⓴ (www.titanicbelfast.com; charge). Opened in 2012, the centennial of the ill-fated liner's launch and sinking, the centre tells the ship's story and also brings to life the wider theme of Belfast's industrial heritage. Civic pride is evident in the scale of the building. Clad in diamond glazing, the bow-shaped facade of the six-storey building reflects the lines of the ship. Its shard-like appearance is created from 3,000 different-shaped panels, each folded from silver anodised aluminium sheets into asymmetrical geometries, which catch the light like a cut diamond.

The SS *Nomadic*, the last surviving White Star Line ship, is moored in Hamilton Dock. She was especially commissioned to tender to the RMS *Titanic* and RMS *Olympic* and although a quarter of their size, she was fitted out to a similarly ornate standard. She ferried 274 passengers to the RMS *Titanic* on 10 April 1912.

A short walk from the Titanic Belfast is the **Titanic Dock and Pump House** (now a whiskey distillery), for many visitors the most memorable of Belfast's *Titanic*-related sites, and an amazing piece of industrial archaeology. The 900ft (274-metre) dry dock where the *Titanic* was built is reached by steps descending 44ft (13.5 metres) to the floor of the dock, retracing the physical footprint of the ship. It took 500 men seven years to build it, working here in all weathers. When full the dock held 21 million gallons of water.

WATERFRONT HALL

Back on the west bank of the Lagan is the copper-domed **Belfast Waterfront Hall** ㉑ (2 Lanyon Place; www.waterfront.co.uk), a forerunner of Belfast's renaissance when built in 1997 and a venue for top international performers.

Beside the Waterfront Hall is the Hilton Hotel; across the road is the grandiose neoclassical 1933 **Royal Courts**

A Titanic Belfast exhibit.

of Justice, fashioned from Portland Stone and still operating as Northern Ireland's judicial centre.

At the corner of Oxford Street and May Street, **St George's Market** ㉒ (www.belfastcity.gov.uk/stgeorgesmarket), built between 1890 and 1896, has been elegantly refurbished and now has many stalls selling superb locally produced food, including cheese, organic meats, fish and seafood, and plants at the **Friday variety market** (8am–2pm) and the **Saturday city food and craft market** (9am–3pm). The **Sunday market, craft and antiques market** (10am–3pm) is a hybrid of the Friday and Saturday markets (plus antiques), with a special emphasis on local arts and crafts.

Head down May Street and turn right into Victoria Street, where you will see the spectacular glass dome of Belfast's biggest and most impressive shopping centre, the **Victoria Square** (https://victoriasquare.com).

On the other side of Victoria Square is the triangular **Bittles Bar** (www.bittlesbar.com) with its literary paintings, the nearby, **Kitchen Bar** (www.thekitchenbar.com) is one of Belfast's most famous traditional pubs. Further along Victoria Street is the excellent **Malmaison Belfast hotel** ㉓ (Nos 34–38; www.malmaison.com/locations/belfast), with its dramatic Gothic meets *Alice in Wonderland* decor, housed in two Victorian warehouses famous for their exterior carvings.

QUEEN'S QUARTER

Based around Sir Charles Lanyon's distinguished Queen's University, Queen's Quarter is a curious mix of student haunts, elegant academia and Belfast's designer-label heartland, the Lisburn Road. **Queen's University** ㉔, its blue-tinged redbrick at its best near dusk, is one of Lanyon's delights, appropriating the Tudor of Oxford's Magdalen College. There are more than a hundred listed buildings around the campus and surrounding area and it's worth picking up the 'Walkabout Queen's' leaflet from the **Queen's Welcome Centre** (www.qub.

Inside Belfast Waterfront Hall.

ac.uk/home/welcome-centre; free) to help you on a signposted tour. In particular, search out the Great Hall, which Lanyon based on the medieval great halls of the Oxbridge universities. Also check out the **Naughton Gallery** (www.naughtongallery.org; free) in the Lanyon Building, which houses the university's own extensive collection and hosts interesting touring exhibitions.

You can find the best of world cinema at the **Queen's Film Theatre** near Queen's University (20 University Square; www.queensfilmtheatre.com), which has two screens and a comfortable bar/lounge. Opposite the University's lawns stands its modernised **Student's Union**. Nearby is the delightful Italianate **Elmwood Hall** (originally, Elmwood Presbyterian Church) which hosts concerts.

Northwards down University Road from Queen's is a selection of atmospheric cafés and restaurants. Many of Belfast's lively younger writers teach creative writing across the road at the **Seamus Heaney Centre for Poetry** (www.qub.ac.uk/schools/seamus-heaney-centre), the centre also organises literary events such as poetry readings, book launches, summer schools and talks.

ROYAL BOTANIC GARDENS

South of the University, the **Royal Botanic Gardens** ㉕ (tel: 028-9031 4762; www.belfastcity.gov.uk/botanicgardens; daily 7.30am–dusk; free) contain another Lanyon gem, his restored curvilinear **Palm House**. In the **Tropical Ravine**, water drips from banana leaves in a miniature sunken rainforest. At the time of writing, both the Palm House and the Tropical Ravine were closed for maintenance, see website for updates.

On the park's Stranmillis Road boundary, the **Ulster Museum** ㉖ (Royal Botanic Gardens; http://nmni.com/um; free), which features a 75ft (23-metre) atrium that leads into fascinating history, art and science galleries. The Belfast-born artist John Lavery (1856–1941) left a major bequest of his work to the museum, which is on

Botanic Gardens.

permanent display. The museum also has an enclosed rooftop gallery to house its glass, jewellery and Belleek collections. Allow at least half a day.

Further south takes you to the pleasant village atmosphere of Stranmillis and the site of the **Lyric Theatre** 27 (www.lyrictheatre.co.uk), at 55 Ridgeway Street, where Antrim-born actor Liam Neeson first trod the boards. Neeson was one of the chief fundraisers for the 390-seat venue completed in 2011 that graces the riverside site. Designed by Dublin architects O'Donnell + Tuomey, the unusual building was a response to the sloping parkland site and the brick streetscape of Belfast. The auditorium's interior uses iroko wood and specially fired brick. It has won many architectural awards.

North from Queen's again is the heavily studenty **Botanic Avenue**, home to a host of lovely cafés and the excellent crime bookshop **No Alibis** (No. 83; https://noalibis.com), a regular haunt of Belfast writer Colin Bateman, it also holds regular book launches.

At the meeting point of Lower Crescent Street and University Road is the **Crescent Arts Centre** 28 (2–4 University Road; www.crescentarts.org; free), a 19th-century building of Scrabo stone, which houses a lively community arts centre. Turn left up University Road for one of Belfast's most enduring restaurants, **Villa Italia** (Nos 37–41; www.villaitaliarestaurant.co.uk), it has been serving Belfast-style Italian cuisine since 1988.

CATHEDRAL QUARTER

Gradually Belfast's historic Cathedral Quarter is becoming a cultural and entertainment district to rival Dublin's Temple Bar. Beginning in the city centre where Bridge Street meets Waring Street is the Soviet-themed **Northern Whig** (2-10 Bridge Street; www.thenorthernwhig.com) with its chunky sofas and fine range of vodkas.

Opposite, the historic 1769 **Exchange and Assembly Rooms** 29 (converted to the Northern Bank by Sir Charles Lanyon) hosted a famous harp festival attended by rebels Wolfe Tone (who

A Belfast blues band play the Kitchen Bar.

disapproved) and fellow United Irishman Henry Joy McCracken.

Across Donegall Street, the lovely facade of the Four Corners building has been preserved as a Premier Inn.

Take a left down Donegall Street, passing two fine pubs, the traditional **Duke of York** (7–11 Commercial Court; https://dukeofyorkbelfast.com/venues/duke-of-york) and the **John Hewitt** at 51 Donegall Street (https://boundarybrewing.coop/pages/the-john-hewitt), a superb community-run pub which features live music and is a key venue in the area's excellent annual Cathedral Quarter Arts Festival (www.cqaf.com).

Also on Donegall Street, **Belfast Exposed** at Exchange Place (www.belfastexposed.org) hosts contemporary photo exhibitions and allows access to its digital archive of 250,000 images of Belfast.

ST ANNE'S CATHEDRAL

Further along, the neo-Romanesque **St Anne's Cathedral** ㉚, dates from the beginning of the 19th century but wasn't completed until 2007 when its striking stainless steel 'Spire of Hope' was added. Check out the mosaic roof over the baptistery, composed of 150,000 pieces of glass. The famed unionist leader Edward Carson is interred here. Opposite, Writers' Square contains sculptural pieces by John Kindness and Brian Connolly, and during the festival hosts musical and comedy events. On the cathedral's east side on Talbot Street is the **Northern Ireland War Memorial** (www.niwarmemorial.org), which gives an in-depth account of wartime Northern Ireland. To the rear, St Anne's Square is home to the **MAC** ㉛ (Metropolitan Arts Centre; www.themaclive.com; free), Belfast's multimillion pound state-of-the-art facility for visual and performing arts. It features regular great shows and exhibitions across its two theatres and three galleries with a café and bar onsite. The opening of this landmark building in 2012 marked an important new stage in the ongoing development of the Cathedral Quarter.

St Anne's Cathedral.

Donegall Street continues past the junction with Royal Avenue and on to **St Patrick's Cathedral** 32 (www.stpatricksbelfast.org), where society painter Sir John Lavery used his beautiful wife Hazel (rumoured to have had an affair with Irish rebel leader Michael Collins) as the face of Madonna in his famous triptych of St Patrick.

Returning east from Donegall Street, along the atmospheric cobbled Hill Street, is one of Belfast's finest pubs, **The Harp Bar** (No. 35; see page 321), while the **Black Box** (Nos 18–22; www.blackboxbelfast.com), a dedicated performance space for new theatre, music and comedy, is another key venue for the Cathedral Quarter Arts Festival, the Belfast Film Festival and many others.

At the junction across the road at the corner of Waring Street and Skipper Street (named for being the lodging place for captains of ships tied up in nearby High Street when the River Farset ran through), is the eclectic and enjoyable tapas bar, **The Spaniard** (tel: 028-9023 2448).

Just along Waring Street is the area's social hub, the **Merchant Hotel** 33 (Nos 35–39; www.themerchanthotel.com), converted from one of Belfast's finest buildings, the 1860s Ulster Bank. The sumptuous five-star hotel, Belfast's finest, radiates luxury from the Great Room restaurant where one of Ireland's largest chandelier hangs beneath a stunning glass cupola. Overnight guests get to stay in one of its 26 lavish rooms or five suites. Wander in for a look at the chandelier (the restaurant is in the main lobby), book for afternoon tea and make a point of sampling one of its swanky bars: there's the cocktail bar and a lively jazz bar, while the adjoining New York-style Cloth Ear gastro pub does great food and opulent Ollie's nightclub in the basement are also part of the hotel.

Opposite the Merchant is **Cotton Court**, the home of **Craft NI** (www.craftni.org). In the same building you can visit the ground-floor gallery of the **Belfast Print Workshop** (http://bpw.org.uk), which has free exhibitions of leading artists.

C.S. Lewis mural.

EAST BELFAST

The largest district of the city, it was here that three of Belfast's most famous sons were born: singer Van Morrison, footballer George Best (after whom Belfast City Airport is now named) and C.S. Lewis, author of the 'Chronicles of Narnia' book series, who was baptised at **St Mark's Church** on the Holywood Road by his formidable grandfather, the Rev. Thomas Hamilton. The area's creative spirit is celebrated at the C.S. Lewis Festival in December, and continually fostered by Eastside Arts (www.eastsidearts.net). Ken Harper of **Harper Taxi Tours** (tel: 028-9074 2711) will guide you on tours exploring locations relevant to the arts, sport and politics.

STORMONT

East Belfast's most famous building is the grand **Parliament Buildings** 34, Stormont, off the Upper Newtownards Road, now home of the frequently fractious and oft-suspended Northern Ireland Assembly (www.niassembly.gov.uk). Visitors don't have access to the building but can walk the 300 acres (120 hectares) of grounds (daily 7.30am–dusk; free), including the impressive one-mile driveway.

Though not exactly dominating the tourist map, East Belfast has some much-visited attractions to offer. Watching sweets and chocolates made in the traditional way will tempt children to **Aunt Sandra's Candy Factory** (60 Castlereagh Road (www.auntsandras.com).

On the outskirts of Belfast, **Dundonald Ice Bowl** (111 Old Dundonald Road; www.theicebowl.com) has Ireland's only Olympic-sized ice rink, one of the biggest indoor play centres in Ireland and 30 state-of-the-art bowling lanes. Adjoining is the American-style mini golf centre the **Pirates Adventure Golf Course** (111a Old Dundonald Road; www.piratesadventuregolf.com), while a short walk away is **Streamvale Open Farm** (38 Ballyhanwood Road; www.streamvale.com; charge) offering lots of farm animals for children to meet.

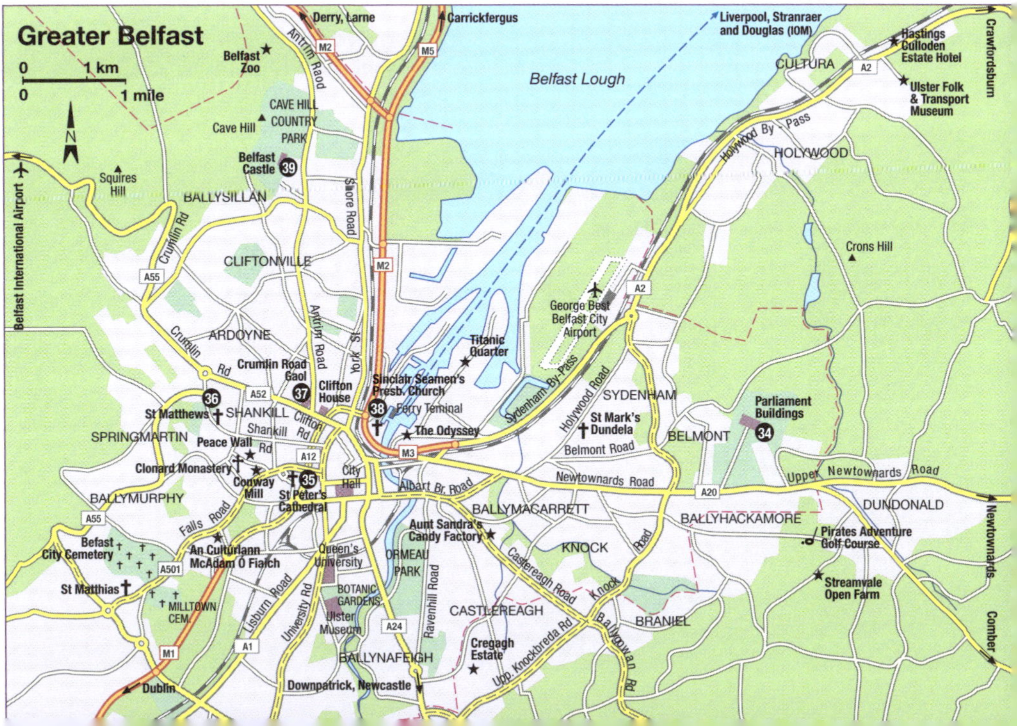

GAELTACHT QUARTER

This is essentially the nationalist part of West Belfast (omitting the Protestant Shankill area) and is focused on the **Falls Road**. A good introduction to the area is to take one of the cheap, shared black cabs that drive along the Falls Road from their headquarters at Castle Junction (TaxiTrax; tel: 028-9031 5777; www.taxitrax.com; charge).

In ascending order up the Falls Road, you should begin your tour at the 1866 **St Peter's Cathedral** ㉟ (Peter's Square; www.stpetersbelfast.ie), whose two great towers with rising spires were used as sightlines by German bombers in the war. The first flax spinning mill in West Belfast, **Conway Mill** (5–7 Conway Street; www.conwaymill.org; free) hosts a Saturday market from 10am to 3pm, as well as community and cultural events. The lovely French-Gothic style **Clonard Monastery** (1 Clonard Gardens; www.clonard.com) is notable for its remarkable rose window, organ and mosaics. Nearby, on Cupar Way, you can still see the 'Peace Wall', erected to separate the nationalist and loyalist communities.

The Irish language arts centre **An Cultúrlann McAdam Ó Fiaich** (216 Falls Road; www.culturlann.ie) with an Irish language book and gift shop, hosts Irish music and theatre and art exhibitions. It has a good-value restaurant, too.

One of the best ways to understand Belfast's rather turbulent history is to investigate **Belfast City Cemetery**, just off the Falls Road, where many of the powerful unionists who made modern Belfast were laid to rest. Over the road, in the **Milltown Cemetery**, is the famous 'Republican Plot' where hunger striker Bobby Sands is buried. He died in 1981 while on hunger strike at HM Prison Maze.

SHANKILL AND NORTH BELFAST

The rundown Shankill area lacks the vitality of nationalist West Belfast but Shankill Road itself is worth visiting for its 'shamrock church', **St Matthews** ㊱,

Belfast Castle.

and its famous political murals. **Taxi Tours Belfast** run a 'Belfast Political & Mural Tour' (www.belfasttours.com; charge), which offers those interested in the city's history a fascinating insight into the Troubles.

Parallel to the Shankill Road is the **Crumlin Road**, highlighted by Lanyon's imposing **Crumlin Road Gaol** 37 (www.crumlinroadgaol.com), which was restored in 2007. An underground tunnel connects it with Lanyon's **Courthouse** across the road.

Further towards the city centre is the most elegant Georgian building **Clifton House** (2 North Queen Street; tel: 028-9089 7534 for group tours; https://cliftonbelfast.com; charge), opened in the 1770s as the Belfast Poor House.

Down in the docks area of North Belfast is Lanyon's nautically themed **Sinclair Seamen's Presbyterian Church** 38 (5–7 Corporation Square; www.sinclairschurch.co.uk). Its pulpit is shaped like a ship's prow and its bell is from the ill-fated HMS *Hood*, sunk by the *Bismarck* in 1941 with the loss of more than 1,400 lives. Further north is the Italianate Harbour Office, which leads into attractive tree-lined riverside plazas at Clarendon Dock.

OUTSIDE BELFAST

Seven miles (11km) east of Belfast on the main A2 road towards Holywood is the excellent **Ulster Folk Museum and Ulster Transport Museum** (www.nationalmuseumsni.org; charge) at Cultra (see page 296).

The 19th-century Scottish Baronial-style sandstone **Belfast Castle** 39 (www.belfastcastle.co.uk; free), scenically sited on the slopes of Cave Hill, is a 30-minute bus ride from the city centre. The adjacent **Cave Hill Country Park** (www.belfastcity.gov.uk/cavehill; free) has several worthwhile archaeological treasures, most notably, McArt's Fort, an ancient ring fort or ráth. If you like plentiful fauna with your flora, **Belfast Zoo** (www.belfastcity.gov.uk/zoo/home; charge), located on the side of Cave Hill, at the top of Antrim Road, is home to more than 500 animals.

The murals in Belfast speak volumes.

IRELAND

TRAVEL TIPS

Transport

A - Z

Further Reading

TRANSPORT

GETTING THERE

By air

Republic of Ireland

There are four international airports in the Republic of Ireland: Dublin Airport, Shannon Airport, Cork Airport, Ireland West Airport and Kerry Airport.

Dublin Airport (www.dublinairport.com), situated roughly 10km north of the city centre, is the largest and busiest of the four and has an extensive route network with direct flights to and from a host of UK and mainland Europe cities and hubs in the Middle East and North America. It has more than 40 partner airlines (see website for full list) and is the home base for Aer Lingus. The airport is a 20- to 30-minute drive from the city centre and is well served by buses – pick-up points are located at Terminal 1, Zone 2, and Terminal 2, Zone 20 (Aircoach; www.aircoach.ie), Terminal 1, Zone 1, and Terminal 2, Zone 21 (Dublin Express; www.dublinexpress.ie) and Dublin Airport Bus Park (Dublin Bus; www.dublinbus.ie) – and taxis.

Shannon Airport (www.shannonairport.com), on the west coast, operates more than 30 routes with direct services to and from Boston, Chicago and New York (Dublin and Shannon airports have full US preclearance facilities) and Birmingham, Edinburgh, Liverpool, London, Manchester and Newcastle, plus several cities in mainland Europe. It is partnered with Aer Lingus, American Airlines, Delta, Lufthansa, Ryanair, Vueling and United. In 2022, Shannon Airport and Ireland West Airport, were the first airports in the world to be certified as Age Friendly Airports by the World Health Organisation (WHO). Located 24km north of Limerick city, the airport is served by buses (Bus Éireann Route 343 and Expressway Route 51; www.buseireann.ie) and taxis (www.shannonairportcab.com).

Cork Airport (www.corkairport.com) is the southernmost airport in Ireland and handles short-haul flights to and from Birmingham, East Midlands, Edinburgh, Liverpool, London, Manchester and Newcastle, and cities across mainland Europe. It is partnered with Aer Lingus, Air France, KLM, Ryanair and SWISS. Bus (Bus Éireann routes 226 and 226A; www.buseireann.ie; and Citylink Route 251/251X; www.citylink.ie) and taxi services connect the airport with Cork city (it's a 20-minute drive).

Ireland West Airport (Knock; www.irelandwestairport.com) operates 20 international routes with short-haul flights to and from Birmingham, Bristol, East Midlands, Edinburgh, Liverpool, London and Manchester and cities in mainland Europe. It is partnered with Aer Lingus and Ryanair. The airport is served by buses (Bus Eireann Route 440 and Expressway Route 64; www.buseireann.ie) and taxis (see airport website for taxi providers).

Kerry Airport (www.kerryairport.ie) has a limited route network with direct flights to and from Dublin, London and Manchester, Berlin and Frankfurt (via Frankfurt-Hahn). It is partnered with Ryanair. Located between Killarney and Tralee, the airport is served by buses (Bus Éireann Expressway routes 14, 40 and 271; www.buseireann.ie) and taxis (see airport website for taxi providers).

Dublin's trams offer a quick way of getting to outlying areas.

Northern Ireland

Northern Ireland has three international airports: Belfast International Airport, George Best Belfast City Airport and City of Derry Airport.

Belfast International Airport (www.belfastairport.com) has services to and from most major cities in Great Britain and mainland Europe. It is partnered with Eastern Airways, easyJet, Jet2, Ryanair and TUI. These will be joined by newcomer Fly Atlantic (www.flyatlantic.com) in 2027; when operational it will cater for more than 30 destinations across the UK, mainland Europe and North America. The Airport Express 300 service shuttles between the airport and the Europa Buscentre. The airport is a 30- to 40-minute bus ride from the city centre.

George Best Belfast City Airport (www.belfastcityairport.com) operates short-haul flights to and from 26 cities in the UK and mainland Europe. It is partnered with Aer Lingus, Aer Lingus Regional, British Airways, easyJet, KLM, Loganair and Lufthansa. The Airport Express 600 service runs from the front of the terminal building to the Europa

Buscentre in the city centre, every 30 minutes during peak times.

City of Derry Airport (www.cityofderryairport.com) has services to and from Glasgow, Liverpool, London and Manchester. It is partnered with Loganair and Ryanair. Situated 7 miles northeast of Derry city, scheduled Ulsterbus (www.translink.co.uk) services run from the airport to the bus depot in the city centre.

Airlines

Aer Lingus (www.aerlingus.com), Air France (wwws.airfrance.fr/en), American Airlines (www.aa.com), British Airways (www.britishairways.com), Delta (www.delta.com), Eastern Airways (www.easternairways.com), easyJet (www.easyjet.com), Jet2 (www.jet2.com), KLM (www.klm.nl/en), Loganair (www.loganair.co.uk), Lufthansa (www.lufthansa.com), Ryanair (www.ryanair.com), SWISS (www.swiss.com), TUI (www.tui.co.uk), United (www.united.com) and Vueling (www.vueling.com).

By sea

Direct ferry routes link the island of Ireland to Great Britain, France and Spain. Travelling from Great Britain, the main routes are Cairnryan (Dumfries and Galloway, Scotland) to Belfast or Larne (County Antrim); Holyhead (Isle of Anglesey, Wales) to Dublin; Fishguard or Pembroke (both in Pembrokeshire, Wales) to Rosslare (County Wexford); Liverpool (Merseyside, England) to Dublin and Liverpool Birkenhead to Belfast. From mainland Europe, you can sail from Cherbourg or La Havre (both in Normandy, France) to Rosslare and from Roscoff (Brittany, France) to Cork; and from Bilbao (northern Spain) to Rosslare. Many routes vary by season; seas can be choppy in winter.

Irish Ferries (www.irishferries.com). Services: Holyhead–Dublin (up to four crossings daily; 3hr 15min); Holyhead–Dublin (Dublin Swift; approx 2hr); Pembroke–Rosslare (two crossings daily; 3hr 45min); Cherbourg–Rosslare (one crossing, usually Wed, Fri, Sat and Sun; approx 15hr).

Stena Line (www.stenaline.co.uk). Services: Holyhead–Dublin (up to eight crossings daily; 3hr 15min); Fishguard–Rosslare (four crossings daily; 3hr 30min); Liverpool–Belfast (up to four crossings daily; 8hr); Cairnryan–Belfast (up to twelve crossings daily; 2hr 15min).

P&O Irish Sea Ferries (www.poferries.com). Services: Cairnryan–Larne (up to seven crossings daily; 2hr); Liverpool–Dublin (two crossings daily; 8hr).

Brittany Ferries (www.brittany-ferries.fr). Services: Bilbao–Rosslare (two crossings weekly; 28hr); Cherbourg–Rosslare (two crossings weekly; 15hr); Le Havre–Rosslare (one crossing weekly; 19hr 30min); Roscoff–Rosslare (one sailing weekly; 13hr) Roscoff–Cork (two sailings weekly; 15hr);

By bus

Bus companies run 'coach and sail' services from various points in Great Britain.

National Express (www.nationalexpress.com). Services: London–Birmingham–Dublin (Fri and Sun; 12hr 30min); London–Belfast (daily; approx 15hr 50min).

Hannon Coach (https://hannoncoach.com) Services: Glasgow–Belfast (Fri, Sun and Mon; 5hr 45 min).

GETTING AROUND

Public transport

Republic of Ireland

Córas Iompair Éireann (CIÉ) is the primary provider of public transport services within the Republic of Ireland. It operates rail and bus services through three subsidiaries: Iarnród Éireann (Irish Rail), Bus Éireann and Bus Átha Cliath (Dublin Bus).

Irish Rail (www.irishrail.ie) provides commuter services in Dublin (between Dundalk, Dunboyne, Longford, Portlaoise and Gorey) and Cork (between Mallow, Cobh and Midleton) and InterCity services between major cities and towns. The Enterprise service (operated in partnership with Translink Northern Ireland Railways) connects Dublin (Connolly Station) and Belfast (Lanyon Place Station). Irish Rail also operates the DART (Dublin Area Rapid Transit system) which runs between Malahide or Howth and Greystones, County Wicklow.

Bus Éireann (www.buseireann.ie) provides town, city and commuter services, plus intercity services nationwide. Intercity bus services are also provided by a host of private bus and coach companies. These include Galway-based Irish Citylink (www.citylink.ie) and Kilkenny-based JJ Kavanagh & Sons (https://jjkavanagh.ie).

Dublin Bus (www.dublinbus.ie) caters for the city and Greater Dublin Area; services include the Airlink Express and Nitelink. Go-Ahead Ireland (www.goaheadireland.ie) operate 25 routes in the Outer Dublin Metropolitan Area.

The LUAS tram system (www.luas.ie) links suburban parts of Dublin via two tramlines that run through the city centre. The Red Line runs from Tallaght to The Point and from Saggart to Connolly Station (Heuston Station and Busáras, the terminal for Bus Éireann, both have stops on this line) and the Green Line runs from Brides Glen to Broombridge.

The National Transport Authority's Transport for Ireland website (www.transportforireland.ie) is a one-stop shop for information on all modes of public transport throughout the Republic. Download the TFI Journey Planner App for free from Apple App or Google Play stores.

Northern Ireland

Translink (www.translink.co.uk) is the primary provider of public transport services in Northern Ireland and operates rail and bus services via its subsidiaries Northern Ireland Railways (NIR), Glider, Goldliner, Metro and Ulsterbus.

NIR's mainline network begins at Newry and runs northward to the Europa Buscentre (the main rail and bus interchange), from here services radiate east to Bangor, northeast to Larne Harbour, and via Ballymena and Coleraine northeast to Portrush and northwest to Derry. The cross-border Express service runs south from Lanyon Place Station to Dublin's Connolly Station.

Ulsterbus provides intercity, town to town and rural bus services. Metro and Glider cater for Belfast city. For bus and/or rail information, call Translink in Belfast, tel: 028-9066 6630 or visit website.

Private transport

Driving

Outside the cities the roads are still amongst the least congested in Europe, although it's hard to believe this when stuck in a traffic jam in Dublin's ever-expanding suburbs or on the ring roads of Galway, Cork or Killarney. All traffic drives on the left on both sides of the border, although there is a predilection in some rural areas for the middle of the road. All passengers, front and back, are legally required to wear seatbelts.

In the Republic, the speed limit is displayed in kilometres per hour: 45km/h, 60km/h or 80km/h (28mph, 37mph or 50mph) in urban areas, and 80km/h or 100km/h (50mph or 62mph) on national roads (green signs with 'N' numbers), with 120km/h (75mph) permitted on motorways (blue signs with 'M' numbers). On-the-spot fines can be issued for speeding offences.

There are 11 toll roads in Ireland (see www.etoll.ie for locations and toll charges), with the exception of the toll point on Dublin's M50 motorway – eFlow operates barrier-free tolling between Junction 6 and Junction 7 – you'll need to pay at barrier toll plazas (keep some loose change handy as some toll plazas don't accept card payments). The eFlow M50 toll must be paid by 8pm the following day, you can either pay online at www.eflow.ie or at any Payzone retail outlet (see www.payzone.ie for your nearest outlet).

Drink-driving laws are strict. It is an offence to drive with a Blood Alcohol Concentration (BAC) exceeding 50mg (over 50mg of alcohol per 100ml blood).

In Northern Ireland, speed limits are displayed in miles per hour so pay attention if you cross the border as you may not realise you have. The limit for country roads is 60mph (96km/h), and 70mph (113km/h) for motorways and dual-carriageways.

Cyclists in Whitehead, Co. Antrim

Taxi

In Dublin, taxis can be hailed on the street and from ranks. Multiple independent operators provide taxi services across the city.

Cabs operate exclusively from taxi ranks and do not stop when hailed. Belfast's main city centre taxi rank is in front of City Hall, but there are also ranks at the airports and main stations. There are two types of taxi: London-style hackneys and saloon cars operated by 'radio cab' companies such as Value Cabs (tel: 028-9080 9080; www.valuecabs.co.uk), or fonaCAB (tel: 028-9033 3333; www.fonacab.com).

Car rental

At peak periods, hire cars can be hard to find. Once you know your travel dates, shop around for the best quotes and book early. To hire a car, you will need to meet the age requirements of the rental company (the minimum age ranges from 21 to 25; drivers aged 21 to 24 will typically incur a young driver surcharge), have a valid driving licence and a credit card.

Republic of Ireland

Alamo, Dublin Airport, tel: 01-460 5042, www.alamo.ie.

Avis, Cork Airport, tel: 021-432 7460; Dublin Airport, tel: 01-605 7500; Kerry Airport, tel: 066-976 4499; Shannon Airport, tel: 061-715 600; www.avis.ie.

Budget, Cork Airport 021-431 4000; Dublin Airport, tel: 01-844 5150; Kerry Airport, tel: 066-976 3199; Shannon Airport, tel: 061-715 600; www.budget.ie.

Enterprise, Cork Airport 021-483 8973; Dublin Airport, tel: 01-460 5042; Shannon Airport tel: 061-704 914; www.enterprise.ie.

Europcar, Cork Airport tel: 021-240 0100; Dublin Airport; tel: 01-812 2800; Shannon Airport, tel: 061-206 040; www.europcar.ie.

Hertz, Cork Airport, tel: 021-496 5849; Dublin Airport, tel: 01-844 5466; Shannon Airport, tel: 061-471 369; www.hertz.ie.

National, Dublin Airport, tel: 01-460 5042, www.nationalcar.com.

New Way Car Hire, Dublin Airport, tel: 01-605 7588, www.newway.ie.

Sixt, Cork Airport tel: 01-235 2030; Dublin Airport, tel: 01-844 5689; www.sixt.ie.

Northern Ireland

Avis, Belfast International Airport, tel: 028-9445 2642; George Best Belfast City Airport, tel: 084-544 6028; City of Derry Airport, tel: 0781-621 3522; www.avis.co.uk.

Budget, Belfast International Airport, tel: 028-9442 3332; George Best Belfast City Airport, tel: 028-9045 1111; www.budget.ie.

Enterprise, Belfast International Airport, tel: 028-9445 1940, www.enterprise.co.uk

Europcar, Belfast International Airport, tel: 028-9445 9747; George Best Belfast City Airport, tel: 037-1384 1007; www.europcar.co.uk.

Hertz, Belfast International Airport, tel: 028-9442 2533; George Best Belfast City Airport, tel: 028-9073 2451; City of Derry Airport, tel: 028-7181 1994; www.hertz.co.uk.

Sixt, George Best Belfast City Airport, tel: 0330-002 2666, www.sixt.co.uk.

Cycling

Cycling is enormously popular in Ireland. In Dublin, visitors can hire a NOW dublinbike from stations across the city by purchasing a one- or three-day ticket (see www.dublinbikes.ie). TFI Bikes operate a similar self-service bike-rental system in Cork, Galway, Limerick and Waterford, and offer a three-day subscription (see www.bikeshare.ie). In Belfast, either pay as you go or buy a casual subscription (3-day hire) for Just Eat Belfast Bikes (see www.belfastbikes.co.uk).

For cycling events across the island of Ireland see www.cyclingireland.ie.

ACCESSIBLE TRAVEL

While progress has been made in making the island of Ireland more accessible to persons with disabilities, this is very much an ongoing process. Venue accessibility varies, especially in buildings of architectural or historical interest, and there is a shortfall of accessible toilets and Changing Places.

Transport for Ireland's website is a good resource for general information on accessible travel (www.transportforireland.ie/getting-around/accessible-travel-information), Translink, Northern Ireland's main bus and rail operator, also provides information on its website (www.translink.co.uk/usingtranslink/accessibility).

The **Irish Wheelchair Association** (Áras Cúchulainn, Blackheath Drive, Clontarf, Dublin 3; tel: 01-818 6400, www.iwa.ie) provides practical information for wheelchair users, including wheelchair sales and rental, parking permits and holidays.

The official government body responsible for the rights of persons with disabilities is the **National Disability Authority** (25 Clyde Road, Ballsbridge, Dublin 4; tel: 01-608 0400, www.nda.ie). They will have up-to-date information on disability issues. The Head Office of **Fáilte Ireland** can advise on accessible attractions and accommodation (88–95 Amiens Street, Dublin 1; tel: 01-884 7700, www.discoverireland.ie). In Northern Ireland the campaigning body **Disability Action** (Portside Business Park, 189 Airport Road West, Belfast; tel: 028-9029 7880, www.disabilityaction.org) also offers practical advice.

ACCIDENTS AND EMERGENCIES

For **emergency services**, such as police, ambulance, fire service, lifeboat and coastal rescue, tel: 999 or 112 in the Republic of Ireland; tel: 999 in Northern Ireland.

Support services

Alcoholics Anonymous, Republic of Ireland, tel: 01-842 0700; Northern Ireland, tel: 028-9035 1222; www.alcoholicsanonymous.ie.
Crime Victims Helpline Republic of Ireland, tel: 116-006, www.crimevictimshelpline.ie.
Lifeline freephone helpline, Northern Ireland, tel: 0808-808 8000, www.lifelinehelpline.info.
Rape Crisis Centre, Republic of Ireland, tel: 1800-788 888, www.rapecrisishelp.ie.
Rape Crisis Northern Ireland tel: 0800-0246 991, https://rapecrisisni.org.uk.
Samaritans freephone helpline, Republic of Ireland, tel: 116-123 or text: 087-260 9090, www.samaritans.org.
Tourist Assistance Service (ITAS) Pearse Street Garda Station, Pearse Street, Dublin 2, tel: 01-666 9354, www.itas.ie.
Victim Support Northern Ireland tel: 028-9024 4039, www.victimsupportni.com.

ACCOMMODATION

In June 2022, the average daily rate for a hotel in Dublin was €202. For the same period, the average daily room rate in Northern Ireland was £107. It is possible to pay considerably more for a room in a top-rated hotel, or considerably less for budget accommodation in a hostel or B&B. Expensive is not necessarily better, of course, but generally speaking the more you pay, the more facilities are on offer. Most B&Bs have 'en suite' rooms with a shower or bath, as well as TV, phone and wi-fi. Some – especially farmhouses – offer first-class food. Both the Republic and Northern Ireland classify hotels on a star rating. Guesthouses is a category for B&Bs with over five rooms. Some, but not all, have restaurant facilities. Guesthouses are not licensed to sell beer and spirits (unless the guesthouse is also a pub), but some have wine licences.

Hostels

An Óige, the Irish Youth Hostel Association (61 Mountjoy Street, Dublin 7; tel: 01-830 4555, www.anoige.ie), has hostels throughout Ireland and offers a 10 percent membership discount on all hostels. Hostels in Northern Ireland are run by Hostelling International Northern Ireland (22–32 Donegall Road Belfast, BT12 5JN; www.hini.org.uk). Members of the International Youth Hostel Federation can use any of these.

Independent Holiday Hostels of Ireland (IHH; Fairview, Dublin 3; www.hostels-ireland.com) is an umbrella organisation for more than a hundred privately owned hostels. Like An Óige, these are relaxed places, with no curfews. Bed linen is supplied, but towel hire is usually extra. As well as traditional dormitory accommodation, many also have private double and family rooms, and offer cooked breakfast as an optional extra, as well as kitchen facilities. For a brochure, contact the IHH (preface the above address with PO Box 11772).

All independent hostels are privately owned, and can vary from scenic organic farms to a tiny townhouse stacked with bunk beds. The one drawback is a tendency to overcrowding in July and August and at festival times. Some hostels prefer not to belong to any organisation, and may not have been inspected for compliance with fire regulations.

Budget accommodation

Kinlay House (www.kinlayhouse.ie) offers year-round centres in Dublin (tel: 01-679 6644) and Galway (tel: 091-565 244). Prices start at around €35 for dorm accommodation. During the long vacation from mid-June to mid-September, they also offer self-catering apartments in UCD Village, Belfield Campus, Dublin 4 (tel: 01-269 7111). Brookfield Holiday Village (twww.brookfieldvillage.ie) offer summer self-catering apartments at College Road, Cork.

Self-catering accommodation

This is available in houses, cottages (some thatched), apartments, caravans and even a few castles. If you are looking for a 'traditional Irish cottage' be warned that many are newly built in artificial 'clusters', and used solely for holiday rentals. Be sure you are getting what you want when you book. If touring the Republic, you can ask one of the local tourist offices to book ahead for you; a small charge is made for telephone costs.

BUDGETING FOR YOUR TRIP

Ireland is in the Eurozone, and has relatively high levels of VAT at 23 and 13.5 percent (20 percent in Northern Ireland). Restaurant meals, pub prices, wine, sweets and even newspapers all come under the 23 percent band, making everyday life more expensive than in many other European countries. Two people should budget using the guidelines below (though variables in meals and hotels can cause prices to rise considerably). Prices in Dublin will be higher than in rural areas. Most hotels and some B&Bs outside Dublin raise their rates in July and August. Major sporting fixtures, bank holidays and other big events also mean you'll be charged premium rates.

Double room per night in a three-star hotel: €150–200
Simple lunch for two: €20–25
Two-course dinner for two: €45–60
Car hire per week: €500–900
Miscellaneous (drinks etc.): €40 per day (for two).

CHILDREN

Ireland is a child-friendly destination. Baby supplies are easily obtained from supermarkets and smaller shops. Children are usually welcome at hotels and B&Bs, and most can supply cots or babysitting services. Many hotels allow children under a certain age to stay in their parents' room at no extra charge, but the age limit varies. Most middle-range restaurants can supply highchairs, and there is usually a children's menu. The bigger restaurants should have nappy-changing facilities. Some of the grander establishments will only accept children over a certain age, usually about 12. Children are usually welcome in pubs frequented by visitors, but expected to be under the supervision of an adult at all times. Some publicans like children to be off the scene by early evening, and the law prohibits under-18s on any premises that serve alcohol after 9pm. Young people cannot drink alcohol until they are 18, and photo ID should be carried. During holiday periods, there are plenty of child-oriented activities designed by museums, local festivals and outdoor centres (check with the local tourist information centre for details). Look out for family tickets, offering good-value deals.

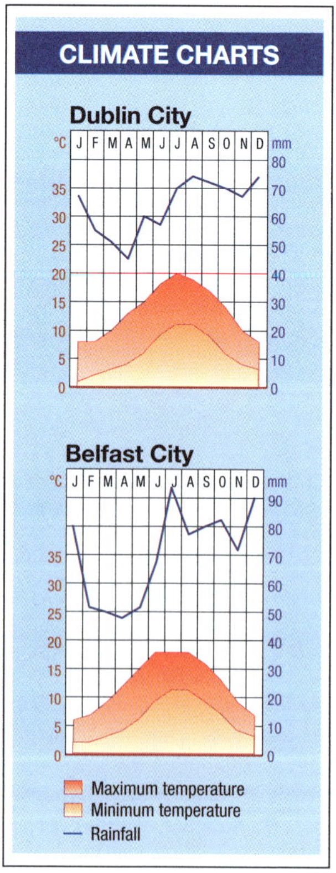

CLIMATE

Although Ireland lies at roughly the same northerly latitude as Newfoundland, it has a mild, wet climate, because of the prevailing southwesterly winds and the influence of the warm Gulf Stream along its western coast. As no part of the island is more than 70 miles (110km) from the sea, temperatures are fairly uniform over the whole country.

Average air temperatures in the coldest months, January and February, are mainly between 4°C and 7°C (39°F and 45°F). The warmest months, July and August, have average temperatures between 14°C and 16°C (57°F and 61°F), but occasionally reaching as high as 25°C (77°F). The sunniest months are May and June, with an average of between 5.5 and 6.5 hours a day over most of the country. The sunniest region is the extreme southeast.

Parts of the west of the country, with annual rainfall averaging 59in (1,500mm), are twice as wet as the east because of the prevailing Atlantic winds.

CLOTHING

Casual clothing is acceptable almost everywhere in Ireland, including smart hotels and restaurants. Because of the unpredictability of the weather, pack an umbrella, some rainproof clothing and a warm sweater, even in summer. But bring the suntan cream as well: when the summer sun shines, the ozone-laden winds from the Atlantic can intensify the burning effect of its rays.

CRIME AND SAFETY

While rural Ireland is generally a low-risk area for crime, visitors are often considered easy pickings. Hired cars are easy targets for criminals, and thefts from cars are commonplace in Dublin, other major towns and cities, and also in the car parks of visitor attractions. Never leave anything in sight in your car. Pickpockets operate in small gangs in central Dublin. Avoid O'Connell Street late at night.

If you experience any difficulties, contact The **Irish Tourist Assistance Service** (ITAS; tel: 01-666 9354, https://itas.ie), a national service that offers free support and practical help to victims of crime, or call the **Crime Victims Helpline** (tel: 116 006, www.crimevictimshelpline.ie).

CUSTOMS AND ENTRY REGULATIONS

Whether you require a visa to travel to the Republic of Ireland is determined by your nationality. You do not need a visa if you are a British, EEA or Swiss national but must have a passport or valid national identity card (under the Common Travel Area arrangements, UK citizens can travel 'passport free' but as you may be asked by an immigration officer for proof that you are a UK citizen it is advisable to travel with your passport). American, Australian, Canadian and other non-visa required nationalities (you can check online at www.irishimmigration.ie if a visa is required) can enter for tourism stays of up to 90 days with a valid passport. If you are from a visa required country you will need to apply for a Short Stay 'C' (Tourist) Visa. Unless you qualify for the short-stay visa waiver programme or have a visa issued as part of the British Irish Visa Scheme (BIVS), you may need to also apply for a UK visa (you can check online at www.gov.uk/check-uk-visa) if you plan to travel to Northern Ireland.

If you are coming from outside the Eurozone, you must now fill in a customs declaration form for cash sums of over €10,000 taken in or out of the Republic of Ireland or Northern Ireland.

If you are arriving in Ireland from another EU country, you can bring in the following items without paying further duties, as long as they are for personal use: 800 cigarettes, 200 cigars, 1kg of tobacco, 110 litres of beer, 90 litres of wine, 10 litres of spirits and 20 litres of fortified wine.

If you are travelling from outside the EU you can bring in 200 cigarettes or 50 cigars or 250g tobacco, plus 16 litres of beer, 4 litres of still wine, 1 litre of spirits or 2 litres of sparkling or fortified wine. For further information on customs regulations, visit www.revenue.ie.

ELECTRICITY

The standard mains power supply is 230V at a frequency of 50Hz. Type G plugs (three rectangular flat pins in a triangular pattern) are used. To use their own small appliances, visitors may need a transformer and a plug adaptor. Hotels usually have a two-pin, dual voltage 'shaver only' socket in the bathroom.

EMBASSIES AND CONSULATES

Dublin

Australia: 3rd Floor, 47–49 St Stephen's Green, Dublin 2; tel: 01-664 5300; www.ireland.embassy.gov.au.

Britain: 29 Merrion Road, Ballsbridge, Dublin 4; tel: 01-205 3700, www.britishembassyinireland.fco.gov.uk.

Canada: 7–8 Wilton Terrace, Dublin 2; tel: 01-231 4000, www.canada.ie.

US: 42 Elgin Road, Ballsbridge, Dublin 4; tel: 01-668 8777, https://ie.usembassy.gov.

South Africa: Alexandra House, Earlsfort Terrace, Dublin 2; tel: 01-661 5553.

Belfast

American Consulate General, 223 Stranmillis Road, Belfast; tel: 028-9038 6100, https://uk.usembassy.gov/embassy-consulates/belfast.

EVENTS

The number of events and festivals, big and small, increases every year. There are folk festivals, music festivals, food festivals, walking festivals, regattas, angling competitions, drama festivals, sporting competitions of all kinds, beauty contests, song contests, parades, car rallies, boat rallies, literary festivals, jazz festivals, agricultural shows, horse shows, commemorations, celebrations, hunt meetings, marathons, summer schools, community festivals, *céilithe* ... the list seems endless. The biggest growth area is arts festivals – theatre and film in winter, and multidisciplinary summer events, including the Cork Midsummer Festival (June), Galway Arts Festival (July) and Kilkenny Arts Festival (August).

In many cases, dates and venues are variable and some festivals – particularly the smaller, local ones – may appear and disappear from year to year according to the availability of funds, enthusiasm or organisers.

Here is a small selection, listed in calendar order. Exact dates often vary, but local tourist offices can provide precise dates and details.

Temple Bar Traditional Irish Music & Cultural Festival, in unique historical venues, Dublin. January. https://tradfest.ie

Out to Lunch Arts Festival, Black Box, Belfast. January. https://cqaf.com.

Six Nations Rugby Championship (Ireland versus England, Wales, Scotland, France, Italy), home matches at Aviva Stadium, Dublin. February/March. www.sixnationsrugby.com.

Audi Dublin International Film Festival, Irish premieres of a selection of Irish and international cinema. Late February. www.diff.ie.

Tedfest, celebration of *Father Ted* TV show, Aran Islands, County Galway. February. www.tedfest.org.

Killarney Mountain Festival, guided walks, outdoor adventures, speakers and live music. March. www.killarneymountainfestival.com.

St Patrick's Day, festival of Ireland's national saint, celebrated throughout Ireland and much of the world. 17 March.

World Irish Dancing Championships, attracts over 4,000 international competitors. Early April. www.clrg.ie.

Mountains to the Sea dlr Book Festival, Dun Laoghaire, Dun Laoghaire–Rathdown. March. www.mountainstosea.ie.

Irish Grand National, this steeplechase (a race over jumps) is the ultimate test for Ireland's finest sports horses, and a thrilling spectacle at Fairyhouse. Easter Monday.

The Cathedral Quarter Arts Festival, lively celebration of the arts in Belfast's vibrant 'left bank' district. First two weeks in May. https://cqaf.com.

Belfast City Marathon, some 3,000 runners take to the streets. May. www.belfastcitymarathon.com.

Northwest 200, the fastest motorcycle road race in Britain or Ireland, runs along the Portrush–Causeway Coast, County Antrim. May. www.northwest200.org.

Feile na Bealtaine, bilingual festival of culture and debate on the Dingle Peninsula, County Kerry. Throughout May. www.feilenabealtaine.ie.

Kinsale Sevens by the Sea, Europe's largest rugby 7s festival takes place in Kinsale, County Cork. May Bank Holiday weekend. www.kinsale7s.com.

Ballyhoura International Walking Festival, guided walks for all levels of hill walkers in the rolling country of the Cork–Limerick–Tipperary border. Early May.

Balmoral Show of the Royal Ulster Agricultural Society, Belfast. Mid-May. www.balmoralshow.co.uk.

Listowel Writers' Week, this large friendly literary festival in Listowel, County Clare, features readings and workshops and is popular with aspiring authors. Late May/June. www.writersweek.ie.

The Cat Laughs Comedy Festival, international festival of stand-up comedy, with over 50 comedians hoping to bring a smile to the medieval city of Kilkenny. June bank holiday – late May to early June.

Dublin International Chamber Music Festival: Great Music in Irish Houses, held in various mansions near Dublin. Early June. www.greatmusicinirishhouses.com.

Bloomsday Festival, is held on the date on which Joyce's *Ulysses* takes place, Dublin-wide celebration with free street entertainment, including breakfast some years. 16 June. www.bloomsdayfestival.ie.

Walk the Glens, walking festival in the breathtakingly scenic Glens of Antrim. Early June.

Rory Gallagher International Tribute Festival, Ballyshannon, County Donegal. June. www.rorygallagherfestival.com.

Bulmer's Forbidden Fruit, electronic dance festival at the Royal Hospital Kilmainham, Dublin. June. www.forbiddenfruit.ie.

Irish Derby, this one-mile flat-race for three-year-old colts is the highlight of the most glamorous festival weekend in the Irish racing calendar. Late June. www.curragh.ie.

Westport Festival of Music and Food, family-friendly two-day celebration in Westport, Mayo's most charming town. Late June.

Irish Oaks, the equivalent of the Derby for fillies. Early July. www.curragh.ie.

West Cork Chamber Music Festival and **West Cork Literary Festival**, culture reigns in Bantry town as the highly esteemed music festival rolls into the literary event. Late June to early July. www.westcorkmusic.ie.

Kinsale Arts Festival, seaside arts extravaganza with many family-friendly events and street entertainment. Late June. www.kinsale.ie.

Willie Clancy Summer School, seaside celebration of traditional Irish music, workshops and performances at Miltown Malbay, County Clare. July. www.scoilsamhraidhwillieclancy.com.

Galway International Arts Festival, celebration of world and Irish theatre, film, art, literature and music. Mid-July. www.giaf.ie.

Féile an Phobail, massive community festival with concerts, debates, tours, exhibitions and street theatre in West Belfast. July–August. www.feilebelfast.com.

Galway Races, heady, often hilarious, holiday horse-racing festival. Late July/August. www.galwayraces.com.

Yeats International Summer School, enthusiasts from all over the world come to listen, learn and explore Yeat's much-loved Sligo. Late July to early August. www.yeatssociety.com.

Beatyard, open-air music and entertainment in Dun Laoghaire, Dun Laoghaire–Rathdown. August. www.the-beatyard.com.

Dublin Horse Show, greatest event in the show-jumping calendar in the RDS, Ballsbridge. August. www.dublinhorseshow.com.

Puck Fair, Killorglin, County Kerry. Ancient pagan festival at which a goat is crowned and horses are traded in the traditional manner amid much merry-making. August. www.puckfair.ie

Kilkenny Arts Festival, Ireland's answer to the Edinburgh Festival with big international names from the worlds of drama, music and visual arts. Mid-August. www.kilkennyarts.ie

The Auld Lammas Fair, Ballycastle, County Antrim. Northern Ireland's most popular old fair, at which you traditionally 'treat your Mary Ann to some dulse and Yellow Man'. August.

Ulster Grand Prix (motorcycling). The world's fastest road race, near Belfast. August. www.ulstergrandprix.net.

Merriman Summer School, a stimulating week of intense intellectual debate about the nation's culture in Lisdoonvarna, County Clare. Mid-August. www.merriman.ie.

Fleadh Ceoil na Éireann, a massive All-Ireland festival of Irish music, song and dance, centred on competitions. Venue variable. August. www.fleadhcheoil.ie.

Rose of Tralee Festival, young women of Irish origin from around the world compete in a pageant based on personality in Tralee, County Kerry; its popularity amazingly endures, even among the younger generation. Late August. www.roseoftralee.ie.

Electric Picnic, Stradbally, County Kildare. Ireland's biggest open-air music and arts festival. Early September. www.electricpicnic.ie.

Matchmaking Festival, good-natured low-key event in the small, friendly town of Lisdoonvarna, County Clare, mainly for the more mature soulmate seekers. September. www.matchmakerireland.com.

Hurling and Gaelic Football All-Ireland finals, Dublin. September. www.crokepark.ie.

Galway Oyster Festival, Galway city celebration of the new season for the native bivalve, traditionally accompanied by stout and soda bread. Late September. www.galwayoysterfestival.com.

National Ploughing Championships, one of Europe's biggest agricultural shows with livestock arena, food and lifestyle villages. Late September. www.npa.ie.

Dublin Theatre Festival. Late September/October. www.dublintheatrefestival.com.

Banks of the Foyle Halloween Carnival, Halloween events for all the family and spectacular carnival parade in Derry. October. www.derryhalloween.com.

Cork Jazz Festival, Cork City takes over the city, with top names concerts and free pub jazz. October Bank Holiday. www.guinnessjazzfestival.com.

Wexford Festival Opera, two weeks of full-scale productions of lesser-known operas in Wexford. Late October–November. www.wexfordopera.com.

Dublin City Marathon, the big one for Irish runners, with a large international contingent, too. Late October. https://irishlifedublinmarathon.ie.

Visit www.dublinbus.ie to help you navigate the city's buses and find your way around.

St Patrick's Cathedral, Dublin.

Bram Stoker Festival, celebration of the legacy of the Dublin-born Gothic author and creator of Dracula in Dublin, Late October. www.bramstokerfestival.com.

Belfast International Arts Festival, ambitious, event-packed two weeks of music, drama, folk song and cinema at Queen's University, Belfast. Late October/early November. www.belfastinternationalartsfestival.com.

Leopardstown Christmas Festival, festive four-day filly racing festival in Dublin. www.leopardstown.com.

HEALTH AND MEDICAL CARE

Medical services

Medical insurance is highly advisable for all visitors. However, visitors from the UK and the EU/EEA and Switzerland with a valid Global Health Insurance Card or European Health Insurance Card are entitled to immediate and necessary medical treatment in across the island of Ireland, free of charge. Ireland and the UK also have reciprocal healthcare agreements with some non-EU countries.

LGBTQ+ TRAVELLERS

There should be no major problems for LGBTQ+ travellers in Ireland. Be as safety-conscious as you would in any foreign city or country. Ireland has become an inclusive, non-discriminatory society in recent years, as reflected by the landslide victory for 'yes' in the referendum over legalising same-sex marriage in 2015. The development of the Irish LGBTQ+ scene is relatively recent, though, and most openly gay Irish are young. Discrimination does still exist, and you are more likely to encounter it the further you get from the main cities. In the North, attitudes can be more negative. Gay men looking for a double room may find that all rooms in the B&B have suddenly been booked. Openly gay couples may also attract unwanted attention in small-town pubs.

The following LGBTQ+ resource centres offer advice and contacts:

Dublin: Outhouse, 51 Capel Street, Dublin 1; www.outhouse.ie; **Switchboard**, www.theswitchboard.ie.

Cork: www.gaycork.com is Cork's LGBTQ+ portal.

Belfast: Belfast LGBT Centre, 23–31 Waring Street, Cathedral Quarter, Belfast; https://en-gb.facebook.com/BelfastLGBTCentre.

Information on bars, clubs, accommodation and friendly contacts can be found at www.gcn.ie, a lively magazine and information service for Ireland's LGBTQ+ community based in Dublin's Temple Bar area.

LIQUOR LAWS

The legal drinking age is 18, but some pubs will only serve patrons over 21 carrying photo identity. Pubs in the Republic of Ireland are open seven days a week, from 10.30am. Opening time is at the discretion of the landlord, and can vary from 12.30pm to 4 or 6pm depending on local trade. Closing time, in contrast, is defined by law, but can vary depending on what sort of licence the pub has. Normal closing time is 11.30pm, but this can extend to 3am on Fridays and Saturdays and during festivals. Sunday opening hours are 12.30pm to 11pm. You are allowed half an hour 'drinking up time' after the official closing time, before you have to leave the premises. All bars in the Republic of Ireland are smoke-free, but heated outdoor 'smoking decks' are often provided. Since 2018, pubs in both the Republic and the North can legally open on Good Friday, although not all will. Christmas Day you'll only find hotel bars open for guests. Persons under the age of 18 are not allowed in the bar areas of licensed premises after 9pm (until 10pm May–September).

Opening hours in Northern Ireland are, generally, 11.30am to 11pm Monday to Saturday and 12.30pm to 11pm Sunday. Many pubs have extended opening hours at weekends.

MAPS

If you intend to do the sort of driving that takes you off the main routes, it is worth buying the *Complete Road Atlas of Ireland* (Ordnance Survey Ireland and Ordnance Survey Northern Ireland) which sells for about €10. Cyclists and walkers may want smaller scale maps: these can be bought locally from tourist information centres, newsagents and bookshops.

MEDIA

Magazines

Hot Press (www.hotpress.com) is a lively local pop culture paper. Totally Dublin (www.totallydublin.ie) is a freesheet and website covering Dublin's lively cultural scene, 'high and low'. The *Irish Arts Review* (www.irishartsreview.com) is a quality glossy magazine published four times a year covering all aspects of fine and decorative arts in Ireland.

Newspapers

The Irish Times (www.irishtimes.com), is the most serious and comprehensive, and the best option for foreign news, arts and business, it also has a great letters page. The *Independent* (www.independent.ie) broadly supports the Fine Gael Party and aims for a hard-hitting style. The *Irish Examiner* (www.irishexaminer.com) is the staple diet of business and farming people in the southwest. Two morning papers are published in Belfast: the Unionist/Protestant *News Letter* (www.newsletter.co.uk) and the Nationalist/Catholic *The Irish News* (www.irishnews.com); it's interesting to compare their respective treatment of a controversial story.

There are three evening papers: the *Evening Herald* from the *Independent* stable in Dublin, the *Echo* (www.eveningecho.ie) from Cork and the *Belfast Telegraph*, (www.belfasttelegraph.co.uk), which also publishes a tabloid Saturday morning edition. All contain lots of sport and showbiz.

All bars are smoke-free.

The *Independent* has a Sunday version; also published from Dublin are the *Sunday World* (www.sundayworld.com), a lurid tabloid (pin-ups, shocks, scares and scandals) and the *Sunday Business Post* (www.businesspost.ie), which concentrates on business and politics. The London *Sunday Times* Irish edition is published in Cork and distributed nationally. From Belfast, there is *Sunday Life* from the *Belfast Telegraph* stable.

All the British dailies and Sundays are readily obtainable on both sides of the border, and UK readers can expect an 'Irish edition' of their usual paper, with a focus on Irish topics.

Like everywhere else, local papers are struggling, but some still survive, providing an interesting window into regional affairs.

Radio

RTE1 is the main station for news, current affairs and drama; 2fm has a staple output of pop music and Lyric FM is for lovers of classical music. There are also a number of independent local radio stations. In Northern Ireland, the commercials-free BBC Radio Ulster has full local coverage, as do the advertising-funded Downtown Radio and Cool FM.

Television

The national broadcasting service, Radio Teilifís Éireann (RTÉ) has three TV channels (one of them, TG4, broadcasts exclusively in the Irish language). Ireland's first independent television network TV3, was launched in 1998 to provide an alternative to 'a middle-of-the-road service aimed at Middle Ireland', in other words RTÉ.

In addition, the British TV channels (both BBC and commercial channels) can be received by satellite, as can many satellite channels including Sky, ESPN, Setanta Sports and Eurosport. In Northern Ireland, BBC1 includes local coverage, as does its commercial counterpart, UTV.

MONEY

In 2002 Ireland became one of the first 12 countries to adopt the euro (€). It is divided into 100 cents. The coins used are 1¢, 2¢, 5¢, 10¢, 20¢, 50¢, €1 and €2. The notes are €5, €10, €20, €50 and €100.

In Northern Ireland, the British pound (£) is used. Exchange rates vary but many shops in border areas will accept either currency.

In the Republic, banks are open between 10am and 4pm, Monday through Friday. Branches in small towns may close from 12.30 to 1.30pm. Most Dublin banks are open until 5pm on Thursday. In Northern Ireland, bank business hours are from 9.30am to 4.30pm, Monday through Friday.

Traveller's cheques are accepted at all banks.

MasterCard and Visa are the most commonly acceptable credit cards, followed by American Express and Diners Club. But many small guesthouses and B&Bs places will expect payment to be made in cash.

OPENING HOURS

Shops and department stores usually open at 9.30am and close at 6 or 7pm, Monday through Saturday. In smaller towns, some shops close for lunch between 1 and 2pm. **Supermarkets** and convenience stores generally open daily until 9pm, and some until much later, Dublin has a number of 24-hour shops. In many towns and smaller cities, shops close one day a week or observe early closing (1pm, usually on Wednesday or Thursday). **Post Offices** open from 9am to 5.30pm weekdays and from 9am to 1pm on Saturdays; some of the smaller ones close for lunch. **Government offices** are open to the public Monday through Friday from 9am to 5pm.

Museums and other tourist sights are often closed on Monday, and outside Dublin and Belfast most have restricted opening hours between November and Easter or late May.

In hotels and B&Bs, **breakfast** is generally served between 8 and 10am, and in restaurants and pubs until noon. **Restaurants and pubs** generally serve a lunch menu between 12.30 and 2.30pm, and dinner from 6 to 9.30pm.

POSTAL SERVICES

At the time of writing, letters and postcards weighing 100g cost €1.25 within Ireland and Northern Ireland, €2.20 to the rest of the world. In Northern Ireland, British postal rates apply.

Most newsagents and postcard outlets also sell stamps. Philatelists may obtain information on Irish stamps from the Controller, Philatelic Section, GPO, Dublin 1.

PUBLIC HOLIDAYS

1 January, 17 March (St Patrick's Day), Good Friday (Northern Ireland only), Easter Monday, first Monday in May, Spring Holiday (last Monday in May in Northern Ireland, first Monday in June in the Republic), 12 July (Northern Ireland only), Summer Holiday (first Monday in August in the Republic, last Monday in August in Northern Ireland) last Monday in October (the Republic only), Christmas Day and 26 December (St. Stephen's Day/Boxing Day).

RELIGIOUS SERVICES

All hotels and B&Bs will have details of nearby Roman Catholic and Church of Ireland services.

Roman Catholic

Dublin's principal Catholic cathedral is the place to hear the Palestrina Choir, which showcases the best Irish male voices. Latin Mass is sung here every Sunday morning at 11am. Pro-Cathedral, Marlborough Street, off O'Connell Street; www.procathedral.ie.

Church of Ireland

At 6pm on Wednesday and Thursday you can enjoy a choral evensong in Dublin's oldest church. Christchurch Cathedral, Christ Church Place; tel: 01-677 8099, www.choralevensong.org.

Muslim

The Islamic Cultural Centre (19 Roebuck Road, Clonskeagh, Dublin 14; https://islamireland.ie) provides services and information for Ireland's rapidly growing Muslim population, now the third largest congregation after the Church of Ireland. Dublin Mosque, 163 South Circular Road, Dublin 8; https://islamicfoundation.ie.

Presbyterian

The Presbyterian Church of Ireland serves the whole island of Ireland and has a membership of about 300,000 in over 560 congregations, 527 of which are in Northern Ireland. The Information Office, Presbyterian Church in Ireland, Assembly Buildings, 2–10 Fisherwick Place, Belfast, BT1 6DW, Northern Ireland; www.presbyterianireland.org.

Methodist

There are about 250 Methodist congregations in Ireland. See website for contact details and meeting times. Secretary of Conference, 1 Fountainville Avenue, Belfast, BT9 6AN; www.irishmethodist.org.

Other churches

Unitarian

A lively congregation meets on Sundays at 11am in this handsome 19th-century church in the centre of Georgian Dublin to share a bond of religious sympathy rather than a creed-bound faith. There are also lunchtime talks series. Contact Rev. Bridget Spain, Minister, Unitarian Church, 112 St Stephen's Green West, Dublin 2; tel: 01-478 0638.

Quaker

There are meetings every Sunday at 11am at the Quaker Meeting House, Frederick Street (off York Street), Belfast. In Dublin meetings are held at 11am on Sundays and 6.15pm on Thursdays at the Quaker Meeting House, 4–5 Eustace Street, Temple Bar, Dublin 1. There are about 30 other meeting houses in Ireland. For details see www.quakers-in-ireland.ie.

Jewish

The Terenure Hebrew Congregation, 32a Rathfarnham Road, Dublin 6W, welcomes visitors to join them for daily Shabbat (8.30am) or Yom Tov services conducted according to the Ashkenazi tradition. Check website (www.dublinhebrew.org) for details or contact The Jewish Community Office, Herzog House, 1 Zion Road, Rathgar, Dublin 6; www.jewishireland.org.

SMOKING

Since 2004 smoking has been banned in all enclosed places of work in Ireland, including public transport, airport terminals, cinemas, banks, offices, shops, pubs, restaurants and cafés. Hotels and B&Bs may allow smoking in some bedrooms, or may opt to have smoke-free bedrooms. Ask about their policy when booking.

Tourist information centres are a good source of free local maps.

Most pubs and some restaurants have adapted existing beer gardens or patios to cater for smokers.

TELEPHONES

The international dialling code for the Republic of Ireland is **353**. Northern Ireland's code is **44**. If you are calling the North from the Republic, just substitute the code 028 with 048, rather than using the international dialling code.

There are several telecommunications companies operating in Ireland – the largest one being Eir (www.eir.ie).

International calls can be dialled direct from private phones, or dial 11818 for the international operator. To contact the local operator, dial 11811. The long-distance services of AT&T, Sprint and MCI are also available.

Telephone services in Northern Ireland are operated by British Telecom; dial 100 for the operator.

Mobile (Cell) phones

Only mobile phones with GSM will work in Ireland. If your phone is non-GSM, consult with your provider before travelling. It may be cheaper to buy a local SIM card and top up with prepaid calls. Local providers include 3, Meteor, O2, Tesco Mobile and Vodafone.

If you are coming from the UK, your mobile should work in Northern Ireland, but you will need international roaming in the Republic.

TIME ZONE

Ireland follows Greenwich Mean Time (GMT). In spring, the clock is moved one hour ahead for Summer Time to give extra daylight in the evening; in autumn it is moved back again to GMT. At noon according to GMT, it is: 4am in Los Angeles; 7am in New York; 1pm in Western Europe; 8pm in Singapore; 10pm in Sydney; midnight in New Zealand.

TOURIST INFORMATION

Irish Tourist Board (Fáilte Ireland)

General enquiries: Fáilte Ireland, 88–95, Amiens Street, Dublin 1; tel: 01-884 7700, www.ireland.com. For accommodation offers visit website.
Dublin City: Discover Ireland Visitor Centre, 4 Upper O'Connell Street Upper, North City, Dublin, D01 WP59; www.discoverireland.ie.
Fáilte Ireland Tourist Information Office, 3 Palace Street, Dublin, D02 T277; tel: 1800-230 330.

Regional offices

Local tourist offices can be found throughout Ireland. A number are mentioned in the 'Places' chapters. For details see www.discoverireland.ie.

Northern Ireland Tourist Board

Belfast: Floors 10–12, Linum Chambers, Bedford Square, Bedford Street, Belfast, BT2 7ES; tel: 028-9023 1221, www.discovernorthernireland.com.

Tourism Ireland offices abroad

Australia: Level 16/109 Pitt Street, Sydney NSW 2000; tel +61 477-009 224.
Britain: Nations House, 103 Wigmore Street, London W1U 1QS; tel: 020-7518 0800.
Canada: 2 Bloor Street West, Suite 3403, Toronto, ON M4W; tel: +1 416-925 6368.
US: 345 Park Avenue, New York, NY 10154; tel: +1 212-418 0800.

WEBSITES

General

www.ireland.com is the official marketing website of Tourism Ireland, it covers both the Republic of Ireland and Northern Ireland, and is designed to help you plan your holiday.
www.discoverireland.ie is the website to use in the Republic of Ireland to plan your day-to-day activities, book accommodation and find out about festivals and other events.
www.discovernorthernireland.com provides information on Northern Ireland.
www.ireland-information.com is a free information service covering everything from genealogy to Irish jokes.
www.irelandofthewelcomes.com carries extracts from Tourism Ireland's excellent magazine, *Ireland of the Welcomes*.

Accommodation

Accommodation can be booked though Ireland.com, discoverireland.ie and discovernortherieland.com, all of which are run by government-funded official Irish tourism organisations.
www.irelandhotels.com for online hotel booking via the website of the Irish Hotels Federation.
www.nihf.co.uk Northern Ireland Hotels Federation.
www.hostels-ireland.com for a Fáilte Ireland-approved holiday hostel online.

Eating out/Food

www.bordbia.ie to locate the nearest farmers' market.

Genealogy

www.nli.ie for family historians. The Genealogy Office of the National Library is the best starting place.

Heritage

www.heritageireland.ie gives details of the National Monuments, historic houses, parks and gardens in State care. Buy a Heritage Card on day one for great savings on admission fees.

Leisure and sport

www.irishtrails.ie for information on walking in Ireland from long-distance waymarked trails to a stroll in the park.
www.gaa.ie to track down a game of hurling or Irish football.
www.discoverireland.ie/things-to-do has a wealth of information on walking, cycling, angling, golf, horse riding and cruising the Shannon and the canals.

Transport

www.theaa.ie for driving advice, time and distance between cities, etc.
www.irishrail.ie for timetables and book tickets on Ireland's railways.
www.buseireann.ie for local and intercity bus services outside Dublin.
www.dublinbus.ie for bus services within Dublin.
www.dublinairport.com live flight information and links to all airlines.

Weather

www.met.ie for the latest forecast.

What's On

www.entertainment.ie will tell you what's on in theatres, cinemas, clubs and at festivals.

IRISH CLASSICS

Castle Rackrent by Maria Edgeworth. Published in 1800, Edgeworth's novel uses pointed humour to question Anglo-Irish identity and absentee landlords.
The Vicar of Wakefield by Oliver Goldsmith. A graduate of Trinity College Dublin, like many others he headed for London where his comic novel about a hapless vicar, and his hilarious play *She Stoops to Conquer* gave him enduring fame.
Portrait of the Artist as a Young Man; ***Dubliners***; ***Ulysses***; ***Finnegans Wake*** by James Joyce. His coming-of-age novel and collection of short stories will help you decide whether to tackle his magnum opus, *Ulysses* and swan song *Finnegans Wake*.
The Life and Opinions of Tristram Shandy, Gentleman by Laurence Sterne. Sterne's bawdy, fictional autobiography of the unfortunate Tristram Shandy is arguably the first postmodern novel.
Dracula by Bram Stoker. Stoker's memorable count spawned an entire genre of literature and film.
Gulliver's Travels by Jonathan Swift. The Dean of Dublin's St Patrick's Cathedral was a noted satirist, and his best-known work *Gulliver's Travels* is a savage indictment of mankind's folly, far removed from the many children's adaptations.
The Picture of Dorian Gray by Oscar Wilde. Dorian Gray sells his soul for eternal youth and beauty. Wilde's only novel was greeted with a flurry of disapprobation on publication.

FICTION

The Book of Evidence and ***The Sea*** by John Banville. A leading intellectual as well as a novelist, his 1989 novel is the disturbing story of a sleazy Dublin murderer, while his 2005 Booker Prize-winner is a tender account of lost love.
There are Little Kingdoms and ***Dark Lies the Island*** by Kevin Barry. Short stories that use anarchic comedy to skewer the absurdities of post-Celtic Tiger rural Ireland.
More Pricks than Kicks and ***Murphy*** by Samuel Beckett. People are often surprised at how funny the Nobel laureate's first story collection is, with its cast of outrageous Dublin characters. *Murphy*, his comic first novel, was rejected by 41 publishers.
Collected Short Stories and ***The Last September*** by Elizabeth Bowen. One of the last writers in the Anglo-Irish tradition, her compelling novel is set during the Troubles.
The Ginger Man by J.P. Donleavy. Exuberant, often hilarious, account of postwar Dublin, as seen by a hard-living American.
Langrishe, Go Down by Aidan Higgins. The last great Irish 'big house' novel, chronicling its decline, championed by Samuel Beckett and Harold Pinter.

Send us your thoughts

We do our best to ensure the information in our books is as accurate and up-to-date as possible. The books are updated on a regular basis by destination experts, who thoroughly review all the information included. However, we know that things change while the book is on the shelf, and we are ultimately reliant on our readers to put us in the picture.

We really welcome your feedback, especially your experience of using the book "on the road" and if you came across a great new attraction we missed.

We will acknowledge all contributions and offer an Insight Guide to the best messages received. Please email us at: hello@insightguides.com

All Names Have Been Changed by Claire Kilroy. A wry look at 1980s Ireland and its literary culture, set at Trinity College Dublin in a tight-knit group of creative writing students.
Creatures of the Earth: New and Selected Stories by John McGahern. McGahern was one of the most understated and highly rated chroniclers of rural Ireland.
The Country Girls; ***A Fanatic Heart: Selected Stories of Edna O'Brien***; ***Saint and Sinners*** by Edna O'Brien. While Ireland's leading female author's first novel is a witty picture of Dublin in the 1950s, her short stories are darker and deeper.
The Third Policeman by Flann O'Brien. Straight-faced novel of absurdist humour.
The Islandman by Tomás O'Crohan. Vivid memoir of a Great Blasket Island farmer-fisherman, written originally in Irish.
An Old Woman's Reflections by Peig Sayers. Memoir written in Irish by a natural storyteller about life on the Great Blasket Island.
The South by Colm Tóibín. Now an internationally known novelist and travel writer, his first novel about an Irishwoman's love affair with Spain remains one of his best.
Collected Short Stories by William Trevor. Set in both England and Ireland, among the plain people. Trevor was a master of the quiet epiphany.

POETRY

The Penguin Book of Irish Poetry edited by Patrick Crotty. Well-balanced selection of the greatest Irish poets.
A Snail in My Prime by Paul Durcan. Popular, readable poet, known for his quirky humour and often agonising honesty.
Finders Keepers: Selected Prose 1971–2001 and ***100 Poems*** by Seamus

Heaney. Superb collection of the Nobel laureate's incisive literary essays and lectures; and a collection of poems hand-picked by the Heaney family.
Collected Poems by Patrick Kavanagh, edited by Antoinette Quinn. One of Ireland's most influential poets, Kavanagh chronicled the country through the everyday in his poetry and prose. This collection includes his most famous works 'The Great Hunger' and 'On Raglan Road'.
Collected Poems by Michael Longley. At his best, his perceptive lyrics, often nature-inspired, can stand beside fellow Ulster poets, Heaney and Mahon.
New Selected Poems by Derek Mahon. A major 20th-century poet in the metaphysical mode, his more sophisticated oeuvre is considered by many to be superior to Heaney's.
The Complete Works of W.B. Yeats. As a poet and dramatist, Yeats played a key role in promoting Irish nationalism, was cofounder of the Abbey Theatre, and a Senator. He was awarded the Nobel Prize for Literature in 1923.

HISTORY

How the Irish Saved Civilization by Thomas Cahill. A humorous look at Irish achievements down the years, with a serious core.
Atlas of the Great Irish Famine edited by John Crowley, William J. Smith and Mike Murphy. Computer generated graphics and authoritative essays elucidate the causes of the Great Famine and its effects.
Modern Ireland 1600–1972 by R.F. Foster. Readable academic history with many new insights.
The Story of Ireland: In Search of a New National Memory by Neil Hegarty. Book of the 2012 RTÉ TV series in which journalist Fergal Keane takes a fresh look at Irish history.
Twilight of the Ascendancy by Mark Bence Jones. Well-informed social history documenting the demise of the 'big house'. Wonderful old photos.
Ireland: A History by Robert Kee. Readable illustrated history, good on disentangling the Troubles.
The Course of Irish History edited by T.W. Moody and F.X. Martin. General narrative history, by established experts in each period, revised and updated.
The Great Hunger: Ireland 1845–1849 by Cecil Woodham Smith. The classic account of the Famine is a harrowing but compelling narrative.

BIOGRAPHY

Michael Collins by Tim Pat Coogan. The life of the pro-Treaty politician on which Neil Jordan's 1996 film was based.
James Joyce by Richard Ellman. One of the finest literary biographies.
W.B. Yeats, a Life by R.F. Foster. Definitive two-volume life of the poet by a leading historian.
Damned to Fame: A Life of Samuel Beckett by James Knowlson. The official biography.

MEMOIRS

Borstal Boy by Brendan Behan. Autobiographical account of time spent in a young offender institution, discovering the working-class kids of England and Ireland have more in common than their differences.
My Left Foot and ***Down All the Days*** by Christy Brown. Two lyrical accounts of growing up with cerebral palsy in a huge, poor family in Dublin in the 1930s and 1940s.
Are You Somebody by Nuala O'Faolain. O'Faolain was admirably candid about her problems with alcohol and sex in her emotionally stark memoir. The commemorative edition includes a foreword by Frank McCourt and extra archival materials.
McCarthy's Bar: A Journey of Discovery in Ireland by Pete McCarthy. Humorous account of an Englishman's discovery of his Irish roots. Excellent on pubs.
Angela's Ashes by Frank McCourt. Bestselling account of a miserable childhood in Limerick, subsequently filmed in 1999.
To School Through the Fields by Alice Taylor. A quiet account of a rural childhood in the 1940s, which became an international bestseller.

CURRENT AFFAIRS

A Place Apart by Dervla Murphy. Her 1978 account of Northern Ireland is still first-rate.
Wasted: A Sober Journey through Drunken Ireland by Brian O'Connell. An interesting look at the human cost of Ireland's famous love of alcohol-fuelled partying.
Heroic Failure: Brexit and the Politics of Pain and ***Three Years in Hell: The Brexit Chronicles*** by Fintan O'Toole. Clever and entertaining analysis of Brexit by one of Ireland's sharpest cultural commentators.

GENEALOGY

Surnames of Ireland by Edward McLysaght. There are numerous pocket books, but this is the standard work.

ARCHITECTURE

The Architecture of Ireland by Maurice Craig. An early account of the uniqueness of Irish architecture and still one of the best.
Georgian Dublin by Desmond Guinness. Enduring illustrated study of Dublin's 18-century architecture.
The Irish Round Tower by Brian Lalor. Scholarly but highly readable guide to Ireland's round towers.

ART AND DECORATIVE ARTS

A Concise History of Irish Art by Bruce Arnold. The definitive account, updated to include more on Irish modernism.
Art in Ireland since 1910 by Fionna Barter. Survey of contemporary Irish art at home and in the diaspora.
Irish Country Furniture and Furnishings 1700–2000 by Claudia Kinmonth. A beautifully illustrated study of vernacular furniture across the island of Ireland.

COOKERY

Avoca Café Cookbook by Hugo Arnold and Georgia Glynn featuring wonderful salads and lunch ideas from the award-winning Avoca group.
Irish Traditional Cooking by Darina Allen. Authentic recipes from the doyenne of Irish cooking.
Nevin McGuire's Complete Family Cookbook by Nevin McGuire. Filled with quick recipes for busy lifestyles from the acclaimed chef.
The Ballymaloe Cookbook (edn, 2014) by Myrtle Allen. Revised and updated edition of Ireland's farm-to-table pioneer's 1970s classic cookbook.
The Irish Beef Book by Pat Whelan and Katy McGuinness. Definitive guide to beef with nose-to-tail recipes.
Wild Food by Evan Doyle and Biddy White Lennon. Tips on foraging in the Irish countryside and plenty of

Bookshop at the Dublin Writers Museum.

recipes for Irish wild goods, including seaweed.

DRAMA

The Complete Dramatic Works by Samuel Beckett. Includes the famous *Waiting for Godot.*

Plays: One and ***Plays Two*** by Brian Friel. Includes *Dancing at Lughnasa* and *Translations.*

David Ireland Plays 1: Half a Glass of Water; The End of Hope; Ulster American; Cyprus Avenue; Sadie by David Ireland. Provocative dramas punctuated by Ireland's trademark dark humour.

McPherson: Four Plays by Conor McPherson. Eerie dramas, including *The Weir*, set in the west of Ireland.

Three Dublin Plays: The Shadow of a Gunman, Juno and the Paycock, The Plough and the Stars by Sean O'Casey. His trilogy of tragicomedies are set in the Dublin tenements, and deal with the problems of ordinary families caught up in historic events.

The Playboy of the Western World by J.M. Synge. The masterpiece of a multifaceted writer who invented a new language using the poetry inherent in the Irish vernacular. Its earthy realism caused riots at its Abbey premiere.

FOLKLORE

In Ireland Long Ago by Kevin Danaher. A highly readable account of the fast-disappearing old ways.

Irish Folk Ways by Estyn Evans. Pioneering ethnographical study.

Irish Trees: Myths, Legends and Folklore by Niall Mac Coitir. An engaging blend of natural history, mythology and folklore.

MUSIC

Irish Traditional Music by Ciaran Carson. Complete guide to playing techniques, singing and instruments, including pub etiquette.

Bringing It All Back Home: The Influence of Irish Music by Nuala O'Connor. Charts the evolution of Irish traditional music at home and abroad.

TRAVEL

Belfast: A Pocket History by Jonathan Bardon and David Burnett. Bestselling account of 13 centuries.

Dublin edited by Peter Somerville Large. History of the city, rich in anecdote.

In Search of Ireland by H.V. Morton. Wallow in nostalgia as an Englishman gets to grips with 1938 Ireland.

The Aran Islands by J.M. Synge. First published in 1907, it is the best book to read on a first visit.

A Place Near Heaven by Damien Enright. A calendar year in west Cork as observed by an amiable nature lover.

The Height of Nonsense: The Ultimate Irish Road Trip by Paul Clements. Light-hearted account of climbing the highest peak in each county.

Connemara: Listening to the Wind; ***Connemara: The Last Pool of Darkness*** and ***Connemara: A Little Gaelic Kingdom*** by Tim Robinson. Magisterial and mesmerising travel and topographical trilogy, from polymath mathematician and artist turned map-maker and author.

Eating Scenery: West Cork, the People and the Place by Alannah Hopkin. A close look at a scenic corner of rural Ireland, concentrating on the huge social changes of the past few decades.

LANDSCAPE AND TOPOGRAPHY

The Shell Guide to Reading the Irish Landscape by Frank Mitchell and Michael Ryan. Explaining the natural, historical and geological factors that have shaped the Irish landscape.

Atlas of the Rural Irish Landscape (2nd edn, 2011) edited by F.H.A. Allen, Kevin Whelan, Matthew Stout. Case studies of the effects on the landscape of changes in land use from prehistoric times to the present day.

Farming and the Burren by Brendan Dunford. Analysis of the impact of agricultural practices on this strange limestone landscape from Neolithic times to the present.

Handbook of the Irish Seashore by Matt Murphy. What lurks in the rock pool.

Blasket Islands: Next Parish America by Joan and Ray Stagles. The story of the hardy inhabitants of a small island off the coast of Dingle who persisted in the old way of life until 1953.

OTHER INSIGHT GUIDES

More than 180 **Insight Guides** cover every continent, with information on culture and all the top sights, and superb photography.

CREDITS

PHOTO CREDITS

All images **Shutterstock** except:
Allen Kiely 165
Belfast VCB 311
Belfast Waterfront 314
Bibliothèque nationale de France/
Bigstock 42BR, 146, 148, 163, 184, 218BL, 219ML, 320
Break Out Pictures 29TR
Brian Morrison/Fáilte Ireland 25R, 246
Cashel Palace Hotel 11B
Chris Hill/Fáilte Ireland 9TL, 42/43T, 43ML, 108/109, 248, 250, 260, 307, 310, 313
Conor McCabe Photography 25L, 140/141T, 140B, 141BR
Corbis 34B, 34T, 70L, 72
Corrie Wingate/Apa Publications 9MR, 9TR, 11TL, 12BR, 26, 46, 83, 85, 89, 103BR, 110, 125, 131, 201, 203, 210, 211, 212, 216, 219BC, 223, 224, 227, 231, 232, 253, 255, 257, 258, 259, 326/327, 337
Dreamstime 94, 103ML, 149, 187, 188, 195, 217, 228, 268
Fotolia 43TR, 219BR
Fáilte Ireland 23, 27, 67, 68, 74, 76/77T, 76BR, 76BL, 77BL, 77TR, 96, 98, 99, 138, 147, 151BR, 162, 169, 189, 193, 198, 207, 215, 233, 242, 243, 256, 264/265, 266
Fáilte Ireland/Derek Cullen 132
Fáilte Ireland/James Fennell 151ML
Gardiner Mitchell/Failte Ireland 269
Getty Images 36, 41, 47, 50, 55, 56, 57, 58, 59, 61, 62, 65, 70R, 75L, 75R
Glyn Genin/Apa Publications 10T, 120, 121, 123, 126, 127, 128, 129, 130, 133, 134, 135, 136, 139, 142, 143, 145, 150BR, 150BL, 151BL, 151TR, 153, 156, 158, 160, 164, 166, 167, 168, 173, 175, 176, 178, 179, 180, 181, 183, 190, 194, 196, 197, 204, 209, 229, 230, 240, 241, 247, 261, 324B, 330
Irish Museum of Modern Art 78, 79, 80
iStock 32B, 33TL, 33MR, 33BR, 37, 40, 119, 206, 213, 218MC, 262
Kate Drynan/Apa Publications 77BR
Kevin Cummins/Apa Publications 8BL, 11TR, 12TL, 13B, 35B, 60, 66, 69, 87, 104/105, 170, 199, 273, 275, 285, 288, 294, 295, 309, 316, 318
Kobal 28BC, 29ML
Leon Farrell/Photocall Ireland 77ML
Library of Congress 39, 44, 48
Mid and East Antrim council/Grafters Media 326
National Library of Ireland/Wikimedia Commons/public domain 52BL, 52/53T, 53ML
National Photo Company/Library of Congress/ 53BR
Northern Ireland Tourist Board 12TR, 71, 81, 82, 93, 276, 277, 279, 280, 281, 282, 283, 286, 287, 296, 297, 298, 299, 300, 301, 302, 303, 312, 317
Public domain 38, 45, 49, 51, 52BR, 53BL, 54
Ronald Grant Archive 28BR, 28/29T
Sipa Press/Rex Features 141ML, 141BL
Stephen Power/Fáilte Ireland 205, 225
The Boston Post/Wikimedia Commons/public domain 53TR
Tourism Ireland 13T, 24, 42MR, 73, 84, 88, 1100, 01, 106/107, 155, 272, 332
Tourism Ireland/Brian Morrison 95
Tourism Ireland/John Redmond 97
Tourism Ireland/Stephen Power 9B

COVER CREDITS

Front cover: Cobh Cathedral
Shutterstock

Back flap: The burren region
Shutterstock

INSIGHT GUIDE CREDITS

First Edition 1986
Thirteenth Edition 2026

Distribution
UK, Ireland and Europe
Apa Publications (UK) Ltd;
sales@insightguides.com
United States and Canada
Two Rivers; ips@ingramcontent.com
Australia and New Zealand
Woodslane; info@woodslane.com.au
Worldwide
Apa Publications (UK) Ltd;
sales@insightguides.com
Special Sales, Content Licensing and CoPublishing
Insight Guides can be purchased in bulk quantities at discounted prices. We can create special editions, personalized jackets and corporate imprints tailored to your needs. sales@insightguides.com
EU Representative
LOGOS EUROPE, 9 rue Nicolas Poussin, 17000, LA ROCHELLE, France;
Contact@logoseurope.eu;
+33 (0) 667937378
www.insightguides.com

Printed by Finidr in Czech Republic
ISBN: 9781839054617
This book was produced using **Typefi** automated publishing software.

A catalogue record for this book is available from the British Library.

Editor: Kate Drynan
Author: Kate Drynan
Picture Editor: Piotr Kala
Picture Manager: Tom Smyth
Cartography: original cartography Berndston and Berndston, updated by Carte
Layout: Claire Armstrong
Production Operations Manager: Katie Bennett
Publishing Technology Manager: Rebeka Davies
Head of Publishing: Sarah Clark

CONTRIBUTORS

This new edition of Insight Guide: Ireland was updated by Kate Drynan. It builds on the editions written by Patrick Kinsella, Alannah Hopkin and Brian Bell. Other contributors include Norm Longley, Biddy White Lennon for the Food chapter, Maxmedia Communications for the chapters on Sport, Golf and Angling, Mary, John Daly, Paul Clements, Jane Powers and Tina Neylon.

The chapters on Northern Ireland and Belfast were reworked by Seth Linder, editor of a listings magazine in Belfast.

Thanks also go to Penny Phenix who indexed the guide.

ABOUT INSIGHT GUIDES

Since 1970, Insight Guides has provided a unique perspective on the world's best travel destinations. With a focus on illuminating text written by local expert authors who are passionate about their destinations, Insight Guides brings places to life through absorbing coverage of their history and culture, backed up by stunning photography.

These books offer a unique combination of the inspirational and practical: an easy-to-use travel guide – with detailed maps and a free eBook to take wherever you go.

Now in our sixth decade of publication, Insight Guides is committed to a sustainable travel approach and is the perfect companion for travellers who want to really get under the skin of their destination.

Legend

City maps

Freeway/Highway/Motorway
Divided Highway
Main Roads
Minor Roads
Pedestrian Roads
Steps
Footpath
Railway
Funicular Railway
Cable Car
Tunnel
City Wall
Important Building
Built Up Area
Other Land
Transport Hub
Park
Pedestrian Area
Bus Station
Tourist Information
Main Post Office
Cathedral/Church
Mosque
Synagogue
Statue/Monument
Beach
Airport

Regional maps

Freeway/Highway/Motorway (with junction)
Freeway/Highway/Motorway (under construction)
Divided Highway
Main Road
Secondary Road
Minor Road
Track
Footpath
International Boundary
State/Province Boundary
National Park/Reserve
Marine Park
Ferry Route
Marshland/Swamp
Glacier
Salt Lake
Airport/Airfield
Ancient Site
Border Control
Cable Car
Castle/Castle Ruins
Cave
Chateau/Stately Home
Church/Church Ruins
Crater
Lighthouse
Mountain Peak
Place of Interest
Viewpoint

INDEX

D

G

J

K

L

N

O

P

Q

R

S